The dominant public figure in Brazil from 1930 until 1954 was a highly contradictory and controversial personality. Getúlio Vargas, from the pampas of the southern frontier state of Rio Grande do Sul, became the dictator who ruled without ever forgetting the lower classes.

Vargas was a consummate artist at politics. He climbed the political ladder through seats in the state and national legislatures to the post of federal Finance Minister and to the governorship of Rio Grande do Sul. His career then took him to the National Palace as Provisional President and as Constitutional President, and later as the dictator of his "New State." After his deposition in 1945 and a period of semiretirement, his continuing widespread popularity resulted in his successful come-back campaign in 1950 for the Presidency on the Labor Party ticket.

Vargas' contributions to Brazilian political and economic life were many and important. Taking advantage of the power which his political magic provided him, he brought Brazil from a loose confederacy of semifeudal states to a strongly centralized nation. He was a great eclectic, welding into his social, political, and economic policies what he found good in various programs. He was also a great opportunist in the sense that he adroitly took advantage of conditions and circumstances to effect his ends. He was intimately related to the revolutionary changes in Brazilian life after 1930.

Vargas, "Father of the Brazilians," attributed achievements such as these to power in his own hands. His foes, however, still feared the political wizard, and they cheered the military when it deposed him. After his return, "on the arms of the people," Vargas saw that the armed forces were determined to repeat history, and in 1954 he chose another path—suicide.

All of these exciting events are related in Professor John W. F. Dulles' *Vargas of Brazil: A Political Biography*. Despite its emphasis on Vargas the politician and statesman, the reader comes to know Vargas the man.

For this new portrait of Vargas and of Brazil the author has drawn much material from State Department papers in the National Archives and from other public sources, and from interviews with numerous persons who were participants in the events he describes or observers of them. The result is an interesting, revealing, valid account of an important people. Many illustrations supplement the text.

VARGAS OF BRAZIL

Getúlio Vargas during his last term in the Presidency, 1951–1954.

VARGAS

OF BRAZIL

A POLITICAL BIOGRAPHY

By John W. F. Dulles

UNIVERSITY OF TEXAS PRESS : AUSTIN & LONDON

Library of Congress Catalog Card Number 67–20502
Copyright © 1967 by John W. F. Dulles
All Rights Reserved

Printed by the University of Texas Printing Division, Austin
Bound by Universal Bookbindery, Inc., San Antonio

ACKNOWLEDGMENTS

This book about Getúlio Vargas owes its existence to Alfred A. Knopf. After he suggested that such a book would be useful I decided to try to write one.

What appears in these pages is largely based on information collected during a three-month visit to Brazil in 1963. I had the great good fortune of being assisted there by Daphne F. Rodger. Had it not been for her, the amount of information collected would have been only a small fraction of what it was, and a part of that fraction would have been rather inaccurate. Since that trip Miss Rodger has removed numerous flaws from the manuscript. Much of what is good about this book is due to her.

On that visit in 1963, and also during a visit to Brazil in 1965 (to prepare the sequel to this volume), we listened to many people, some of whom are named in the Sources of Material. It was a joy to accept the warm hospitality which was always offered with much interesting information. Hélio Silva, Newton de Siqueira Campos, and others went far out of their way to supply introductions and to help in every possible manner.

In Washington I spent almost three weeks looking over Department of State records in the National Archives, and I found them enlightening. The late E. Taylor Parks, who was chief of the Research Guidance and Review Division of the Historical Office of the Department of State, guided me wisely.

For reading the manuscript and submitting suggestions, I am indebted to Charles A. Gauld, Estanislau Fischlowitz, Paul Vanorden Shaw, and Herbert Weinstock. For typing, and just as cheerfully retyping, and for helping in numerous ways, I want to thank Eleanor MacMillan.

This project would not have been possible except for financial assistance provided by the Brown-Lupton Foundation, the Foreign Area Fellowship Program, and the Organization of American States; also by the Institute of Latin American Studies and the Humanities Research Center,

both of The University of Texas. Frances Hudspeth, of The University of Texas, encouraged the work and did a great deal to arrange that it could be carried out.

J.W.F.D.

CONTENTS

ILLUSTRATIONS

MAPS

VARGAS OF BRAZIL

BRAZIL

VENEZUELA
COLOMBIA
BR. GUIANA
SURINAM
FR. GUIANA
AMAPÁ

EQUATOR

ECUADOR

Amazon River   Manaus   Belterra   Belém   São Luís

FERNANDO DE NORONHA ISLAND

AMAZONAS   PARÁ

BRAZIL

Pôrto Velho

ACRE
GUAPORÉ (RONDÔNIA)

PERU

BOLIVIA

MATO GROSSO

Corumbá

MARANHÃO   CEARÁ

R.N.   Natal
Pa   João Pessoa
Pe   Recife

PIAUÍ

GOIAS

Francisco River

Paulo Afonso Falls
Al
Se

BAHIA

ATLANTIC

OCEAN

Salvador

Brasília
FEDERAL DISTRICT (after April 1960)

São

MINAS GERAIS

Itabira

0 100 200 300 400 500 Miles

Belo Horizonte

E.S.   Vitória

PACIFIC

OCEAN

Pres. Epitácio   SÃO PAULO

Juiz de Fora

R.J.

PARAGUAY

Campinas   São Lourenço

PARANÁ   Itararé   São Paulo   Rio de Janeiro

Senges

Catanduvas   Ribeira

Santos

Campinas   Cruzeiro

Volta Redonda
Petrópolis

São Paulo

Niteroi
Rio de Janeiro

Senges   Itararé
Ribeira   Santos

ILHA GRANDE

Ponta Grossa
Curitiba

Tropic of Capricorn

CHILE

Iguaçu Falls

Paraná R.

Pelotas R.

Florianopolis
SANTA CATARINA ISLAND

SANTA CATARINA

Santo Tomé
RIO GRANDE DO SUL

Santo Ângelo
São Luís
São Borja

Paso de los Libres
Alegrete
Pôrto Alegre

Santo Tomé

Santa Maria

Uruguay R.

ARGENTINA

URUGUAY

Paso de los Libres

Uruguaiana

Cachoeira

Pôrto Alegre

Pedras Altas

Al   Alagoas
E.S.   Espírito Santo
Pa   Paraíba
Pe   Pernambuco
R.J.   Rio de Janeiro
R.N.   Rio Grande do Norte
Se   Sergipe

Buenos Aires

Montevideo

VMB

1966

0 100 200 Miles

CHRONOLOGICAL TABLE

April 19, 1883: Birth of Getúlio Vargas in São Borja, Rio Grande do Sul.

March 29, 1909: Vargas elected to Rio Grande do Sul state Assembly.

April 13, 1919: Presidential election won by Epitácio Pessoa (of Paraíba) over Rui Barbosa (of Bahia).

July 28, 1919: Inauguration of President Epitácio Pessoa.

March 1, 1922: Presidential election won by Artur Bernardes (of Minas) over Nilo Peçanha (of Rio de Janeiro).

July 5–6, 1922: Revolt of the "Eighteen of the Fort" in Rio.

November 15, 1922: Inauguration of President Artur Bernardes.

January 25, 1923: A. A. Borges de Medeiros starts his fifth term as governor of Rio Grande do Sul. Civil war breaks out in the state.

May 3, 1923: Vargas takes seat in Rio as federal congressman.

December 15, 1923: Treaty of Pedras Altas ends Rio Grande do Sul civil war.

July 5–27, 1924: Uprising in São Paulo by discontented military men, who later go to Paraná.

October 24–December 1924: Uprising in Rio Grande do Sul by discontented military men. Later they join São Paulo rebels in Paraná.

April 1925: Miguel Costa-Prestes Column (about 1,500 men) leaves Paraná to cross Paraguay, beginning the Long March in the Brazilian interior.

March 1, 1926: Presidential election won by Washington Luís Pereira de Souza (of São Paulo). There was no opposition candidate.

November 15, 1926: Inauguration of President Washington Luís. He names Vargas his Finance Minister.

February 3, 1927: The Long March ends when 620 men enter Bolivia.

January 25, 1928: Getúlio Vargas inaugurated governor of Rio Grande do Sul.

Early January, 1930: Vargas, presidential candidate of Aliança Liberal, reads manifesto in Rio and São Paulo.

March 1, 1930: Presidential election won by Júlio Prestes de Albuquerque (of São Paulo) over Getúlio Vargas.

July 25, 1930: Assassination of João Pessoa (Vargas' Aliança Liberal running mate from Paraíba).

October 3, 1930: Outbreak of revolution against Washington Luís Administration.

October 24, 1930: Rio military junta overthrows Washington Luís.

November 3, 1930: Getúlio Vargas becomes Chief of Provisional Government.

July 9–October 2, 1932: Unsuccessful Constitucionalista revolution (mostly in São Paulo) against Vargas regime.

May 3, 1933: Election of members of Constitutional Assembly.

November 15, 1933–July 16, 1934: Constitutional Assembly draws up Constitution.

July 17, 1934: Constitutional Assembly elects Vargas President.

October 14, 1934: Congressional elections.

November 23–27, 1935: Communist rebellion in Natal, Recife, and Rio. Congress declares martial law.

July 1937: Armando de Sales Oliveira (of São Paulo) and José Américo de Almeida (of Paraíba) formally open their campaigns for the Presidency.

October 18, 1937: Flôres da Cunha, forced out of Rio Grande do Sul, goes to Uruguay.

November 10, 1937: Vargas decrees Estado Nôvo with himself as President under a new autocratic constitution. This ends the presidential election campaign.

December 3, 1937: Vargas decree outlaws political parties and the Integralistas (Green Shirts).

January 1938: Start of intensive campaign against foreign political and cultural influences.

May 11, 1938: Unsuccessful Integralista attempt to overthrow Government.

September 1938–June 1939: Short break in diplomatic relations between Brazil and Germany.

May 1, 1940: Vargas decrees minimum wages.

June 1940: Italy enters World War II. Germany overwhelms France.

August–September 1940: United States Congress passes bill increasing Export-Import Bank capital by $500 million for loans to Latin America.

September 26, 1940: Announcement of Export-Import Bank financing for Volta Redonda steel plant.

March 1941: United States enacts Lend-Lease Act. In April, 1941, its terms come to include Latin American nations.

August 14, 1941: Announcement of Roosevelt-Churchill "Atlantic Charter," mentioning, among other things, "the right of all people to choose the form of government under which they will live."

December 7, 1941: Pearl Harbor attacked by Japan (resulting in United States declaration of war).

January 1942: American foreign ministers meet in Rio and recommend that their governments break relations with Axis powers. Brazil breaks relations with Axis.

February–March 1942: Souza Costa Mission to Washington.

August 22, 1942: Brazil declares war on Germany and Italy after over six hundred lives are lost in a sudden attack on Brazilian ships.

January 28, 1943: Vargas-Roosevelt meeting in Natal.

July 2, 1944: First contingent of Brazilian Expeditionary Force sails from Rio to fight in Italy.

February 1945: End of government control over press. Vargas calls for elections.

March 1945: Vargas publicly agrees to diplomatic recognition of Soviet Union.

April 1945: Political prisoners freed. Death of F. D. Roosevelt.

May 9, 1945: End of European hostilities.

May 1945: Vargas sets elections for December 2, 1945, and decrees that political parties must be national. PSD supports Eurico Gaspar Dutra for President; UDN supports Eduardo Gomes.

June 7, 1945: Brazil declares war on Japan.

August 15, 1945: Surrender of Japan.

October 29, 1945: Armed Forces depose Vargas. Supreme Court Chief Justice José Linhares becomes Acting President.

December 2, 1945: Eurico Gaspar Dutra elected President. Vargas elected senator.

January 31, 1946: Dutra inaugurated. Constitutional Assembly starts work on 1946 Constitution.

September 18, 1946: Constitution promulgated.

1947: Brazilian Communist Party outlawed. Diplomatic relations with Soviet Union broken.

October 3, 1950: Getúlio Vargas (PTB) elected President over Eduardo Gomes (UDN) and Cristiano Machado (PSD).

January 31, 1951: Vargas starts presidential term under 1946 Constitution.

July 1951–July 1953: Technical studies by Joint Brazil-United States Economic Development Commission.

October 5, 1953: Vargas signs bill creating Petrobrás.

August 5, 1954: Assassination of Major Rubens Vaz.

August 24, 1954: Suicide of Getúlio Vargas. João Café Filho (Vice-President) assumes Presidency.

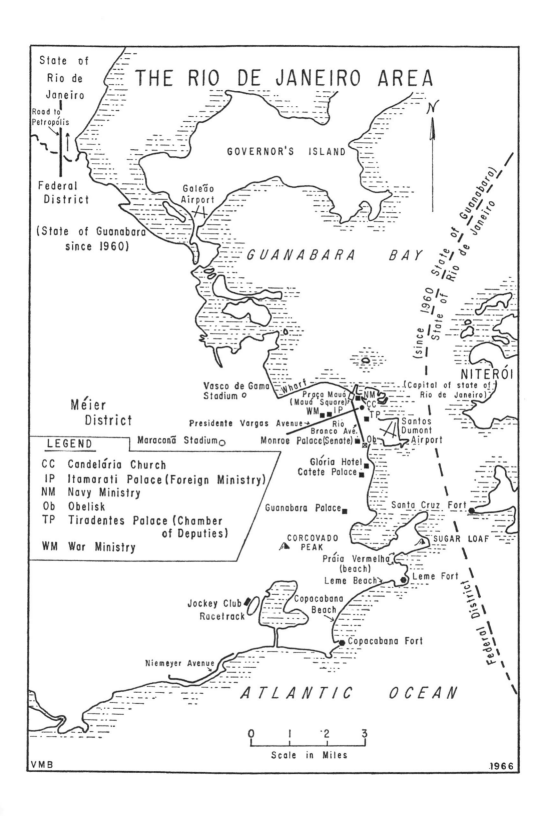

THE RIO DE JANEIRO AREA

State of
Rio de
Janeiro

Road to
Petropolis

Federal
District

(State of Guanabara
since 1960)

GOVERNOR'S ISLAND

Galeão
Airport

GUANABARA BAY

(since 1960) State of Guanabara
State of Rio de Janeiro

NITERÓI

Méier
District

Vasco de Gama
Stadium

Wharf

(Capital of state of
Rio de Janeiro)

Praça Mauá
(Mauá Square)
WM   IP

NM
CC
TP

Santos
Dumont
Airport

Presidente Vargas Avenue

Rio
Branco Ave.

Monroe Palace (Senate)   Ob

Maracanã Stadium

LEGEND

CC   Candelária Church
IP   Itamarati Palace (Foreign Ministry)
NM   Navy Ministry
Ob   Obelisk
TP   Tiradentes Palace (Chamber
     of Deputies)
WM   War Ministry

Glória Hotel
Catete Palace

Guanabara Palace

Santa Cruz Fort

CORCOVADO
PEAK

SUGAR LOAF

Práia Vermelha
(beach)
Leme Beach

Leme Fort

Jockey Club
Racetrack

Copacabana
Beach

Copacabana Fort

Niemeyer Avenue

Federal District

ATLANTIC OCEAN

0   1   2   3
Scale in Miles

VMB

1966

PROLOGUE

"'Everything about him is medium, mediocre. He never had the picturesqueness of a Flôres da Cunha, the brilliance of an Osvaldo Aranha, the eloquence of a João Neves. He is not known for a single unselfish gesture, a single passionate impulse. He is a cold, reserved, cautious, impersonal man. His literary style is empty and lacks character. His physical appearance is unimpressive . . .'

"'But listen. Listen all of you. Above all, the biography of Getúlio Vargas must take into account certain traits which make him a unique figure in this country, giving him advantages over other politicians. He is a calm man in a land of hotheads. A disciplined person in a land of undisciplined people. A prudent person in a land of imprudent people. A temperate person in a land of squanderers. A silent person in a land of parrots. He dominates his impulses, which was never the case of Flôres da Cunha. He controls his flights of imagination, a thing which Osvaldo Aranha does not know how to do. . . . João Neves uses his splendid words to say things . . . things which sometimes compromise him.' "

In 1954, nine years after Erico Verissimo has his characters make these comments,[1] Cariocas were surrounding the gates of the presidential palace in Rio de Janeiro, shouting epithets against Getúlio Vargas. Then came the news of his suicide, followed by farewell words: "This people whose slave I was will no longer be slave to anyone. My sacrifice will remain forever in your soul, and my blood will be the price of your ransom." The mobs around the palace, swept by sentiment, began re-echoing the old refrain which first shook Brazil in 1930: "We want Getúlio."

A prominent lawyer of Rio de Janeiro writes:

I like to compare Vargas with a Napoleon from the countryside, playing his role far away from his native Corsica (in this case the frontier town of São Borja) . . . spreading the *caudilhismo* of the remote southern frontier until it covered the vast continentlike expanse of Brazil . . . and bringing to those placid lands, once conquered by Portugal, an Indian-Hispanic unrest which was unknown to Brazil until 1930 . . . all of this accompanied by the tumult of horses from the pampas and of men of song and drawling accents. Like Bonaparte, who dreamed of unifying Europe by reviving the empire of Charlemagne, Vargas grasped the reins of the Federation which the Republic had held so loosely. Arrogant regionalisms, semiconfederate states with their own small local armies, their Senates patterned after legislatures in the United States, and their feudal baronies dominated by "colonels" . . . all of these tumbled before the unifying magnetism of Vargas, who made use of the Brazilian Revolution (as Napoleon did of the French Revolution), Plínio Salgado's green nationalism, Lindolfo Collor's ideas about social legislation, etc. Like the Little Corsican, who advanced from soldier to consul, and from consul to emperor, Vargas was the democratic candidate of the Aliança Liberal, chief of the Revolution, Chief of the Provisional Government from 1930 to 1934, Constitutional President until 1937, dictator from 1937 to 1945, and again Constitutional President some years later. Deposed in 1945, he made his Itu Ranch his Island of Elba. . . . From there he returned to his Hundred Days, which lasted a few more years, and to his final Waterloo in Catete Palace ("The Old Guard dies but does not surrender").[2]

[1] Erico Verissimo, *O Arquipélago*, III, 711, 731.
[2] Thomas Leonardos, *Palestra Proferida na Escola Superior de Guerra, em 9 de Junho de 1964*, pp. 13–14.

BOOK I

THE REVOLUTIONARY
BACKGROUND, 1922–1929

1. The Steam Roller

PEDRO II, overthrown by some Brazilian Army chiefs in 1889, sailed sadly from beautiful Rio de Janeiro, his wife having kissed the beloved sand she was leaving behind. Now tired and ill, Pedro had ruled as emperor for almost fifty years; his bearded face had become synonymous with benign monarchy, and, in many minds throughout the world, almost synonymous with Brazil itself.

After thus belatedly following the vogue of becoming a republic, Brazil soon found itself with a political machine solidly replacing old Pedro. In spite of regular "elections" it was not democratic, but on the whole it worked well for the country. It shone with particular brilliance around the turn of the century, when the state of São Paulo provided as Presidents some outstanding statesmen who had been trained under the Empire. They surrounded themselves with other high-collared statesmen and discovered that the golden key to peace, prosperity, and railway construction lay in a strong currency. In the legislative branch, too, Brazil had some excellent men, even if a few represented states they had never visited.

Rui Barbosa, the balding orator from the eastern state of Bahia, often seemed to be the only man in Brazil with a penchant for butting his head against the national political machine. The enthusiasm he stirred up as opposition candidate for the Presidency in 1910 was something people talked about long afterward. In an unheard-of fashion he stumped the nation. The candidate of the official machine was awarded only two thirds of the total vote that year, and this, too, was something unheard of.

Four years later the machine recaptured its old smoothness, limiting Rui Barbosa to about 8 per cent of the vote. It did even better in 1918, running a highly respected Paulista, an ex-President of the Republic, who obtained over 99 per cent of the vote in a race in which Rui Barbosa did not participate. But the fine old gentleman who was so substantially elected died shortly after inauguration day.

It was for the resulting special election of 1919 that Rui Barbosa flexed his muscles. He was looking forward to stirring the nation as he had in 1910, and for this reason he declined an appointment to head the Brazilian delegation to the Paris Peace Conference.

That in this, probably his last effort, he would be declared loser he well knew. The federal machine, which was really a collaborative union of most of the state machines, held all the trump cards. One of these was known as the "Golden Rule": an arrangement whereby Minas Gerais and São Paulo, the two wealthiest and most populous of Brazil's twenty states, took turns supplying Presidents of the Republic. Of further assistance was the mechanism of voting. Votes were reported by the local political bosses, known as "colonels," whose powerful positions were the reward of supplying election returns satisfactory to the state machines. The country had no secret vote, and if the vote on a ballot was ever a secret from anyone it was secret only from the person recorded as casting that particular ballot. Not infrequently districts reported the results before the voting was done, and there was plenty of well-founded doubt as to the currency of the lists of electors.

With Rui Barbosa's decision in 1919 not to go to Paris, the office of leader of the Brazilian peace delegation fell to Senator Epitácio Pessoa, a distinguished little man whose speaking ability gained him renown as "the songbird from the north." In public life Epitácio, who had a good legal mind, had advanced as far as conditions seemed to allow, having served in the federal Cabinet and on the Supreme Court. For a man from the small northeastern state of Paraíba, the going on the national scene was not easy, top plums being reserved for the politicians from Minas Gerais and São Paulo, the two great states which lie in the southeast. Occasionally the state which provided the third most votes, boisterous Rio Grande do Sul, in the far south, managed to be heard nationally.

In Paris the "songbird" raised his voice to suggest that the new world organization be known by some name other than the League of Nations, and presently a cable reached him from Brazil, a somewhat rare occurrence for February 1919. But it did not, as Epitácio expected, concern this matter of his speech about the League. Instead, this and other messages brought unbelievable news. Brazil's political leaders had picked him to be the official candidate for the Presidency. In other words, he was to be President of Brazil.

Back in Rio this unprecedented compromise had been suggested by an old senator whose keen political sensitivity brought him fame as a "political seismograph." By straying from the Golden Rule for a partial term, the machine took most of the wind out of the sails of the hard-campaigning Rui Barbosa. Pessoa won easily, without campaigning, and learned in Paris of his electoral victory in Brazil.

This unusual choice for the Presidency gave Brazil an unusual administration. For the first time civilians headed the republic's War and Navy Ministries, in a difficult experiment which irked many a military officer. Politicians of São Paulo and Minas came to regret their compromise choice, resenting the large expenditures with Epitácio authorized for works against droughts in his home area, Brazil's Northeast. The service charges on the large loans which the President was contracting from abroad would fall mainly on the taxpayers in their two states.

The rough electoral contest, which the "seismograph's" sagacity had helped avoid in 1919, began two years later when the political machine got back on the old track and prepared to place Artur Bernardes, the polished governor of Minas, in the Presidency. It would be Bernardes of the Partido Republicano Mineiro in the election of March 1, 1922, and Washington Luís Pereira de Souza of the Partido Republicano Paulista four years later.

The work in 1921 went forward in the traditional manner, with the politicians of the two large states sounding out the governors of the smaller ones. The only unusual feature was the failure of President Epitácio Pessoa to introduce himself into the negotiations regarding his successor, but these were entirely cut and dried.

While this was going on, two of Brazil's former heads of state returned from Europe and were warmly greeted by those who wanted to protest the arrangements being made by the machine. The first to arrive was Nilo Peçanha of the state of Rio de Janeiro (which surrounded the Federal District and the capital city of Rio). He had served as Chief Executive of Brazil in 1909 and 1910, having been Vice-President when an incumbent died, and later he had made a name for himself as Foreign Minister. Now it was expected from his recent statements that when his boat reached Brazil he would do the usual thing and support Bernardes. But instead he found himself greeted as a hero of the opposition, and, although he was not one of Brazil's great orators, he was drafted to carry on the fight for "Representation and Justice."

When Marshal Hermes da Fonseca docked in Rio this bemedaled chieftain received so enthusiastic a reception that it seemed his six-year absence had dimmed memories of his none-too-successful four years in the national Presidency. Now he listened to Army officers who had complaints against Pessoa's Administration and against the civilian War and Navy Ministers, and he resolved to support Nilo Peçanha against Bernardes. The old soldier would doggedly defend the honor of the military.

One of the factors which brought about the compromise selection of Epitácio Pessoa in 1919 was the refusal of the Republican Party of Rio Grande do Sul (Partido Republicano Riograndense) to go along with the Republican parties which dominated Minas and São Paulo. In 1921 when it saw them staking out the Presidency for Bernardes from 1922 to 1926 and São Paulo's Washington Luís from 1926 to 1930, the Rio Grande do Sul state machine came out in support of Nilo Peçanha. The election battle was on.

2. Deputado Getúlio Vargas[1]

Rio Grande do Sul's decision to support Peçanha in the election of March 1, 1922, was made by "old" Antônio Augusto Borges de Medeiros, who had made all the decisions of the Republican Party of his state since the death of its founder, Júlio de Castilhos, in 1903.

Known by his friends for his integrity and by his enemies as "the vulture," Borges de Medeiros had the undistinguished appearance of a not-

---

[1] João Neves da Fontoura, *Borges de Medeiros e Seu Tempo (Memórias, I)*; Paul Frischauer, *Presidente Vargas: Biografia*; André Carrazzoni, *Getúlio Vargas*; Olmio Barros Vidal, *Um Destino a Serviço do Brasil*; Alzira Vargas do Amaral Peixoto, *Getúlio Vargas, Meu Pai*; Alzira Vargas do Amaral Peixto, "A Vida de Getúlio Contada por Sua Filha, Alzira Vargas, ao Jornalista Raul Giudicelli" (the *Fatos & Fotos* series starting June 15, 1963) ; Agildo Barata, *Vida de um Revolucionário*, Ch. 3.

too-well-fed scarecrow. He ran a state machine which was as undemocratic as the national one and which achieved the zenith in autocracy. In no uncertain terms Borges let his Cabinet secretaries know who did all the thinking in his state, and when he disliked mayors he would replace them with *intendentes provisórios,* some of whom, in spite of the nature of the appointments, stayed on permanently. They and the Brigada Militar, the state militia of about 2,000 fighters, had for years contributed to the successful struggle against the state Federalist Party, traditional enemy of the Republican Party of Rio Grande. Whereas other states followed the example of the federal government in not allowing immediate re-election of chief executives, the Gaúcho state was an exception and so Borges planned to be re-elected on November 25, 1922, to his fifth five-year term as governor.

Borges' authoritarian concepts were those which Júlio de Castilhos had learned from the Positivism of Auguste Comte and had infused into the party and the state constitution. Assemblymen found that they had very limited duties when they met in Pôrto Alegre, the state capital.

One of these Gaúcho state assemblymen in 1921 was Getúlio Dorneles Vargas, thirty-eight–year–old member of Borges' Partido Republicano Riograndense, and, like the party president, a strong admirer of the gospel of Júlio de Castilhos. Getúlio's father, Manoel do Nascimento Vargas, had fought in the Paraguayan War during the Empire, had been named an honorary general in the Army, and later had supported the cause of Júlio de Castilhos. At the suggestion of Borges de Mcdeiros the General served for a while as mayor of São Borja, and he made a point of instilling in his five sons a devotion to Republican Party principles as practiced in the state.

Getúlio, the General's third son, was born on April 19, 1883, in the town of São Borja, which, separated by the Uruguay River from the Argentine town of Santo Tomé, was in a cattle-raising district famed for contraband and border feuding. When he was away from São Borja, Getúlio would recall fondly the green grass of the region and the days spent there on horseback.

Getúlio had not led a remarkable life. His early dream of following his father in a military career was shattered when he backed some students charged with indiscipline and was thrown out of military school; and later, when at twenty he participated in an expedition to the territory of Acre, the scene of a dispute with Bolivia, he discovered that Army life was miserable. The law school at Pôrto Alegre was much more to his liking, and as a student there he wrote and campaigned as a true disciple of Júlio de Castilhos. When he was chosen orator of his class at graduation in 1907, his long address on Greek culture, Nietzsche, sociology, and other subjects revealed his wide reading.

Soon after getting his degree Getúlio was a state assemblyman doing political work for Borges in Pôrto Alegre. In São Borja, where he spent part of his time, he married Darci Sarmanho as soon as she became fifteen, and they raised a family of three boys and two girls. Getúlio's career in the legislature at Pôrto Alegre was interrupted by his resignation of his mandate when his boss disciplined two of his colleagues. But in 1917, after an interval limited to the practice of law, a lesson in the senselessness of opposing the system, Getúlio was back in the good graces of the autocrat and by 1921 was majority leader in the state Assembly and secretary of its budget commission.

Such, in brief, had been his career. What about the man? The General once remarked that, of all his five sons, this one caused him the least trouble. A quiet person who possessed a good memory and read a wide variety of philosophical works, Getúlio was one whose closing remarks at the end of a discussion were likely to carry much weight.

Getúlio the politician was a short, somewhat heavy-set man who was often smoking a cigar with an air of contentment. An attentive listener, he developed an engaging smile and used it so frequently that visitors spoke of his "proverbial affability." No extrovert, he was friendly, patient, and apparently unemotional. Inclined to display genuine appreciation for the opinions which opponents might advance in a discussion, he came to be regarded by fellow legislators as one who excelled at reasonable compromise.

The facade of friendliness and calm hid considerable tenseness, and he often felt less cheer than his surface indicated. Vargas was inwardly impatient, resenting late-comers and tellers of stories he already knew, but self-discipline so dominated impatience that he would hold off moving until his shrewd analysis of a situation told him that the best time had come. Nor, for this man who could not abide any unnecessary gamble, was the best time likely to come as quickly as associates might wish. When the youthful Vargas, in a welcoming speech for Rio Grande's greatest senator, praised the hero of the occasion for being able to "await the march of events, placing yourself at their head, to direct them,"[2] he was admiring a quality he himself would perfect.

Self-reliant, he was inspired by reason, not by religion. Finding him-

[2] Paul Frischauer, *Presidente Vargas*, p. 103.

self in a setting which demanded the ability to bide one's time, he made himself a champion at it and became extra careful not to make a wrong move. Behind what Sumner Welles was to call a "singularly impassive face," a good mind sized up situations in a practical, sensible manner which foes would come to define as "cold."

3. The "Eighteen of the Fort," 1922[1]

Rio Grande state assemblymen Getúlio Vargas and João Neves da Fontoura, "the golden boy of Borgismo," set to work on Borges' orders to fill the state with propaganda for Nilo Peçanha. Three other state governments supported the opposition candidate: those of Pernambuco, a state in the Northeast which was squabbling with the Pessoa Administration; Bahia, home of Peçanha's running mate; and Rio de Janeiro, the presidential candidate's home state. Peçanha's popularity in the Rio de Janeiro district was great and most of the capital's press helped turn this feeling into one of dislike for Bernardes.

Thus, unlike Rui Barbosa in 1910, Nilo Peçanha in 1922 had behind him the four most populous states after Minas Gerais and São Paulo. There was another difference: Army officers in 1909–1910 had supported the dominant political machine, but in 1921–1922 many of them were going along with Marshal Hermes da Fonseca in his opposition to it, leading observers to speculate on the possibility of a military revolt after the announcement of the returns.

The most passionately discussed campaign issue involved the Armed Forces. In October 1921 the *Correio da Manhã*, a Rio morning newspaper which opposed the Bernardes candidacy, published facsimiles of two letters grossly insulting to the military, apparently in the handwrit-

[1] Hélio Silva, *1922: Sangue na Areia de Copacabana*; Juarez Távora, *À Guisa de Depoimento*, I; João Vicente, *Revoluçao de 5 de Julho* [1922]; Plinio Reys, *A Sedição Militar de Matto Grosso em 1922*; last chapters of Brígido Tinoco; *A Vida de Nilo Peçanha*; Glauco Carneiro, "A Revolta dos Tenetes," *O Cruzeiro*, July 18, 1964 (part of the series of articles, "Revoluções Brasileiras," by Glauco Carneiro in *O Cruzeiro*); Glauco Carneiro, "Eu Também Sou Sobrevivente dos '18 do Forte' " (Manoel Ananias dos Santos interview), in *O Cruzeiro*, September 5, 1964; Newton de Siqueira Campos, interviews, July–September, 1963; Emídio da Costa Miranda, interview, July 19, 1963; Eduardo Gomes, interview, July 20, 1963; and Hermes Ernesto da Fonseca, interview, September 7, 1963. The last-named provided a copy of a thirty-two-page government accusation against 1922 revolutionaries: Heraclito Fontoura Sobral Pinto (Procurador Criminal da República), *Por Libello-Crime Accusatório*.

ing of Bernardes and with his signature. The set of five letters which the *Correio* received had earlier been offered for sale to Bernardes, but he had rejected the offer, and after the publication of the two letters he declared them forgeries.

When the Military Club refused to accept this explanation Bernardes and his campaign manager agreed to send representatives to a commission which the Club set up to judge the authenticity of the letters. The wording of the famous "false letters" lacked the educated phraseology characteristic of the governor of Minas, but whoever had forged them had done an excellent job on the handwriting. As the experts carefully analyzed minute details of penmanship there were reports that the finding would be favorable to Bernardes. It was, then, a surprise when the commission suddenly declared the letters genuine, just after Bernardes' representatives quit the commission.

The nation was still discussing the letters, and feeling among Army officers was running high, when, after considerable delay, the outcome of the March 1 election came to be known: roughly 467,000 votes for Bernardes to 318,000 for Nilo Peçanha. The losers and the Military Club demanded that the result be checked and, although this was done by a *Tribunal de Honra* on orders of Epitácio Pessoa, it gave no comfort to the opposition.

Late in April, Epitácio Pessoa came down from the summer resort of Petrópolis to Rio. In what was supposed to be a triumphal march, the President, well protected by bayonets, passed the Military Club, the windows of which had been boarded up as a show of protest. Tenseness increased with the arrest and jailing of four aviators, in whose planes bombs had been found.

Although the President was among those who were convinced that his Administration was strong enough to turn the government over to Bernardes, he had doubts that peace would follow. Hoping to prevent a catastrophe, he suggested that Bernardes step aside, but the President-elect had the full support of São Paulo's Washington Luís and rejected the advice.

To Pernambuco, one of the states which had supported Nilo Peçanha, federal troops were sent under a commander apparently determined to bring the state into the orbit of the country's dominant political group. When state authorities resisted, serious incidents occurred, among them a political assassination, the work of Army men; these were not left unforgotten by enemies of the federal Government.

A number of Army officers in Pernambuco resented carrying out orders which went against their political views, and late in June 1922 they appealed to Hermes da Fonseca, president of the Military Club. In reply the Marshal sent a controversial telegram to the commander in Pernambuco, stating that the Military Club was saddened that "our glorious Army" was placed in "the odious position of being hangman of the people of Pernambuco." He asked the recipient to heed the officers who objected to such conduct and he concluded with a reminder that "political administrations pass on but the Army continues."

This was too much for President Epitácio Pessoa, who denied that the federal government was illegally intervening in Pernambuco and who characterized the Marshal's telegram as a "flagrant act against discipline." He placed the Marshal under arrest for twenty-four hours and closed the Military Club for six months.

Young Army officers in Rio then started planning a revolt which was to break out at midnight between July 4 and 5, 1922. As they saw it, not only the honor of the Army was at stake but also "Representation and Justice," the slogan of the Peçanha people. Men of brains and strong character, many had turned to the Army for a career because the cost of education in other professions was prohibitive, but they could not isolate themselves from political developments and were resolved to upset the national machine in the only way possible.

The most elaborate planning took place at Copacabana Fort, which adjoins Rio's famed Copacabana Beach. As early as July 3 Captain Euclides Hermes da Fonseca, commander of the fort and son of the Marshal, was supervising the stacking of sandbags and the acquisition of large supplies of food. Conspiring officers at nearby Vigia and Praia Vermelha, unable to get the units there to go along with the plans, joined the rebel leaders at Copacabana Fort, who presently found themselves with over 200 men.

On the fourth, when trenches were being dug at the Fort, high authorities became concerned, and Euclides da Fonseca received a visit from a general accompanied by an officer bearing an order to take over the command of the Fort. But Euclides and a determined twenty-four–year–old lieutenant, Antônio de Siqueira Campos, made prisoners of them both. Said Siqueira Campos, the handsome hothead and leading spirit of the rebellion: "Brazil's eyes must be opened."

About fifteen miles to the west of the Fort officers who backed the coup were busy at Realengo Military School and at the important Army barracks at Vila Militar. Just before midnight the conspiring officer-instructors at the School had everything ready to go. The first shots were fired, the legalists fled, and the officers led 600 cadets on the early morning of July 5 to join the rebels at Vila Militar, who were scheduled to march on Catete, the presidential palace. But Vila Militar's conspirators were subdued after vainly waiting for Marshal Hermes da Fonseca himself to lead them and after unsuccessfully trying to make prisoners of loyal officers. The cadets, marching under their instructors to Vila Militar, were met by a strong Government force which opened fire on them and then led them back to the School.

Thus Copacabana Fort stood alone in the Rio area in defying the regime of Epitácio Pessoa. At 1:20 A.M. on July 5, while things were going poorly for the cadets, one of the Fort's cannons sent out a shot, a sign for the rebellion to start at all the forts. The only reply was silence, interrupted by Siqueira Campos' shout: "Cowards, all of you! But we have begun and will carry on to the end." The cannon shot at other forts and later in the day fired on the city, aiming at strategic points such as the Navy Arsenal. This caused so much consternation that the Government ordered Santa Cruz Fort to bombard Copacabana Fort.

Even after phoning to point out that resistance was useless and that the rebellion had failed at other points, the Government was unable to get the leaders at Copacabana Fort to surrender. However, on the morning of July 6 Euclides released all who wished to leave, he and Siqueira Campos explaining that those who stayed would defend the cause until death. The Navy Ministry then had its two principal warships, the *Minas Gerais* and the *São Paulo,* shoot at the Fort, and two hydroplanes dropped bombs from the air, whereupon the Fort shot back at the warships and fired in the direction of Catete Palace.

With the Fort's power and water about to be cut off, Euclides left to negotiate with the authorities, but on his way to Catete was made prisoner. Back at the Fort, where Siqueira Campos took command, the idea of surrender was dismissed, and the Fort's flag was cut into twenty-eight pieces, one for each of the remaining men to carry with him on a suicide show of protest. Unable to hold out where they were, they would battle the federal troops in the open.

Those who did this on the sands of Copacabana Beach have been immortalized as the "Eighteen of the Fort." In fact they were fewer than eighteen, and they included one civilian, who was killed in a burst of Army machine-gun fire. Of the four rebelling officers, two were killed and Lieutenants Siqueira Campos and Eduardo Gomes ended up badly wounded in a military hospital, where they received an unexpected visit from President Epitácio Pessoa.

The only other evidence of indiscipline occurred 750 miles away at an Army unit in Mato Grosso, to which generals displeasing to the central power were likely to be relegated. After the commanding general there, another relative of the Marshal, received a telegram on July 5 from the capital with news of the outbreaks, he and his subordinates decided to join the revolt. The troop, naming itself the Divisão Provisória Libertadora and issuing a proclamation attacking Bernardes for having insulted the military, set out for the state of São Paulo. But still in Mato Grosso these rebels learned of the outcome in Rio and surrendered to Government forces.

4. Gaúcho Civil War, 1923[1]

On November 15, 1922, Artur Bernardes took over the nation's Presidency amid hostile demonstrations and reports of danger to his life. From his predecessor he inherited a "state of siege" applicable to the Federal District and the state of Rio de Janeiro, and Bernardes had Congress prolong this limitation of individual freedoms before it closed its session at the end of 1922. Deeply hurt by the recent campaign, he turned his attention to states which had supported his opponent, among them Rio de Janeiro and, in the south, Rio Grande do Sul.

Raul Fernandes, an associate of Nilo Peçanha, had received in July 1922 the most votes for governor of Rio de Janeiro. But after Fernandes moved into Ingá Palace on December 31, Brazil's new President pointed out that another candidate had also declared himself elected governor. Bernardes proposed that the federal Congress, on whose support he could rely, handle the matter upon reconvening in May. In the meantime he appointed an *interventor* to administer the state on behalf of the federal government. Raul Fernandes was out.

In Rio Grande do Sul on July 3, 1922, Borges de Medeiros decried what he called federal intervention in Pernambuco and backed fellow Gaúcho Hermes da Fonseca. This he did by means of an opinion pub-

---

[1] Hélio Silva, *1922: Sangue na Areia de Copacabana*; João Neves da Fontoura, *Borges de Medieros e Seu Tempo* (*Memórias*, I); Agildo Barata, *Vida de um Revolucionário*, Ch. 3; Glauco Carneiro, "A Revolta dos Libertadores," *O Cruzeiro*, July 25, 1964 (part of the series of articles, "Revoluções Brasileiras" by Glauco Carneiro in *O Cruzeiro*); Alzira Vargas do Amaral Peixoto, *Getúlio Vargas, Meu Pai*; Alzira Vargas do Amaral Peixoto, "A Vida de Getúlio Contada por Sua Filha, Alzira Vargas, ao Jornalista Raul Giudicelli" (the *Fatos & Fotos* series starting June 15, 1963).

lished by *A Federação,* organ of the Partido Republicano Riograndense. But four days later, after the uprising at Copacabana Fort had been subdued, *A Federação* carried Borges' important editorial, called "Pela Ordem," condemning the use of violence. Borges, about to be re-elected to his fifth term as his state's chief, supported the regime of Epitácio Pessoa and recognized that Bernardes had been elected. Foes of the federal machine would get no more help from him.

The Rio Grande state constitution, elaborated by Júlio de Castilhos and often praised by Getúlio Vargas, prescribed that the governor could succeed himself if he received three quarters of the vote. Gaúcho students, seeking a candidate to run against Borges, got a favorable response when they called on Joaquim Francisco de Assis Brasil, former Brazilian minister to Washington. They found this member of the dissident Republican wing working on agricultural projects at his Pedras Altas ranch, his great mop of white hair flowing in the wind. On October 19, with the election a little more than a month away, an appropriate manifesto declared that Assis Brasil would campaign as candidate of a new party, the Aliança Libertadora, to whose banner he hoped to attract all the anti-Borges forces in the state, including the Federalistas.

On November 25, 1922, ten days after Bernardes occupied Catete Palace, both parties in the Rio Grande contest took what advantage they could of the state election law: it allowed anyone who had a voting certificate to cast a ballot without investigation as to whether he was the man named on the certificate.

The results reported by the municipalities went for checking to a commission of the state Assembly headed by Getúlio Vargas. For a while the commission seemed to find it impossible to show that Borges had the necessary three quarters, and so Republicans were delegated to discuss the problem with their party president. But when they were admitted to his august presence they heard him exclaim, "I know what you're here for: to advise me that I have been elected for the fifth time." They quietly filed out and the commission went ahead more assiduously with its work, reporting on January 16 that Borges had 106,360 votes to 32,216 for Assis Brasil. With Artur Bernardes refusing to act as arbitrator in the dispute which followed, the state Assembly approved the work of the Vargas Commission, and on January 25, 1923, Borges commenced his fifth term.

Civil war broke out at once between the Maragatos, as the Borges people had for years depreciatingly called their local foes, and the Chimangos, supporters of "the vulture."

It was a bloody affair, more typical of Rio Grande do Sul than of Brazil as a whole. After Borges contracted 500 well-mounted mercenaries from Uruguay to assist his blue-uniformed Brigada Militar, engagements continued, each side using the services of professional throat cutters who reposed during the engagements and afterwards set to work on unhappy Maragato or Chimango prisoners.

High-spirited Maragatos, who as Federalists had fought Republicans in the days of Júlio de Castilhos, now referred to themselves as Libertadores (supporters of Assis Brasil's Aliança Libertadora). Gladdening their hearts, assistance came from some of the prominent Riograndense families. Vargas' mother was a Dorneles, and when various members of the Dorneles family took up arms on behalf of Assis Brasil, relatives stopped speaking to each other. To help combat this opposition Borges called up provisional units which were organized by members of the Vargas and Aranha families and by men like José Antônio Flôres da Cunha, an *intendente provisório* who had anticipated the new civil war by purchasing four hundred rifles in Argentina. By living dangerously such men were able to keep old Borges from falling, but they could not end the strife.

As a lieutenant colonel of the São Borja provisional unit Getúlio Vargas early sought to participate in the conflict, setting out with some companions wielding knives to rescue the Aranhas, beleaguered by Maragatos near the Argentine border. But before the rescue squad could perform this service the Aranhas escaped and joined Flôres da Cunha.

As it turned out, Getúlio saw little action, for he had work to do in the national capital, having been elected a federal *deputado* in October 1922. His predecessors in the Gaúcho delegation in Congress were demoralized and not very helpful now to the Governor; they had spent their energy speaking in favor of Nilo Peçanha until "Pela Ordem" had forced them tearfully—too tearfully to suit Borges—to reverse their position. What concerned the old autocrat was that the Bernardes Government might intervene in his state, and he hoped that Vargas in Rio could make this seem unnecessary.

Getúlio found himself and his family some modest quarters not far from the federal Câmara dos Deputados, and settled down in his unfrivolous manner to try to charm his fellow congressmen with his reasonableness. When Congress convened on May 3, 1923, he went along with the majority in approving the decree by which Bernardes had extended the "state of siege" to the end of the year. Overcoming what he called his "timidity and incapacity" as a new federal *deputado,* Getúlio spoke early in favor of Bernardes, arguing that the intervention in the state of Rio had been justified by the existence there of two governors and two Assemblies. Asked whether the situation in Rio Grande was not similar, he disagreed, saying that the Gaúcho government had the material force to put down the rebels. He did, however, speak highly of the bravery of both Rio Grande's Republicans and Libertadores. There was nothing narrow-minded about Getúlio.

Bernardes had behind him not only the largest bloc of federal *deputados,* that of his own state of Minas, but with one exception all members of the São Paulo representation. The exception, son of Brazil's first civilian President, voted against the intervention in Rio de Janeiro, and for his temerity he lost his seat in the next election. Nilo Peçanha, a defender of the rebels of July 5, blamed the federal government for having created the situation in which Rio de Janeiro found itself with two state governments, but his political fortunes were at a low ebb and the Senate, like the Câmara, supported Bernardes.

In spite of Vargas' statements there was doubt in Rio that the Borges Administration could end the hostilities in Rio Grande. The fighting strength on each side had been built up to about 10,000 and, although the Libertadores were not so well armed, they effectively harassed the Chimangos in the countryside. Borges, who on principle preferred not to resort to loans, had to borrow money from Uruguay. The federal government was pleased enough with Pela Ordem and the sentiments being expressed by Vargas, but it could not ignore the Gaúcho conflict.

As early as May 1923 Bernardes suggested peace terms, under which Borges' recent election would be recognized but further re-elections would be ruled out. Other changes in the state constitution were proposed and, although Borges agreed to place a few of his opponents in Congress, he refused to tamper with the revered creation of Júlio de Castilhos. So Bernardes threatened to put the matter in the hands of Congress if peace were not restored in Rio Grande. Then, after some months of continued strife, he directed his Minister of War, General Setembrino de Carvalho, to try to negotiate a settlement.

An armistice was worked out for November 7, 1923, with the understanding that all fighting forces would remain in their positions during the negotiations. A relief to many, the armistice was particularly agreeable to the Maragato military leader, Honório Lemes, who was being mercilessly hounded by Flôres da Cunha.

The War Minister found old Borges less difficult to deal with than Assis Brasil, who simply kept insisting that Borges must get out, forcing

Setembrino to repeat more than once that the state election results would be respected. After the armistice Setembrino got Borges to agree to practically everything originally suggested by Bernardes, thus leaving it up to the Libertador leader to accept the terms or be held responsible for the renewal of hostilities. Assis Brasil finally signed at his Pedras Altas ranch on December 15, 1923.

Although Borges steadfastly refused to increase the authority of state assemblymen, the treaty did include some radical changes in the Rio Grande constitution. Gubernatorial re-elections were barred and restrictions were placed on the governor's power to appoint *intendentes provisórios* to administer municipalities. From each state district the minority party was guaranteed at least one representative in the state and federal legislatures. Full amnesty was guaranteed to all who had participated in the civil war.

Old Borges had not suffered a fate as bad as that of Raul Fernandes in Rio de Janeiro. He had, of course, lost some prestige, but a fairly good working arrangement had been developing between himself and Bernardes. Borges also appeared to have preserved for himself perpetual domination of the state through his presidency of the Partido Republicano Riograndense.

The Gaúchos settled down to peace. But it was to last for less than a year.

5. Uprising in São Paulo, July, 1924[1]

Deputado Getúlio Vargas co-operated with the Bernardes Administration and served on a congressional commission which helped amend the federal constitution to give the chief executive stronger powers. In this capacity Getúlio had an opportunity to preach the virtues of Rio Grande's constitution.

More importantly for the course of Brazilian history and the career of

[1] Juarez Távora, *A Guisa de Depoimento sobre a Revolução Brasileira de 1924*, I; Hélio Silva, *1922: Sangue na Areia de Copacabana*; Abilio de Noronha, *Narrando a Verdade*; Polícia de São Paulo, *Movimento Subversivo de Julho* [1924]; Procurador Criminal da República, em Commissão no Estado de São Paulo, *Successos Subversivos de São Paulo: Denuncia*; Glauco Carneiro, "A Revolução de Isidoro," *O Cruzeiro*, August 1, 1964 (part of the series of articles, "Revoluções Brasileiras" by Glauco Carneiro in *O Cruzeiro*); Abguar Bastos, *Prestes e a Revolução Social*, Ch. 3; Newton de Siqueira Campos, interviews, July–September, 1963; Emídio da Costa Miranda, interview, July 19, 1963; and Eduardo Gomes, interview, July 20, 1963.

Getúlio, winds of rebellion were blowing fiercely in military circles. Events in the nation's capital had not, in the eyes of the 1922 revolutionaries, borne out Bernardes' pledge that "the President will forget the insults hurled at the candidate." Instead of getting amnesty, they learned that the courts found all the participants in the 1922 outbreak to be criminals in accordance with an article of the Penal Code which they themselves considered inapplicable. These *tenentes* (lieutenants), their military careers already brought to a sudden end in their youth, were now condemned to years of prison, but most of them remained at large, plotting new rebellions and building up a force which came to be known as *tenentismo*. It would turn them into modern Brazil's most legendary figures, hardened by fighting, jailbreaks, and long forced marches. Identified quickly with a desire for change in Brazil's political ways, some of the *tenentes* became gradually and unclearly identified with a desire for social change. Using fictitious names and posing as men engaged in a variety of trades, they were likely to travel constantly in their new work, visiting Army units and developing plans with friends.

Siqueira Campos, the resolute leader of the "Eighteen of the Fort," escaped from the military hospital, and, after hiding in Rio and São Paulo, made his way to the La Plata region just south of Brazil to carry on the conspiracy. But most of the plotters remained in Brazil. Eduardo Gomes, the other officer to survive the slaughter on Copacabana Beach, might be found in vast Mato Grosso, now and then in the company of some who had participated there in the march of the Divisão Provisória Libertadora. Joaquim and Juarez Távora, brothers who had rebelled in 1922, traveled principally between São Paulo and the far south.

The peace pact of Pedras Altas did not help the conspirators, but it meant that War Minister Setembrino de Carvalho would be returning to the national capital from Rio Grande, and the Távora brothers readied plans to capture him as he passed through the state of Paraná, where most of the Army units were expected to rebel. However, the plan failed when word of it reached the Government, and discontented military men in Paraná thereafter acted too cautiously to suit the Távoras.

For that matter, little seemed to favor the revolutionary cause early in 1924. Bernardes, irritated by the press and not unforgetful of the famous "false letters," got Congress to approve a law which was supposed to check improper journalistic behavior, but which his enemies felt would be used against them. Nilo Peçanha's 1922 running mate was forced out of Bahia. And Nilo Peçanha himself died, a piece of the cut-up flag of Copacabana Fort lying against his heart.

The center of the conspiracy had come to be located in the city of São Paulo, more precisely in two houses there. In these might be found many who were wanted by the law, such as those who had led the Realengo cadets to revolt in 1922. But they were joined now by an extraordinarily large number of adventuresome idealists who had not participated in the events of 1922.

An important new member of the group was cavalry major Miguel Costa, converted by Joaquim Távora. A noted sportsman, highly respected in all circles, Costa had more to lose than most of his new companions if things went badly. He commanded a regiment in the powerful Fôrça Pública, or São Paulo State Police, and became responsible for the adherence to the revolutionary cause of much of that well-trained and elite militia. In elaborating plans for the revolt in São Paulo he was invaluable.

When it came to naming a head of the revolutionary movement, the young military opponents of Bernardes turned to a retired colonel who had participated in the uprising of 1893, Isidoro Dias Lopes. Yet Joaquim Távora, revealing all the necessary qualities for leadership, was the one who decided that the new outbreak would honor the memory of July 5, 1922, by occurring on that same day in 1924. Faced with pessimistic reports about the chances elsewhere in Brazil, he declared that the revolt would go ahead on that day even if he had to dynamite Catete Palace alone.[2]

Thus on July 5 the population of the city of São Paulo awoke in the midst of a battle which was to rage for days. Isidoro Dias Lopes and Joaquim Távora quickly captured the commander of the military region but, soon after, some of the top leaders of the rebellion were made prisoners when one of the battalions of the Fôrça Pública backed the Government. The National Telegraph Office changed hands six times early in the fighting, whereas during the whole struggle the rebels were able to control the railroad stations. To make things more alarming for noncombatants, federal troops, sent from the port city of Santos, began to bombard positions held by the revolutionaries.

In the city, legalist Army leaders—and the governor too—were so well impressed with the rebel artillery fire that on July 8 they resolved to withdraw, just when the pessimistic Isidoro Dias Lopes was ordering the rebels to do the same. On the next day Miguel Costa, revolutionary commander of the Fôrça Pública Paulista who chose to fight on instead of obeying Isidoro, suddenly and surprisingly discovered the entire city in the hands

[2] Emídio Miranda, interview, July 19, 1963.

of the revolutionaries. He advised Isidoro, whose men were making their departure, and the veteran of 1893, regretting his recent decision, offered to step down as chief of the movement. Officers around him restrained him, and he called his men back.

From outside the city a full-scale attack to retake it began on the night of July 10, by which time the federal troops had been reinforced by the Rio de Janeiro state militia. On July 15, when the rebels were being pushed back, their outstanding revolutionary, Joaquim Távora, was mortally wounded in combat. The federal bombardment of the great city caused little comment in the pro-Administration Congress, but it alarmed Paulista civilians, some of whom joined the archbishop in directing an appeal to Bernardes. The President, however, insisted that if the government were not to shell the enemy the moral destruction would be worse than damage caused by bombardment. When the Paulistas approached the rebels about an armistice, Isidoro laid down his terms: the Bernardes Government should resign.

Elsewhere in Brazil the only support for "Isidoro's Revolution" was in the tiny northeastern state of Sergipe, and at Manaus in Amazonas. Such a situation hardly indicated that the end had come for Bernardes. Eduardo Gomes made one fragile effort to communicate with the people in the national capital, being flown from São Paulo in a small plane with thousands of copies of a manifesto for the Cariocas, and with a bomb for Catete Palace. But the plane developed mechanical trouble and had to land before it reached Rio.

The São Paulo revolutionary force, consisting at the outset of 2,000 men from the Fôrça Pública and the federal Army, grew to 5,000 with the incorporation of Germans, Hungarians, and Italians, who had originally come to São Paulo in search of work and who were now attracted by wages and plots of land offered by the revolutionaries. Against this assemblage Bernardes flung a force of 18,000, and organized additional columns to advance from Minas, Mato Grosso, and the south.

While the way was still open for escape, the revolutionaries decided to use it. With plenty of arms and munitions, 3,000 of them set out by train on July 27. In Congress, Getúlio Vargas hailed their defeat as they began crossing the state of São Paulo in a westward direction on a trip which took them to the Paraná River, separating São Paulo from Mato Grosso. Reaching the river port of Epitácio Pessoa, they renamed it, calling it Pôrto Joaquim Távora. On their way they picked up a press with which they printed some "war bonds" and several issues of O Libertador.

The motto of this periodical was like that of an opposition paper which Maurício de Lacerda helped manage in Rio: "It is necessary to republicanize the Republic."

6. Luís Carlos Prestes Joins the Revolution[1]

Leading a contingent of Hungarian and Italian veterans of the First World War, Juarez Távora advanced from Pôrto Joaquim Távora into southern Mato Grosso, where the revolutionaries planned to establish the "Free State of the South." But the expedition was a catastrophe. Marching in their accustomed but inappropriate form of a great phalanx, the Europeans could not cope with the enemy fire, nor with an enormous brush fire spread by the wind.

Revising their plans, the revolutionaries, late in August 1924, started descending the Paraná River southward into Paraná state. Some of the men used two river steamships, and these, towing small boats bearing cannon and munitions, occasionally went aground as the revolutionaries hugged one bank or another in the effort to keep hidden.

Tall, white-haired João Francisco Ferreira de Souza, a veteran frontier fighter known as "the hyena of Cati," was an expert at reopening long-abandoned trails at the riverside. While he and Juarez Távora led the vanguard in successful skirmishes with the enemy, the revolutionaries established positions at several of the ports on the Brazilian side of the river which separates Paraná from Paraguay. Finally in mid-September 1924 the Coluna Paulista, as the revolutionaries called their force, reached Iguaçu Falls in southwest Paraná near the Argentina-Paraguay border.

To protect the posts they held on the river, the revolutionaries sent troops eastward; but the federals were building up strength in Paraná and the revolutionaries could not push beyond Catanduvas, a town eighty miles east of the river. João Cabanas, a revolutionary known for his diabolic smile and for his bold deeds during the São Paulo upheaval, led his

[1] Nelson Tabajara de Oliveira, *1924: A Revolução de Isidoro*; Hélio Silva, *1926: A Grande Marcha*; João Alberto Lins de Barros, *Memórias de um Revolucionário*; Lourenço Moreira Lima, *A Coluna Prestes*; Abguar Bastos, *Prestes e a Revolução Social*; Glauco Carneiro, "A Coluna Prestes," *O Cruzeiro*, August 8, 1964 (part of the series of articles, "Revoluções Brasileiras" by Glauco Carneiro in *O Cruzeiro*). Dorval Soares, interview, July 24, 1963; Luís Carlos Prestes, interview, September 5, 1963; Emídio Miranda, interview, July 19, 1963; and Newton de Siqueira Campos, interviews, July–September, 1963.

revolutionary "Column of Death" through large landholdings, and there
he brought terror to *latifundiários*, four of whom were shot on the charge
of torturing and murdering conspiring serfs.

To bolster his movement Isidoro sent Juarez Távora to Rio Grande to
persuade Siqueira Campos and Luís Carlos Prestes to start an uprising in
the far south. Siqueira Campos' Copacabana exploit had made him the
leading revolutionary hero, but Captain Prestes was unknown because
typhoid fever in Rio had prevented his joining the bold "Eighteen." A
small, serious, twenty-six–year–old Army engineer with a brilliant
scholastic record behind him, he was directing the construction of a rail
line in Rio Grande in 1924.

In planning the revolution in Rio Grande, Prestes and Siqueira Campos
were joined by Lieutenant João Alberto Lins de Barros, a lanky youth
from Pernambuco. They were joined, too, by men like Honório Lemes,
who lacked their professional training but who, as veteran Maragatos,
were practiced Gaúcho fighters.

The rebellion broke out, as planned, on October 24, 1924, at points
bearing saintly names in the old Jesuit Missões region: Santo Ângelo,
São Luís and São Borja. Prestes could count on 2,000 men, many from the
barracks, to face a superior legalist foe, and he himself led the Santo Ângelo railway battalion in revolt. João Alberto, leading 300 rebels against
500 soldiers in the town of Alegrete, got the first of much experience
when he directed artillery fire on the town's strategic points, careful to
miss the building where he had left his wife and their nine-day-old first-
born child.

João Alberto's shots went straight, but the battle went badly. Federal
soldiers, assisted by Borges' state militia, forced João Alberto's men to
Uruguaiana, on the Argentine border, and there they were joined by
Honório Lemes.

The border town, full of colorful Gaúcho horsemen who had added
the revolutionary red ribbon to their characteristic garb, seemed surprisingly festive to Juarez Távora and João Alberto, both from the
Northeast. They learned that Gaúchos recuperate quickly from defeat.
But they could not persuade them to adopt the more scientific battle
strategy taught in school. Instead, they heard "General" Honório Lemes
counsel Távora not to use spurs. The riding methods of the northerners
did not set well with the Gaúchos.

Honório Lemes was the leader whom 2,500 revolutionaries in Uruguaiana followed early in November 1924 to make a surprise attack on
their foe. Although not more than 1,000 were properly armed, they set

forth at night, determinedly if not carefully—musical instruments and all. But early the next morning, while enjoying a hearty *churrasco* (barbecue) breakfast, they themselves were surprised by the troops of Flôres da Cunha. As long as they could they followed the instructions of "General" Honório, who was shouting from horseback, indifferent to bullets. But the battle was lost. Defeated warriors retired to Argentina to get their breath.

The death of a rebel Army captain left Prestes the revolutionary with the highest Army rank, and thus top revolutionary commander, in the state. Until he grew a beard he looked to be about twenty-one. After allotting detachment commands in a way which upset informally high-ranking Gaúchos, he concentrated on getting his men out of the enemy circle being formed around São Luís. In a maneuver which soon brought him fame, he had João Alberto's Second Detachment act as a decoy, luring the enemy so as to allow an opening, and later, when the legalist ring closed in on São Luís, the Prestes Column had vanished.

Outnumbered and outarmed in Rio Grande, Prestes decided to join the rebels in Paraná. As 1924 ended he was leading 2,000 poorly armed men and twice as many horses on the first part of the march north, an experience so rough that half his men dropped out when the Column passed through a town on the Argentine border. The pampas gave way to difficult trails through thick forests, which had to be penetrated while the enemy was being held off. The horses had to be abandoned, and, as cattle became scarce, the *churrasco* lovers of Rio Grande had to change their eating habits. When the Column was crossing the 500-meter-wide Uruguay River, between the states of Rio Grande and Santa Catarina, Prestes gave orders that the twenty or thirty women should remain behind. But Prestes, the last to cross, found all the women on the other side when he got there.[2]

For much of the march João Alberto's Second Detachment was in the vanguard. Prestes, the frail little man with the new-grown beard, bore little resemblance to the elegant chiefs the Gaúchos were used to. But he seemed to be everywhere, studying the maps he carried with him, planning where to go and when to attack, resolving innumerable problems. In a letter to Isidoro he asked for better maps, ones showing the positions occupied by the enemy. He wrote: "War in Brazil, whatever the terrain, is war of movement. For us revolutionaries, movement is victory."[3]

[2] Luís Carlos Prestes, interview, September 5, 1963.
[3] Lourenço Moreira Lima, *A Coluna Prestes*, pp. 108–111.

At the end of March 1925, when the Prestes Column joined the Paulista rebels in Paraná near Iguaçu Falls, it consisted of about 800 revolutionaries, in pitiful condition but high spirits. However, the news was far from bright. To allow the Prestes Column to join the Coluna Paulista at the river, Paulista rebels at Catanduvas had been fighting from trenches, under deplorable conditions, holding off a great federal force. Just as the two revolutionary columns joined, the defenders of Catanduvas were forced to surrender, the federals making prisoners of the 400 survivors.

Fifteen thousand legalists then approached the river, where the combined São Paulo and Prestes Columns had 1,600 men.

Prestes and Miguel Costa proposed to march through eighty miles of unknown Paraguayan forests and hills, re-entering Brazil in southern Mato Grosso. After their followers had agreed to this, a new command was worked out. Ailing Isidoro was finally persuaded that he could best serve the revolution by conspiring from Argentina. Top command would go to Miguel Costa, a major who was named revolutionary general. There would be two brigades of nearly 800 men each: the Rio Grande Brigade, under Prestes; and the São Paulo Brigade, under the Greek-god figure of Juarez Távora.

7. The Long March[1]

When tall João Alberto, in his familiar role of vanguard leader, embarked with 150 men on the *Assis Brasil* in April 1925 to cross the stiff currents of the Paraná River, he began an adventure which ended in Bolivia early in 1927. The "Long March" of fourteen thousand miles throughout the vast interior of Brazil presented almost every conceivable problem and cost the revolutionaries hundreds of lives. The federal Army, out to break up the march, was assisted by state militias and, most effectively, by groups of *cangaceiros,* or bandits, supplied with Government arms and money. In addition to the difficulties often presented by

[1] Lourenço Moreira Lima, *A Coluna Prestes*; Hélio Silva, *1926: A Grande Marcha*; Juarez Távora, *À Guisa de Depoimento sobre a Revolução Brasileira de 1924*, III; João Alberto Lins de Barros, *Memórias de um Revolucionário*; Abguar Bastos, *Prestes e a Revolução Social*; Jorge Amado, *O Cavaleiro da Esperança*; Lourival Coutinho, *O General Góes Depõe*; Glauco Carneiro, "A Coluna Prestes," *O Cruzeiro*, August 8, 1964 (part of the series of articles, "Revoluções Brasileiras," by Glauco Carneiro in *O Cruzeiro*); G. M. Dyott, "Miranda, o Salteador, Sanguinario, Implacavel, Culto e Cavalheiresco," *O Cruzeiro*, June 22, 1935; Dorval Soares, interview, July 24, 1963; Emídio Miranda, interview, July 19, 1963; and Luís Carlos Prestes, interview, September 5, 1963.

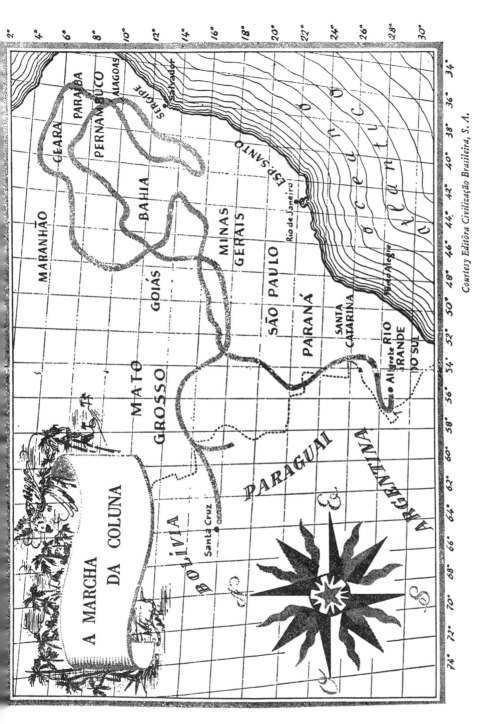

The Long March. Map used to illustrate *Memórias* of João Alberto Lins de Barros, who participated in the rebellion at Alegrete in October 1924 and joined Luis Carlos Prestes in the Long March (1925–1927).

Courtesy Editôra Civilização Brasileira, S. A.

the terrain, and shortages of food and water, serious attacks were made by malaria. Local inhabitants, for the most part terror-stricken, were usually stubbornly hostile. The problem of preserving harmony and discipline within the ranks of the revolutionaries themselves was always present.

Outstanding leadership was called for, and this was consistently provided by Luís Carlos Prestes, who became Miguel Costa's chief of staff when Juarez Távora became assistant chief of staff in an early reorganization which sought to eliminate rivalry between the Rio Grande and São Paulo Brigades. The troops, by then reduced to 1,200, were divided into four detachments commanded by João Alberto, Siqueira Campos, Osvaldo Cordeiro de Farias, and Djalma Dutra. All these top officers gained great stature as revolutionaries, but by the time the March was over and seeds of unrest had been widely sown, the revolutionaries knew they had a remarkable leader whose name was on tongues throughout Brazil: Luís Carlos Prestes.

After passing through Paraguay, the revolutionaries eluded a force of 2,000 truck-driven soldiers brought to Mato Grosso by German-trained Major Bertoldo Klinger. Commander-in-Chief Miguel Costa favored a decisive battle with Klinger's troops, whereas Prestes, wanting to use quick movements to stir up the revolutionary spirit in the Brazilian interior, preferred to avoid a showdown. At staff meetings the plans advocated by Prestes invariably prevailed. Among the common soldiers, also, his prestige was already enormous, and they wished to acclaim him as a revolutionary general. But for this they had to wait until early 1926, when, at a ceremony in northern Brazil, Miguel Costa promoted his chief of staff to this rank.

Before the Column left Mato Grosso, the high alcoholic content of *cachaça* provided an unfortunate experience. One hundred drunken revolutionaries engaged in large-scale depredations, and then the ringleader deserted, knowing that officers of the revolution were dead-set against such misbehavior. Members of the Column had no money and anyone found with any was presumed to have stolen it and was whipped or, sometimes, forced to walk several days while companions rode on horse.[2] The vanguard was ordered to destroy any *cachaça* stills it found. But in spite of everything a few cases of notorious indiscipline arose, as when one drunken soldier tried to shoot Prestes and when another member of the

[2] Dorval Soares, interview, July 24, 1963.

Column pulled a knife on Siqueira Campos; in such cases strong measures were taken, the offender sometimes being shot.

Siqueira Campos firmly opposed having any women with his troops, but other detachment commanders were more lenient, and one soldier's wife, who started her travels when Prestes and his men left Rio Grande do Sul, gave birth on three occasions before the Long March ended in 1927.[3]

In Goiás in June 1925 the Column made the mistake of attempting an assault on its pursuers, and thirty revolutionaries were killed. Artur Bernardes, well pleased, sent a congratulatory message to the governor of Minas, whose state militia was assisting in southern Goiás; Klinger expressed satisfaction with the "preliminary phase" of his operation.

However, not far from what is now Brasília, the revolutionaries bested the federals and in August 1925 lost contact with Klinger's force. The Miguel Costa-Prestes Column invaded parts of Minas and Bahia, returned to Goiás, and made the trek to the far northern state of Maranhão. Klinger, suspected of having conspired in São Paulo before being selected to crush the Column, was to be tried by the Supreme Military Tribunal for his failures in southern Goiás; the ill will existing between him and one of his superiors was the first example of a lack of harmony which would help the rebels.

The Column met with encouraging receptions only in the backlands of the two northern states of Maranhão and Piauí (directly east of Maranhão). When it prepared to cross a river into Maranhão it was met by friendly anti-Government politicians, who provided a boat. The revolutionaries were brought up to date on the "state of siege" which Bernardes had extended to cover all the country, and some of them took time out to print another issue of their journal, O Libertador. New adherents in Maranhão and Piauí increased the Column's strength from 900 to 1,300.

But malaria affected 60 per cent of the Column's men, and General João Gomes was present with 6,000 federal soldiers, many of whom contributed to the successful defense of Piauí's capital. At the end of 1925 Prestes decided that it would be a good time to move into Brazil's northeastern bulge.

With the capture of Juarez Távora in Piauí, near the border of his home state of Ceará,[4] the fortunes of the Column took a decided turn for

[3] *Ibid.*
[4] Juarez Távora, interview, May 20, 1965.

the worse. The Northeast was infested with groups of *cangaceiros*. These outlaws, whose leaders were appointed reserve officers in the federal Army, were organized into battalions to fight the Column. If at the same time they sacked the countryside such ravagement was usually blamed on the revolutionaries. An Army barracks rebellion was supposed to break out in Pernambuco with the Column's arrival there, but it never materialized; its organizer was shot and his chief accomplice beheaded. The Column, described as a bunch of barbarians, found itself too busy fighting to worry about where the next meal might come from.

Disappointed, weary, and reduced in number, the revolutionaries outfought the Pernambuco state militia and used Prestes' strategy to gain a crossing of the São Francisco River into Bahia. Their horses lost, the bedraggled men made their way on foot to the harsh backlands of southern Bahia, where the main fight was against thirst and the "patriotic troops" of "Colonel" Horácio de Matos, whose *jagunços* (ruffians) ruled the high regions.

Federal troops stuck largely to the pleasanter river banks, and federal officers squabbled. During an altercation with Colonel Álvaro Mariante, General João Gomes quit, and the former, who had defeated the Paulista rebels in Paraná, concentrated on finding assistance from local military units. This effort involved time-consuming arguments about who gave orders to whom, and when the revolutionaries invaded Minas Gerais again a real scrap developed between Mariante and Minas Governor Fernando Melo Viana.

In Bahia in June 1926 the Column was in no condition to resist serious attack. Malaria had struck again and many of the thirsty, hungry men, plodding on foot, were bearing the sick and wounded. But Prestes and his associates wanted to hold out at least until Bernardes left office in November 1926, making the Column one thing in Brazil he had been unable to dominate.

A possible exit from Brazil had to be gained. This objective required going back through much of the territory already covered on the march from Mato Grosso. For the Column it was fortunate that more horses were found and that the Pernambuco militia was mainly concerned with defensive measures. The most formidable attacks were made by bands led by "Colonel" Franklin de Albuquerque and "Colonel" Horácio de Matos, *caudilhos* of the interior. In a surprise assault in northern Goiás, the "patriots" of Horácio de Matos killed 5 revolutionaries before Siqueira Campos and his detachment drove them away. Among the seriously wounded was Miguel Costa, and the Column's busy doctor, a veterinary, was called to apply his remedies on the commander in chief.

President Bernardes, disappointed in the Army, looked to São Paulo's renowned state militia of 4,000. But again the legalists guarded towns and roads which the Column avoided, and again there were conflicts of authority. What most upset the Paulista militia was finding itself attacked by the "patriots" of Horácio de Matos. Bernardes turned once more to the Army, making Mariante a general.

From Mato Grosso, Miguel Costa and Prestes sent emissaries to Libres, Argentina, to get Isidoro Dias Lopes' ideas about the future of the revolution. An escort of 12 of the boldest conducted the envoys to the Paraguayan border while Siqueira Campos' detachment of 80 men enticed the enemy away from the route of the envoys. After this Siqueira Campos and his followers never could relocate the main Column and carried on their own march.

With no word coming from Isidoro or Siqueira Campos, Prestes proposed that the Column divide itself into autonomous bands to carry on the campaign. The soldiers, however, favored emigrating to Bolivia. Miguel Costa agreed with them, and thus took, as he rarely did, a position contrary to that of Prestes.

The last lap of the Long March followed a trail through dense forest. It was not unusual to see Gaúcho riders astride oxen, and when the forest gave way to swamps near Bolivia, the beasts were invaluable for drawing heavy canoes. The men of Franklin de Albuquerque and the Mato Grosso militia killed 7 revolutionaries with some of their final shots before the Column of 620 entered Bolivia early in February 1927. Siqueira Campos and his remaining 65 men got to Paraguay late in March.

8. The Revolutionaries Cope with Peace

While the Miguel Costa-Prestes Column was engaged in its rugged adventure, "Marshal" Isidoro Dias Lopes, chief of the revolution, was obsessed with the idea of organizing an invasion of Rio Grande.

Help for his mission stemmed from events late in 1924 in Rio, where some naval officers resolved to play a part in trying to overthrow the Bernardes regime. A few of these seafaring revolutionaries picked up a supply of chloroform at the Rio clinic of Dr. Pedro Ernesto Batista, a civilian conspirator, and sought to put unco-operative shipmates into a long sleep.[1] Although this trick failed, in November 1924 the rebel seamen on the battleship *São Paulo* were able to overpower the loyal men aboard, and the ship, exchanging shots with the Rio forts, set out under the command of Herculino Cascardo. It proved impossible for the *São Paulo* to land its 600 sailors in Rio Grande do Sul and so it went on to Montevideo. Thirty of the more irrepressible sailors crossed from Uruguay to join discontented Gaúchos in rebellion, but they were badly overwhelmed, and the men of Borges de Medeiros, showing the newcomers that Rio Grande meant business, cut the throats of 11 invaders.[2]

As soon as he was established at the Argentine town of Libres on the Rio Grande border, Isidoro began plotting with Maragato fighters and ex-officers of the *São Paulo*. Still working on plans in November 1926, on the eve of Washington Luís' inauguration, the exiles were surprised to learn of an uprising in Rio Grande by the Etchegoyen brothers. Apart from wounding the dashing Osvaldo Aranha, who headed a band of Borges *provisórios*, the Etchegoyens accomplished little, and the exiles decided to help them in December, 1926, by invading Rio Grande at several points in what they called a "lightning campaign."[3] Some who did this feared that Brazil's new President might hurt the revolutionary cause by declaring a general amnesty, and they hoped the unrest they were creating would make this unlikely.[4] But the unrest was short-lived. Outnumbered by men fighting under Flôres da Cunha and a brother of Aranha, the battle-weary revolutionaries recrossed the frontier in disorder at the end of 1926, with only half their force remaining. That seemed to be the end of the revolution in Rio Grande.

With the inauguration of fifty-six–year–old President Washington Luís Pereira de Souza, and with the emigration of the Miguel Costa-Prestes Column, Brazil came to enjoy a peace unknown during the Bernardes administration. No cry of election fraud was possible, for the robust and majestic ex-head of São Paulo had been the only candidate offered to the people in the presidential "contest" of 1926. Showing his appreciation of the political support given him by Borges de Medeiros, the new President appointed Getúlio Vargas as his Finance Minister in the federal Cabinet.

Washington Luís, another member of the cultured group which had

---

[1] Augusto Amaral Peixoto, interview, August 17, 1963.
[2] *Ibid.*
[3] Nelson Tabajara de Oliveira, *1924: A Revolução de Isidoro*, pp. 67–86.
[4] Augusto Amaral Peixoto, interview, August 17, 1963.

been providing Brazil with Presidents, appeared more affable than his predecessor, who was almost injured by irate mobs when he appeared in Rio to take his Senate seat in 1927. But, like Bernardes, Washington Luís believed in treating the opposition severely and, after receiving an unflattering telegram from Siqueira Campos about his "election victory," he rejected all suggestions of granting amnesty to revolutionary officers. The government did absolve civilians and soldiers below the rank of sergeant who had gone on the Long March; but Washington Luís maintained that a general amnesty would be a sign of weakness on the part of his Administration, and he was certainly no respecter of weakness. Lindolfo Collor, leader of the Gaúcho Republicans in Congress, joined the congressional majority in backing the President, whereas Assis Brasil, recently elected opposition *deputado* from Rio Grande, agreed with much of the press that in denying full amnesty Washington Luís was blocking a popular cause of humanitarian character.

In 1927 "Marshal" Isidoro was right when he told eager Maragatos that it was not the time to take up arms. But Column leaders Siqueira Campos and João Alberto, highly impressed with their recent experience in northern and central Brazil, wanted to make Prestes supreme commander of the revolutionary movement. Isidoro, they felt, was old and pessimistic. Assis Brasil, who had received a few opposition votes in the 1926 presidential election, agreed that the switch be made. So did exiles in Argentina who were being asked to contribute funds to help sustain Prestes and his men in Bolivia. Then when Isidoro acquiesced, Prestes succeeded him as the military head of the revolution.

Prestes, who became known as the "Cavalier of Hope," was caring for his veterans, most of whom, like himself, were suffering from malaria. A few of the men died, but others made their way to a charity hospital in Corumbá, Mato Grosso. The circumstances of the 400 remaining in the lake district of southeast Bolivia were much improved when Prestes arranged a contract for them to work on the lands of a large British concession.

The studious "Cavalier of Hope," who might be found reading Karl Marx when he was not supervising work, remained about a year, leaving Bolivia only after the last of the Column's veterans who wanted to return to Brazil had done so. Then he settled down in Buenos Aires. Working as an engineer with a road-construction firm, he soon tired of Miguel Costa's proverbial patience and got into the habit of carrying on long discussions with Rodolfo Ghioldi and other Argentine Communists.

At Prestes' suggestion an attempt was made to further the cause in Rio, and there for a while Juarez Távora, who had escaped from prison, joined Siqueira Campos and João Alberto in fanning the revolutionary flames with young new Army *tenentes*. But the outlook for overthrowing the great Brazilian political steam roller appeared bleak.

Optimistic and self-assured, Washington Luís was giving Brazil an administration which gained popularity from the start by terminating the nationwide "state of siege." The federal budget in 1927 showed itself in balance, while new loans from London and Wall Street, bringing Brazil's public indebtedness abroad to over a billion dollars, helped promote the President's favorite objectives—highway construction, and a stable currency backed by plenty of gold. The no-nonsense formulae with which Paulistas had brought progress and prosperity to Brazil early in the century were felt to have eternal value. Banning trade unions and strikes, the administration called the "labor problem a problem for the police."

In the Rio clinic of Dr. Pedro Ernesto conspirators found little to cheer about. The most hopeful sign seemed to lie in the work of the Partido Democrático which, having been founded in São Paulo the previous year, decided in 1927 to work on a national scale; calling itself the Partido Democrático Nacional, it joined forces with Assis Brasil's Partido Libertador in Rio Grande. In 1928, after a group of Paulista Democrats had gone to Argentina to speak with Prestes, Isidoro, and Miguel Costa, the new national party sent caravans of speakers around the countryside to preach its gospel of electoral reform, "Representation and Justice."[5] The caravan which made its way by boat to the north in July 1928 featured Assis Brasil, who proclaimed that his title of "Civilian Chief of the Revolution" had been conferred by Luís Carlos Prestes and Isidoro Dias Lopes.

[5] Paulo Nogueira Filho, *Ideais e Lutas de um Burguês Progressista; O Partido Democrático e a Revolução de 1930*, I, 152–238.

9. The Republicans Rule

Both inclination and training gave Getúlio Vargas a high respect for a balanced budget, and he ran the Finance Ministry in a manner which brought him praise "for his probity in handling public money" and for his show of "character by refusing to permit payment of irregular accounts.''[1] But the post had disadvantages for the politician who sought always to be understanding, friendly, even charming. It was not a pleasant job. Political developments in Rio Grande, however, made Getúlio's role of Finance Minister a short one. A new state election was due late in 1927 and Borges de Medeiros, now ineligible to serve a sixth term as governor, was seeking an appropriate figure to take over the office he would have to relinquish.

The *caudilho* had certain concepts about the dignity of the office which may have influenced his decision. The mayor of Uruguaiana liked to sip wine with cronies at the Clube dos Caçadores and was said to admire a dancer. Flôres da Cunha gambled for high stakes. João Neves da Fontoura, majority leader in the state Legislature and devoted Borges follower, seemed a good bet, but he had youthful ideas which did not appeal to the influential Old Guard.[2] When the "old man" drew up the slate of Vargas for governor and João Neves for vice-governor, their elections were assured, and they took office in January 1928.

Vargas, governor of Rio Grande do Sul, always showed the greatest respect for the head of his state party, consulting him with deference. In matters of party policy Borges' word was final; yet as an administrator Vargas was able to steer pretty much his own course, and state Cabinet selections were his. These included Osvaldo Aranha, the exuberant idea-man who took over as Secretary of Justice and the Interior, the number-one post. In a clean break with the past Vargas healed old wounds by including in his Administration men of the Partido Libertador, by studying Assis Brasil's suggestions for increasing agricultural production, and by ordering a recount which reversed the result of a municipal election declared fraudulent by the opposition. As an officer of the party organ, *A Federação,* Vargas spent evenings going over articles for publication, submitting changes and comments designed to promote the new ideas he advocated and the state harmony he deemed essential.

Much that he did was regarded as heresy by the Republican Old Guard, which would have given trouble had the Legislature enjoyed more constitutional power. But Vargas' unifying efforts had positive results. When his uncle, Modesto Dorneles, was on his deathbed, this member of a family which had long fought the Republicans called in his followers,

[1] Communication (1927), American Embassy, Rio, to U.S. State Department, Washington.

[2] Paul Frischauer, *Presidente Vargas: Biografia,* pp. 218–219.

asking them to support Vargas and end the state's long tradition of fratricidal war. Thus, in an atmosphere of unprecedented political harmony, Getúlio was able to concentrate on Gaúcho economic development. As a means of promoting this end the Banco do Rio Grande do Sul was founded in 1928 with a special department to provide credits for cattlemen.

São Paulo, too, had a change of governors, occasioned by the unexpected death of the incumbent in 1927. Washington Luís, whose financial policy seemed off to a good start, sped to his home state in a special train and arranged that his leading admirer would become the new governor. Júlio Prestes de Albuquerque, somewhat Bohemian in his tastes, and as hearty as Washington Luís himself, took office in July 1927, causing uneasiness in Minas because he seemed just the sort of man Washington Luís might want to carry on his work in Rio. "A sort of *dauphin* or Prince of Wales," one Mineiro wrote of Júlio Prestes.[3]

Antônio Carlos de Andrada, the attractive, shrewd, and ambitious governor of Minas, could expect to be Brazil's next President under the São Paulo-Minas pattern of *café com leite* (São Paulo coffee with Minas milk). He came to be credited with saying "Let's make the revolution before the people make it," thus recalling a position taken by his famous forebear when Brazil became independent in 1822. Not only did Minas in 1928 extend the suffrage to women, but also Antônio Carlos himself took special pride in opening the door to a chief demand of liberals and revolutionaries, the secret vote. As a test, he picked a contest for a seat on the Belo Horizonte city council, inviting prominent journalists from São Paulo and elsewhere to witness the historic event. To his own satisfaction and to the surprise of many, the "opposition" candidate defeated the man backed by the mayor.[4]

In the eyes of Washington Luís all this was foolishness. Nor was the President pleased that the Minas governor, a former Finance Minister and author of several financial studies, had strong reservations about the currency-stabilization program.[5] Although Antônio Carlos tactfully came around to accepting the President's financial views as the 1930 election approached, Washington Luís did not trust him.

Ruling with an iron hand and riding a high tide of success, Washing-

[3] Virgilio A. de Mello Franco, *Outubro, 1930*, p. 111.
[4] Lucas Lopes, interview, July 9, 1963.
[5] Alexandre José Barbosa Lima Sobrinho, *A Verdade sôbre a Revolução de Outubro*, pp. 34–35; João Neves da Fontoura, *A Aliança Liberal e a Revolução de 1930* (*Memórias*, II), 25.

ton Luís seemed in a position to put the capstone on his career by installing a successor who would be a devoted pupil, fully sympathetic with his
glorious program. Early in 1929 those who spoke to the President about
the succession were told that a four-year term was altogether too short
and that plans for the election of March 1930 should first be considered
in September 1929. But no politican was really ignoring the question.
While most of them spoke of the President's favoritism for his fellow
Paulista, Júlio Prestes, the Gaúchos appreciated that if they played their
cards well their big moment might finally be at hand. The split between
Washington Luís and Antônio Carlos meant that each would look to Rio
Grande, a state now united behind a leader who was on warm terms with
Washington Luís and had been his Finance Minister. Deputado Flôres da
Cunha, busy furthering his state's good relations with the federal adminis-
tration, advised Vargas confidentally that the President admitted to
some opposition to Júlio Prestes and had decided that if the difficulties
made it impossible to launch his candidacy he would pick Vargas.[6]

Antônio Carlos, besides playing for the support of those favoring more
liberal political ways, was scheming with the air of a distinguished man
who enjoys scheming; but he was more desperate than he seemed. Unable
to get Rio Grande to agree to support him in case Washington Luís broke
the political "Golden Rule,"[7] he conversed with newspaper publisher
Assis Chateaubriand in January, 1929, letting it be known that if the
Júlio Prestes candidacy was presented he would veto it and offer the
support of Minas to a candidate from Rio Grande.[8] This message was to
serve as a warning to Washington Luís.

Borges and Vargas, both mentioned as possibilities in case Antônio
Carlos had to make good his threat, could see no merit in breaking with
the federal Government, and even oppositionist Assis Brasil agreed with
Vargas that the wisest course was to wait until September.[9] In a letter of
May 10, 1929, to Washington Luís, Vargas put aside any concern his
friend the President might have had. Repeating assurances given in
December, he added:

I have remained silent about the presidential succession because I do not wish
to contribute to disturbing the atmosphere, wanting to leave Your Excellency

[6] Letter, Flôres da Cunha to Getúlio Vargas, November 29, 1928. See Hélio
Silva, *1926: A Grande Marcha*, pp. 195–197.

[7] Affonso Henriques, *Vargas, o Maquiavélico*, p. 36.

[8] João Neves da Fontoura, *A Aliança Liberal*, pp. 52–53.

[9] Hélio Silva, *1926: A Grande Marcha*, p. 228.

entirely free to take the initiative when you judge it opportune. Your Excellency may rest assured that the Republican Party of Rio Grande do Sul will not fail you with its support at the proper moment. We are seeking no personal advantages.[10]

[10] Affonso Henriques, *Vargas*, pp. 40–11.

BOOK II

THE ELECTION AND
REVOLUTION OF 1930

"... placing yourself at their
head to direct them."

1. Preparing for the Election

VARGAS, playing his first role on the national political stage, acted carefully and wisely. Yet he lost the battle. He felt he lost it because of fiery little João Neves, who, after becoming vice-governor of his state, was assigned the crucial post of leader of the Gaúcho Republicans in Congress. The dispute which João Neves carried on with fellow *deputado* Flôres da Cunha early in 1929 represented the conflict between the paths which seemed open to Rio Grande. Flôres was betting that Washington Luís would turn to Vargas—perfect "candidate of national conciliation"—as the conflict developed between the two big aspirants, Júlio Prestes and Antônio Carlos. João Neves, fraternizing with Mineiros who were unloved by Washington Luís, wanted to confront the President with a Vargas candidacy backed by Antônio Carlos and others. Vargas himself knew the value of waiting.

Neves, told by his Gaúcho bosses not to initiate anything, found the national capital seething when Congress convened on May 3, 1929. Hearing that agriculturalists in São Paulo planned to honor Júlio Prestes, Antônio Carlos agreed to be honored by a parade in Belo Horizonte.

In his room at Rio's elegant new Glória Hotel, João Neves' Mineiro friends wooed him with favorable, but not quite accurate, reports. Minas, they said, was completely united, and Antônio Carlos sent word that he was persuading the governor of Pernambuco to join the anti-Júlio Prestes front.

Vargas became increasingly worried about Neves and on June 15, 1929, wrote to advise him against making a secret pact with the Mineiros. But just as this warning was being written, Francisco Campos, Interior Secretary of Minas, called Neves in Rio to ask whether Rio Grande would put up an opposition candidate to face Júlio Prestes if Minas would provide full support. The impulsive Neves replied in the affirmative, and two days later, on June 17, he was presented with a pact to be signed by himself and Antônio Carlos' brother, head of the Minas Republican bloc in Congress. This stipulated that in case Washington Luís did not present a Mineiro for the Presidency, Minas and Rio Grande would support either Borges or Vargas, the choice to be made by Rio Grande. Neves signed with the proviso that the agreement be ratified by Borges as head of the party.

Getúlio received the pact coldly and sent Aranha to discuss it with Borges at his ranch. Instead of pulling the rug from under his man in Rio, Borges went along with what had been done, but he counseled that the pact should be put into operation only if every effort at conciliation failed, in which case the Gaúcho candidacy should be presented to Washington Luís by Antônio Carlos and ratified by a national convention. He removed himself as a possibility, explaining that Vargas corresponded more closely to the national desires.

The Minas-Rio Grande alliance having thus been precipitously formed, Vargas wrote Washington Luís, pointing out that he had to abandon commitments given earlier because, as a member of the Partido Republicano Riograndense, he was obliged to conform to the decision of the head of his party. Getúlio's letter kept quoting Borges: in the absence of national political parties it was up to the President to avoid disasters such as had occurred in 1922 when Epitácio Pessoa had failed to act; Washington Luís had shown preference for no name, and, under the circumstances, Vargas should not dismiss an opportunity which might benefit Rio Grande.

Flôres da Cunha, on the best of terms with the ruling Paulista Republicans, was chosen in mid-July 1929 to deliver this letter, but before doing so he went to confer with Antônio Carlos and Afrânio de Melo Franco,[1] one of Minas' outstanding men in public life. The Mineiros

[1] Virgilio A. de Mello Franco, *Outubro, 1930*, p. 124.

decided that Antônio Carlos would also prepare a letter for Washington Luís, and in it, following the suggestion of Borges, the Vargas candidacy would be proposed.

Both letters proved highly irritating to the President. He had taken comfort from Vargas' letter of May 10, and the majority leader in Congress had been whispering that the President's plans had the full support of Rio Grande. "It can't be!" Washington Luís now exclaimed to Flôres da Cunha, who seemed as crushed as the President.

The Vargas candidacy, once a possibility for avoiding a shattering national political struggle, was not something Washington Luís was going to have thrust down his throat by Antônio Carlos and João Neves. In the face of the new development he did not abandon his partiality for Júlio Prestes, but he did give up the idea of waiting until September. Still in July 1929 he sent replies to Vargas and Antônio Carlos, letting it be known that he had sounded out state political parties and had found those dominating seventeen states favored Júlio Prestes. The only ones not going along were Minas, Rio Grande do Sul, and Paraíba, the small northeastern state which, according to the President, had not been heard from.

Antônio Carlos and João Neves were seeking a vice-presidential candidate who would increase the size of their two-state coalition. After the governor of Bahia agreed to be Júlio Prestes' running mate, and after it developed that Antônio Carlos' earlier optimistic report about Pernambuco's governor had been wrong, they turned to Paraíba. Ex-President Epitácio Pessoa, Paraíba's most distinguished son, had indicated that Minas could name the successor of Washington Luís if it would itself desist from presenting a candidate. Now a cable went to Epitácio at The Hague proposing that Vargas' running mate be João Pessoa, governor of Paraíba and Epitácio's favorite nephew. Epitácio agreed.[2] And so on July 30 the slate of Getúlio Vargas and João Pessoa was announced at Belo Horizonte by the Executive Committee of the Partido Republicano Mineiro.

João Pessoa, like Getúlio Vargas, had been critical of those who had led revolts in the 1920's; as a member of the Supreme Military Tribunal, he had urged severe punishment for these rebels.[3] An eloquent speaker, in nine months as governor of Paraíba he had broken with local politicians

---

[2] João Neves da Fontoura, *A Aliança Liberal e a Revolução de 1930* (*Memórias*, II), p. 98.

[3] Agildo Barata, *Vida de um Revolucionário*, p. 92.

he considered corrupt and had built up a reputation for integrity and administrative ability. A Pessoa, he was a fighter.

Joined by Flôres da Cunha, the opposition to the Government opened the campaign in Congress on August 5 with a flood of impassioned speeches. The new movement was called the Aliança Liberal. João Neves, theatrical orator, accused Washington Luís of seeking to impose a President without consulting the people. When it became known that a Bank of Brazil director from Minas was heading the Júlio Prestes campaign in that state, the opposition sought to show that the bank's credits were being used to influence the election.

The unifying work of Vargas in Rio Grande now bore fruit. Deputado Assis Brasil and his Libertadores, decorated with their revolutionary red ribbons and neckerchiefs, covered the country blasting the Júlio Prestes candidacy. So did members of the Partido Democrático. *O Estado de S. Paulo,* the daily which had sponsored the Partido Democrático, sought to get an assurance from Júlio Prestes that, if elected, he would put the secret vote into effect; but Washington Luís would not allow his candidate to agree to any such thing.[4]

In spite of enthusiastic support which the Aliança Liberal was receiving —and this included the backing of numerous well-known newspapers— Getúlio was realistically pessimistic. Uncomfortable as an oppositionist, he repeatedly advocated a solution in which he and Júlio Prestes would withdraw in favor of a compromise candidate. João Neves maintained that Washington Luís would turn a deaf ear, while Antônio Carlos warned that vacillation would hurt the cause. At length Vargas insisted on getting the judgment of Epitácio Pessoa, and Afrânio de Melo Franco, the Mineiro, wrote him in Europe. It was fortunate for the Aliança that Afrânio did not reflect the full pessimism of Vargas, for a copy of the letter fell into the hands of the Administration and was widely circulated.

Before Epitácio returned from Europe on November 1, 1929, and vainly tried to persuade Washington Luís that the country needed a compromise candidate, the parties held their nominating conventions. On September 21, when the Aliança Liberal met, handsome Antônio Carlos was the man most acclaimed; had traditional political practices prevailed in 1930 his triumphal reception in Rio at this time would have heralded his advancement to the top of the national political ladder.

However, the date was approaching for Antônio Carlos to step aside as governor of Minas, and one of his preoccupations was the selection of

---

[4] Júlio de Mesquita Filho, interview, August 7, 1963.

a successor. Fernando Melo Viana, Vice-President of the Republic, wanted to head the state again and broke with the Antônio Carlos faction in the Partido Republicano Mineiro when he could not get its support. Antônio Carlos tried to smooth things out by naming old Olegário Maciel, whose chief merit seemed to be that Melo Viana was a friend of his. But even this nomination left Melo Viana dissatisfied, and he and his friends, including the vice-governor of Minas, joined the Concentração Conservadora, a movement backing Júlio Prestes in their state.

Vargas, still in Rio Grande and apparently primarily concerned with governing there, told João Neves firmly that when he had accepted the presidential candidacy it had been with the understanding that Minas would be united; he now considered himself free to drop out whenever he judged it opportune.[5]

To the casual observer it might have seemed that it had become less appropriate than ever for the reluctant leader of the opposition to hint at throwing in the towel or to persist with the idea of a compromise solution. The great Wall Street crash, disastrous for coffee and financial circles centered in São Paulo, was wrecking the Government's currency stabilization program. Those who pointed out that Washington Luís had the backing of all the Army generals now heard it said that the most powerful general of all, "General Coffee," had turned against him. In Congress, *deputados* of the opposition had a new issue.

But the ways of elections had not changed, and Vargas, more than most Gaúcho representatives in Congress, was concerning himself about the situation of Rio Grande after an Administration victory. General Firmino Paim Filho, sent by Vargas to negotiate with Washington Luís, made no headway toward a compromise candidate or toward having Júlio Prestes accept the main demands of the opposition, but he did not return to Pôrto Alegre empty-handed. A secret agreement reached early in December 1929 about a *modus vivendi* provided that after the election the relations between the federal government and Rio Grande would revert to their previous harmonious condition, and that Gaúchos elected to Congress would be seated. Vargas agreed that he would not campaign outside Rio Grande, and that the election results would be respected.[6]

Assis Brasil and some of his friends in the Democratic Party, also con-

---

[5] João Neves da Fontoura, *A Aliança Liberal*, p. 198.

[6] Alexandre José Barbosa Lima Sobrinho, *A Verdade sôbre a Revolução de Outubro*, pp. 127–128; see also *Manifesto* of Senator Paim Filho published in *O País*, October 9 and 10, 1930.

sidering the postelection period, liked the idea of approaching the revolutionaries. But Antônio Carlos displayed no fervor for an armed insurrection,[7] and Borges definitely stood Pela Ordem. At the suggestion of Siqueira Campos, Luís Carlos Prestes visited Vargas in November 1929. By this time the "Cavalier of Hope" had developed ideas so radical that they made no sense to the Aliança candidate, and Vargas told the military chief of the revolutionaries to see Aranha. But Luís Carlos Prestes had no confidence in politicians; back in Buenos Aires, he told his followers that he trusted Aranha least of all.[8] He sized up Vargas as one who would assume no responsibility, leaving himself in a position where, if an armed revolt failed, everyone but Vargas would fail.[9]

Late in December, Washington Luís was surprised to note that the Aliança was making plans to receive Vargas in Rio. By then Congress, about to recess, had become a bitter scene of debate about the election. To avoid having sessions take place the congressional majority saw to it that no quorum showed up; Aliança *deputados* resorted to speaking on the steps of Tiradentes Palace to get the publicity they wanted. Their audience, however, came to include thugs whose insults and provocations turned these affairs into something less than orderly. After one such "meeting" on December 26 a prominent Gaúcho *deputado* who had served as Epitácio Pessoa's Agriculture Minister strode onto the floor of Congress with his son. Strong words with a Pernambuco *deputado* were followed by the use of canes and fists. When the Pernambucano drew a knife, the Gaúcho killed him with a bullet,[10] committing the first political murder in Congress. Newspapers which supported the Aliança tried to explain that the underlying cause of the tragedy was autocratic action by the Government.

[7] Virgilio A. de Mello Franco, *Outubro, 1930*, p. 214; Lucas Lopes, interview, July 9, 1963.

[8] João Alberto Lins de Barros, *Memórias de um Revolucionário*, p. 215.

[9] Emídio Miranda, interview, July 19, 1963.

[10] See Ildefonso Simões Lopes Filho, *Defendendo Meu Pai*.

2. The Election and Its Aftermath

On December 29, 1929, three days after the shooting in Congress, Getúlio Vargas arrived by plane in Rio, and on the next morning a steamer brought João Pessoa from the Northeast. To Vargas at the Glória Hotel, but not to Pessoa, Washington Luís sent his military aide with greetings, and early on the thirty-first Vargas had a secret session at Guanabara Palace. He explained to Washington Luís that he was anxious to observe the *modus vivendi* and had made his trip only because of pressure within his party.[1]

Festive banquets held no appeal for Getúlio, but he attended a lunch for the Liberal candidates at which Epitácio Pessoa presided. The high point was the mass meeting late on the afternoon of January 2, 1930, at the Esplanada do Castelo, a large square in downtown Rio. There, in the open air, Vargas read the program of the Aliança to the enormous crowd, which was wildly enthusiastic even though most of the people were too far from the speaker to hear him. Nor did they have a dramatic performance to watch. Looking neither right nor left, Vargas read the rather long and carefully worded manifesto. For reformers it made good reading when they saw it in the newspapers.

The Aliança Liberal called for amnesty for all the 1922–1926 revolutionaries and offered fuller guarantees of individual liberties and of autonomy for the states. It wanted a new election law and the reorganization of justice and education. It proposed the enactment of such daring social legislation as allowances for invalids and the aged, annual vacations for workers, plus a guaranteed minimum of nourishment; also opportunities for workers to participate in sports and cultural activities. The Aliança promised economic development for the nation, serious attention to the afflicted regions of the Amazon (suffering from the rubber collapse of 1912) and the arid Northeast. Federal "protection" for the coffee and cattle-raising industries was offered.

When Vargas and João Pessoa took a train for São Paulo early on January 4 many were surprised, but most of all Washington Luís, who had understood from Vargas that he would keep out of both Minas and São Paulo.[2] At the stations along the way Vargas was acclaimed, and in São Paulo he was received as the savior of Brazil by crowds chanting "We want, we want, we want Getúlio." Amid a tumult he again read the platform of the Aliança Liberal, and, soon after, went with João Pessoa to another triumph in the nearby port city of Santos.

This concluded Getúlio's few days of campaigning, but the result was terrific. Before returning to Rio Grande, Vargas became convinced that

[1] Alexandre José Barbosa Lima Sobrinho, *A Verdade sôbre a Revolução de Outubro*, pp. 130–131.

[2] Hélio Silva, interview, August 24, 1963; Paulo Nogueira Filho, *Ideais e Lutas de um Burguês Progressista: O Partido Democrático e a Revolução de 1930*, II, 403.

the movement he was leading had the majority of the people behind it. And what the people saw in Getúlio they liked.

Back in Pôrto Alegre, Vargas governed Rio Grande for a few more weeks and then suddenly took a leave of absence. Announcing that "scruples of a moral order" prevented him from holding his post during an election, he retired temporarily to São Borja, naming Interior Secretary Osvaldo Aranha interim head of the state.

Vice-Governor João Neves was away campaigning. Late in January, after touring Minas with João Pessoa, he and other speakers from Rio Grande, São Paulo, and Minas participated in one of those "caravans" to the Northeast. At Natal some were hurt in the riots which followed a hostile demonstration organized by supporters of the Administration. But when João Pessoa spoke in Recife the enthusiasm he inspired contrasted markedly with the cool reception given there to Júlio Prestes. It was an eloquent tribute to Pessoa, particularly as his policy favored giving Paraíba its own port facilities, making it less dependent on Recife.[3]

There was nothing one-sided about the use of force that February, the last month of campaigning. In northern Minas five pro-Government campaigners were killed and Vice-President Melo Viana, candidate for governor of Minas, was among the wounded. Several days later, at Vitória, on the east coast, the Caravana Liberal ran into trouble when one of its members, waving his red neckerchief, cried out that the Government stole so many votes that the people had no faith in election results. In the shooting which followed, six lives were lost.

The March 1 election coincided with the annual *carnaval*, but the festivities were well over before the slow count ended. By telegraph from the state capitals Washington Luís followed the returns, satisfactory for Júlio Prestes. Replying to one of his wires, Osvaldo Aranha expressed his pleasure at the President's assurance that the Brazilian people "would be governed only by the one elected by their sovereign will."[4] But Aranha went on to advise Washington Luís that he was calling election irregularities to the attention of governors so that figures could be corrected, and he added that the latest Rio Grande results showed Vargas with 287,321 votes and Júlio Prestes with 789.

The national count put Júlio Prestes well ahead, and Foreign Minister Otávio Mangabeira was having Brazilian diplomats proclaim the victory abroad. Aliança leaders, Aranha in particular, were crying fraud when, on

[3] Barbosa Lima Sobrino, *A Verdade*, pp. 169–170.
[4] Virgilio A. de Mello Franco, *Outubro, 1930*, pp. 210–211.

the front page of *A Noite* on March 19, they read a sensational interview given by Borges de Medeiros.

The old man said:

According to the latest data Júlio Prestes has over a million votes and Vargas fewer than 700,000. With frankness and loyalty then we must recognize that Júlio Prestes is elected. Perhaps many votes will have to be subtracted from these totals, because of frauds which the commissions will check. There will be proportional reductions, because there are frauds from north to south, including here.

Borges stated that both he and Vargas recognized that Júlio Prestes had won. Revolution, he said, would be "a monstrous crime."[5]

Paim Filho, who had negotiated with Washington Luís in December, warmly supported Borges and spoke highly of Júlio Prestes. But the reaction of most of the younger Aliança party workers was different. João Neves respectfully disagreed with Borges, and the emotional Flôres da Cunha was visibly upset by the *A Noite* interview.

Vargas, enigmatic, returned to governing the state, leaving it to Aranha to keep the spirit of the Aliança alive.

Paraíba was becoming the focus of the nation's attention, as changes instituted by João Pessoa before the election were beginning to provoke an upheaval there. José Pereira, wealthy strongman in Paraíba's interior Princesa sector, liked neither Pessoa's political ways nor his effort to build up Paraíba's seaport by taxing imports coming overland from other states.[6] While Gaúcho leaders played a careful game, Pessoa, a thorn in the side of the old political bosses, seemingly went out of his way to annoy the Washington Luís Administration. In drawing up his slate to represent Paraíba in Congress, he threw out all those who were friendly to Rio and to strong man José Pereira, calling them corrupt and replacing them with new Liberals. "What he stood to gain," the United States consul reported to Washington, "is a mystery . . . A more astute politician would have compromised."[7]

Soon after the election, Pereira and his pro-Júlio Prestes friends organized their followers into groups of *cangaceiros*, or "professional outlaws," took control of the Princesa sector, and worked to spread their influence to neighboring towns. The state police force, ordered by João Pessoa to put the rebellion down, was handicapped when the federal government

[5] Affonso Henriques, *Vargas, o Maquiavélico*, pp. 59–64.
[6] Barbosa Lima Sobrinho, *A Verdade*, pp. 169–172.
[7] Despatch from U.S. consul, Recife, September 10, 1930.

took measures to prevent it from receiving arms. The governor of Pernambuco would not allow the Paraíba police to enter his state, which had a common boundary with the Princesa sector, nor would he stop the inflow of arms at this point to Pereira and his rebels.

When federal legislative leaders convened to rule on the credentials of incoming members prior to the opening of Congress on May 3, 1930, the entire Paraíba slate favored by Pereira and opposed by João Pessoa was seated. Aliança Liberal leaders had just issued a manifesto, which neither Vargas nor Antônio Carlos signed, promising to fight for its principles through its congressmen; but it was clear that the Aliança congressional group would be small. In the case of Minas the authorities accepted the credentials of twenty-three Antônio Carlos *deputados*, but threw out fourteen, among them Afrânio de Melo Franco, whose letter to Epitácio Pessoa had hardly been esteemed by Washington Luís. The only Liberal state left unmolested was Rio Grande, blessed with Borges' recent statement and Vargas' postelection behavior.

Late in May this new Congress studied the election results and declared Júlio Prestes President-elect. Then the victor sailed aboard a warship to the United States and Europe.

Getúlio Vargas' long-awaited pronouncement, dated May 31, was considered "calm and statesmanlike" by foreign observers. Although disappointing to ardent Aliancistas and such vociferous dailies as Rio's *Correio da Manhã,* it closed no doors and summarized the situation in a particularly disinterested manner. Vargas' brief reference to fraud, "inherent in the system," was followed by the announcement that as governor of Rio Grande he was compelled to restrict himself to his duties of office, while as a politician he would subordinate himself to the will of his party. Hoping that his scruples would not be taken for weakness, he added that "it now rests with the people to show whether or not they are in accord with the result." Going on to reaffirm the nation's need to modify its laws and political practices, he expressed his belief that the necessary changes would not be long in coming. Order, for which all good patriots were working, was, he said, seriously threatened by arbitrary acts practiced against Paraíba and Minas, acts which "show deplorable ignorance . . . Two states are punished for wishing to elect the candidate they preferred."

3. The *Tenentes* Break with Their Leader

The federal government had been rather ineffective in rounding up rebel *tenentes*. Shortly before the election, Siqueira Campos had managed to avoid capture by scaling a wall in São Paulo; Juarez Távora, although recaptured in January 1930, escaped with companions on election day by dropping out of a Rio fort onto rocks and seashells.

These men were disappointed by Getúlio's cautious ways. But in Osvaldo Aranha, a very different sort of person, they found all the encouragement they wanted. He closely followed revolutionary plans being developed by João Alberto in the south, Siqueira Campos in São Paulo, and Juarez Távora in the north.

Aranha also kept in touch with Luís Carlos Prestes, supplying him generously with funds for a future outbreak. The "Cavalier of Hope," hero of the Long March, was as important for his prestige among the discontented as for being military chief of the revolution. During the recent campaign people had swarmed around the Aliança caravans, vowing to revolt under him if their candidates were declared losers.[1] São Paulo's *Diário Nacional* emphasized its anti-Government position with front-page photographs of Aliança leaders around a larger one of the "Cavalier of Hope." Admirers carried in their wallets the picture of the bearded figure on horseback and exhibited it to establish their credit in the eyes of other revolutionaries.

Luís Carlos Prestes in Buenos Aires was aware that Francisco Campos, Interior Secretary of Minas, had flown to Pôrto Alegre in April and pledged to Aranha that his state would join Rio Grande and Paraíba in a revolution at a date to be determined. Prestes may not have known that Minas was promising to supply Aranha's war chest with six thousand contos[2] and that Paraíba was committed to contribute two thousand, but it was clear enough to the revolutionaries that Aranha had funds available. All his old followers, Prestes knew, were being attracted to the ideas of revolt-minded Aliança politicians.

But Prestes saw an Aliança uprising as nothing more than a traditional power struggle. When he declined Aranha's offer that he be its

[1] Paulo Nogueira Filho, *Ideais e Lutas de um Burguês Progressista: O Partido Democrático e a Revolução de 1930*, II, 438.

[2] One conto de reis (one thousand milreis, or one million reis) was worth roughly $120 at the time.

military leader, with Vargas the civilian chief, Prestes was visualizing another sort of movement, of which he would be both military and civilian leader. In Buenos Aires he told a follower that if an Aliança rebellion were successful they would have to wait two years before carrying out their own revolution; that if the Aliança effort failed they could go ahead in one year.[3] "Their own" revolution, as Prestes' intimates knew, would have much in common with the Communist movement which Prestes had been studying.

After several sleepless nights Prestes finished work on a declaration calculated to stir up enthusiasm for the cause he held dear. In this "Manifesto of May" Prestes classified the program of the Aliança Liberal as "insignificant." The new Government, he wrote, should be entirely in the hands of peasants, workers, soldiers, and sailors. It should seize lands and parcel out plots to those who worked them. Foreign debts should be repudiated. Mines, banks, public services, concessions, and all means of communication should be confiscated and nationalized.

A Prestes emissary took a copy of this proclamation to Siqueira Campos, who was fabricating bombs in São Paulo. But the leader of the Eighteen of the Fort, feeling that it would estrange Paulistas on whose co-operation he was counting, insisted that it not be shown around São Paulo and prepared to see Prestes about it in Buenos Aires. After this rebuff, Prestes' emissary went to Rio to discuss the manifesto with revolutionaries in Pedro Ernesto's clinic; although he tried to convince his hearers that the manifesto was not Communist, they too, gave it a chilly reception.

Alighting in Buenos Aires, Siqueira Campos and João Alberto joined Prestes and Miguel Costa. Juarez Távora, too busy preparing barrack revolts to make the trip from Paraíba, had earlier warned Prestes against seeking assistance from the Soviet Union.[4]

Of the eight hundred contos which Prestes had received from Aranha, six hundred remained, and Prestes declared his unwillingness to return them for an Aliança rebellion. Maintaining that the funds had come from the Rio Grande treasury and therefore belonged not to the Aliança but to the people, he felt they should be used for the people's revolution he would someday lead.

More serious than these money matters was the ideological struggle, straining the close friendships forged in the 1920's among the courageous

[3] Emídio Miranda, interview, July 19, 1963.
[4] *Ibid.*

leaders of the Long March. Nerves were on edge, Prestes becoming fanatic as he tried to convince the others that he had found the right way and that the Aliança politicians, who now included ex-President Artur Bernardes, merely sought to replace other politicians. In one tense moment, when Prestes was accusing the absent Juarez Távora of being a false revolutionary, Miguel Costa asked why he was excepting his three listeners.[5]

Prestes was inflexible, and the others, convinced that the masses could not be galvanized by his program, regretfully broke with the chief who had once so inspired them. But before they parted, Siqueira Campos, the closest to Prestes, persuaded him to postpone publication of his manifesto for a month.

On the rainy night of May 10 Siqueira Campos and João Alberto, shattered by their experience, boarded the five-passenger plane that was to take them back. It crashed into the ice-cold sea off Uruguay before dawn. As it sank beneath them, João Alberto, who had received a gash on the head, handed ten contos to Siqueira Campos, a strong swimmer. But the hero of the Eighteen of the Fort drowned, as did everyone aboard except one: João Alberto reached shore after a two–and–one-half–hour swim.

Prestes rushed to Uruguay and would not leave until the body of his dearest friend had been recovered. Before João Alberto departed, Prestes asked whether he planned to carry on without Siqueira Campos. João Alberto, still very shaken, was undecided, but he agreed that Prestes need not hold up publication of the manifesto.

Thus while the Rio funeral of the legendary revolutionary was the occasion of anti-Government demonstrations, Prestes was sending copies of his manifesto to associates in Brazil with urgent pleas that it be published quickly. When it appeared in print it shocked most of the revolutionaries. Carlos de Lima Cavalcanti, the sugarland and newspaper owner named by Prestes in 1928 to represent the revolution in Pernambuco, refused to publish it, and his comments to Prestes provoked a reply signed "your adversary." Juarez Távora analyzed with "sadness" Prestes' ideas; in a letter to his former chief he remarked that 99 per cent of the readers of the manifesto would consider it Communist. He published a long rebuttal, and degraded the revolutionary general in a telegram which referred to the "disastrous manifesto of Captain Prestes."[6]

[5] João Alberto Lins de Barros, *Memórias de um Revolucionário*, p. 219.
[6] Papers of Carlos de Lima Cavalcanti, shown in interview with Lima Cavalcanti, August 1, 1963.

Members of Brazil's small Communist Party were also unhappy, resenting the manifesto's failure to mention Communism, and wondering whether its author proposed to substitute Prestismo for their party.[7] Their fear seemed justified in August when Prestes, finding himself outside all movements, launched his Liga de Ação Revolucionária with two remaining devotees.

[7] Leoncio Basbaum, *História Sincera de República*, II, 408.

4. Aliança Politicians Are Wary

To obtain funds for an Aliança revolution, Minas state officials sold Belo Horizonte's modest power system to the American & Foreign Power Company.[1] About to remit an installment to Rio Grande, ideally located for smuggling arms, Mineiros reviewed developments at Antônio Carlos' home in Juiz de Fora, the small second city of overwhelmingly rural Minas Gerais. To the party leaders gathered around him, the Governor described the commitment to the revolution which he had authorized Francisco Campos to make in Pôrto Alegre in April. All present approved.

With this reassurance Aranha and his friends went ahead, their target date being late June. Besides exchanging coded messages, making small munitions, and importing arms, they persuaded the formidable Major Pedro Aurélio de Góis Monteiro to take the place they once had in mind for Luís Carlos Prestes. A Northeasterner, Góis had been an outstanding trainee in 1921 when a French military mission gave courses for Brazilian officers. Later he had helped harass the Miguel Costa-Prestes Column, and early in 1930 he had been sent to bolster the federal government's position in Rio Grande do Sul. Asked by Aranha to assume the military leadership of the revolution, he listed so many conditions, and specified so many uprisings, that one of the *tenetes* laughingly remarked that the only thing Góis was not requiring was the adherence of Washington Luís.[2] The conditions were accepted, at least in theory, and while Rio still considered him loyal, Góis set about methodically perfecting plans and organizing a "secret society" within the Army.

But June was a month of frustration for the would-be revolutionaries. Góis, who favored careful but time-consuming military planning, almost

[1] Lucas Lopes, interview, July 9, 1963.
[2] Augusto Amaral Peixoto, interview, August 17, 1963. The *tenente* mentioned was Newton Estilac Leal.

resigned when Aranha "appeared intransigent" in his insistence on launching the revolt late that month.[3] However, the main trouble came from Antônio Carlos. Flôres da Cunha and João Neves, dropping in at Juiz de Fora to get some inspiring words from the Governor of Minas, heard him say that perhaps the best thing would be a political combination among the three states of the Aliança. Later, when emissaries of the Paulista revolutionaries came to Juiz de Fora to tell of preparations in their state, Antônio Carlos was displeased with the report. Claiming that he had been misinformed earlier, he took a position favoring an alliance exclusively for political action and had his Interior Secretary, Francisco Campos, so advise Aranha on June 21.[4]

Aranha shot back a hot wire to Minas blaming Antônio Carlos for the collapse of their plan. "Negroes suffered slavery with less ridicule."[5] João Alberto wired Juarez Távora, who had things ready in the Northeast: "Minas has just declared it will not support the movement. Have decided suspend conspiracy considering this stage ended. Believe you have no more to do there . . ."[6]

Aranha was exasperated, and on June 27 he dramatically resigned from the Rio Grande Cabinet. One of the top *tenentes* in Pôrto Alegre advised Dr. Pedro Ernesto in Rio that after Antônio Carlos had opposed an armed uprising Vargas had done likewise.[7] But Rio Grande's Partido Libertador, replying to an inquiry from the north, spoke only of "the hesitations of Getúlio Vargas, gripped by the conservative current headed by the spirit of Borges and assisted by Paim Filho."[8]

Tenentes of past movements reaffirmed the poor opinion they had of politicians, and many of them returned to exile. Maurício Cardoso, of the Partido Republicano Riograndense, went to Rio and Minas to get a fresh report, particularly on the attitude of Olegário Maciel, who would become governor of Minas on September 7. There was no reason to believe that the septuagenarian was a revolutionary; he had, in fact, expressed the thought that revolution would be a calamity. Maurício Cardoso armed himself with letters from Artur Bernardes and other prominent Mineiros who felt that revolution was the only worthy cause to follow, and then he

[3] Lourival Coutinho, *O General Góes Depõe*, p. 72.
[4] Virgilio A. de Mello Franco, *Outubro, 1930*, p. 256.
[5] Papers of Carlos de Lima Cavalcanti, shown in interview with Lima Cavalcanti, August 29, 1963.
[6] *Ibid.*
[7] Virgilio A. de Mello Franco, *Outubro, 1930*, p. 262.
[8] Affonso Henriques, *Vargas, o Maquiavélico*, p. 70.

called on Olegário in the federal Senate. The future head of Minas, after hearing a forthright statement by Cardoso, replied without the sonorous expressions typical of Antônio Carlos. He simply said that if Minas had made an agreement he would, as governor, see that it was kept.[9] But he wanted the revolution to start before Antônio Carlos left office.[10]

Before Cardoso got back to Rio Grande the politicians there were flocking to Pôrto Alegre's Clube do Comércio on the evening of July 25 to attend a banquet honoring Osvaldo Aranha on his retirement from the state government. The speakers had just about finished when the group was electrified by news from Recife—a report of the assassination of João Pessoa.

[9] João Neves da Fontoura, *A Aliança Liberal e a Revolução de 1930* (*Memórias*, II), p. 366.
[10] Virgilio A. de Mello Franco, *Outubro, 1930*, p. 282.

5. The Assassination of João Pessoa

João Pessoa, it was said, visited Recife to seek the co-operation of Pernambuco's Governor Estácio Coimbra in dealing with the uprising of José Pereira; but Coimbra remained incommunicado on his ranch. In any case, Pessoa's main interest in Recife was a girl friend, a well-known singer due to arrive from Rio.[1] Her ship not yet having docked, Pessoa was enjoying refreshment in a crowded ice-cream parlor. There João Duarte Dantas shot him dead.

Dantas had once worked with Pereira against Pessoa in the Princesa sector, but he had been forced out of Paraíba when Pessoa's men, after ransacking his property, had published letters involving an amorous scandal. A month before killing Pessoa, Dantas had threatened his life in a telegram, and as soon as he was arrested for murder he declared the matter an "affair of honor." Comfortably imprisoned in Recife, he felt confident of being absolved.

"My God," exclaimed Coimbra, "Now they have a martyr!"[2]

In Paraíba the assassin's family was slaughtered. Homes and business houses of Pessoa's most prominent local opponents were damaged by irate mobs.

In Congress, Rio Grande's *deputado* Lindolfo Collor cried out: "Mr.

[1] Hélio Silva, interview, August 3, 1963.
[2] U.S. Consulate, Recife, report of December 9, 1930.

President, what have you done to the governor of Paraíba?" From Pôrto
Alegre came the voice of Vargas, speaking of the "revolting crime in
which political vengeance armed a hired assassin." At The Hague, Epitácio said that his nephew's murder was due to the Princesa situation,
"nourished by the systematic and criminal hostility of the federal government toward the governor of Paraíba." But words such as these, it was
felt by the Administration, could worsen the situation, and so telegraph
companies were warned against handling messages which might incite
public disorder.

Washington Luís declared three days of mourning, but the Pessoas
were quick to reject what they called "hypocritical homage," and they and
their supporters went ahead with their own plans, which included bringing the body by ship for burial in Rio. At Recife and ports along the way
appropriate religious services were held and moving speeches delivered
before multitudes. The capital of Paraíba was renamed João Pessoa in a
ceremony during which some of the dead man's enemies sought refuge
in the federal customhouse. A defiant expression of the late leader became
a motto on the state flag. The João Pessoa Hymn was soon being sung
throughout Brazil: "The whole Nation awaits your resurrection."

The grand climax was the coffin's arrival on August 7 in Rio, where
the throng at the dock included some of the most vehement orators of the
opposition. As the casket, covered with the national flag, moved to the
church, enormous crowds tied up Carioca traffic, defying the police. They
heard Maurício de Lacerda call the dead man's body "the corpse of the
Nation." "João Pessoa," he cried out, "God wants you to be immortal, the
martyr of liberty. You are the red banner of our revolt. Citizens, this man
died for you . . . You, Gaúchos and Mineiros, fulfill your promise. The
people are ready to die for liberty." Pessoa became "This Christ of patriotism."[3] His body was buried on August 8, four days after the return of
Júlio Prestes from his "preinauguration" trip abroad.

Speculation about a general outbreak was ridiculed by the confident
Washington Luís, who told friends that nothing had happened after a
little excitement late in June, and who was reassured by telegrams from
loyal Army commanders throughout the nation. In a show of strength the
Government deported some European Communists who had been exploiting the growing unemployment in São Paulo, and it sent more troops to
Paraíba.

But the President might have been less smug had he decoded the ex-

---

[3] Affonso Henriques, *Vargas, o Maquiavélico*, pp. 79–82.

cited wires which revolutionaries were now exchanging. João Pessoa's murder, generally considered a political act, rekindled a dying spark, turning it into a great flame. *Tenentes* returned from exile and found Aranha optimistic about the Aliança politicians.

After Antônio Carlos wired Vargas, suggesting a manifesto to the nation holding Washington Luís responsible for the assassination and therefore an outlaw, Getúlio told Aranha: "We would be crazy to do that. Such a manifesto without the next logical step would be suicide and a crime."[4] The calm Getúlio had a better idea. In reply to an inquiry of August 18 from Olegário Maciel, he affirmed that the Republican Party and government of Rio Grande would initiate the planned movement, but at a time to be chosen by himself "so as to assure victory."

Juarez Távora found determined conspirators in the troops sent by Washington Luís to Paraíba, and he wired Aranha advising when such men would be on duty as officers of the day at barracks. Aranha, reviewing things with Góis and João Alberto, settled on August 26. This would satisfy Olegário Maciel and others in Minas, where conspirators in the Belgo-Mineira steel mill were making hand grenades.

But another crisis upset this plan. A former director of *A Federação* came from seeing Borges and prepared to issue a statement, with the old man's blessing, opposing an armed revolt. Aranha himself then rushed to Borges' ranch. Armed with a rare persuasiveness and more information on the subject than any visitor Borges had received, Aranha convinced the party president that the Washington Luís Government was about to be toppled quickly and without the bloodshed which Borges wanted to avoid. Soon after, Borges signed a letter instructing the state's Military Brigade, subordinate to the Partido Republicano Riograndense, to support the forthcoming movement.

By September 11 even the careful Góis agreed that all was ready. Olegário Maciel, who had become governor of Minas four days earlier, was resolved to honor the commitment made by his state. In Rio, in the meantime, Washington Luís was encouraged by wires which reached him twice daily from Rio Grande, and he assured American Ambassador Edwin V. Morgan that talk of political unrest in the south was entirely unfounded. The ambassador, after advising the Department of State to take with reserve the messages in which the consul at Pôrto Alegre was predicting an uprising, sailed for a vacation in Europe confident that the President of Brazil had everything under control.

[4] Virgilio A. de Mello Franco, *Outubro, 1930*, p. 275.

Vargas, responsible for setting the date for the revolt, was aware that the federal commander in the south might wake up and that Távora was finding it difficult to delay further in the Northeast. But in spite of every pressure, Getúlio was not ready. As a last precaution, Lindolfo Collor was sent to see Army men in the national capital. There three generals who commanded no troops agreed that if the Administration should fall before the revolution reached Rio they would try to step in on behalf of the Aliança to prevent the government from falling into the hands of "adventurers."

Collor also visited Belo Horizonte, giving an enthusiastic account to Olegário Maciel. When the governor of Minas still seemed unsatisfied, Collor asked if anything had been left undone. "Yes," said the old Mineiro, "you have not set the date."

6. The Revolution Breaks Out

Collor returned to Rio Grande, and Aranha exchanged wires with Juarez Távora and the Mineiros about suitable days and hours. Then on September 25 Vargas agreed that the revolution was to commence at 5:30 p.m. on October 3. Messages at once went out from Pôrto Alegre, one on cigarette paper from Aranha and Collor to friends in Rio advising of the "final and irrevocable decision." The Rio adherents were asked to promote disturbances in the capital.[1]

Accident, human design, and human failure had brought together almost every element necessary to overthrow a regime. Washington Luís, whose inflexibility had done so much to doom his Administration, was off-guard because nothing had come of earlier rumors. On the morning of October 4 he was completely surprised to learn of outbreaks in the far south, in Minas, and in parts of the Northeast. Ineffectively (it was too late to do anything) he suppressed that morning's edition of Assis Chateaubriand's *O Jornal* and dispatched cruisers to Pernambuco and Santa Catarina.

In Rio Grande on the morning of October 3 Vargas had a manifesto ready to be issued the next day: "Not in vain has our state brought about the miracle of sacred union. Each of her sons must become a soldier of a great cause. Rio Grande, arise for Brazil. You cannot fail your heroic destiny." All the state's revolutionaries had their orders.

---

[1] Note of September 25, 1930, signed by Lindolfo Collor and Osvaldo Aranha; photostat provided by Augusto Amaral Peixoto, August 17, 1963.

Aranha and Flôres da Cunha, who was wearing his general's uniform, started things off on the afternoon of October 3. They led 50 members of a "Civilian Guard" in a well-planned attack on the headquarters of Brazil's Third Military Region, and the commanding general quickly surrendered. The most important federal stronghold in Pôrto Alegre was on Menino Deus Hill, but the defenders of the large storehouse of armaments there were infiltrated by revolutionaries. After half an hour of shooting, the insurgents, including men of the State Military Brigade, captured the hill; João Alberto, who had led the assault, reported the victory to Vargas and Góis in the State Government Palace.

By that night Pôrto Alegre had been dominated at a cost of twenty lives.[2] On the morning of October 4 it was learned that the two strategic barracks at Santa Maria, the rail crossroads in the center of the state, had fallen without a shot's being fired; one had already been won over by the Etchegoyen brothers, and the loyalist officers at the other found that key pieces of the cannon had been removed.[3]

Some barracks held out longer than others, but within forty-eight hours Rio Grande was entirely in the hands of the revolutionaries, and the Gaúchos became mainly preoccupied with moving north. Already Miguel Costa and his men were invading the state of Santa Catarina. Alcides Etchegoyen's heavy detachment of 2,800 was sent by train from Pôrto Alegre to join them, this being the start of a great rail movement north supervised by João Alberto, the revolution's military administrator in Santa Catarina and Paraná.

In Minas the principal struggle took place in Belo Horizonte. Part of the capital became a battleground when 385 loyal soldiers in the 12th Infantry Regiment could not be persuaded to join the revolution, choosing instead to resist attacks by the state police and civilian units. No federal troops came to the Regiment's relief and after four days it surrendered, its water and communications cut off and 16 of its soldiers killed.

In the Brazilian Northeast the element of surprise was less effective than it might have been because a misunderstanding led Juarez Távora to believe that the uprising was scheduled for the early morning of October 4. Conspiring *tenentes* at Paraíba's important 22nd Infantry Battalion

[2] Article by André Carrazzoni, "O Dia Tres de Outubro em Porto Alegre," in *Revista do Globo*'s *Revolução de Outubro de 1930: Imagens e Documentos*, pp. 45–58.

[3] Article by Walter Jobim, "A Revolução em Santa Maria," in *Revolução de Outubro de 1930: Imagens e Documentos*, pp. 70–72.

learned of the outbreak in Rio Grande when they intercepted a government wire. In a skirmish in which 8 were killed, including the general commanding the military region, the revolutionaries quickly dominated the battalion and set off to lend a hand in Recife.[4]

Pernambuco's Governor Coimbra had taken strong precautionary measures in Recife, and the rebels there, made up of groups of civilians and cadets, accomplished little in the first hours.[5] But the picture changed when Muniz de Farias, a retired captain of the state police, led 15 men in a successful attack on the Quartel da Soledad, the poorly guarded arms depot. While Coimbra was frantically trying to get the state police commander to recapture the Quartel, Muniz de Farias was successfully building up his defenses, recruiting from streetcars the laborers he found on their way to work at dawn.

With news of the approach of the revolutionaries from Paraíba under Juraci Magalhães, a contingent of the Pernambuco state police set forth from Recife to turn them back. After the failure of this half-hearted bid, the officers and most of the local Army men put to sea for Bahia, where forces loyal to Washington Luís were congregating. Coimbra and his staff decided to do likewise.

In Recife about 35 had been killed, most of them in the battles for the arms depot.[6] Streetcars had been overturned and burned. But order was quickly restored. On October 5 Juraci Magalhães, speaking in the name of Távora, appointed Carlos de Lima Cavalcanti to head the government of Pernambuco. Dantas, the assassin of Pessoa, committed suicide in his Recife cell to escape being lynched.

Loyal Army men in the northern state of Ceará resisted in an uncommonly determined way but were unsuccessful. The governor of Ceará then joined the local general in steaming around the Brazilian bulge to Bahia, stopping at Natal to pick up another fleeing governor. Since Bahia, home of Júlio Prestes' running mate, had given the Aliança Liberal little backing, the federals hoped to rally strength there to resist the optimistic revolutionary columns which Juarez Távora was leading south from Recife.[7] That this hope was frail was evident when the first battalion sent north from Bahia decided to join the revolution instead of fighting.[8]

---

[4] See Agildo Barata, *Vida de um Revolucionário*, pp. 89–113.

[5] Annibal Fernandes, *Pernambuco no Tempo do "Vice-Rei,"* p. 20.

[6] Carlos de Lima Cavalcanti, interview, August 29, 1963; U.S. Consulate reports from Recife, October 15, 1930, and November 1931.

[7] Joaquim Ribeiro Monteiro (MS) "A Revolução de 30 na Bahia," p. 4.

[8] Agildo Barata, *Vida de um Revolucionário*, pp. 137–141.

7. On the Wings of the People

Within two days of the outbreak Washington Luís decreed a "state of siege" in all Brazil and called up Army reservists. In Rio and São Paulo, which were quiet, the only news of the military situation came from the Government, which confidently explained its strategy of isolating Minas and then crushing the south. Reservists ordered to defend the increasingly unpopular regime, however, displayed a distinct lack of enthusiasm.

Washington Luís announced that in the south he could count on tens of thousands of loyal soldiers, but he had reports only from generals who could do nothing. Displaying the red neckerchiefs of the revolution and vowing to hitch their horses to the obelisk in downtown Rio, crowds of Gaúchos grabbed any available space on the slow meter-gauge trains moving north. The state of Santa Catarina virtually joined the great march, contributing more men to be moved. Then the Army unit at the rail center of Ponta Grossa in Paraná rejoicingly turned against the Government; after that, the conspirators prevailed at the unit in Paraná's capital of Curitiba.

In Pôrto Alegre on the evening of October 9, Vargas, wearing a uniform which showed no rank, and assuming the supreme command of the revolution, got aboard the train in which Góis and his staff were headed for the north. The frenzied crowd around the train's back platform heard Aranha address them stirringly and salute Vargas as the revolution's leader. The tall, debonair speaker, however, did not remain aboard to join the galaxy of revolutionary stars who planned to participate in the invasion of São Paulo. He had reassumed his state Cabinet position and was to remain behind, having been named acting governor of Rio Grande by Vargas.

João Neves, Rio Grande's explosive vice-governor, had a letter from Vargas asking him to stay in Rio Grande as a federal *deputado* rather than as acting head of the state. Taking violent exception to Vargas' request, he resigned his posts and prepared to go to the front as a simple soldier.[1] But when the Vargas train passed through Cachoeira and João Neves got aboard, Getúlio, addressing the crowd, hailed him as "the great planter of the revolutionary idea."

The track was cluttered with trains and the trip north allowed Góis, Flôres da Cunha, and their associates plenty of time to work over maps,

---

[1] João Neves da Fontoura, *A Aliança Liberal e a Revolução de 1930. (Memórias,* II), p. 433.

preparing in detail the attack on São Paulo. The jubilation with which Vargas was greeted at stations along the way helped slow the pace and showed his extraordinary popularity. Made "on the wings of the people," the trip turned out to be a series of unscheduled stops, all of them marked by the offering of flowers and red neckerchiefs and the singing of the João Pessoa Hymn. A Paulista representing the Partido Democrático described the reception of Getúlio at Ponta Grossa as "simply fabulous," with the delirious populace incessantly chanting

> João Pessoa, João Pessoa, bravo filho do sertão
> Tôda a Pátria espera um dia a tua ressurreição.

From Ponta Grossa, where the general headquarters of the revolution were set up, Góis kept in touch with his massive force, stationed along the São Paulo border. Close to Capela da Ribeira, from which a dirt road ran to São Paulo city, the revolutionary troops were commanded by João Alberto. But the largest concentration was the division commanded by Miguel Costa near the railroad station of Senges, facing loyalists at Itararé. Beside Miguel Costa rode Flôres da Cunha on his beautiful black horse.

On October 23 orders came from Góis for an attack on the 25th against Itararé's defenders. These were better armed than the revolutionaries but their morale was low and they were outnumbered, partly because members of São Paulo's "Civilian Guard" refused to accept service in the regular Army. If Itararé could be taken by the revolutionaries the way would be open to ride the Sorocabana Railroad into the city of São Paulo.

8. Golpe in Rio

Meanwhile much was happening in Rio. The War Minister, subject to all sorts of criticism, based his hopes on the superiority of arms at Itararé and planned after a victory there to invade Minas and the north. The President suspended airline service in Brazil, imposed a censorship of cables, and then unexpectedly declared a fifteen-day bank holiday.

Such was the situation on October 19, when popular Cardinal Sebastião Leme reached Rio from Rome. Two days earlier, when his ship was off Recife, a message from Lima Cavalcanti had convinced the new cardinal that in the interest of peace he should urge Washington Luís to resign. In Rio he found an opportunity to discuss the matter with the President, but Washington Luís simply remarked: "What! Then Your Eminence doubts the loyalty of my generals!"[1]

[1] Article by André Carrazzoni, "O Cardeal D. Sebastião Leme e a Revolução de

There were, however, numerous generals in Rio who felt that Washington Luís' stubbornness was useless. One of these was a former Chief of Staff, Augusto Tasso Fragoso, who earlier had told Lindolfo Collor that he might co-operate with the revolution if it were a nationwide movement. Now, after attending a Mass for the soul of the general killed in the Paraíba revolt, he told General João Mena Barreto, inspector of the First Military Region, that the revolution would triumph and that a rebellion seemed imminent in Rio. Mena Barreto then had Bertoldo Klinger, the 1925 pursuer of the Miguel Costa-Prestes Column, draft an ultimatum for Washington Luís. Klinger found many reluctant to sign it, but he did get the adherence of important members of the Army's general staff.[2]

A "pacification coup" was what these Rio officers proposed to carry out. On October 23 Tasso Fragoso agreed to head it, and he reworded Klinger's document to make it more of an appeal than an order to Washington Luís. Meeting that night at Copacabana Fort to draw up plans for Brazil's first Army ouster of a President, Tasso Fragoso, Mena Barreto, and their associates got favorable news from the Military Police and the outlying barracks at Vila Militar.

The operation which began on the morning of October 24 was under the direction of another of the generals Collor had seen. The movement of troops from the regiment at Praia Vermelha to Guanabara Palace, the President's residence, was hindered only by the crowds of armed civilians who wanted to join the march. The ultimatum (or appeal) which the generals had signed appeared early in the press with the result that mobs were soon gleefully burning pro-government newspapers.[3]

Unable to hold back the multitude, the police brigade charged with defending Guanabara Palace decided not to resist. When Tasso Fragoso and Mena Barreto found Washington Luís he was sitting solemnly in a small, gloomy room, surrounded by his Cabinet, sons, and a few friends and congressmen. From outside could be heard the taunting cries of the crowd, bedecked in red.

The President remained every inch the proud man who would fulfill his duty as he saw it. Tasso, after bowing, offered him full guarantee of

Outubro," in *Revista do Globo's Revolução de Outubro de 1930: Imagens e Documentos,* pp. 443–447.

[2] Bertoldo Klinger, *Parade e Desfile duma Vida de Voluntário do Brazil,* pp. 330–331.

[3] Tristão de Alencar Araripe, *Tasso Fragoso,* pp. 562–563.

his life, but Washington Luís explained in a firm, dry tone: "The last thing I cherish at a time like this is my life. My blood will soak the soil so that a better Brazil may emerge, a true national regeneration."[4] Tasso, learning that the President was not surrendering, said: "Your Excellency will be responsible for the consequences." With dignity the President said he assumed full responsibility. Tasso bowed again and left.

Cardinal Leme, calling on the President at Tasso Fragoso's request that afternoon, noted that the generals had already established their provisional government, the Junta Pacificadora, on the first floor of Guanabara Palace. Seeing the ugly mood of the crowd, he conceded that Copacabana Fort would be the safest place for Washington Luís, but he got the generals to agree that the fallen man be permitted to sail for Europe without delay.[5]

Washington Luís placed himself in the Cardinal's hands. "Since this morning," he explained, "I have been a prisoner in this room, with the palace and garden invaded by troops. I leave, bowing to violence." After receiving guarantees for those who had stood by him, he was driven to Copacabana Fort and held there.

[4] Cicero Marques, *O Ultimo Dia de Governo do Presidente Washington Luis no Palacio Guanabara*, p. 57.

[5] Laurita Pessôa Raja Gabaglia, *O Cardeal Leme*, p. 224.

9. The Junta Pacificadora

Manifestos were quickly issued calling for a suspension of hostilities, and from these Brazil learned that the Washington Luís Administration had been replaced by a three-man Junta Pacificadora made up of Tasso Fragoso (its head), Mena Barreto, and Admiral Isaias de Noronha. The new War Minister was General José Leite de Castro, a supporter of the movement of October 24. Afrânio de Melo Franco's assumption of the direction of the Foreign and Justice Ministries meant that in addition to the telegrams exchanged between the Junta and the revolutionaries at Ponta Grossa there would also be an informal line of communication, Afrânio keeping in touch with Vargas through his son, Virgílio de Melo Franco, who was serving with Góis and João Alberto.

The Junta's initial message to the fighting fronts briefly advised of the occurrences in Rio, but gave nothing to indicate that the way was being prepared to pass Brazil's leadership over to those who had started things on October 3. As instructed, antirevolutionary troops, including the defenders of Itararé, laid down their arms. But from northern Bahia Juarez Távora wired that he did not recognize Rio's new military junta, and he kept right on marching, leading his troops into Salvador, the state capital.

Between the Ponta Grossa revolutionaries and the Junta a telegraphic duel was taking place, with Góis laying down his conditions, one of which was that Vargas should head the new government. Góis went on to advise that "our forces of over 30,000 are occupying the south of São Paulo state and will continue the advance until there has been complete submission." A message from Tasso Fragoso to Vargas explained that the coup in Rio had been made with the high ideal of Brazilian fraternal unity. Vargas replied that such fraternal unity depended solely on full acceptance of the revolutionary program. He wired Afrânio that members of the Rio Junta would be accepted as collaborators but not as leaders, as they had joined the revolution only when it was virtually victorious.

On October 15, when Tasso Fragoso was advising Vargas that his idea all along had been to turn the government over to him, the Junta unexpectedly received a long message from Pôrto Alegre. In it Aranha emphasized the strength of the revolutionary movement and declared that "we cannot stop in the middle of the road." Aranha, at Vargas' request, then sped with Lindolfo Collor to Rio to work out the transfer of the government to Vargas.

Tremendous acclaim greeted the flamboyant Aranha when he reached Rio on October 27, and the reception for Távora, long the embodiment of *tenente* daring, was equally impressive. A strong bond developed between these two heroes, Aranha recognizing the key role of the *tenentes,* and the modest Távora seeing in Aranha a politician of vast style and ability, who had perservered more than his fellow politicians to bring about co-ordination and success.

Aranha's arrival coincided with the worst of the disorders which followed the fall of Washington Luís. As in other cities, mobs filled Rio's streets, throwing aside restraints which had annoyed them in the past. Inflamed by orators, they sacked stores and the installations of *O País,* *Gazeta de Notícias,* and other dailies which had supported the late government.[1] The Junta's bulletin of October 27 noted that "pernicious elements" sought to influence laborers with "ideas which are harmful to public peace"; the Armed Forces, it was announced, would severely punish those who were caught "distributing seditious manifestos."[2]

[1] Leoncio Basbaum, *História Sincera da República,* III, 13; Bertoldo Klinger, *Parade e Desfile duma Vida de Voluntário do Brazil,* pp. 347–348.
[2] Tristão de Alencar Araripe, *Tasso Fragoso,* p. 582.

Bertoldo Klinger, the Junta's police chief, created a furor with his note to the press on October 28. He declared that, being conversant with the wishes of those who directed the military fronts, he could say that there was nothing to "the false rumor that the Junta Governativa will be summarily replaced and will turn over the reins of government to Getúlio Vargas."[3] This declaration, made while Aranha was conferring with the Junta, was promptly contradicted in a note issued by the Junta itself. Thus it became public knowledge that Vargas, chief of the triumphant revolution, would receive the government from the Junta. Aranha did, however, agree that the forthcoming administration would retain some who were serving the Junta, although certainly not Klinger. Besides the War and Navy Ministers, these came to include Afrânio de Melo Franco as Foreign Minister and Adolfo Bergamini, mayor of the Federal District.

[3] Bertoldo Klinger, *Parada e Desfile*, p. 349.

10. Vargas in São Paulo

When the Junta appointed a Washington Luís general, friendly to Júlio Prestes, to govern São Paulo, it was easy enough for Vargas to send word from Ponta Grossa advising the Partido Democrática that the revolution did not recognize the appointment. More difficult was the problem of deciding what to do about São Paulo. No mere foretaste of difficult decisions lying ahead, this one would mark the course of the regime. Vargas made up his mind before he left Ponta Grossa, choosing João Alberto, the *tenente* from the Northeast, to administer the state.[1] When the decision emerged during Vargas' one-day stay in São Paulo, it was evident to the unhappy Partido Democrático that the *tenentes* had won their first victory in the new order of things. Many came to feel that Vargas attributed the success of the October movement not to the Aliança but to the revolutionaries in the Army.[2] Anyway, knowing men and forces well, he was acting to strengthen his forthcoming regime, and this meant satisfying *tenentismo.*

Emissaries, sent by Vargas from Ponta Grossa on the twenty-seventh

[1] Paulo Nogueira Filho, *Ideais e Lutas de um Burguês Progressista: O Partido Democrático e a Revolução de 1930*, II, 537.
[2] Aureliano Leite, *Memórias de um Revolucionário: Revolução de 1930*, p. 182.

to prepare his own entry into São Paulo city, found Partido Democrático President Francisco Morato in a dilemma. The Junta in Rio, with second thoughts about its original appointee to head the state, had told Morato to take over from him. But Morato also had a message from Vargas telling him to hold off.[3] For the moment São Paulo's affairs were in the hands of a state Cabinet of civilians. Highly satisfactory to the Partido Democrático, it was headed by Finance Secretary José Maria Whitaker pending the expected inauguration of Morato as chief executive of the state.

João Alberto's letter from Vargas simply named him the revolution's "delegate" to São Paulo, but, as soon as he reached the city of depressed industry and coffee bankers, he established himself in the government palace, Campos Elíseos. The popular Isidoro Dias Lopes, returning for the first time since heading the 1924 revolt, took command of the São Paulo-based Second Military Region.

On October 29 the city was filling with revolutionary soldiers. The colorful ways of the Gaúchos were giving it a changed aspect,[4] not much appreciated by the cultivated rulers of the past. That evening, after Vargas and his staff reached the city, the stocky little leader of the revolution had to be picked up and carried to a car to avoid being crushed by the wildly enthusiastic mass of humanity welcoming him at the city's new Sorocabana Railroad Station.

The short ride to Campos Elíseos was made between throngs madly shouting "Nós temos Getúlio . . . Getúlio . . . Getúlio" ("We have Getúlio"). It took two hours.

In the palace garden, to another sea of rejoicing people, Getúlio praised the revolution. His words were followed by a speech by João Neves, who shouted "São Paulo for the Paulistas," thus making one point which Vargas had carefully avoided, and for this expression the ex-vice-governor of Rio Grande received a tremendous ovation.

But the Partido Democrático's Morato learned nothing from Vargas or João Alberto to give him confidence in Neves' alluring exclamation. Approached by João Alberto about a possible ministry in Rio, the irritated Morato explained that he was not seeking a job but was upholding the position of his party and the right of São Paulo to govern itself. Vargas told him that João Alberto's tenure might not be long and that per-

---

[3] *Ibid*, p. 162.
[4] *Ibid*, p. 167.

haps he would take over later,[5] but the distinguished Paulista professor was poorly impressed with the Gaúcho chief of the revolution.

In the palace which had once housed Júlio Prestes (now in asylum in the British Consulate), Getúlio had plenty of opportunity to be the good listener. The conflict was not simply between those favoring a political leader for the state and those favoring the *tenentes*. The Democratic Party itself had been suffering from a split. And as for the *tenente* candidates, Miguel Costa, a Paulista, had received louder acclaim than João Alberto on arrival in São Paulo.

The announcement told the people that João Alberto would have full powers "to consolidate the revolutionary work in São Paulo." The state Cabinet was told that it would govern "autonomously" with João Alberto. Since Whitaker was to be the new Finance Minister in Rio, the Cabinet chose Justice Secretary Plínio Barreto to be its presiding officer.

With these decisions made, Vargas and his staff left for Rio after dinner on October 30. At every station in the Paraíba Valley crowds chanted "Nós queremos Getúlio," demanding to see the man to whom all had turned for the salvation of Brazil.[6]

[5] *Ibid*, p. 176; Paulo Nogueira Filho, *O Partido Democrático e a Revolução de 1930*, p. 583.

[6] Articles by Manuel Vargas Netto, "De Pôrto Alegre ao Rio de Janeiro com o Getúlio Vargas," in *Revolução de Outubro de 1930: Imagens e Documentos*, pp. 292–303.

11. Vargas Takes the Helm with Cautious Hand

The Cariocas, too, were "mad with enthusiasm" in their greeting.[1] When Catete Palace was finally reached on the night of October 31, Getúlio addressed the nation by radio, reviewing the events leading up to the revolution, "the bitterness born with patience" and the "oppression by violence and brutality which could no longer be tolerated." As for his plans, he spoke of keeping a close watch over public funds, and, more signifiicantly, of "the need to end the profession of politics."

Getúlio decided not to take over from the Junta until November 3, one month following the outbreak. During the intervening days Góis established the headquarters of his revolutionary army in Rio, where some of the Gaúchos did hitch their horses to the obelisk, and he ordered a rapid

[1] Despatch, U.S. ambassador, Rio, to U.S. Secretary of State, November 5, 1930.

demobilization of the "provisional" forces to prevent Brazil from having a "double army."

Temperamentally Vargas was hardly a revolutionary. He was not attracted to the use of violence for what might be a lost cause. However, it would have been difficult to find one as well equipped as he to handle the conflicting forces now seeking satisfaction.

Aside from men who would be unhappy because there were not enough plums to go around, some on ideological grounds would feel let down or betrayed by Vargas. Disappointments could not be avoided considering the constraining effects of the world economic collapse, and, above all, considering that by November 1930 practically every group in Brazil seemed to have backed the revolution. Bernardes, bitterest foe of the *tenentes* of the 1920's, had done notable work in Minas. There were extreme leftists, and there were very proper, orthodox, but determined people like some of the São Paulo Democrats. Among the revolutionaries in the Armed Forces was a large group which favored startling changes but had only vague ideas of what should replace the old order. As Ambassador Morgan wrote, the new administration "will meet with great difficulty in harmonizing the different points of view."[2]

Vargas felt that Brazil was ripe for reforms—reforms which seemed more radical in 1930 than they do today. In the course of bringing them about he concentrated on avoidance of becoming the pawn of any force; and he made sure that groups which would inevitably become irate would not constitute a preponderance of power.

Never making decisions hastily, Vargas had an aptitude for listening to the opinions of others and for letting solutions develop, an aptitude which led one of his associates to conclude that Vargas himself never made decisions.[3] Defining the status of the new regime was a question which Vargas, after hearing many suggestions, settled in a manner which differed from his first idea. Although he originally saw the revolution as correcting a fraudulent election, making him President for one term under the 1891 Constitution,[4] and although the Partido Libertador's influential Raul Pilla argued that the revolution should be followed by

[2] Despatch, U.S. ambassador, Rio, to U.S. Secretary of State, November 12, 1930.

[3] Francisco Campos, interview, September 3, 1963.

[4] Alzira Vargas do Amaral Peixoto, Ch. 5 of "A Vida de Getúlio Contada por Sua Filha . . .," in *Fatos & Fotos,* July 13, 1963; Agildo Barata, *Vida de um Revolucionário,* pp. 151, 153.

a new and honest election,[5] the view which prevailed was that of *tenentes* wanting a complete break from the past. The Constitution was suspended, Congress was closed down, and Vargas became Chief of the Provisional Government of the Republic with legislative as well as executive powers.

As for the judiciary, Aranha was quoted in the press as favoring the abolition of the "reactionary" Supreme Court. Most of the lawyers disagreed.[6] In the end Vargas dismissed various lower-court judges and retired four justices of the Supreme Court, reducing it from fifteen judges to eleven.

Turning over the government to Vargas at Catete Palace on the afternoon of November 3, Tasso Fragoso assailed Washington Luís, the "betrayer" of ideals who had "had no foresight" and had "acted as a veritable king, with complete disdain for everything and everybody."

Getúlio, subdued, admitted that "this government may not end up as it has just established itself, amid general acclamation."[7] After praising the Junta for having avoided the further sacrifice of lives, he announced concisely a broad seventeen-point program, which included some of the platform of the Aliança Liberal and stressed the strictest economy in government. Two new Cabinet posts were to be created: a Ministry of Labor, Commerce, and Industry; and a Ministry of Education and Public Health.

The indispensable Aranha became Justice Minister, this Cabinet appointment being described by Vargas' daughter Alzira as the only one of the nine which was freely made by her father.[8] Actually Aranha suggested that the post go to João Neves, who wanted to remain in Rio, but Vargas was not impressed with the suggestion and Neves said he preferred practicing law and acting as counselor to the Bank of Brazil.

Reassuring abroad were the appointments of Afrânio de Melo Franco as Foreign Minister, and Whitaker, the São Paulo coffee banker, as Finance Minister. Assis Brasil, Borges' long-time foe, was pleased to head the Agriculture Ministry, which, according to Vargas, needed complete reorganization.

Some said the two new ministries were created to permit appointments necessary for placating two influential old men, Borges and Olegário

[5] João Neves da Fontoura, *A Aliança Liberal e a Revolução de 1930 (Memórias,* II), p. 440.

[6] Levi Carneiro, interview, June 26, 1963.

[7] "A Revolução Liberal," *O Cruzeiro,* August 15, 1964.

[8] Alzira Vargas do Amaral Peixoto, Ch. 4 of "A Vida de Getúlio . . .," in *Fatos & Fotos,* July 6, 1963.

Maciel. Olegário had not been consulted about Afrânio and did not regard him as "his man," although he was a Mineiro.[9] So Francisco Campos, the lawyer who had helped define positions taken by Minas before the revolution, became Brazil's first Minister of Education and Health. Borges was momentarily mollified by Lindolfo Collor's appointment to the new Labor Ministry, commonly described as "the Ministry of the Revolution."

Finally, the Northeast had to be represented, and the organizers of the new government were highly pleased when Juarez Távora accepted the post of Minister of Communications and Public Works. But in the eyes of Távora's followers, who pictured him as the real chief of the revolution, the acceptance of a ministry reduced him to a secondary position. Some of these urged that he turn the revolution into a "real revolution" rather than an "invasion by the Gaúchos" or a victory of Aliança politicians.[10] When Távora left his Cabinet post after holding it only fifteen days, it was with the recommendation that it be filled by an engineer who had more experience than he.[11] However, his successor was José Américo de Almeida, a writer who had worked closely with João Pessoa in Paraíba. Távora himself, as the Provisional Government's delegate in the north, attempted to promote reforms and progress in that neglected, backward region. Informally referred to as the "Viceroy of the North," he determined important appointments and policies in the vast area which included Espírito Santo and all states north of it.

[9] Carolina Nabuco, *A Vida de Virgílio de Melo Franco*, p. 64.
[10] Agildo Barata, *Vida de um Revolucionário*, p. 154.
[11] Juarez Távora, interview, May 22, 1965.

BOOK III

FIRST TWO YEARS OF THE
PROVISIONAL GOVERNMENT

"... not in obedience to the exclusive desire of politicians."

1. Troubled *Interventores* in the Northeast

THE VICTORIOUS *tenentes,* wanting to organize so as to use their weight as effectively as possible, established the Clube 3 de Outubro. Góis, the club's president, saw the organization as one which would form the basis of a political party backing the revolution, and he hoped the *tenentes* would use the club facilities, rather than the barracks, for their political work.[1] Alzira Vargas has written that to be a *tenente* belonging to the Clube carried more prestige at this time than being a general or a Cabinet minister.[2] The club's voice, carefully heeded by Vargas, was the nation's strongest political force.

Interventores were named by Vargas to run the states on behalf of the Provisional Government, and early battles of the Clube 3 de Outubro involved some of these nominations. The *tenentes* directed their fire at Bergamini, the Junta-appointed mayor of the Federal District. Although the tribunal probing the administration of the now-exiled Washington Luís

[1] Lourival Coutinho, *O General Góes Depõe,* p. 157.
[2] Alzira Vargas do Amaral Peixoto, *Getúlio Vargas, Meu Pai,* p. 53. (All references to this book are to pocket-book edition.)

was producing no sensations, the Clube sought to establish another investigating commission—one which would complicate Bergamini's life by looking into his alleged corruption. Opposed by the Clube, Bergamini found it impossible to run the Federal District, and in 1931 he was replaced as mayor by Dr. Pedro Ernesto, vice-president of the Clube.

Vargas, with Borges' approval, named Flôres da Cunha *interventor* of Rio Grande do Sul. Juarez Távora, an Army captain after relinquishing the title of revolutionary general, recommended to Vargas the names of the *interventores* chosen in his "viceroyalty." These were usually *tenentes* with good revolutionary records, but they lacked administrative and political experience and none of them had the formidable machines which had served their predecessors, the state governors. In 1931 Távora toured the north to help the *interventores* deal with their many problems and rivals, but it seemed to be a thankless task. After two *interventores* had tried their hand in Bahia, the office, still in 1931, fell to Juraci Magalhães, the *tenente* from Ceará who had been serving as secretary of the "Viceroyalty of the North."

The Brazilian Northeast was suffering not only from the world Depression but also from one of the longest droughts in Brazil's history; although Vargas had approved a public-works program there, little was done in 1931 because Finance Minister Whitaker was trying to balance a budget affected by reduced revenues.

The very success of the 1930 movement invited challenges to authority. Thus in isolated Piauí, the northern state in which the Long March had been welcomed in 1925, rebelling corporals dominated the local Army battalion until subdued by the state police. The corporals had recently been stirred by messages sent from Argentina by Luís Carlos Prestes.[3]

In restless Recife, Interventor Lima Cavalcanti was constantly troubled by riots caused by conditions which were general in the Northeast. Workers, expecting immediate improvement to follow the revolution, found that the drought raised prices, while the economy program of the state government increased unemployment. Old political foes took advantage of the situation and joined with Army rebels and discontented laborers in making the Recife eruption of October 1931 more bloody than the uprising there a year earlier. The Pernambuco state police, hated by local Army men, was finally victorious after troops loyal to Vargas had been rushed in from neighboring states. The vessel which might have been

[3] Landri Sales Gonçalves, interview, September 2, 1963.

used for Lima Cavalcanti's escape was used, instead, to carry rebels to the island prison of Fernando de Noronha.[4] Nevertheless, the picture in the Northeast was far from comforting to the Vargas Government.

[4] Recife 1931 revolt, based on U.S. Consulate reports of 1931 and the following 1963 interviews: Carlos de Lima Cavalcanti, August 29; Joaquim Ribeiro Monteiro and João Costa, August 29; Malvino Reis, September 2; Landri Sales Gonçalves, September 2; Luís Carlos Prestes, September 5; Carlos da Costa Leite and Meireles family, September 6; and Afonso de Albuquerque Lima, September 12.

2. The Case of Minas

In Minas old Olegário Maciel insisted that he had been legally elected and that his title should reflect this. Prior to the 1930 revolution the governors had been known as "presidents" of their states. Now that the word "president" was less fashionable Olegário became known as "governor" as well as *interventor*.

More was at stake than a title. Olegário, although he had kept Minas true to her word in 1930, found himself attacked by the strongest force in the nation. *Tenentes* were using the expression *carcomido* (worm-eaten) to describe old politicians, and they liked to apply it to Olegário, pointing out that nothing in him would bring the state into what they called the "renovating current" made popular by the revolution. *Tenentes* and Aranha, a mighty force in the Clube 3 de Outubro, supported young Virgílio de Melo Franco, the Foreign Minister's son, who was yearning to head a new deal in Minas.

When three of Olegário's four state Cabinet secretaries proposed that they and the Governor offer their resignations to Vargas, Olegário fired all three.[1] Then his opponents, surprised to find the old man so formidable, planned to get tough. They were joined by Artur Bernardes, who controlled the Partido Republicano Mineiro and was trying to rebuild his political fortunes by espousing liberal ideas for which his presidential administration had not been famous.

Francisco Campos, Olegário's man in the Vargas Cabinet, came quickly to the Governor's support, setting up a semifascist khaki-shirt organization, the Legião Liberal de Minas. Minas state Cabinet officers wore khaki shirts and the Secretary of Public Safety declared that the Minas govern-

[1] Carolina Nabuco, *A Vida de Virgílio de Melo Franco*, p. 66.

ment considered all enemies of the Legião to be enemies not only of the state government but also of the state itself.[2]

Early in May 1931, after Campos' *legionários* had put on an impressive parade in Belo Horizonte, Bernardes and his cohorts countered by using a special train for a trip to promote love for the PRM (Partido Republicano Mineiro) throughout the state. Disregarding snubs of PRM leaders who supported the Governor—among them Antônio Carlos—Bernardes' men prepared to hold a well-publicized congress of the PRM in Belo Horizonte.

Olegário's foes, especially the friends of Virgílio de Melo Franco, planned a conspiracy to coincide with the party congress. When Artur Bernardes spoke to the delegates in Belo Horizonte's Teatro Municipal on August 15, outsiders cheered him on, eager to report disorders to their friends in Rio. By August 17 the congress had become thoroughly offensive to the Governor, but, as he had not yet arbitrarily closed it down, that night his opponents kidnapped his Agriculture Secretary, whose administration the PRM congress was attacking.[3]

Reports of "tremendous unrest" were reaching Aranha in Rio. On August 18, shortly after midnight, the colonel commanding the Army's 12th Infantry Regiment in Belo Horizonte received Aranha's order to take over the state government from Olegário. After the conspirators learned that instructions to the colonel should have come from the Army, a second telegram went to the colonel, this one forged by men who had seized telegraph offices in Minas.

While Olegário slept at the Palácio da Liberdade, his young Justice Secretary, Gustavo Capanema, phoned Francisco Campos in Rio. But before Campos could act, the colonel sent a subordinate with a small force to the Governor's Palace to take over. The only thing that saved the Governor was a state police contingent, loyal to Olegário, which met the Army men at the Palace door. Its leader threatened to shoot any federal soldiers who tried to enter, regardless of messages from federal officers. The Army men, neither willing nor instructed to shoot their way in, withdrew, and Olegário's sleep went undisturbed.

Later in the day four Cabinet ministers met with Vargas at Guanabara Palace. Foreign Minister Afrânio de Melo Franco, backed by Aranha, favored making his son Virgílio *interventor* of Minas, but the discussion

[2] Paulo Nogueira Filho, *Ideais e Lutas de um Burguês Progressista: A Guerra Cívica, 1932* I, 115–117.

[3] Carolina Nabuco, *A Vida de Virgílio de Melo Franco*, p. 76.

reached an impasse when Francisco Campos and War Minister Leite de Castro took a contrary position. Vargas, as was often his way, simply listened.[4] Ostensibly nothing was decided, but Olegário stayed on, and, soon after, Vargas announced that the federal government backed the Governor. Virgílio, contenting himself with the thought that time was on his side, mourned the fact that the Minas state police (Fôrça Pública Mineira) was busy making arrests of those, including Bernardes, who had actively opposed Olegário.[5]

Aranha, trying to establish peace in Minas, succeeded mainly in getting into a scrap with Francisco Campos. Olegário Maciel stubbornly refused to accept a Bernardista in his state Cabinet, and the only step taken toward harmony was artificial. A new state political party was formed, its executive committee made up of men who continued at odds. Into it were herded members of the PRM, its prestige tarnished and its future unpromising, and of the khaki-shirt Legião, in which Vargas had lost interest.

[4] Francisco Campos, interview, September 3, 1963.
[5] Carolina Nabuco, A Vida de Virgílio de Melo Franco, p. 77.

3. The Provisional Government at Work

The tenentes, having lost out in Minas, fought to hold São Paulo, unleashing attacks against politicians there or elsewhere who favored quick restoration of constitutional government in Brazil. And they kept up a barrage against conservative Finance Minister Whitaker.

While criticism of the new administration mounted, Getúlio astonished and disappointed observers. Entirely unlike his predecessors, he seemed weak. "The efficiency of the Provisional Government has broken down," Ambassador Morgan reported in April, 1931.[1] A little earlier, when Vargas had relaxed for three weeks at a spa in Minas, he had been pictured by another American Embassy official as "fiddling while Rome burns."[2]

In Rio, Getúlio would preside at night over his tenente-oriented "black Cabinet": Aranha, Távora, Góis, Pedro Ernesto, José Américo, Leite de Castro, and João Alberto (when he was not in São Paulo). During its discussions, which often lasted until after 2:00 A.M., Getúlio sometimes seemed to fall asleep. When Aranha would finally get his attention and remark that a problem had been discussed and settled, Getúlio would

[1] Despatch to Washington from U.S. Embassy, Rio, April 13, 1931.
[2] Despatch to Washington from U.S. Embassy, Rio, March 12, 1931.

smile pleasantly and observe that, from what he had been able to note, no complete agreement had been reached, and so the question ought to be considered at the next meeting.[3]

A bone of contention to occupy the attention of divergent groups, all of which he knew were ambitious, did not necessarily displease Getúlio. The principal debate now was over constitutionalizing the nation. Politicians generally favored this, and early in 1931 Vargas asked Agriculture Minister Assis Brasil to head a commission to draw up an election law.

But Góis, speaking on behalf of the Clube 3 de Outubro, warned Vargas that the national political, economic, military, social, and educational structure first needed reforming. Those who had rebelled in the 1920's under the slogan "Representação e Justiça" now felt that, before returning to something which might resemble the political set-up of the past, Brazil should somehow be remade by them.

In public utterances Vargas reflected their ideas. On May 4, 1931, he emphasized that a new Magna Carta, enacted too quickly, would bring bitter disappointment. Often criticized for being slow to go ahead, Vargas would say that he found himself much less free to act than he wanted to be. While some came to feel that the central government had no plans at all, politicians, particularly those in São Paulo, feared that Vargas, Aranha, and Góis, with *tenente* backing, were interested mainly in continuing in power indefinitely.

Vargas had entered office with the conservative financial ideas of one who had studied budgets and had been Washington Luís's Finance Minister. For a full year *tenentes* writhed while Whitaker stubbornly persevered in balancing the budget, increasing taxes and holding down expenditures. They criticized Sir Otto Niemeyer's British financial mission, which arrived in February 1931 and after five months recommended a stable currency and a true central bank, "free of government influence." Whitaker had his eye on new foreign loans and another of those Brazilian "Fundings" whereby the old ones would be renegotiated. But when he sought to preserve the nation's credit by shipping abroad all the remaining gold, including rare old coins, nationalists let out a howl.

Something had to be done about coffee. Brazilian warehouses were bulging with twenty-seven million bags, enough to supply exports for almost two years. The main feature of Whitaker's coffee program was the decision to purchase and keep off the market the seventeen million bags which São Paulo had pledged as security for a London loan in May

<hr>

[3] Lourival Coutinho, *O General Góes Depõe,* p. 163.

1930. To finance a part of the purchase of this unsold mountain of coffee, which blocked the sale of recent production, Whitaker exchanged coffee for United States wheat which he sold locally.[4]

At a São Paulo coffee congress, supporters of *tenentismo* claimed that the purchase of the huge surplus was being made too slowly, and advocated burning the stock and forgetting about the "London money barons."[5] Contemplating the disastrous coffee prices, they attributed them to the shipments made in return for wheat.

Although on October 1, 1931, it did become necessary to stop servicing foreign debts while refunding negotiations were being carried on, Whitaker proposed setting local currency deposits aside for this service. In November, after most of the Cabinet objected to keeping up these deposits, Whitaker resigned.

Aranha, less inclined than Whitaker to balance budgets, took over as Finance Minister. But Vargas did not give the *tenentes* full victory, wanting always to counterbalance any force which showed signs of achieving control. A continuation of the struggle in top political circles was assured in December 1931, when Aranha turned the Justice Ministry over to Maurício Cardoso, representing Borges and other Gaúcho politicians eager for a constitution.

Judiciously, usually cautiously, Vargas was gaining support elsewhere. Tasso Fragoso became Army Chief of Staff, and, as he and Mena Barreto had much say in important military promotions, almost always these benefited officers criticized by the *tenentes*.[6]

But if decisions about a constitution and Army promotions had to be handled with care, neither *tenentes* nor politicians who had adhered to the Aliança Liberal could object to social legislation. Labor had never been a factor in the game of power plays in Brazil. But Vargas, who saw that it might, issued decree after decree, convincing many an urban worker that he had a government actively attending his interests. To protect Brazilian labor, a restriction was placed on immigration, and a decree ruled that the workforce at plants should be at least two-thirds Brazilian. Retirement and pension arrangements, formerly limited to

[4] José Maria Whitaker, interview, August 7, 1963. See Ministério da Fazenda, *Relatório da Administração Financeira do Govêrno Provisório de 4 de Novembro de 1930 a 16 de Novembro de 1931; Exposição apresentada pelo Dr. José Maria Whitaker em 4 de Fevereiro de 1933.*

[5] U.S. Consulate, São Paulo, report of November 16, 1930; also report from U.S. Embassy, Rio, November 16, 1930.

[6] Lourival Coutinho, *O General Góes Depõe*, pp. 162–163.

railroad, telegraph, and port workers, were extended to other urban workers in decree-laws which sought to provide further protection for those with more than ten years of service: dismissal should be restricted to cases in which an inquiry proved an extremely serious fault.

In March 1931 much publicity attended the issuance of a decree, signed by Vargas, Collor, and Aranha, organizing syndicates, or unions. To be recognized, each syndicate—whether of workers or employers— was to submit satisfactory statutes to the Labor Ministry, which planned to organize the syndicates into statewide federations, and the federations into national confederations.[7] Although this was a far cry from what had once been an official spirit of hostility toward labor-union activities, some who were interested in labor organization, among them Communists, decried the control over unions given to the new Labor Ministry.[8]

[7] Alfredo João Louzada, *Legislação Social-Trabalhista: Coletânea de Decretos.*
[8] Leoncio Basbaum, *História Sincera da República,* III, 33.

4. João Alberto in São Paulo

During the first two years of the Provisional Government the situation in São Paulo required most of the attention of Rio's leaders and produced the biggest story.

The trouble started on November 8, 1930, when Vargas, yielding to Aranha and the *tenentes,* named João Alberto *interventor* of São Paulo. That the fight did not involve the coffee state alone was clear when the nomination ran into objections from three Borges followers: Maurício Cardoso, Batista Luzardo (Federal District police chief) and João Neves ("São Paulo for the Paulistas").[1]

Upset about the *interventor,* São Paulo politicians were equally disturbed when Miguel Costa, state Secretary of Public Safety, established a "legion," the Legião Revolucionária de São Paulo. The bitterly disappointed Partido Democrático looked askance at the unemployed who flocked to join Miguel Costa's noisy legion, and it identified many of them as Communists.[2] The discovery that João Alberto's brother was di-

[1] Debate in Câmara dos Deputados, June 16, 1935, reproduced in Affonso Henriques, *Vargas, o Maquiavélico,* pp. 119–120.
[2] Paulo Nogueira Filho, *A Guerra Cívica, 1932,* I, 42; Carlos Castilho Cabral, *Tempos de Jânio e Outros Tempos,* p. 14; Paulo Duarte, *Que É Que Há?,* p. 122.

recting Communist propaganda in São Paulo[3] simply confirmed that the *interventor* was a bolshevik. When it became known that the amount of money spent at the drab Campos Elíseos Palace was almost double that expended in the days of Júlio Prestes, rumor had it that João Alberto had installed a gold bathtub for himself.

Before the end of 1930 the Paulista state Cabinet resigned in disgust, becoming known as the "Secretariat of forty days." The well-meaning *interventor* went ahead with his work, decreeing a 5-per-cent wage increase and breaking up some of the bankrupt *fazendas* (plantations) to give small parcels to members of the demobilized "provisional force" which had fought for the revolution. His enemies were quick to point out that those receiving the tracts failed to work them and sometimes stole from hard-working neighbors.

By March 1931 the Partido Democrático had decided to make a dramatic break with the *interventor* and thus lead the campaign for the locally popular idea of substituting a Paulista for João Alberto. Party President Morato drew up a manifesto proclaiming João Alberto guilty of "administrative incompetence, assigning most of the positions to military agents who are confidants of the *interventor*, squandering the people's money, multiplying expensive and unnecessary departments, creating government bureaus to censure the press, bypassing the sons of São Paulo and other notable people, and expanding Communist ideas."[4]

After consulting Vargas, who spoke pleasantly about "solving the case of São Paulo," the Partido Democrático agreed to hold up publication of its manifesto. But knowledge of the document spread and members of the Fôrça Pública Paulista, under the direction of Miguel Costa, raided residences to find writings offensive to the *interventor*. They detained eighteen prominent Democrats, including a former member of the "Secretariat of forty days," whereupon students staged indignation meetings.[5] The Partido Democrático officially broke with João Alberto and released its manifesto.

Although the Fôrça Pública Paulista reported to Public Safety Secretary Miguel Costa, it was full of officers who resented the use being

---

[3] Paulo Duarte, *Que É Que Há?*, p. 122; Paulo Nogueira Filho, *O Partido Democrático e a Revolução de 1930*, II, 587.

[4] Aureliano Leite, *Memórias de um Revolucionário: Revolução de 1930*, p. 223.

[5] Paulo Nogueira Filho, *A Guerra Cívica, 1932*, I, 69–71; Paulo Duarte, *Que É Que Há?*, pp. 133–136.

made of their famous corps. They prepared a proclamation mentioning the Fôrça's desire to see the nation constitutionalized and ending with these words: "Paulistas, arise in a united front for the liberation of São Paulo and the increased greatness of Brazil." This they showed to the commander of the region's federal troops, General Isidoro Dias Lopes, whom they wanted to put in Miguel Costa's place.[6] The experienced rebel doubted that the planned revolt would succeed, but he agreed to be away from the city so as to play no part in putting it down.[7]

As Isidoro had warned, the state government was too well informed of the plans of the conspirators to allow them success. The rebellion of April 28, 1931, was a curious affair in which the rebel leader ordered his men to desist after they had barely started making prisoners of Miguelista officers.[8]

[6] Paulo Nogueira Filho, *A Guerra Cívica, 1932,* I, 104.
[7] Heliodoro Tenorio and Odilon Aquino de Oliveira, *São Paulo contra a Dictadura,* p. 84.
[8] Euclydes Figueiredo, *Contribuição para a História da Revolução Constitucionalista de 1932,* p. 22; Heliodoro Tenorio and Odilon Aquino de Oliveira, *São Paulo contra a Dictadura,* pp. 79–108.

5. João Alberto Resigns

The brief outbreak in the Fôrça Pública Paulista cost Isidoro Dias Lopes the command of the Second Military Region. After a week in Rio, where he faced the fury of the *tenentes,* he relinquished his post late in May 1931. At Vargas' insistence it was assumed by Góis. Góis, who had risen in a matter of months from major to general in the Army, turned over the presidency of the Clube 3 de Outubro to Dr. Pedro Ernesto and set out to play a part in the São Paulo hassle.

The hand of censorship, heavy in São Paulo following the events of April, was gradually lightened. Paulistas learned that Rio Grande's Frente Única—the united front of the Libertadores and Republicanos—opposed the *tenentes* and wanted constitutional government for the nation.

For the harassed João Alberto the situation continued to deteriorate. The failure of the revolt hardly reduced the opposition in the Fôrça Pública to the *interventor* from the Northeast, and members of the Legião Revolucionária, crying "We want Miguel Costa," began to hear and spread stories of divergences between their hero and João Alberto.[1]

Among those who acclaimed Isidoro after he lost his Army command were hard-pressed industrialists whom the *interventor* had alienated by advocating an increased work week and a 5-per-cent profit distribution to workers. Overwhelmingly the São Paulo press battled João Alberto, some of the writers joining students to organize a Liga de Defesa Paulista (League for São Paulo's Defense). Two thousand Paulista women joined the crusade, signing an impassioned proclamation calling for a constitution and São Paulo's autonomy.

In July, 1931, when João Alberto made known his decision to step aside, *tenentes* throughout the nation protested. At Pedro Ernesto's home they resolved that he had revealed the highest administrative qualities and they offered to back him with the military power of the states they controlled.[2] But his mind was made up, and on July 12 he signed a moving message "to the Paulistas," reviewing his role as a revolutionary since leaving military school and citing his two personal losses of May 1930: the death of Siqueira Campos, and the separation of Luís Carlos Prestes, "who, more than leader, was my best friend." Defending the regime he was bringing to a close, he mentioned that he had found agricultural work for sixty thousand urban unemployed, and added that for the second half of 1931 he had prepared a balanced budget.

Reflecting on his recent experience, João Alberto suggested that his successor be Paulista and civilian. With such a suggestion coming from a *tenente*, Getúlio was perfectly agreeable. But when João Alberto delighted the Partido Democrático by picking Plínio Barreto, who had headed the "Secretariat of forty days," he unintentionally provoked a storm. It came to light that in July 1922 Barreto had published an article, "Heroes, No! Bandits!" describing the revolutionaries of Copacabana Fort as training their guns on a defenseless city. Notwithstanding a revised opinion which Barreto now rendered about this affair, little else could have been so calculated to anger the *tenentes*.

But the fundamental issue was whether the scholarly Paulista politicians (most of the top ones were professors) should run their state with a freedom from interference such as that enjoyed by the Minas and Rio

---

[1] Leven Vampré, *São Paulo: Terra Conquistada*, p. 118; Paulo Nogueira Filho, *A Guerra Cívica, 1932*, I, 122–123; Heliodoro Tenorio and Odilon Aquino de Oliveira, *São Paulo contra a Ditadura*, pp. 109–110.

[2] Heliodoro Tenorio and Odilon Aquino de Oliveira, *São Paulo contra a Ditadura*, p. 113.

Grande governments. While members of the Legião Revolucionária Paulista were reviving the chant "We want Miguel Costa," Barreto asked Rio to transfer the Fôrça Pública Paulista from Costa's hands to those of a civilian state government.[3] The *tenentes* were unwilling to go that far, and so Barreto lost interest in becoming *interventor*. Aranha, sent by Vargas to São Paulo to unravel the situation, turned to another Paulista civilian, Judge Laudo de Camargo.

Serving as *interventor* for less than four months, the judge spent his time trying to persuade Aranha that Costa should leave either the Fôrça or the Legião. Costa accused the *interventor* of behaving more like a representative of an autonomous São Paulo than was fitting for an agent of the federal government. The *interventor*'s last illusions were shattered in November 1931 when João Alberto, accompanied by Miguel Costa, strode into his office and told him that the state cabinet would have to "correspond more closely with the orientation of the revolution." The *interventor* vainly tried to reach Vargas and then resigned, told by Góis that João Alberto's mission had been authorized by the Provisional Government.[4]

While the powers in Rio sought a "Paulista and civilian" who would be more to their liking, the job went temporarily to Colonel Manoel Rabelo, who had been filling in for Góis as interim commander of the Army's Second Military Region. Rabelo, uncertain of the Fôrça Pública, asked Góis to increase the Army's strength in São Paulo.

[3] Leven Vampré, *São Paulo: Terra Conquistada*, pp. 126–141; Euclydes Figueiredo *Contribuição*, p. 23.

[4] Lourival Continho, *O General Góes Depõe*, p. 172; Leven Vampré, *São Paulo: Terra Conquistada*, p. 240.

6. The Diário Carioca Affair

Early in 1932 Paulistas made full use of Rabelo's reluctance to stifle expression. Groups vied with one another in issuing manifestos. In the forefront was the Partido Democrático, which broke with the Rio government on January 13, citing unfulfilled promises of Vargas. A group known as the Separatistas advocated that São Paulo become an independent nation and thus relieve itself of the burden of supporting the rest of Brazil. When Góis, who enjoyed making off-the-cuff observations, told his soldiers to develop their initiative and abilities like the "resolute and vigorous Japanese" so as to be able to act *nipônicamente,* São Paulo saw in the remark a comparison between itself and China, then being invaded by Japan.

At the suggestion of the recently formed Liga pró-Constituinte, a holiday was declared for January 25, the 378th anniversary of the founding of São Paulo city. The celebration turned into a mass demonstration, with orators shouting: "São Paulo for the Paulistas," "São Paulo free," "All for São Paulo," "São Paulo stands alone," and "Down with the dictatorship."[1]

Thus stirred, ardent Paulistas went to the Centro Gaúcho, whose flag arrangement was irritating: the Rio Grande flag to the right of the national flag with the São Paulo flag to the left.[2] The shield of the Gaúcho state was torn down by Paulistas, but a torrent of rain ended the incident, to the relief of those with cooler heads. Though not above heckling Aranha and Vargas, they saw no point in offending Rio Grande, where Borges was becoming increasingly provoked at Vargas.

Nothing better demonstrated the tension in São Paulo than the decision of the state's Partido Republicano and Partido Democrático to join forces to create a new Frente Única against the Provisional Government. This done on February 17 in a document speaking of "danger and adversity," the new Frente asked old Isidoro Dias Lopes to plan a conspiracy. He sent emissaries to other states, not forgetting Artur Bernardes.[3]

Vargas, with the help of Justice Minister Maurício Cardoso and Assis Brasil's commission, had been carefully steering toward democracy, going too slowly for some and too fast for others. An announcement on January 23, 1932, spoke of the secret vote, proportional representation with full guarantees for minorities, the creation of an electoral justice system, and the extension of voting rights to women. But, to water down the strength of Minas and São Paulo in future federal legislatures, the planners in Rio were increasing from 150,000 to 300,000 the number of inhabitants required for each *deputado* over the first twenty-five from any one state.[4] Paulistas, seeing in this a confirmation of the "conquered territory" status of their state, were cold about the election-law project decreed by Vargas on February 24, anniversary of the Constitution of 1891.

[1] Paulo Nogueira Filho, *A Guerra Cívica, 1932,* I, 361.
[2] *Ibid.,* p. 362.
[3] Agildo Barata, *Vida de um Revolucionário,* p. 180.
[4] Paulo Nogueira Filho, *A Guerra Cívica, 1932,* I, 353.

One week earlier the Clube 24 de Fevereiro had been organized in Rio to oppose the Clube 3 de Outubro. But a rally planned by the new club for February 24 was banned after the military ministers decided that the would-be demonstrators were inspired more by opposition to the regime than by pleasure at getting an election law.[5]

The Provisional Government's most serious Cabinet crisis developed from dinner-table conversation at Rio's Lido Restaurant late in February, 1932.[6] Justice Minister Maurício Cardoso, who had wanted the Clube 24 de Fevereiro to hold its demonstration, expressed his views to other discontented Gaúchos—João Neves, Lindolfo Collor, and Batista Luzardo. Also present was the director of the *Diário Carioca*, a daily which regularly attacked the Government, and he quickly published an article highly offensive to the *tenentes*.

In retaliation, Pedro Ernesto's son and other *tenente* supporters led three truckloads of soldiers on the night of March 1 in a destructive assault on the offices of the *Diário Carioca*. Two of the newspaper's employees were injured.

After midnight Justice Minister Cardoso and Police Chief Luzardo went to Guanabara Palace to express their indignation. They were with Vargas and Aranha when War Minister Leite de Castro phoned in to say that he would have participated in the assault had he been twenty years younger. And then Vargas told his visitors that he could hardly oppose "these young people who did this because the *Diário Carioca* was attacking me."[7]

This provoked the wrath of Rio Grande's Frente Única. After its men in Rio had exchanged telegrams with Pôrto Alegre, Getúlio had to look for a new police chief, Justice Minister, and Labor Minister. The revolution, Collor wrote Getúlio, had become a "movement for suffocating liberty."[8] When Collor and his companions were met at the Pôrto Alegre airport, Interventor Flôres da Cunha remarked that a new revolution seemed inevitable.[9]

The statement which Getúlio now addressed to the Clube 3 de Outubro led observers to regard him as a figurehead whom the club would soon

[5] Augusto Amaral Peixoto, quoted in Affonso Henriques, *Vargas, o Maquiavélico*, p. 119.

[6] Paul Frischauer, *Presidente Vargas: Biografia*, p. 287.

[7] Batista Luzardo, quoted in Affonso Henriques, *Vargas, o Maquiavélico*, pp. 124–125.

[8] U.S. Embassy, Rio, report to Washington, March 4, 1932.

[9] Paul Frischauer, *Presidente Vargas*, p. 301.

drop.[10] "You represent," he said, "the vibrant civilian and military youth who do not wish to see the revolution disappear in a mire of compromises, agreements, and accommodations with reactionaries and false advocates of democracy." Although he promised a return to constitutional ways, he stated that this would be done "under the guidance of the revolutionary government and not in obedience to the exclusive desire of politicians."[11]

Getúlio kept the door open for a reconciliation with Rio Grande's leaders, but without much hope, for, as he saw it, the struggle was one for power and the practiced politicians were rougher than the *tenentes* and more resolved than they to make him their puppet.

Rio Grande's Frente Única began submitting lists of conditions for Getúlio to meet. First there was a "decalogue," but finally the Frente settled on seven points, a "heptalogue." The authors, pleased with their wording, sent copies to all the *interventores*.[12] The demands were for an inquiry into the *Diário Carioca* affair, the immediate re-establishment of individual rights in accordance with the 1891 Constitution, a decree guaranteeing press freedom, a preliminary draft of a constitution, the election of a Constitutional Assembly before the end of the year, the federal government's assumption of state and municipal debts owed abroad, and the creation of a board to determine economic and financial policy.

Vargas told Assis Brasil, who had helped formulate the "heptalogue," that to govern was not easy. He added that much was being done along the lines suggested, and that it would be helpful if Maurício Cardoso would return to the Justice Ministry. But neither Borges nor the Partido Libertador's Raul Pilla would consider co-operating unless Getúlio bent before their demands.

The *tenentes* scored handsomely when João Alberto replaced Luzardo in the key post of Rio police chief. And they liked the new Labor Minister, Joaquim Pedro Salgado Filho, a Gaúcho who was out of sympathy with his state's Frente Única. Ever mindful of the working masses, Vargas and Salgado kept turning out social legislation, such as decrees establishing a forty-eight–hour week and bettering the conditions of women workers. Their decree of May 12 instituted mixed commissions to settle labor disputes; it provided that if the commissions could not reach agreement the final decision would be made by judges working under a presiding officer named by the Labor Ministry.

[10] U.S. Embassy, Rio, report to Washington, March 11, 1932.
[11] *Jornal do Commercio,* Rio, March 7, 1932.
[12] Paulo Nogueira Filho (MS), "Ideais e Lutas de um Burguês Progressista: Pródromos da Guerra Cívica dos Paulistas," p. 456.

The post of Justice Minister was left open, in view of the possibility of filling it by negotiation with the Frente Única Riograndense.

7. Conspirators at Work

Vargas, just before the *Diário Carioca* affair, found another "Paulista and civilian" to serve as *interventor* of São Paulo. This was ex-Ambassador Pedro de Toledo, a man in his seventies who had been in retirement in Rio for twenty years. The appointment was poorly received in São Paulo, where political leaders wanted a member of their Frente Única. The new *interventor*'s announcement that he would continue with most of his predecessor's Cabinet neither surprised nor pleased the *autonomistas*.

Juarez Távora was on another tour of the Northeast and frequent press releases were issued to remind would-be rebels that the Vargas Administration had a lot of support in that region. Távora's trip, suggested by Vargas as a prelude to a trip he planned for himself, was a success, because of sizable federal aid now going to combat the drought.

But the principal step taken by Vargas to prevent an explosion was to have his Cabinet announce on April 7, 1932, that an election for a Constitutional Assembly would take place on May 3, 1933.[1] Although he had not submitted to the demands sent from Rio Grande, he was making rebellion senseless. There was, after all, no point in holding out indefinitely against a popular wish, or in provoking a civil war and the possible inglorious end of the regime. Vargas was finding that the pressure created by political oratory allowed him to free himself from the domination of diehard *tenentismo*.

Getúlio had no intention of ending up at the mercy of any powerful group, and in avoiding this situation would see to it that none became too strong. Smoking his cigar and presiding benignly, he was the conscientious and unhurried moderator. Preserving his own independence in this way, he was at the same time helping the nation reach a decision based on the will of no one group.

The *tenentes* considered Getúlio their ally in the fight being waged by conspiring politicians against Getúlio and themselves. The election decree

[1] Paulo Nogueira Filho, "Pródromos da Guerra Cívica dos Paulistas" (MS), p. 539.

apparently resulted from the strength of the politicians, and *tenentes* aimed their fire at them, working at the same time to persuade Vargas to cancel the decree.[2] Paulistas and Gaúchos who had been scolding Vargas ignored the decree or expressed doubt that it would ever become effective. In Rio members of the Federation of Constitution-Supporting Paulista Students greeted the election decree with an anti-Government demonstration which João Neves excitedly compared with the great Aliança Liberal meetings of January 1930.[3]

Later in April, Borges (*Pela Ordem*) sent Glicério Alves to size up opportunities in São Paulo, Minas, and Rio for overthrowing the Vargas regime. In São Paulo, Glicério was briefed by Isidoro Dias Lopes, the rebellion's chief military planner, and by Júlio de Mesquita Filho, the dapper director of the daily *O Estado de S. Paulo,* who was emerging as the leader of the conspirators. The visitor was deeply impressed by the reports of representatives of all the military units which planned to rebel in the state. Artur Bernardes, approached by Glicério in Rio, offered to assist a rebellion in every way possible.[4] Although Bernardes saw a possibility of Olegário Maciel's remaining neutral, he doubted that the old *interventor* of Minas would help the conspirators.

Over 10,000 federal soldiers were in the state of São Paulo, compared with 3,000 before the 1930 revolution.[5] But Góis, finding his men plotting, became worried.[6] Calling in the local politicians, he expounded at length, as he liked to do, on the national situation. São Paulo, he said, could obtain its objectives peacefully, and he proposed that the "São Paulo case" be solved by having the state government placed in the hands of its Frente Única.

The Frente had no objection to this, and some of its members thought Góis would make a splendid leader of the planned rebellion. São Paulo's *Separatista,* in its second issue, was less complimentary to Góis. After reminding its readers that Santos each day contributed to the federal government more than Rio Grande contributed in a month, it scoffed at reaching any understanding with Góis, that "fleshy drunkard."[7] Nothing

---

[2] Augusto Amaral Peixoto, interview, August 17, 1963.

[3] Paulo Nogueira Filho, "Pródromos da Guerra Cívica dos Paulistas," p. 539.

[4] *Ibid.,* p. 505.

[5] U.S. Embassy, Rio, report to Washington, March 18, 1932; Paulo Nogueira Filho, "Pródromos da Guerra Cívica dos Paulistas," p. 478.

[6] Euclydes Figueiredo, *Contribuição,* p. 41.

[7] Paulo Nogueira Filho, "Pródromos da Guerra Cívica dos Paulistas," pp. 525–526.

should be done which involved recognition of the "little roly-poly dictator" in Catete Palace.

The Góis formula was running into trouble anyway. Miguel Costa sped to Rio to attack it in the Clube 3 de Outubro, and was assisted by Pedro Ernesto, Aranha, Juarez Távora, and Manoel Rabelo.[8] Rebuked by the club, Góis resigned the command of the Second Military Region.

In the meantime the São Paulo Frente Única was busy cementing bonds with allies. One of these was Bertoldo Klinger, the general relegated to the command of 5,000 soldiers in the wild western state of Mato Grosso. As police chief of the Junta Pacificadora he had revealed his low opinion of Vargas, and since that time had forbidden his men to join the Clube 3 de Outubro. Late in April 1932, when old Isidoro asked him to be military leader of the forthcoming rebellion, Klinger accepted.[9]

A political pact between the Frentes Únicas of São Paulo and Rio Grande was signed by João Neves, Júlio de Mesquita Filho, and others early in May. This sustained the "Heptalogue of Pôrto Alegre" and prohibited either Frente from entering into agreements with the "Dictatorial Government" unless the other approved. More dangerous to the nation's peace was a pact which Júlio de Mesquita Filho was negotiating with Flôres da Cunha. This would list the *casus belli*, the developments which the two states would regard as reasons for jointly declaring war on the Vargas Government.

[8] Lourival Coutinho, *O General Góes Depõe*, p. 176; Euclydes Figueiredo, *Contribuição*, p. 43.

[9] Bertoldo Klinger, *Parada e Desfile duma Vida de Voluntário do Brazil*, p. 441.

8. Aranha Visits a Bellicose São Paulo

For those who were overlooking or disparaging the announcement to hold an election for a Constitutional Assembly, Getúlio set the record straight in a widely publicized manner. At a ceremony in the Chamber of Deputies building he and his Cabinet signed the decree. Then, speaking as one with a mission conferred on him by the people, he reviewed the steps taken to provide the electoral reform promised by the Aliança Liberal. If there had been some delay, he noted dourly, it could be attributed to the Cabinet crisis and disturbances which followed his signing the election law in late February.

Raul Pilla had once said that "the constitutionalist campaign will have lost its *raison d'être* the moment the Government sets its course definitely toward constitutionalization."[1] Now he decided the campaign was worthy of backing even if it had no *raison*. And Borges, after the Rio ceremony, appeared more disgruntled than ever. Departing from his usual custom, he gave a press interview at his ranch, acidly attacking Vargas. "We are working for the solution of the case of São Paulo," he added.[2] Collor said that "in no hypothesis whatever will Rio Grande return to co-operation with the dictatorship."[3] Interventor Flôres da Cunha lived under the shadow of the Frente Única and often seemed to agree with its leaders. At the same time he set himself the impossible job of reconciliation and spoke of leaving office if it could not be achieved.

When Aranha, his personality as magnetic as ever, visited Rio Grande in April 1932 he was received in demonstrations which made it clear to his good friend Flôres da Cunha that Vargas as well as Aranha had loyal supporters among the Gaúcho people. Borges and Pilla could make no case for their state's being "conquered territory."

Cheered by this reception, Aranha went to São Paulo on May 22. But there he was regarded as responsible for the selection of João Alberto as *interventor* and for every sin practiced against the state's Frente Única. On the day of his arrival students distributed the Frente's bulletin, advising that the "special envoy of the dictator" was coming, and urging that a continuous demonstration against his "uncalled-for-meddling" start that very day.

The mammoth meeting was at its peak late in the afternoon with Ibraim Nobre shouting that São Paulo had for too long been crushed by outsiders and adventurers. Immediate popular action, he cried, was needed. More than ready, the mass of almost delirious humanity swarmed to the main Army barracks and then swept on to the headquarters of the state's Fôrça Pública. There, because of the presence of Miguel Costa supporters, a student was wounded in a scuffle.

At Campos Elíseos Interventor Pedro de Toledo opened the garden gates to the crowd, which was shouting "Death to Vargas" and "Death to Aranha." Nobre, in a reference to the wounded student, exclaimed that "São Paulo blood has begun to be spilled." The old *interventor* was given the choice of "besmirching" all his honored past, or becoming worthy of a statue, and he selected the latter, promising to give his listeners the

---

[1] U.S. Consulate, Pôrto Alegre, report, May 14, 1932.
[2] U.S. Consulate, Pôrto Alegre, report, May 19, 1932.
[3] U.S. Consulate, Pôrto Alegre, report, May 14, 1932.

government they demanded or leave office. The elated crowd went home, filled with a sense of what mass demonstration could accomplish.

Aranha had more than this to worry about. He found Army officers arguing violently about the position to be taken in case of a Paulista rebellion. None of them favored firing on the people.

The next day, May 23, was another "glorious" one for Paulistas. Officers of the Fôrça Pública issued a manifesto supporting a truly Paulista Cabinet. The stores closed and the multitude again surrounded Campos Elíseos, wildly cheering Francisco Morato when he announced the names of those who would make up the new Cabinet. Aspirations, it seemed, were being realized one after the other. That evening scholarly, pugnacious Valdemar Ferreira became Justice Secretary, and a state-government decree retired Miguel Costa from the Fôrça Pública. Jubilant Paulistas tore down the plaques of João Pessoa Street, renaming it "May 23."

But that night brought tragedy. Overexcited youths, many of them students, destroyed the offices of two newspapers, one belonging to relatives of Aranha, and the other to the Miguelistas. Then the mob, its orators assailing the Legião Revolucionária, went on to Miguel Costa's political headquarters, where a few defenders tried to hold off thousands. During five hours of fighting with rifles and hand grenades four of the attackers were killed and one was so badly wounded that he died five days later. When the Army intervened on the morning of the twenty-fourth the Miguelistas surrendered their arms.[4]

Funerals for the fallen were attended by large crowds, and in this somber atmosphere São Paulo's new Cabinet began its work. The initials of the dead, MMDC, were used to designate a civilian militia organized on May 24.

Accompanied by well-known *tenentes* who had served João Alberto, Manoel Rabelo returned to São Paulo, this time to command the Second Military Region. Cordially greeted by Miguelistas, he had a tart exchange of words with Pedro de Toledo and lost any goodwill he had earlier earned, especially after he announced the incorporation of the Fôrça Pública into his command. When he brought more troops into the city—troops which Paulistas described as molesting their women—he was pictured as eager to re-establish the control of the Vargas Government over São Paulo.

But Aranha had been shocked by his visit. Back in Rio he urged cau-

[4] Paulo Nogueira Filho (MS), "Pródromos da Guerra Cívica dos Paulistas," pp. 580–592; Carlos Castilho Cabral, *Tempos de Jânio e Outros Tempos,* p. 16.

tion, with the result that Manoel Rabelo was told to go easy, and the Fôrça Pública was disincorporated from his command. João Alberto, irritated by Aranha's attitude, made sure that disorders would not occur in Rio. Public meetings were strictly controlled and press reports about São Paulo were censored. To bolster the Rio police, poorly regarded since the events of 1930, João Alberto organized a new body, the Polícia Especial, whose five hundred athletic young men, picked from student groups and sports associations, were trained to act boldly.[5]

Flôres da Cunha conferred with Borges, whose confidential report from São Paulo spoke optimistically of the chances of a successful rebellion. Returning from Borges' ranch to Pôrto Alegre, Flôres was received by an inquisitive crowd. He had, he exclaimed, just been telling his "Great Chief" that even if Rio Grande should mistakenly take the road to disaster, he would, loyal to Rio Grande, go along that road. Heavily applauded, the emotional *interventor* wept.

At Aranha's suggestion, Flôres wired Vargas to say that the São Paulo Cabinet changes were "a happy solution" which had the full backing of Borges and Pilla. But Getúlio annoyed the *interventor* with his reply. The new Paulista Cabinet, he said, would continue only if it co-operated with the Provisional Government along the lines of the revolution's ideology.[6]

[5] Eusébio de Queiroz Filho, interview, June 26, 1963.
[6] Paulo Nogueira Filho, "Pródromos da Guerra Cívica dos Paulistas," pp. 609–610.

9. A Cabinet Reform?

Borges and Pilla directed Gaúcho external relations. Early in June 1932 they concluded their deal with the Paulistas about the *casus belli*, producing a keg of dynamite—a letter from Pilla to the presidents of São Paulo's Democratic and Republican Parties. By this the two states committed themselves to take up arms against the Vargas regime should it modify the São Paulo state government, dismiss the federal military commander in the south, or dismiss Klinger from his Mato Grosso post. The terms had been agreed between Júlio de Mesquita Filho and Flôres da Cunha,[1] and the letter stated that it had been written upon the authorization of both Flôres and Borges. It went on to say that the principal

[1] Júlio de Mesquita Filho, interview, August 7, 1963.

object of any armed movement would be to put Brazil in the hands of a junta which would speedily call a national election.[2]

The indefatigable João Neves, representing the Rio Grande Frente, urged Vargas to solve the"crisis" by reshuffling his Cabinet so as to give the constitution-lovers more influence. The suggestion was unwelcome to Paulista leaders because by now they were accusing Vargas of "deceitfulness" and "doublecrossing," and of "deliberately lying." Seeing a Machiavellian trick in everything he did, they rejected any kind of existence with him in power.

Getúlio, on the other hand, seemed agreeable to Neves' suggestion and so the capital was alive with talk about the new Cabinet. But as the negotiations dragged on during June, more and more people decided that the Vargas philosophy could be summed up in one sentence: leave everything as it is to see how it will turn out (*deixa como está para ver como fica*).

Finally on June 23 the government reported that the entire Cabinet had offered to resign but that Vargas had calmly refused to accept any resignations, pointing out that he could simply offer the vacant Justice Ministry to Flôres da Cunha and the Agriculture post, which Assis Brasil wanted to leave, to a Paulista. After all the speculation this solution, much too unsensational for the Frentes, who were out to humble Vargas, was hailed as a great *tenente* victory.

João Neves, furious at Vargas, reported to Pôrto Alegre. There Pilla considered that it might be nice to have Flôres in the Justice Ministry but that even when Maurício Cardoso had been there the *tenentes* had done well. When the Gaúcho leaders turned to Borges to get the final word they were told that João Neves should reject Vargas' proposal.

With Olegário Maciel giving unconditional assurance that Minas would back the Vargas regime, Getúlio sounded out Flôres da Cunha. The Gaúcho interventor, who had been building up his military strength, was in a difficult position. He was critical of Vargas whenever the *tenentes* got an advantage, but what he really wanted was a formula which would satisfy both his bosses, Borges and Vargas. Flôres' messages to Aranha, with whom he most liked to deal, were so satisfying to the federal government that the Rio Grande Interior Secretary, a Borges man, resigned. After this, Flôres wired Vargas that he would "maintain order in the

[2] Paulo Nogueira Filho, "Pródromos da Guerra Cívica dos Paulistas" (MS), p. 639.

state, particularly if, as you declare, you are willing to constitutionalize the nation."[3]

[3] *Ibid.,* p. 715.

10. Klinger Gets Himself Fired

To dominate Brazil, Getúlio needed the support of generals as well as *tenentes*. While he was being criticized for doing nothing, he was preparing the delicate operation which would gain the loyalty of generals who disliked the Clube 3 de Outubro and who disapproved of War Minister Leite de Castro's interest in it. The Army, these generals believed, could best perform its function by keeping out of politics. General João Gomes, who felt strongly on the matter, had been installed by Vargas to command the Rio military region even though *tenentes* opposed him for his opinions and his record. By resigning this post in the first part of 1932, João Gomes strikingly underlined the feeling of all the old-line "regulars."

Klinger, one of the most resolute critics of the Clube 3 de Outubro, became the center of the storm when an Army captain belonging to the *tenente* group insulted him, calling him a "coward," a "traitor," and an "idiot." Army men who came to Klinger's defense were punished by the War Minister, but the captain who started the fuss remained unpunished on the ground that he was an official in the Rio de Janeiro state Cabinet.

At this point Vargas stepped in, supporting the bulk of the Army generals by signing a special decree which gave an eight-day prison sentence to the captain. Thus it was evident that there would be less Clube politics in the Army and that Brazil would have a new War Minister. But the political artist in the presidential palace did not propose to leave the *tenentes* empty-handed. Much publicity was given to their victory, the collapse of the myth about a sensational Cabinet reform favorable to Paulista and Gaúcho politicians.

Of the Clube's 300 members in Rio, 210 met to back the War Minister. But Aranha, Góis, and João Alberto failed to show up. Góis and Aranha had run into the club's fire on the São Paulo matter and now they resigned from the organization they had helped make influential.

War minister Leite de Castro's successor was not one whose name had been in the rumor mills. Practically everyone was astonished at the appointment of Augusto Inácio do Espírito Santo Cardoso. A general who had retired nine years earlier and not been heard from since, he had no ties to *tenentismo* and was generally acceptable to his predecessor's opponents. But his son, who had worked for Leite de Castro, had close ties with João Alberto. In fact, it was the Police Chief, so influential in *tenente* circles, who had been quietly pushing for Espírito Santo Cardoso. A happy solution, thought Vargas.

But Klinger, who considered the new War Minister's son an "extremist," felt otherwise. The message which he gave to an aide in Mato Grosso for delivery by hand to Espírito Santo Cardoso was hardly the congratulatory greeting of a fond admirer. Nor was it a routine message offering support. It included reflections on what Klinger called the physical and moral deficiencies of the addressee, and went on to say that Brazil was in effect re-experiencing the appointment of a civilian to the post, as had happened in 1919. The new minister, Klinger said, would be a straw man, and generals and colonels would get orders from his office assistants.[1]

On the same day—July 1—Klinger sent off another message bearer, this one to Paulista leaders to inform them of what he was doing. These men, and João Neves in Rio, shaken by the insulting letter to the War Minister, persuaded Klinger to postpone its delivery. If he lost his post the *casus belli* agreement was supposed to go into effect.

But copies of the letter got around, Klinger even sending one to Góis, who unsuccessfully sought to have the author withdraw the original. Klinger, not a man to be turned from his course, telegraphed Góis that Tasso Fragoso or Mena Barreto (both of the 1930 Junta Pacificadora), or Góis himself, would make a good War Minister, and that General Cardoso could well be used as mayor of the Federal District, a solution which would have the merit of getting rid of Dr. Pedro Ernesto.

After a radio broadcast made Klinger's letter public knowledge, the original was rushed to the War Minister on instructions of its signer. On July 8, a few hours after receiving the missive, General Cardoso wired Klinger that Vargas had put him on the retired list and that he should pass his command to the next in line. This Klinger did, recommending order and discipline to the five thousand soldiers.

[1] Bertoldo Klinger, *Parada e Desfile*, pp. 453–454.

11. Paulistas Decide To Revolt

In the series of meetings held on July 8 by Paulista leaders little consideration was given to commitments which, against some pressure, Vargas had
undertaken on behalf of an election and a new constitution; nor to the
fact that the São Paulo political leaders had the state Cabinet they cherished and Rabelo had been instructed to co-operate with it. The circumstances surrounding Klinger's dismissal hardly made this a reason for
civil war. A revolt on this account could only be justified on the basis of
armed strategy, the subject which dominated the discussions of the Paulista leaders on July 8. The military men put great stock in the adherence
of Klinger, who they supposed would bring soldiers and badly needed
weapons from Mato Grosso.

Paulistas were also counting on the Gaúchos leading a great march
north as in 1930. A wire from Lindolfo Collor advised that Rio Grande
would co-operate; Flôres da Cunha might cause some trouble, but, Collor
said, Borges would handle him. The Gaúcho oracle was even reported to
be coming from his farm to Pôrto Alegre.

As it would take time to organize well in Rio Grande and elsewhere,
and as arms ordered from abroad had not reached the port city of Santos,
Paulistas had been planning to have their revolution commence between
July 15 and July 30, after deceptive rumors had been spread fixing the
date for the fourteenth.[1] But after Klinger lost his post on the eighth
the more impetuous military men in São Paulo favored a quick drive to
overthrow Vargas. Isidoro and the Fôrça Pública commander at length
agreed that the outbreak begin on the night of July 9. One of those present reflected the prevailing spirit when he exclaimed: "I, as a Paulista,
will never permit anyone to rob me of firing the first shot against the
dictatorship."

Euclides Figueiredo, a colonel who stood by Washington Luís in 1930,
was chosen to command the outbreak until Klinger arrived. Updating
some plans drawn up prior to the "glorious" events of May 23, the
colonel put them into effect without difficulty. Thanks to infiltration in
local Army barracks and a great reluctance to put up resistance, the federal troops in São Paulo went along with the Fôrça Pública Paulista in
opposing Vargas. However, many Army officers felt differently, and they

---

[1] Agildo Barata, *Memórias de um Revolucionário,* pp. 183–184.

were made prisoners. So was Miguel Costa, who had been calling the most recent São Paulo government an affront to the 1930 revolution.

Although not a shot had been fired, the Constitucionalistas, as the new revolutionaries called themselves, were able to telegraph Klinger at 2:00 A.M. on July 10 that the whole state was under their control. He was urged to come quickly to assume command of forces estimated to include 10,000 federal soldiers in the state, 11,000 members of the Fôrça Pública, and 3,000 Fôrça Pública reservists.[2] In addition, the MMDC, civilian militia, had been mobilized.

Pedro de Toledo wired Vargas his resignation as *interventor* and prepared to turn the state government over to Justice Secretary Valdemar Ferreira, Democratic Party strong man. But as the old ex-ambassador backed the July 9 revolution, the politicians decided to avoid frictions by having him stay on with his Cabinet and with the title of governor.

July 10 was a Sunday. More than 30,000 Paulistas jammed the small square in front of the state government palace under "a brilliant winter sun which flooded everything with golden radiance."[3] They were stirred by the white plumes on the helmets of the cavalrymen of the Fôrça Pública and by the pennants streaming from the lances. A bugle sounded, and Pedro de Toledo, his white head showered with rose petals thrown by the ladies, took his place and heard Valdemar Ferreira pronounce him "president" of São Paulo. All sang the National Anthem and acclaimed the nation, the state, and the "constitution."

The recruitment of volunteers was begun that day amid cheers. In stark contrast to 1930, 70,000 enlisted before the first week was up, and the number grew to 180,000. Women were offering to do all they could at the fighting fronts and elsewhere. Money and all sorts of possessions came pouring in to contribute to the reversal of the series of "humiliations imposed on São Paulo by adventurers." Some factories and metallurgical shops strove to make guns and bullets, and São Paulo's Polytechnic School was described as "a veritable arsenal."[4]

All during July 10 and 11 troops were being rushed to the east, to move quickly through the Paraíba Valley in the direction of the national capital, where they hoped to find an uprising against the Vargas Government. The Paulistas, believing the crusade noble enough to appeal to all patriotic Brazilians, felt there might well be no hostilities from Minas

[2] U.S. Consulate, São Paulo, report, July 30, 1932.
[3] *Ibid.*
[4] Herculano C. e Silva, *A Revolução Constitucionalista*, p. 70.

to the north or from Paraná to the south, and only on the eleventh did they send troops to the borders of those states.

The optimism in the state capital was reflected in its press, always offering stories which would keep spirits high. Allied troops were reported to be arriving from Mato Grosso, and a battalion in Paraná was said to have turned against Vargas. There was talk of how Minas and the federal Navy would be neutral. "Everyone in Minas," it was said in São Paulo, "is favorable to the revolution except Olegário."

General Klinger was greeted by a throng when he reached São Paulo on July 12, but he was accompanied by only a few members of his staff, not 5,000 soldiers. Nonetheless Ibraim Nobre, the greatest orator of the Constitucionalista cause, made a vibrant welcoming speech which was constantly interrupted by applause.[5] When he had finished and a quiet moment arrived, Klinger spoke in the reassuring tone of a military man. Nobre, he said, had spoken "with his heart, the heart of São Paulo, in his mouth . . . We are here with our sword drawn in a salute to legality."

Then, while Colonel Figueiredo went off to direct the attack on Rio, Klinger joined Pedro de Toledo, Isidoro Dias Lopes, and others in signing a manifesto explaining what the revolutionaries would do when victorious. Because the dictatorship had broken the promises of the Aliança Liberal, the new movement proposed turning the national government over to a junta which would immediately operate under the 1891 Constitution. This junta of five men, representing Rio Grande, São Paulo, Minas, the Federal District, and the north, would call an assembly to draw up a new constitution.

[5] Armando Brussolo, *Tudo pelo Brasil!*, pp. 27–28.

12. The Constitutionalist Revolution

Getúlio had no intention of following the example of Washington Luís. No cardinal would lead him, defeated, from the presidential palace. One caller felt it significant that Vargas had a revolver in his office and what appeared to be an appropriate message ready. Vargas' undramatic and businesslike demeanor hid an urge to go down fighting if need be. But to prevent the need from arising he directed Góis to defend the capital and to advance on São Paulo from the east; Góis' rival in the Army, General Valdomiro Lima, was to command the attack on São Paulo from Paraná in the south.

The authorities in Rio had been following developments with care and had detailed information about all who were involved. João Alberto's police picked up Isidoro's agent, sent from São Paulo to lead the rebellion in Rio, and sent him to join other suspicious characters on the prison ship *Pedro I*. This was on July 9, just before the revolt started. Right after the outbreak two important generals were imprisoned, and Tasso Fragoso, who wanted Vargas to open peace negotiations, was dismissed as Chief of Staff. General Álvaro Mariante, Góis' old chief who had opposed the 1930 revolution, took command of the First Military Region so that Góis could lead the advance on São Paulo.

The most critical matter was the position of Flôres da Cunha. Borges' message to him on July 9 evoked "our commitments of honor" in the crusade to recapture liberties.[1] But when Flôres telegraphed Vargas, resigning as *interventor,* Vargas reminded him that he had given his word to maintain order. "I cannot accept your resignation. No one is better than my dear friend to be guarantor of the honor of Rio Grande do Sul at a moment when we are the victims of a treason which seeks to stab us in the back. I will not give in."[2]

Aranha applied his persuasiveness and presently Flôres assured Vargas that he would preserve order in Rio Grande. Vargas might sigh with relief, but the Paulistas supposed that the Frente Única Riograndense reflected Gaúcho sentiment and was in control.

During a moment of confusion the Rio Grande Frente, reporting that it had been "caught by surprise in the avalanche," said that it would back Flôres in seeking a peaceful solution.[3] But after the Paulistas wired that they could not interrupt the operations into which they said they had been "forced,"[4] Borges, Pilla, Luzardo, and Coller broke with Flôres. The *interventor,* they noted with dismay, had become "an unconditional servant of the dictatorship."[5]

They had discovered that Flôres had been arranging to have troops, including volunteers from the interior, leave Pôrto Alegre by ship quietly at night to go north to fight for Vargas.[6] After the break with Flôres the

[1] Euclydes Figueiredo, *Contribuição,* p. 59.

[2] *Ibid.,* p. 60.

[3] Herculano C. e Silva, *A Revolução Constitucionalista,* p. 98.

[4] U.S. Consulate, São Paulo, report, July 30, 1932.

[5] Herculano C. e Silva, *A Revolução Constitucionalista,* p. 100.

[6] U.S. Consulate, São Paulo, report, July 16, 1932; Heliodoro Tenorio and Odilon Aquino de Oliveira, *São Paulo contra a Dictadura,* p. 241.

spirited Luzardo headed a revolt in the north of Rio Grande, but he was virtually without munitions and it was quickly quelled. Even so, Paulistas were ever getting fresh good news from Rio Grande and long kept expecting to see Borges arrive at the head of 10,000 fighters. João Neves went around São Paulo showing joyful telegrams from Raul Pilla, such as the one announcing that the Gaúcho revolutionary movement was "all over the state." About as truthfully, Neves wired back that "the dictatorship, repulsed by the nation, is decaying hour by hour."[7]

The naval blockade made the encirclement of São Paulo complete. During more than two and a half months of defensive warfare the Paulista troops were forced back at the three fighting fronts: the east, the north, and the south.

Colonel Euclides Figueiredo in the east commanded the bulk of the federal troops who had rebelled. At the outset he was near the Rio state border, closer to the national capital than to the Paulista capital. But he hesitated to proceed without reinforcements and sent emissaries to persuade federal troops in Minas to adhere. None did, and Figueiredo, having lost his early opportunity to advance on Rio, spent the rest of the revolution fighting stubbornly from trenches, retreating from one line of defense to another. Góis and his men, advancing slowly along the Central do Brasil Railroad, were joined by the Marines. Major Eduardo Gomes made effective use of the Army Air Force.

General Valdomiro Lima in the south inflicted the first setbacks on the Paulistas, and the news of them was helpful to Flôres da Cunha. Itararé, scene of São Paulo's defensive concentration in October 1930, fell quickly in July 1932, and the federals pushed on rapidly with other victories along the rail line. Then Ribeira, on the highway, fell on July 30. All this took place without much fighting, some Paulista officers entering into agreements with the enemy, so that along both the railway and the highway large numbers of the Fôrça Pública turned themselves and their arms over to pro-Vargas troops.[8]

In the northern sector, the Fôrça Pública withdrew from an advance into Minas territory when one of its officers thought he had a non-aggression pact with the Mineiro state militia.[9] But Olegário Maciel had

[7] U.S. Consulate, São Paulo, report, July 30, 1932.

[8] Gastão Goulart, *Verdades da Revolução Paulista,* pp. 213–214; U.S. Consulate, São Paulo, report, July 30, 1932.

[9] Romão Gomes quoted in Herculano C. e Silva, *A Revolução Constitucionalista,* p. 177.

his state militia commander inform the Paulistas that "without total surrender of all your troops, we shall not reach any understandings."[10] Colonel Eurico Gaspar Dutra, who had rebuffed emissaries of Euclides Figueiredo, joined ex-São Paulo *interventor* Manoel Rabelo in the drive from the north toward São Paulo city. The attacking troop was swelled by the arrival of a group of hard-fighting Gaúcho *provisórios,* who included Benjamim Vargas, Getúlio's younger brother.

While the Vargas forces thus followed the three approaches to the city, private automobiles practically disappeared from São Paulo's streets and the inhabitants, responding to a "campaign for gold," turned in watches and trophies and exchanged their gold wedding rings for iron ones. There was no lack of favorable reports, the most sensational being the radio broadcast of August 3 describing the fall of the Vargas Government and the accompanying ecstatic demonstrations in the streets of Rio. A story of the death of Góis pictured him as losing an arm and dying from the loss of blood before he could be conveyed to Rio. But of such stories the only one which could be confirmed was the death in battle of Góis' brother.

From the very start Constitucionalista soldiers complained of insufficient munitions.[11] In São Paulo's shops the quality of cartridges was improved and production was raised to 200,000 daily, but this increase failed to keep pace with the growing need.

Only 20,000 of the Paulista civilian volunteers could be furnished arms.[12] Those who went to the fronts, their ears ringing with recent speeches, soon experienced the hardships of holding out against the fire of superior forces. Quite untrained, they often disappointed their professional comrades. Late in August the Paulista commander in the north advised the head of the Fôrça Pública: "I have just sent almost 800 men back to São Paulo. I command troops who are irresponsible and cowardly. Truly afraid of the enemy, the men do not hesitate to abandon the lines in mass, seeking at all cost to reach the rear."[13] A few days earlier, Euclides Figueiredo had sent back another of the "patriotic units" of the MMDC. Figueiredo remarked: "Young men of the finest *Paulista* society, they

[10] Herculano C. e Silva, *A Revolução Constitucionalista,* p. 255.
[11] Euclydes Figueiredo, *Contribuição,* pp. 169 (footnote), 183, 204, 224, 299, and *passim.*
[12] Gastão Goulart, *Verdades da Revolução Paulista,* pp. 172–173.
[13] Quotation given in Herculano C. e Silva, *A Revolução Constitucionalista,* p. 142.

were inexperienced and lacked precise military instructions. They had lots of goodwill, but that was not enough."[14]

By the latter part of September, Valdomiro Lima, with 12,000 men in the southern sector, was facing 4,000 defenders eighty miles from São Paulo city. Góis' "Army of the East" had reached 40,000.[15] The Constitucionalistas in the north had been forced back to the strategic city of Campinas, forty-five miles northwest of São Paulo city. Justice Secretary Valdemar Ferreira, determined to fight to the end, visited Campinas in an effort to raise the spirit of the men. Much to his disgust, he noted that while the enemy prepared to attack, exhausted volunteers insisted on returning to the state capital for some rest;[16] the main topic of conversation within the troop was a possible armistice.

[14] Euclydes Figueiredo, *Contribuição*, pp. 219–220. See also p. 205.
[15] Lourival Coutinho, *O General Góes Depõe*, p. 212.
[16] Herculano C. e Silva, *A Revolução Constitucionalista*, p. 335.

13. The End of Hostilities

During the struggle attempts were made to settle the dispute peacefully, and many hoped that Cardinal Leme would come up with a formula. The most publicized effort was that of Flôres da Cunha late in July, when he sent forth Maurício Cardoso, the only well-known politician in the Rio Grande Frente who had not completely broken with him. Paulistas, having just celebrated—briefly—the false report of Vargas' downfall, heard vaguely that Cardoso had in mind a provisional constitution to be effective until an assembly drew up a permanent one.[1] But in the national capital Cardoso could get Vargas to offer nothing attractive to São Paulo, and Cardoso's wire to Valdemar Ferreira advised that a cease-fire would be acceptable only if the Paulistas surrendered.

In the latter part of August, when it was clear that the Cardoso mission had failed, Borges announced a general uprising in Rio Grande. Flôres da Cunha, who had been using the velvet glove, clamped down on anti-Government opinion and exiled remaining political opponents. Although Flôres' desire to avoid bloodshed delayed his superior force in eliminating scattered resistance in the interior, by mid-September the only rebel group remaining in the state consisted of a band of fewer than 100 men led by

[1] Euclydes Figueiredo, *Contribuição*, pp. 196–199.

Luzardo and old Borges himself. Borges, who might have been leading a large force had he had more arms, refused all appeals from Flôres that he desist, and was finally captured on September 20. The famous prisoner, sent by ship to Rio, was greeted by Aranha and then packed off to reside "in exile" on a ranch near Recife. The news of his capture was not believed in São Paulo.

On September 25, after an agent of the Paulistas had unsuccessfully proposed peace on the basis of setting Vargas aside, Valdemar Ferreira visited the headquarters of the Fôrça Pública. There he declared that the fighting must continue even if it meant moving elsewhere, as the Paulista rebels had done in 1924.[2] Officers of the Fôrça had been trying to explain that the soldiers, lacking sufficient munitions, were in no condition to carry on, regardless of all the "idealism" in the state government.

At Campinas two days later Herculano de Carvalho, commander of the Fôrça, presided over a meeting made up largely of his subordinates. They were joined by an Army officer from the eastern front with letters from fellow Army officers who considered it ridiculous to prolong the agony. Everyone at the Campinas meeting signed a document declaring a military victory impossible. Herculano, "backed by the forces of the Army and the Fôrça Pública," was chosen to get the military and civilian authorities to end the fighting, or, should that prove impossible, to enter directly into discussion with the Vargas forces.[3]

The state government had already given Klinger exclusive authority to explore surrender terms when he felt it necessary. On the morning of September 28 he advised that, as there had been no favorable external development, the moment had come. Valdemar Ferreira agreed, remarking that he had learned on the previous night that the Fôrça was in clandestine negotiation with Góis.[4]

That evening a disturbed Euclides Figueiredo reached São Paulo from the east. He had resolved that death in the trenches would be preferable to abandoning the cause and was annoyed that Klinger had decided to act without consulting him. Hoping to get support from Herculano de Carvalho, Figueiredo phoned him at Campinas. This conversation did nothing to soothe Figueiredo. He strode into a meeting at Campos Elíseos and disagreed with the military men who were backing Klinger. The situ-

---

[2] Herculano C. e Silva, *A Revolução Constitucionalista*, p. 355.
[3] *Ibid.*, pp. 356–358.
[4] Bertoldo Klinger, *Parade e Desfile*, p. 532.

ation in the east, Figueiredo said, was not bad, and he insisted that the fight go on.

The Colonel's words lifted civilian spirits, and the Campos Elíseos midnight meeting became turbulent with resolution. It was decided that Romão Gomes, who had won a few skirmishes in the north, should take over the Fôrça Pública. Herculano de Carvalho, who had lately exchanged acrimonious words with Valdemar Ferreira, was to be jailed as a traitor. These decisions made, Ferreira asked Klinger to hold up his telegram to Vargas proposing an immediate cessation of hostilities. But Klinger refused, and at the hour which had been established earlier, 1:00 A.M. on September 29, he went personally to the telegraph office and sent the message with his signature alone. He cut out the Governor's signature and the phrase expressing agreement of the São Paulo government.

João Neves left the Paulistas after advising Isidoro that "with all chances ended here, my duty calls me to join the people of my state." Actually Neves went to Buenos Aires to write *Acuso!,* the story of his role in seeking to overthrow the Vargas Provisional Government.

Romão Gomes, Valdemar Ferreira's new hope, came to São Paulo, but he explained that his "spirited troop of 1,800 men" had become contaminated with the pessimism at Campinas and that all his officers favored an armistice. Declining to head the Fôrça, and pointing out that the cause was lost, he was sent back to Campinas by men who only later learned that he, too, had signed there the September 27 manifesto favoring an immediate truce.[5]

Klinger was dealing with Góis, who, together with Valdomiro Lima, had been named by Vargas to conduct the peace negotiations. Rejecting Góis' first draft as too severe, Klinger sent a counterproposal to the federal headquarters at Cruzeiro. Representatives of the Fôrça Pública, who went to Cruzeiro because they resented being left out, heard Góis warn them that they had better sign a separate peace agreement or else receive the same punishment as rebel federal soldiers.[6] The Fôrça signed, promising no longer to obey the "present state authorities, whose obstinacy in carrying on the struggle is considered against the state's interests." The Fôrça was to maintain order in the state capital and recognize no authority other than that of the federal government.[7]

---

[5] Euclydes Figueiredo, *Contribuição,* pp. 279–280; Herculano C. e Silva, *A Revolução Constitucionalista,* Ch. 21.

[6] Herculano C. e Silva, *A Revolução Constitucionalista,* p. 383.

[7] Gastão Goulart, *Verdades,* pp. 261–262.

In protest against this separate agreement Romão Gomes resigned from the Fôrça Pública, which he had served for twenty years.[8] Klinger's already difficult negotiating position was now hopeless. Valdemar Ferreira, fuming, learned that Góis was giving his instructions to Herculano de Carvalho, the head of the Fôrça Pública, whom the Paulista government had ordered jailed as a traitor. One of these instructions assigned to the Fôrça the task of removing Governor Pedro de Toledo, and stipulated that Herculano himself was to run the state.

Under these conditions the São Paulo government resigned in a public manifesto issued on October 2:

With the failure of the armistice negotiations proposed by the commander of the Constitucionalista forces, who considered the dictatorship's conditions humiliating and unacceptable, a pact was signed separately by the commander of the Fôrça Pública, and he has been named military governor of the state. Thus is ended the Constitucionalista Government, acclaimed by the Paulista people, by the National Army, and by the Fôrça Pública, which today deposes it.

Stating things differently, Herculano wrote: "Thus ended a government imposed by the people, but which did not know how to correspond to that confidence and took them to the bloodiest of civil wars, disillusioning them."[9] Hundreds had lost their lives.

Like Isidoro and the top officials of the revolutionary São Paulo government, Klinger and his staff surrendered at Cruzeiro and went on to Rio as prisoners. After a short imprisonment, chief participants in the Constitucionalista rebellion, 200 in all, were exiled to Portugal late in 1932.

Euclides Figueiredo refused to turn himself over. Being unable to reach Mato Grosso and learning that he could have done nothing had he got there, he left with six companions on a fishing boat for the south. But off Santa Catarina the Navy captured them; and Figueiredo, like Bernardes, Mesquita Filho, Klinger, and Pedro de Toledo, ended up in Portugal. From there, keeping in touch with rebels who had fled to Argentina and Uruguay, he plotted a continuation of the struggle against Vargas.[10]

[8] Romão Gomes' letter given in Herculano C. e Silva, *A Revolução Constitucionalista*, pp. 402–403.

[9] Herculano C. e Silva, *A Revolução Constitutionalista*, p. 421.

[10] Agildo Barata, *Vida de um Revolucionário*, p. 213.

BOOK IV

THE END OF THE PROVISIONAL GOVERNMENT, 1932–1934

"They have forgotten Brazil."

1. The Government Prepares for Democracy

As a victor Vargas was magnanimous, revealing traits he had shown in Rio Grande after becoming governor. On September 20, 1932, before the fighting ended, Vargas addressed a manifesto to São Paulo, offering to have wheat shipments made from Rio. He placed the blame for the tragedy not on the Paulistas, but on those who led the conspiracy. The state's people, he said, were not responsible and would not be humiliated.[1]

In the surrender terms drawn up by Góis, and in other documents, the Vargas Administration recognized the heroic qualities demonstrated by the people of São Paulo. Valdomiro Lima, who became military commander of the defeated state when Góis declined the post, declared that "all resentments are forgotten." The victorious Vargas Government even agreed to redeem the bonds which had been issued by the São Paulo revolutionaries to finance the revolt.

A healthy São Paulo was indispensable for Brazil. Further, a strong link with the Paulistas was interesting to Getúlio, who seldom closed the door to understandings with former foes, and who remarked that he often found it easier to deal with an adversary than an ally.

[1] Getúlio Vargas, *A Nova Política do Brasil,* II, 90–91.

The forces confronting Getúlio had changed considerably by October 1932. The 1931 power struggle between *tenentismo* and state politicians was over. Both groups lost out, the political group because it lost a rebellion, the *tenente* group because, by the time victory had been achieved, Vargas could act without its support. The regular Army came out on top, its poise recovered, and on it Getúlio would have to rely heavily in the future.

Getúlio, moving with the care of a ruler representing no faction, had watched politicians try to grab the leadership of the democratic current and turn it into an anti-Vargas thing. He had known that many pro-constitutional pronouncements had simply reflected a desire to see him thrown out. But he had discerned, too, the strong popular appeal of elections and a constitution.

During the rebellion Getúlio had sought to counter the main Constitucionalista argument by listing the steps his Administration had taken and was taking to implant democracy. Reference had been made to the February 24, 1932, Electoral Code and the decree of April 18, authorizing funds for the newly created system of electoral courts: the Tribunal Superior Eleitoral and the Tribunais Regionais Eleitorais.[2]

The 1932 Electoral Code, besides watering down the representative strength of the two largest states, provided that employees, employers, and professional groups be represented directly (a feature of corporative states which—like mosaic sidewalks—Brazil would share with the Portuguese). Literacy, limited to about 20 per cent of the population, remained a requirement for voting. The new code reduced the minimum age for voters from twenty-one years to eighteen. It extended suffrage to women. And it fulfilled the pledge of the Aliança Liberal by providing for the secret vote.

As early as mid-1931 Aranha was listing names to submit to Vargas for a commission to start drafting a constitution,[3] but it took the outbreak of the 1932 rebellion to prod the Provisional Government into announcing the organization of the commission. To finish its work, it was given until November 15, 1933, when the Assembly to be elected on May 3 was to convene.

After the 1932 rebellion had been subdued, the commission set to work, meeting at the Foreign Office under the chairmanship of Afrânio de Melo Franco. The Constitucionalista rebels thus came to feel that al-

[2] *Ibid.*, p. 53.
[3] Levi Carneiro, *Pela Nova Constituição*, p. xix.

though they had suffered a military defeat they had accomplished their main purpose.

In preparing the Itamarati (Foreign Office) draft of a constitution, the commission met more than fifty times between November 1932 and May 1933. The seasoned diplomat who presided had to face divergences between old-school democratic jurists and those who had less faith in democracy; he came to regard Góis as an extreme advocate of fascism favored by young *tenentes*.

Among the issues which badly split the commission was that of representation by classes or professions. Afrânio de Melo Franco argued against including such representatives in a chamber also made up of representatives elected by the states.

One of Afrânio's sons writes that Vargas "as always, acted ambiguously. He agreed with Melo Franco because he rarely disagreed with a man to his face. But fundamentally, class representation was the irreplaceable capstone in the game of his secret intention."[4] In fairness to Getúlio it must be said that on this matter he was prompt in leaving little doubt about how he felt: he wanted class representatives to sit with those elected in the traditional manner because he wanted to weaken the congressional blocs of the large states.[5] He was disappointed when Afrânio and others prevailed over five commission members (including Góis, Aranha, and José Américo) to get class representation omitted from the draft of the constitution.

[4] Afonso Arinos de Melo Franco, *Um Estadista da República*, III, 1419.
[5] Lourival Coutinho, *O General Góes Depõe*, p. 246.

2. A Rash of Political Parties

Like the prerevolutionary political parties, practically all of those created to participate in the election of May 3, 1933, were state parties. But the situation differed now in that the opponents of state regimes had a better chance to elect representatives.[1] Indeed, in their zeal to eliminate fraud and give Brazil its first democratic experience, the new electoral tribunals devised such strict voting requirements that registration was difficult and slow.

When admirers asked Cardinal Leme to found a party, he became one

[1] Afonso Arinos de Melo Franco, *Estudos de Direito Constitucional*, pp. 165–196.

of the few men to turn down such a suggestion. Arguing that Catholicism was universal and parties were fractional, he refused to organize a Partido Católico, establishing instead a Liga Eleitoral Católica to back candidates who would agree to defend Catholic social principles in the Constitutional Assembly. The indissolubility of marriage was the first on his list.[2]

Only the Communist Party, considered non-Brazilian, was refused registration by the authorities. For the ten Assembly seats allotted to the Federal District, two hundred candidates were sponsored by a score of parties. One of these was the *tenente*-backed Partido Autonomista, whose main objective was to make the 520 square-mile Federal District a state.

Their eyes on the national scene, Pedro Ernesto and other leaders of the Clube 3 de Outubro organized a rally in Rio which was supposed to inspire the establishment of *tenente*-backed Socialist Parties throughout the country.

Miguel Costa, released from jail, founded the Partido Socialista of São Paulo. But his foes were as numerous as ever. What had once been the Frente Única of the old Republican and Democratic Parties now became the Chapa Única pelo Bem de São Paulo (Single Slate for the Good of São Paulo), and, after its supporters resigned themselves to participating in a Vargas-sponsored election, it forged well ahead of its rivals. All the Frente's former leaders had been stripped of their political rights for three years and many of them were in Portugal, but a good new piece of political timber was found in an able and serious-minded engineer, Armando de Sales Oliveira, brother-in-law of newspaper publisher Júlio de Mesquita Filho.

Valdomiro Lima, uncle of Vargas' wife, was having his difficulties, as Góis had expected. *Tenentes* objected that he was too lenient with São Paulo and they criticized Vargas for appointing him *interventor*.[3] Valdomiro, who desperately needed local political support, publicly charged a *tenente*-backed São Paulo police chief with treating prisoners badly, and then he formed a new São Paulo party, the Partido da Lavoura (Farm Party), to get the support of coffee workers.

Of all the parties born at this time, only Ação Integralista Brasileira was destined eventually to play a dramatic role and arouse strong emotions. Its founder was Plínio Salgado, the emaciated intellectual with the Hitler-type mustache who had been producing an abundance of novels, newspaper articles, and essays on social and political matters. One of his crea-

[2] Laurita Pessôa Raja Gabaglia, *O Cardeal Leme*, pp. 310–313.
[3] U.S. Consulate, São Paulo, report, February 10, 1933.

tions had been the first manifesto of Miguel Costa's Legião Revolucionária, but he had broken with the Legião after failing to permeate it with
his philosophy. Since then he had shown extraordinary vitality in attracting interest in his Society of Political Studies.

Plínio's Integralista manifesto, issued in São Paulo in October 1932,
declared that "God directs the destinies of People. Man on earth should
practice the virtues which elevate him and make him perfect. Man has
worth through work, through sacrifice for the Family, Nation and Society." This manifesto, and Plínio's Statement of Integralista Principles of
1933, proclaimed the need of an Integralista state, free of divisions such
as those caused by political parties or a disorganized economy.

Great emphasis was placed on the family, the sacred creator of virtues,
the consolidator of the state, and the most important of all social institutions. Municipalities would become meetings of families, and to give
them more autonomy Brazil should be decentralized.[4] Legislative representation would be only by class or profession.[5]

The state, under the Integralista program, should control theaters,
press, and radio, "which today favor international capitalism and Moscow
agents." Although private property rights would be recognized, the Integralista manifesto rejected "the unrestrained individualism" of capitalism and proclaimed the need of new regulations covering production and
commerce so as to avoid harmful imbalances. Integralismo's archenemy
was Communism, which it said "is based on the same fundamental principles as capitalism but has the disadvantage of reducing the number of
masters to one. . . . Communism destroys the family in order to enslave
the worker."[6]

Some observers found Integralist pronouncements obscure, clerical, or
confusing. But many writers and professors subscribed to them and the
movement gave promise of becoming national, with various "provincial
chiefs."

The Integralistas made much use of fascist trappings. At the São Paulo
headquarters the Greek letter *sigma* (used in integral calculus) was
chosen to be the party emblem, and a uniform was designed: green shirt
with white or black pants. The slogan was "God, Country, and Family."

Plínio Salgado urged that the Liga Eleitoral Católica (LEC) especially
recommend Ação Integralista Brasileira to its members or make Inte-

---

[4] Plínio Salgado, *O Integralismo perante a Nação* (3rd Edition), pp. 17–38.

[5] Olbiano de Melo, *A Marcha da Revolução Social no Brasil*, p. 66.

[6] Plínio Salgado, *O Integralismo perante a Nação*, p. 23.

gralismo the official party of the Catholic Church. When the Liga nevertheless approved candidates of various parties, including those of Integralismo, Plínio remarked: "Very well. I respect the decision of the LEC. But let me tell you one thing: this time the LEC will win; in the next election the Communists will win; and finally we shall win."[7] He went off to organize the first parade of "Green Shirts," which was viewed in São Paulo on April 23, 1933, mainly as a curiosity.

[7] Laurita Pessôa Raja Gabaglia, *O Cardeal Leme*, p. 316.

3. The Vargas Star on the Rise

Like previous Brazilian chiefs of state, Vargas enjoyed spending summers at Petrópolis, high above sweltering Rio. The head of the Provisional Government, approaching fifty, would sometimes stroll through the uncrowded streets of Petrópolis, happy to be greeted by passers-by. He and his family found the old palace, constructed during the empire by the Baron of Rio Negro, in considerable need of modernizing. That they were still there in April, 1933, was owing to work being done to make Rio's presidential palaces, Guanabara and Catete, fit for distinguished visitors, among them Argentina's President Agustín Justo.

One evening late in April 1933, Getúlio, his wife Darci, and one of their sons were returning from Rio on the scenic road up the escarpment to Petrópolis. It was Brazil's longest paved road, an achievement of Washington Luís, "the road-building President."[1] Landslides were not uncommon, particularly after heavy rains, and the presidential car was struck by a 170-pound granite slab. A Vargas aide was killed and the legs of Getúlio and Darci were crushed.

For about two months after this accident, a familiar sight on the Rio-Petrópolis road was the car of good-hearted Pedro Ernesto, calling at first more as a physician than as mayor of the Federal District with business to discuss with the hospitalized head of state. By the time the condition of Getúlio and Darci allowed them to be moved by ambulance to Rio, the winter cold of late June made them glad to leave the unheated old summer palace.

By then the election of May 3, 1933, much more honest than its predecessors, had taken place. Only 1,285,000 had registered to vote. Considering that the minimum age had been reduced from twenty-one to

[1] Charles A. Gauld, written comment to author, March 1965.

eighteen years, and that women were voting for the first time, the number of electors was strikingly lower than the 1,840,000 recorded as having voted in the presidential election of 1930.

The count was slow, occasioning complaints, but when the totals were in it seemed that the Vargas Administration had won a genuine victory. More precisely, it revealed that, except in São Paulo, the *interventores* of important states had things well under their control. A few Vargas foes were elected, such as two on the slate "Bahia is still Bahia." But of the 140 representatives chosen by the Federal District and the six most populous states, 94 were regarded as "pro-Government," 26 as "neutral or undefined," and 20 as "anti-Government."[2] Although many months remained before the members of the Assembly would elect a President to serve under the new constitution, and the outcome would depend on how the *interventores* instructed their men, Vargas' prospects for winning the Presidency were believed good, particularly as the forty "class" representatives were considered likely to support him.

In Rio Grande, Flôres da Cunha's new Liberal Republican Party captured thirteen Assembly seats whereas the Frente Única Riograndense elected only three representatives (among them Assis Brasil and Maurício Cardoso). The largest bloc was that of Minas, its preponderance due in part to its rigged census of 1920 and the failure of Brazil to have any census in 1930. Old Olegário Maciel's Progressista Party smashed the Partido Republicano Mineiro thirty-one to six. After the "Autonomists" of the Federal District won six out of ten places, Góis withdrew from their party. Regretting to see a movement in favor of a constitution which would grant "excessive" autonomy to the states, he reflected the views of *tenentismo* and Vargas when he remarked that "a Brazilian soul no longer exists, having been replaced by a great number of provincial souls."[3]

In São Paulo, the Chapa Única, offspring of the 1932 rebel movement, was the overwhelming victor over Miguel Costa's Socialists and Valdomiro Lima's Partido da Lavoura. This result led Getúlio to agree with Aranha that a new *interventor* had to be found. Valdomiro, retaliating, became involved in a plot to overthrow the Vargas Government, but, after federal troops had been readied to smother his revolt, he prudently left for Europe.

It was time for that tie with the Paulistas which Getúlio wanted, and

[2] U.S. Embassy, Rio, report to Washington, July 26, 1933.
[3] U.S. Consulate General, Rio, report to Ambassador Gibson, August 17, 1933.

so, at long last, he consulted São Paulo political groups about their future *interventor*, asking for lists of men who would govern above parties. He studied them well and selected Armando de Sales Oliveira, the brother-in-law of Júlio de Mesquita Filho. With this excellent "Paulista and civilian," São Paulo felt better about things.

Flôres da Cunha, too, was feeling cheerful. The Gaúcho state militia and "provisional" forces, and a special fund created from the state's take on gambling, all assured that his grasp on Rio Grande was firm. When he lunched with Aranha and Góis in Rio early in August 1933, he was looking forward to becoming a great national figure. Who, he asked Góis, should be Brazil's President under the new constitution? The general from Alagoas, rarely reticent, delivered a discourse on Brazilian history and concluded by saying that, for the sake of national harmony, the federal government should continue in the hands of Rio Grande. The three pillars of Rio Grande, said Góis, were Vargas, Aranha, and Flôres; one should govern the nation, one should govern Rio Grande, and the third should be in the federal government. When Flôres persisted, asking who should head Brazil, Góis chose Vargas; then, he said, Aranha and Flôres, in that order.[4]

A few days after this lunch, Vargas, walking with the help of canes, was well enough to take a ship for the north on a trip which could hardly fail to gain him political support. Accompanying him on the *Almirante Jaceguaí* were the Northeast's representatives in the Cabinet, Agriculture Minister Juarez Távora and Transport Minister José Américo; also Góis (military inspector of the north), and twenty journalists.

In the face of the prolonged drought, the Northeast was receiving federal aid unmatched since the days of President Epitácio Pessoa.[5] By the time Vargas and his party touched their first stopping points, engineers, agronomists, and other experts were launching job-creating works, chiefly roads and hydraulic projects. This program, which was employing over 200,000 drought victims, was supplemented by relief going to millions.[6]

Getúlio was acclaimed by the people and warmly greeted by state *interventores*. Many of these were *tenentes*, and when Góis asked Vargas how long he was going to keep them in their posts rather than return them to the Army, Vargas explained that he found *tenentes*, accustomed to mili-

[4] Lourival Coutinho, *O General Góes Depõe*, pp. 237–238.
[5] Stefan H. Robock, *Brazil's Developing Northeast: A Study of Regional Planning and Foreign Aid*, p. 77.
[6] Anthony Patric, *Toward the Winning Goal*, Ch. 14.

tary discipline, easier to deal with than professional politicians.[7] None, in the private opinion of Vargas, had administrative and political talents equal to those of Juraci Magalhães, the *tenente* who was *interventor* of Bahia.

In Recife, where Borges was in exile, Vargas spoke to the Pernambucanos about the Government's program of assisting sugarcane growers with Bank of Brazil loans for crops. The new Institute of Alcohol and Sugar, he said, was taking over the task of using the sugar production tax to buy and sell sugar to eliminate wide price fluctuations, which he blamed on speculators. Furthermore, the new Institute was to promote the use of sugar alcohol as automobile fuel, a step which Vargas hoped would permit ending the tax.[8]

In João Pessoa, Getúlio lauded his late running mate before a wildly cheering audience, and he let Transport Minister José Américo explain to his fellow Paraibanos the Government's program of drought relief.

Automobiles and trains were used to reach state capitals in the far north and then riverboats and airplanes took the chief of state to more remote spots. In late September the *Almirante Jaceguaí* brought Getúlio to long-depressed Belém, and there he spoke of the rebirth of the Amazon region with Henry Ford's pioneering efforts in plantation rubber.

The last lap of the expedition, from Recife to Rio, was made on Germany's *Graf Zeppelin*, which had inaugurated a seasonal all-air service between Europe and South America two years earlier. Vargas, who relished air travel, had to be in the national capital early in October to receive Argentina's President Justo. He arrived there, tanned and refreshed, cheered by the receptions he had been given, and ready to apply his talent to a thorny new political problem.

[7] Lourival Coutinho, *O General Góes Depõe,* p. 240.
[8] Getúlio Vargas, *A Nova Política do Brasil,* II, 129–140.

4. A Live Coal from Minas

While Getúlio was in Recife early in September 1933, news reached him of the death of Olegário Maciel, governor and *interventor* of Minas. Carrying on with his trip, Vargas planned to handle the matter of Olegário's successor later, and in the meantime Gustavo Capanema, Interior Secretary of Minas, was acting *interventor*.

By November 1933, when Antônio Carlos was presiding over the first sessions of the Constitutional Assembly, the chief talk of politicians was the Minas contest. Capanema, who considered himself well qualified to carry out Olegário's ideas, found that apart from Minas government circles his chief support came from Flôres da Cunha, busy seeking alliances which would strengthen his presidential ambitions.

Virgílio de Melo Franco, who had served the 1930 revolution well, was the outstanding candidate to be *interventor* of Minas. After he, Bernardes, and the *tenentes* had failed to unseat Olegário in 1931, Virgílio had resigned himself to waiting it out and had become well known in Rio society. Now his moment seemed to have arrived. As earlier, he had the support of Aranha and a strong "revolutionary" sector, and Getúlio himself let Virgílio and others know that he favored him.[1] However, Antônio Carlos, who had supported Olegário and thus was presiding over the Assembly, did not conceal his annoyance at Virgílio's book, *Outubro 1930,* which pictured Antônio Carlos as having deserted the revolutionary cause at a decisive moment.

The *Correio da Manhã* joined the campaign against Virgílio with two violent articles headed "Ratos, Ratinho, e Ratices" (Rats, Mouse, and Pranks).[2] These revived sensationally an old charge that the Melo Francos had profited from the expropriation of a railroad in 1919 when Afrânio was Transport Minister and Virgílio was his aide.

In a bitter note to Vargas, Virgílio reminded him of the significance of the *Correio*'s articles during a period of government press control. He added: "I do not wish to be *interventor* of Minas, just as I did not wish to become a notary public, or be minister to Uruguay, or director of the Bank of Brazil, or president of the National Coffee Council, and as I do not wish to become Justice Minister."[3]

Afrânio, who had refuted the 1919 charge long ago, was as incensed as his son, presuming that the *Correio* articles appeared with government permission. He wrote Vargas saying that he could not carry on as Foreign Minister. Vargas replied that an investigation showed that the articles had been published without the knowledge of government censors, and he expressed his full confidence in his Foreign Minister. After Vargas showed him a decree naming Virgílio *interventor,* Afrânio withdrew his resignation and joined other Latin American diplomats at the Montevideo Conference of December 1933.

[1] Carolina Nabuco, *A Vida de Virgílio de Melo Franco,* p. 87; Alzira Vargas do Amaral Peixoto, *Getúlio Vargas, Meu Pai,* p. 94.
[2] Carolina Nabuco, *A Vida de Virgílio de Melo Franco,* p. 85.
[3] *Ibid.*

Flôres da Cunha was frantic about the decree. Taking Góis with him, he rushed to Guanabara Palace and interrupted the viewing of a movie by the Vargas family to explain that if Virgílio were appointed *interventor*, Vargas would not be elected President by the Constitutional Assembly. Flôres pointed out that the large Minas delegation would oppose Getúlio's election, and so would others.

Getúlio was at his best. Expressing surprise that Virgílio's appointment would cause such a crisis, he agreed to hold it up. He emphasized that all who were interested in the Minas matter were friends. A satisfactory solution could, he felt sure, be reached at a meeting of Flôres, Aranha, Góis, Virgílio, Capanema, and the Minas delegates to the Assembly. Getúlio said he would speak with Capanema, even then at the Palace anxiously awaiting his opportunity to see him. Flôres and Góis were asked to call on Aranha, Virgílio, and the Minas delegates.

Flôres and Góis were able to reach Aranha after he left an American Embassy dinner. Angry at Flôres for getting involved in Minas political affairs, Aranha accused him of supporting Capanema, a man Flôres hardly knew, merely to block Virgílio's appointment.[4] The harsh words exchanged between the two ambitious Gaúchos shattered a warm friendship which had been particularly valuable to the Provisional Government when the Paulista rebellion broke out.

Vargas called Aranha, Flôres, Virgílio, and Capanema together.[5] He was charged by Aranha with having broken his word, and by Flôres with being evasive, but the dispute between Aranha and Flôres, involving their political power, became so acrimonious that the charges against Vargas fell by the wayside. Virgílio, irritated at the way things were going, prepared to leave, with the remark that he had sought nothing. Vargas, who had been smoking his cigar and listening, then said he would accept any name on which Virgílio and Capanema could agree.

The two young aspirants lunched together but found themselves at an impasse. And so Getúlio, telling them that they had dropped live coals in his hands, called on Antônio Carlos to draw up a list of names acceptable to the Minas political leaders, directors of the Partido Progressista. The contest thus ceased to be "a Gaúcho free-for-all on Mineiro soil."[6] Antônio Carlos, after long discussions, handed Getúlio his calling card with eight names written on it.

[4] Lourival Coutinho, *O General Góes Depõe*, p. 252.
[5] Carolina Nabuco, *A Vida de Virgílio de Melo Franco*, pp. 87–88.
[6] Francisco Negrão de Lima, quoted by Hélio Silva in Part 1 of "Lembrai-vos de 1937," *Tribuna da Imprensa*, Rio, October 1, 1959.

Looking them over, Getúlio asked his distinguished visitor why the Mineiros had omitted Benedito Valadares, who was one of the relatively unknown members of their delegation to the Assembly. "An oversight," Antônio Carlos is reported to have murmured as he added the name of the Mineiro whose lack of prominence made him eminently suitable to Vargas. Asked by Minas *constituintes* which of the eight names had been chosen, Antônio Carlos replied "the ninth."[7] As a compliment to Minas, Valadares was appointed "governor" instead of *interventor,* and he took office on December 12, 1933.

Virgílio spoke in the Assembly, breaking with Vargas, and his father wired his resignation from Montevideo. Back in Rio, after quitting the diplomatic conference still in progress, Afrânio learned that Aranha had resigned from the Cabinet with the remark to the press that "the choice of the new *interventor* was made by the President to suit himself." "It is unfortunate," Aranha had added, "that the true revolutionaries, the men who risked something to put the present Government in power, are being passed over."[8]

Getúlio let a little time pass and then asked Flôres da Cunha, Góis, and João Alberto to work on Aranha and Afrânio. He himself offered one of Aranha's brothers a position on his staff and took the unusual step of visiting the Aranha home. At Tiradentes Palace early in January 1934, Flôres da Cunha presided over an impressive gathering of Cabinet ministers and important *interventores.* All signed a resolution calling on the Ministers of Finance and Foreign Affairs to return to their posts. Even Afrânio, absent from the meeting, signed later at the request of Pedro Ernesto.

Afrânio, however, was determined not to return to public life, as he made clear in a letter to Vargas. He had signed the resolution in the hope that it would help persuade Aranha to change his mind.[9] Perhaps it did contribute to Aranha's decision to remain in the Cabinet at least for a while. But Aranha, who was not without political ambition, had been badly hurt by Vargas and Flôres in the Minas affair. Speaking to his successor as majority leader of the Assembly, Aranha admitted that his own influence had been "decidedly impaired."[10]

[7] Alzira Vargas do Amaral Peixoto, *Getúlio Vargas, Meu Pai,* p. 96.
[8] U.S. Embassy, Rio, report to Washington, December 15, 1933.
[9] Afonso Arinos de Melo Franco, *Um Estadista da República,* III, 1505–1506.
[10] U.S. Embassy, Rio, report to Washington, December 15, 1933.

Correio da Manhã

Nilo Peçanha, Acting President of Brazil, 1909–1910. This photograph was taken shortly after his arrival in Brazil from Europe in 1921.

Correio da Manhã

Marshal Hermes Rodrigues da Fonseca, President of Brazil, 1910–1914.

Correio da Manhã

Epitácio da Silva Pessoa, President of Brazil, 1919–1922.

O Estado de S. Paulo

Artur da Silva Bernardes, President of Brazil, 1922–1926.

Heroes of Copacabana. Left, Eduardo Gomes; right, Antônio de Siqueira Campos. Photo taken in military hospital after they had been wounded and some of their companions killed in the revolt of the "Eighteen of the Fort," July 1922.

Supporters of Borges de Medeiros in the Gaúcho civil war of 1923. Left to right: Arlindo Duarte, Osvaldo Aranha, Nepomuceno Saraiva, José Antônio Flôres da Cunha, Guilherme Flôres da Cunha (killed in action), José Alvares, and Aires Maciel.

Sacking a warehouse in São Paulo during the 1924 revolt.

O Jornal

Washington Luís Pereira de Souza, President
of Brazil, 1926–1930.

O Estado de S. Paulo

The "Cavalier of Hope," Luís Carlos Prestes.

Correio da Manhã

Isidoro Dias Lopes.

Correio da Manhã

João Neves da Fontoura as vice-governor of
Rio Grande do Sul, 1928.

Brazilian revolutionaries at Paso de los Libres, Argentina, April 3, 1927. Seated (left to right): Dr. João Batista Remão (representative of *O Combate* of São Paulo), General Bernardo de Araújo Padilha, Marshal Isidoro Dias Lopes, General Miguel Costa, Colonel João Alberto Lins de Barros. (These military ranks, or titles, were those in the Revolutionary force.)

The first directorship of the Partido Democrático de São Paulo, 1926. From left to right: Professor Valdemar Ferreira, Dr. Paulo de Moraes Barros (front), Dr. Paulo Nogueira Filho (in rear), Professor Francisco Morato, Dr. Prudente de Moraes Barros (in rear), Conselheiro Antônio Prado (center, front, with beard), Dr. Antônio Cajado de Lemos (in rear), Professor Gama Cerqueira, Professor Cardozo de Melo Neto, Dr. José Adriano Marrey Júnior (in front), Dr. Luís Aranha.

O Cruzeiro

Acclaim for Vargas during the 1930 revolution.

O Jornal

Belo Horizonte, Minas Gerais. Flag of surrender on the battered headquarters of the 12th Infantry Regiment, October 1930.

A platoon of revolutionary fighters.

O Cruzeiro

Correio da Manhã

Aranha conferring with the Junta Pacificadora in Rio, October 28, 1930. Left to right: Admiral José Isaías de Noronha (mostly hidden), General João de Deus Mena Barreto, General Augusto Tasso Fragoso, and Osvaldo Aranha.

Correio da Manhã

Aliança Liberal leaders gather before a Rio lunch at which Epitácio Pessoa presides. Early January, 1930. The face of Epitácio Pessoa (with white mustache) can be seen between shoulders of presidential candidate Getúlio Vargas and vice-presidential candidate João Pessoa (with flower in buttonhole).

Correio da Manhã

A group of 1930 revolutionaries. Seated, front row (left to right, after the small boy): Virgílio de Melo Franco, Osvaldo Aranha, Getúlio Vargas, Batista Luzardo, Florencio de Abreu, and Alcides Etchegoyen.

Juarez do Nascimento Fernandes Távora, "Viceroy of the North."

Antônio Carlos de Andrada, governor of Minas Gerais, 1926–1930.

General Bertoldo Klinger.

Antônio Augusto Borges de Medeiros, governor of Rio Grande do Sul, 1898–1908 and 1913–1928.

Finally on November 1, 1930, the revolutionaries from Rio Grande do Sul hitch their horses to the obelisk at one end of Rio Branco Avenue in Rio.

Artur Bernardes (with glasses) and A. A. Borges de Medeiros.

President Herbert Hoover and President-elect Júlio Prestes de Albuquerque in Washington, 1930.

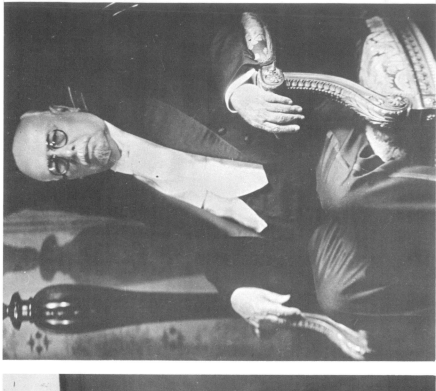

Correio da Mambã

Olegário Maciel, governor of Minas Gerais, 1930–1933. (Last photograph, taken September 5, 1933.)

Albertino Cavalieiro

Pedro Aurélio de Góis Monteiro.

Getúlio Vargas and Cardinal Leme.

Correio da Manhã

Correio da Manhã

"Old *caudilho*" Borges de Medeiros (center) arrives in Rio on way to enforced exile in Pernambuco, September 1932.

The Governor of Minas Gerais with Khaki-Shirt leaders, 1931. Seated, left to right: Gustavo Capanema, Francisco Campos, Governor Olegário Maciel, and Amaro Lanari.

On the streets of Petrópolis. Vargas, center, chats with Antônio Silvino ("Volta Sêca"), who had been a bandit leader in the Northeast and who seeks a job from Vargas. At far right is Vargas' younger brother, Benjamim.

Manchete

Osvaldo Aranha (with cigarette), Afrânio de Melo Franco, and Getúlio Vargas.

Correio da Manhã

Vargas and General Góis Monteiro, October 1932.

Getúlio Vargas with his brothers and parents. Left to right, standing: Viriato, Manoel do Nascimento Vargas (father), Getúlio, Protásio, Spartacus, and Benjamim; seated: Cândida (mother). Photo taken in 1934.

Getúlio and Darci Vargas, July 19, 1934.

Correio da Manhã

At the Guinle *fazenda*. Front row: far left: Lutero Vargas and "Getulinho" Vargas; far right: Alzira Vargas; middle: Darci and Getúlio Vargas. Above Darci: José Américo de Almeida (with glasses); above Getúlio Vargas: Juraci Magalhães.

Correio da Manhã

Taking coffee just before the inauguration of War Minister João Gomes. Left to right: Police Chief Filinto Müller, General Gomes, Justice Minister Vicente Ráo, and Federal District Mayor Pedro Ernesto Batista, 1935.

O Jornal

Dr. Pedro Ernesto Batista, mayor of the Federal District, 1931–1936.

Correio da Manhã

Integralistas, October 1934.

Correio da Manhã

The 3rd Infantry Regiment barracks (at Rio's Praia Vermelha) in flames after the Communist uprising there on November 27, 1935.

O Jornal

Green Shirt funeral. Plínio Salgado (with mustache).

O Jornal

Start of Integralista (Green Shirt) parade, Rio, November 1, 1937.

Correio da Manhã

Second floor of the 3rd Infantry Regiment barracks at Praia Vermelha after the Communist revolt there had been put down, November 27, 1935.

Correio da Manhã

Virgílio de Melo Franco, federal congressman from Minas Gerais, 1933.

Correio da Manhã

José Antônio Flôres da Cunha, interventor of Rio Grande do Sul, 1930–1934, and governor, 1934–1937.

O Estado de S. Paulo

Júlio de Mesquita Filho.

Correio da Manhã

José Américo de Almeida.

O Estado de S. Paulo

Armando de Sales Oliveira.

O Estado de S. Paulo

Luís Carlos Prestes as a prisoner.

Correio da Manhã

A contingent of Marines arriving at Catete Palace to guard the Palace.

O Estado de S. Paulo

Góis Monteiro, Gustavo Capanema, and Getúlio Vargas.

Getúlio Vargas at Campos Elíseos Palace in São Paulo. Seated at left in photo (on Vargas' right) is Ademar de Barros.

Left to right: Ambassador Jefferson Caffery, Undersecretary Sumner Welles, and Foreign Minister Osvaldo Aranha. Rio, January 1942.

Correio da Manhã

President Getúlio Vargas at his desk.

O Estado de S. Paulo

Vargas, golfer.

Correio da Manha

The Estado Nôvo Cabinet meets at Rio Negro Palace in Petrópolis in January 1942 and resolves that Brazil will break diplomatic relations with Germany, Italy, and Japan. From left to right at far side of table: Labor Minister Marcondes Filho, Navy Minister Henrique A. Guilhem, Foreign Minister Osvaldo Aranha (reading), Finance Minister Artur de Souza Costa; at right end of table: Getúlio Vargas; at far right, at Vargas' left: Education Minister Gustavo Capanema.

Manchete

Vargas posing for bust by Jo Davidson, sent in 1942 by F. D. R. to make busts of the heads of the states of the Pan American Union.

Manchete

Vargas with daughter Alzira (1941 or 1942).

Correio da Manhã

Lourival Fontes and Vargas.

Correio da Manha

At Campos Elíseos Palace in São Paulo. Finance Minister Souza Costa (left) and Economic Mobilization Co-ordinator João Alberto Lins de Barros (center) in conference with São Paulo Interventor Fernando Costa.

O Cruzeiro

O Estado de S. Paulo

General João Batista Mascarenhas de Morais, commander of the Fôrça Expedicionária Brasileira.

The Cabinet resolves that Brazil will declare war on Germany and Italy. Alexandre Marcondes Filho, Minister of Labor and Acting Minister of Justice, shakes hands with Vargas. From left to right, behind Marcondes Filho: Agriculture Minister Apolônio de Sales (smiling), Communications and Public Works Minister Mendonça Lima (partly hidden), War Minister Dutra (partly hidden), Education Minister Capanema (wearing glasses). August 1962.

Crowd at Vasco de Gama Stadium to hear Luís Carlos Prestes, May 23, 1945.

Correio da Manhã

O Jornal

Osvaldo Aranha, Góis Monteiro, and Eurico Gaspar Dutra.

Manchete

Agamenon Magalhães, Minister of Justice, 1945.

General Eurico Gaspar Dutra.

O Cruzeiro

"Take me with you," says Vargas on accepting the candidacy for the Presidency on April 19, 1950, at Goulart's São Borja ranch. Goulart (in dark suit) appears in center of photograph, his head just to the right of that of Vargas; Samuel Wainer appears immediately in front of the tree at the left.

Otávio Mangabeira, Finance Minister of President Washington Luís and long-time Vargas foe. He returned from exile in 1945 to become president of the UDN, and in 1947 became governor of Bahia.

O Estado de S. Paulo

Tancredo Neves. *O Estado de S. Paulo*

Francisco Campos. *Manchete*

O Estado de S. Paulo

Osvaldo Aranha.

Manchete

Benedito Valadares.

O Estado de S. Paulo

General Newton Estilac Leal.

Manchete

Carlos Lacerda.

Vice-President João Café Filho.

Getúlio Vargas.

Vargas at Mannesmann steel-tube plant inauguration, Belo Horizonte, August 12, 1954. Governor Juscelino Kubitschek at center.

Gregório Fortunato being decorated by War Minister Zenóbio da Costa.

O Cruzeiro

Getúlio Vargas during his last term in the Presidency, 1951–1954. These two photographs and the eight following are from a series published by *O Cruzeiro*.

O Cruzeiro

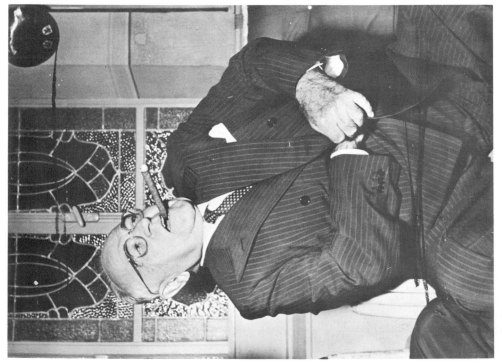

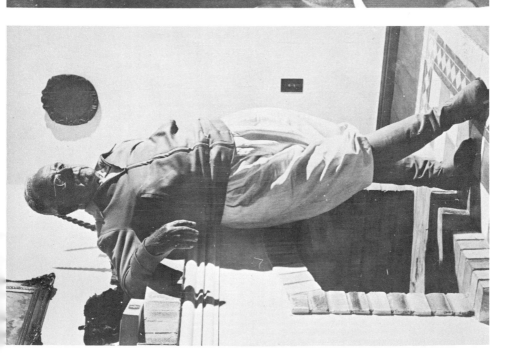

5. Writing a Constitution

Vargas was polite enough to call the "Itamarati draft" of a constitution "a useful basis for discussion by the Assembly."[1] Although the draft opposed the idea of having "class representatives" serving with regularly elected legislators, Vargas followed the ruling of the Electoral Code in arranging to have such representation in the Constitutional Assembly. Soon after the election of May 3, 1933, he signed a decree in his Petrópolis sickbed explaining how the selections would be made.

Syndicates of workers in the cities and towns were asked to send "elector delegates" to Rio. They would meet as arranged by the Labor Ministry to choose eighteen representatives to the Assembly. Similarly, "elector delegates" of employers' syndicates would choose seventeen from their group. The bureaucrats were to get two representatives, and delegates of the associations of the "liberal professions" were to choose three.

In this way the formation of syndicates was stimulated. By early June, after "elector delegates" from such groups as the hotel proprietors of Minas, the stevedores of Belém, and the barbers and hairdressers of the Federal District had been heard from, the full contingent of forty class representatives had been chosen to meet with the 214 *constituintes* elected on May 3.

Those who opposed the whole idea included many who felt that the class representatives would be amenable to the wishes of the Provisional Government and would, when the time came, vote for Vargas for President. One cynic referred to the forty class representatives as the "forty thieves of the national sovereignty." Complaining that voting requirements in the syndicates were less stringent than those used in the May 3 election, he went to the courts to get the class representatives in the Assembly ruled ineligible to vote for President; but the Superior Electoral Tribunal gave him no comfort.[2]

The Assembly, which met in Tiradentes Palace in Rio on November 15, 1933, heard an opening address in which Vargas reviewed the accomplishments of the Provisional Government and stressed the importance of

[1] Luiz Vergara, *Fui Secretário de Getúlio Vargas*, p. 95. See also Alzira Vargas do Amaral Peixoto, Ch. 5 of "A Vida de Getúlio . . .," in *Fatos & Fotos*, July 13, 1963.

[2] Affonso Henriques, *Vargas, o Maquiavélico*, pp. 223–226.

class representation.[3] Then it waited for the report of its Committee of Twenty-Six, assigned the task of reviewing in thirty days the Itamarati project. But the Committee, bogged down with over 1,200 suggested alterations, had to turn its work over to a subcommittee.[4] After toiling in daily sessions in the heat of February 1934, the subcommittee completed its recommendations early in March. Then the Committee of Twenty-Six made important last-minute changes, advocates of alterations collecting support for what they wanted in return for backing the favorite alterations of others.

While all this went on, the full Assembly became so restless that during February it came close to choosing a new "President of the Republic, whose term of office shall be established in the future Constitution."[5] In support of this resolution, whose twenty-eight signers were mostly from the Northeast, the majority leader joined with leaders of Minas, Rio Grande do Sul, and Pernambuco in citing the delay in completing a constitution. Opponents, unable to agree on a name to put up against Vargas, maintained that the resolution was inspired by Vargas' concern lest coolness develop toward giving him a new term.

After Justice Minister Antunes Maciel stated that two-thirds of the Assembly members favored Vargas, João Alberto violently opposed taking a vote before adopting a constitution, observing that although he planned to vote for Vargas when the time came, an early vote might provoke a new rebellion. Vargas followed this up with an autographed statement in João Alberto's *A Nação* disavowing any effort to force an election. He had, he said, nothing to do with the controversy and made it his policy to keep out of political questions which were brought up by troublemakers who would later become favor-seekers.[6] Early in March the proposal was set aside in favor of a resolution calling on the Committee of Twenty-Six to transmit its projected constitution to the Assembly within forty-eight hours.

Vargas, admirer of Júlio de Castilhos, wanted a constitution which would unify Brazil under a strong chief executive. For a short while he tried through Gaúcho representatives and through Raul Fernandes, secretary of the Committee of Twenty-Six, to introduce suggestions.[7] But his

[3] Getúlio Vargas, *A Nova Política do Brasil*, III, 33.
[4] Levi Carneiro, *Pela Nova Constituição*, p. xxv.
[5] *Ibid.*, p. xxviii.
[6] U.S. Embassy, Rio, report to Washington, February 23, 1934.
[7] Alzira Vargas do Amaral Peixoto, *Getúlio Vargas, Meu Pai*, p. 249.

predicament was much the same as that of the heads of state who had been in office when Brazil got its first two constitutions. In 1823 the antagonism between the Assembly and Pedro I reached such proportions that Pedro had the military close the Assembly; in 1891 Marshal Deodoro da Fonseca so upset the Assembly with his interference that, despite his prestige, he very nearly missed being elected the first President of Brazil.

Vargas soon concluded that he would have to exercise his well-known care, not opposing what he called "the ardors of the members" of the Assembly.[8] He received praise for his "hands-off" attitude.

After the draft reached the full Assembly, *constituintes* spent from mid-March to mid-April proposing two thousand amendments. Many had already been turned down by the Committee of Twenty-Six but were believed to have better prospects in the plenary session, where the large states had more influence.

While eight new subcommittees reviewed the two thousand suggestions, attacks on the work of the Committee of Twenty-Six were heard outside and inside Tiradentes Palace. The Clube 3 de Outubro published a manifesto against the draft, and leftist João Mangabeira, who had been a member of the Itamarati Commission, condemned the draft vehemently in the press. Friends of Vargas said the draft left the Presidency too weak. There were rumors that the Provisional Government might submit, as a substitute, its own project for the Assembly to work on, and even wilder rumors forecast a repetition of 1823: the Assembly would be closed by a military *golpe*.

In May and June, during what was supposed to be the final discussion by the full Assembly, the influence of the heavily populated states became pronounced. Success on the floor depended on the decisions of a "Coordinating Committee" made up of the leaders from Minas Gerais, São Paulo, Rio Grande do Sul, Bahia, Pernambuco, and Rio de Janeiro.

A drafting committee completed its work on June 29, but during July 1–7, while the Assembly was taking a last look at its achievement, seven hundred additional suggestions were dealt with. This brought to over five thousand the number of proposed amendments to the Itamarati Project which were considered by the Constitutional Assembly and its committees in the course of hammering out the Constitution of 1934.

[8] *Ibid.*

6. Contest for the Presidency

In the months preceding the election of the President by the Assembly, the Administration was generous with funds to appease interest groups. The new American ambassador, Hugh Gibson, reported that no one was more aware than Vargas that his election depended on the support of henchmen who would desert him instantly if they felt they had anything to gain thereby; that even Vargas could not be sure of not being double-crossed; and that neither São Paulo nor Minas leaders could be trusted to support him should political exigencies indicate that a withdrawal could cause his downfall.[1] That he was maintaining his balance, the Ambassador added, was a tribute to his ability.

And where lay his ability? Earlier in 1934 Ambassador Gibson had observed that Vargas had an advantage in his unusual capacity for silence, keeping his views and activities to himself "while the other conspicuous members of the Government are frittering away their influence and prestige in a steady stream of speeches, interviews, and semipublic intrigue."[2]

The interest of many politicians picked up as the Assembly members prepared to add the long-awaited and controversial "transitory clauses" to the somewhat hodge-podge Constitution. Democracy had put Vargas at the mercy of the *interventores*, but they too had their Achilles heel, as did most of their representatives in Rio. From top to bottom, few cared for the idea of leaving office. Although over a year earlier the Justice Minister had pointed out that the tasks of the Assembly did not include turning itself into an ordinary legislature, most of the *constituintes* preferred to go on serving until a new Congress had been installed; against some stormy opposition, they arranged this in one of the "transitory clauses."

Interventores, agreeing they would make admirable governors, got a "transitory clause" making themselves eligible. In elections to be carried out ninety days after the effective date of the Constitution, *deputados* for the federal Câmara and for the state assemblies would be chosen by the people. Then the state assemblies would select the first state governors and the first federal senators.

When Góis called on Vargas, objecting to what the *interventores* were doing on their own behalf, Vargas told him to accept "the consummated fact." Otherwise, Vargas said, the secret vote by Assembly members, and

---

[1] U.S. Embassy, Rio, report to Washington, July 6, 1934.
[2] Letter, U.S. Embassy, Rio, to U.S. Secretary of State, January 24, 1934.

other "complications," would "put in jeopardy" Vargas' election to the Presidency.[3]

Vargas had other reasons, too, for not wishing to rock the boat. He wanted, and finally got in the form of a "transitory clause," approval of all the acts which had been carried out by the Provisional Government and its *interventores*. This meant that over fifty decrees which the Provisional Government was hastening to enact before the Constitution went into effect would stand up.[4]

Those interested in defeating Vargas could find no candidate to agree on, particularly after the Minas squabble had taken its toll, cutting Aranha from Flôres da Cunha, weakening Antônio Carlos, and splitting Minas. Aranha and Flôres da Cunha were both blamed by Paulistas for their troubles in 1931 and 1932. Small states were wary of the two large ones.

The powerful Góis, who had Clube 3 de Outubro support, was considered from time to time, but his distrust of a "regime of liberal democracy"[5] held no appeal for the constitution makers. Soon after the Minas case had been settled, Vargas called in Góis and, all smiles, insisted he take over the War Ministry from old General Espírito Santo Cardoso. In fact, Góis learned, his appointment was already being published in the *Diário Oficial.*[6]

Getúlio surprised his bright and talkative general by pulling out from the files a memorandum about Army reorganization which Góis had written and thought that Vargas had forgotten. Now, explained Vargas, Góis, as War Minister, was to put it into effect. A principal feature was to bring state militias and "provisional" troops under federal command. In the months that followed, as Góis prepared to implement his scheme, he hardly enhanced his popularity among *interventores*. In particular, trouble developed between the new War Minister and Flôres da Cunha, who was reported to have the allegiance of twenty thousand *provisórios* in addition to the state Brigada.

When there was still talk of Góis' getting some of the votes, Góis assured Vargas that this would only help split the opposition. After hear-

---

[3] Lourival Coutinho, *O General Góes Depõe*, p. 267.

[4] Ernest Hambloch, *His Majesty the President of Brazil*, p. 95.

[5] Alberto Byington report to Council on Foreign Relations, New York, July 30, 1934.

[6] Lourival Coutinho, *O General Góes Depõe*, p. 255.

ing rumors that Góis had more than that in mind, Alzira Vargas expressed concern; but she found her father completely unworried.[7]

Although Armando de Sales had been finding co-operation with the Vargas Government useful to São Paulo, the Paulista delegation, regarded as the largest "opposition" bloc, could not be expected to vote for Getúlio. It turned, however, to none of the ambitious men who were playing a role on the political stage; it gave its votes to old Borges de Medeiros, a tribute to his behavior in 1932. He was still in exile in Pernambuco, but his unsatisfactory existence there was about to end, for the Constitution provided full amnesty to all who had committed political crimes.

The forecast of Vargas strength made by the Justice Minister in February was confirmed when the *constituintes* cast their secret votes on July 17, 1934. Vargas received 175, Borges 59, and Góis 4. Eight men received one vote each, among them three Mineiros: Bernardes, Afrânio de Melo Franco, and Antônio Carlos.

On July 20, amid applause and flower petals, Vargas entered the Assembly, took his place beside Antônio Carlos, and promised to support the new Constitution. In a manifesto he had prepared, he pointed out that he had never, directly or indirectly, indicated any desire to be chosen. "Bowing to the duty of completing the programs carried out in the last three years," he discussed in a professorial manner what most needed to be done. The keys to Brazil's progress, he maintained, lay in health, education, communications, and opening up new areas. He recommended a "university" for training farm and factory workers.[8]

Vargas' public promise to support the Constitution was hardly a reflection of his private opinion about the document, expressed to a visitor at Guanabara Palace. Abandoning his usual calm and emphasizing that neither he nor the majority leader had influenced the Assembly in its work, he spoke of the Constitution's lack of unity. It included, he said, both reactionary features and impractical reforms. Above all, Vargas was distressed at its failure to promote national cohesion. Fearing that Brazil would again fall prey to the ambitions of powerful states, he declared that "the *constituintes* have forgotten Brazil." "I believe," he concluded, "that I shall be the first to revise the Constitution."[9]

The new document, reflecting the many voices heard during its crea-

[7] Alzira Vargas do Amaral Peixoto, *Getúlio Vargas, Meu Pai,* p. 102.

[8] Getúlio Vargas, *A Nova Política do Brasil,* III, 245–246.

[9] Paul Frischauer, *Presidente Vargas,* p. 315.

tion, embodied wishes of those who favored a collectivist or corporative state and wishes of old-line "liberal" jurists who, in the words of Vargas, "turned their eyes to the past."[10] Out of the Babel came a charter which, more than the 1891 Constitution, looked to the federal government to solve social problems. However, the presidential authority was not as great as that which Bernardes and Washington Luís had enjoyed.

When the *constituintes* went to Catete Palace to congratulate Vargas for having promulgated the Constitution, he said to one of them that he had been in the habit of writing on unruled paper. "You are obliging me to use ruled paper." The *constituinte* smiled and said that it would be graph paper, with lines up and down as well as across.[11]

The powers of the Chief Executive were carefully defined, and Cabinet ministers could be called on to report to the legislature. Except for the recent election by the Assembly, Presidents were to be elected by the people for terms of four years without the possibility of immediate re-election.

The Itamarati Commission's idea of a single legislative body was accepted in the sense that although there were to be two houses, the legislative power would be in the hands of the Chamber of Deputies.[12] This was to be made up of *deputados* elected every four years from the states on the basis of one for every 150,000 inhabitants; however, 250,000 inhabitants were necessary for each *deputado* beyond twenty from any one state. In addition, the Chamber of Deputies was to have fifty "class" representatives (one-fifth of the membership elected in the usual manner).

The other house, made up of two senators from each state for eight-year terms, had novel functions. A watchdog of the Constitution, it was to be the "co-ordinator" of the governmental powers. Not only could it authorize federal intervention in the states, and authorize foreign loans by state and municipal governments, but also it had the formidable task of suspending the "federal force in the states when such force is not justified by the needs of public order."[13]

[10] Alzira Vargas do Amaral Peixoto, *Getúlio Vargas, Meu Pai*, p. 249.

[11] Hélio Silva, Part 1 of "Lembrai-vos de 1937," *Tribuna da Imprensa*, Rio, October 1, 1959.

[12] Waldemar Martins Ferreira, *História do Direito Constitucional Brasileiro*, pp. 95–96.

[13] 1934 Constitution, Ch. V, Sec. II, Art. 90d.

BOOK V

THE CONSTITUTIONAL
GOVERNMENT, 1934–1937

> "I believe that I shall be the first
> to revise the constitution."

1. Flôres da Cunha's Bid for Power

BRAZIL having become democratically constitutionalized, Vargas awaited the disturbances he expected, and abided by the rules which had been drawn up. The traditional way of doing things was reflected in the new appointments to all the nonmilitary Cabinet posts. São Paulo's *interventor* rushed to offer the new administration his full support, and São Paulo received, like Minas, two of the federal civilian ministries. The remaining three were allotted to Bahia, Rio Grande, and Pernambuco.

Aranha left to become ambassador to the United States. After his political setback he had been devoting particular attention to modifying the terms of the Third Funding of 1931. The "Aranha Plan," which became effective in April 1934, divided foreign obligations of the federal, state, and municipal governments into eight categories. Servicing was to vary depending on these classifications; full payments would be made on issues in the top category and none at all on those considered poorest grade.

Behind him, in Brazil, Aranha left politicians who were as attracted as he to the "blue fly," the presidential bug which was considered beautiful until caught. All of them knew that the October 1934 election for state and federal *deputados* would largely determine where the power lay in the next four years.

The election was a disaster for the *tenentes,* who lost their hold on the Northeast. In Pernambuco, João Alberto was badly beaten by the pro-Vargas Lima Cavalcanti. Juarez Távora in his home state of Ceará saw his candidates lose to those of the Liga Eleitoral Católica, and in three other northeastern states the *interventores* were defeated. The only results comforting to the *tenentes* were the victories of the forces of Pedro Ernesto in the Federal District and Juraci Magalhães in Bahia.

But the election was a triumph for Vargas. Of the 250 federal *deputados* elected 76 were classified as belonging to the opposition and 32 were regarded as independent.

In Minas the Partido Progressista polled 73,000 votes to 54,000 for the opposition Partido Republicano Mineiro. Before the campaigning had started there Partido Progressista President Antônio Carlos had wanted the election of state assemblymen who would choose a new governor favorable to his presidential aspirations. But Vargas had spoken a few words to Antônio Carlos and to Gustavo Capanema, the Mineiro who had been named Education Minister to please Flôres da Cunha;[1] and so the Progressista victory in Minas assured the continuance of Vargas' newly installed "governor," Benedito Valadares.

One of the other key races was in São Paulo, where the Republicans, disapproving of co-operation with the federal government, had dropped out of the coalition. Armando de Sales' Constitucionalista Party, which included the Democrats, triumphed over the Republicans 123,000 to 91,000. The Integralistas, in their birthplace, polled an insignificant 4,600 votes.

Although Flôres da Cunha's fourteen Liberal Republican federal *deputados* were listed as pro-government and the Frente's six as opposition, the trouble with classifying in this way soon became clear. Even before the Constitution went into effect, Flôres, out to preserve his control over the Gaúcho military units, was accusing Góis, an admirer of Napoleon, of Bonapartism. Presently the War Minister ran into every sort of trouble, much of it stimulated by the *interventor* of Rio Grande. Congressmen reacted unfavorably to Góis' proposal for increasing military salaries. Newspapers unfairly blamed him for political shootings in Alagoas because his close relatives were involved. Flôres da Cunha got some Army officers to disobey the War Minister, and, when Góis punished them, the

[1] Benedicto Valladares, *Tempos Idos e Vividos: Memórias,* pp. 81–97.

boss of Rio Grande went farther, ordering his representatives in Congress to break with Góis.[2] For this reason Góis resigned as War Minister early in 1935, but he remained a power behind the scenes.

Following this victory, Flôres submitted his suggestions about who the new War Minister should be. But the President accepted instead the recommendation of Armando de Sales, thus furthering his alliance with São Paulo. As a result, General João Gomes, who had fought the *tenentes* in the 1920's and opposed the 1930 revolution, became War Minister.

While Flôres was getting the better of Góis, he was preparing for the January 1938 presidential election by building up support in all states possible. *Interventores* who had done their political work well found it easy to get their state assemblies to choose them governors. But there were hard-fought battles, too, with some assemblymen selling their support to the highest bidder. In Pará one pro-Flôres da Cunha assemblyman was kidnapped. After Flôres' candidates for the governorships of Pará and Santa Catarina were defeated, *A Nação,* the Rio newspaper which Flôres had purchased to further his ambitions, published his charge of "treachery."

Flôres was reaching for a bigger prize than either Santa Catarina or Pará. His candidate for the governorship of Rio de Janeiro had the backing of twenty-two of that state's assemblymen, and the other twenty-three were split. But in this case Flôres was foiled by four machine guns used by his opponents to guard the Rio de Janeiro assembly hall in Niterói while they tried to reach agreement on one name to place in opposition to Flôres' man. After they had recruited the Navy Minister, and Vargas had urged the admiral "not to refuse this service," Flôres' opponents were ready to vote and the machine guns were withdrawn. By then it was September 1935, and Rio de Janeiro was the only state not to have elected a governor. Further delay, however, resulted as the balloting progressed, for one of the twenty-three who voted for the Navy Minister was shot and seriously wounded by an onlooker, prompting the Flôres da Cunha people to go to the courts. The Superior Electoral Tribunal annulled the Navy Minister's election on the ground of coercion, but in November 1935 the twenty-three assemblymen elected him all over again. This time Justice Minister Vicente Ráo, an Armando de Sales man, declared the election legal, whereupon Flôres da Cunha demanded Ráo's resignation. After Vargas stood by Ráo, Flôres announced that his support of the Administration would henceforth be "conditional."

---

[2] Lourival Coutinho, *O General Góes Depõe,* p. 261.

Getúlio's visit to Pôrto Alegre in September 1935 did nothing to ease the relations between the President and the Governor. Flôres da Cunha, working to make himself Vargas' successor, began to feel that Vargas was uninterested in having a successor.[3] The occasion for Getúlio's visit was the centennial of Rio Grande's cherished Ragamuffin's Revolution (Revolução Farroupilha). The sentimental Governor, wearing his general's uniform, presided over ceremonies which were financed out of his cut on gambling and which recalled that Rio Grande had once been an independent nation.

Vargas gave a speech about inter-American co-operation and then sped to São Borja to visit his parents and recapture, for a moment, life in the green fields. The information he carried back to Rio confirmed that Flôres was purchasing arms abroad for his 20,000 *provisórios*. It would be well, Getúlio told his brothers before leaving, to build up a strong opposition to the Governor in the state legislature.

From Rio early in October, 1935, Getúlio wrote to his older brother, Protásio, the São Borja cattle raiser.

Recently Flôres has been giving me serious reasons for concern. I have been putting up with all this patiently, in view of our old friendship, considering his great services, and also because I know of the corrosive work by intriguers who take advantage of his temperament. The systematic campaign by Flôres or by people close to him seeks to show that the federal government does nothing for Rio Grande do Sul . . ., nor for the rest of the country. Another prejudicial attitude of Flôres is his obsession with pretending, there in Pôrte Alegre, to be directing federal policy, intervening in the politics of other states. Besides this there is the early agitation of the problem of the presidential succession, causing misunderstandings which are entirely unnecessary. I have put up with all of this, but am reaching the limit of my patience.[4]

[3] Hélio Silva, Part 3 of "Lembrai-vos de 1937," *Tribuna da Imprensa,* Rio, October 6, 1959.
[4] Paul Frischauer, *Presidente Vargas,* p. 319.

2. Integralismo versus the Aliança Nacional Libertadora

Much of the world in the mid-1930's was the scene of struggles between two forces, each claiming to be the wave of the future. While Red Shirts clashed with Gold Shirts in Mexico, a somewhat similar struggle developed in Brazil on a much more serious scale. Conditions for the growth of each camp were good because of the new democratic era, the demise of old political parties, and the absence of new national parties. The vacuum attracted the clerical-fascist Ação Integralista Brasileira and the Communist-backed Aliança Nacional Libertadora.

Green-shirt parades became familiar sights, as did the special manner used by Integralistas to greet each other: with the raised right arm and the Indian word *anauê*. "No Brazilian home," said an Integralista publication in January 1935, "should be without the picture of the NATIONAL CHIEF" (Plínio Salgado). More and more came to profess their allegiance to him and to "God, Country, and Family."

The parades, stirring the antipathy of left-wingers, were likely to end in disorder. In September 1934, three thousand green-garbed men and women, marching three abreast in São Paulo in response to a call of the national chief, were shot at from the building occupied by a number of the trade unions. Six were killed in the turmoil.

Integralistas looked forward to the day when Brazil would have a single national party—their own—and when there would be no direct elections. In the meantime, by their statutes of March 1935, they proposed to work within the 1934 Constitution to create "a new philosophic and juridical culture" which would assure numerous blessings. These included "the grandeur and prestige of the armed forces."[1] In its abundant literature, Integralismo quoted War Minister Góis as saying: "Integralismo is a Brazilian party . . . and its effort to expand should be respected."[2]

During his term in the Cabinet, Góis saw little to impress him about democracy. After the Constitution became effective and politicians were battling for control of states, strikes broke out in Brazil as seldom before. In São Paulo foreign agitators (Lithuanian, Hungarian, and Polish) pushed for Trotsky or Stalin and joined with Brazilian Socialists in provoking unrest. Stories about planned violence helped create an atmosphere favorable to the passage of a National Security Law which men like Góis hoped would discourage subversive activities.

In March 1935, during heated discussions about the Security Law, the Aliança Nacional Libertadora (ANL) was launched in Rio with a great flourish. Members of Brazil's weak and illegal Communist Party were pleased to learn from a publication of the Third International that the ANL could help "Brazil rise on the basis of a popular revolutionary program against imperialistic bandits and against internal reactionary op-

[1] Plínio Salgado, *O Integralismo perante a Nação*, pp. 45–46.
[2] *Ibid.*, p. 76.

pressive governments, represented by the government of Getúlio."[3] By this new "popular front" the masses were to create unrest on behalf of the ANL's five basic demands: 1) an end to payments on the "imperialistic" debt of Brazil; 2) nationalization of all "imperialistic" companies (for their profits enrich foreign magnates); 3) protection of small and medium-sized farms, and division of large properties among those who work them; 4) fuller liberties; and 5) establishment of a "popular" government.[4] People heard a lot about "imperialism." "We want Brazil emancipated from imperialistic slavery."[5]

Brazilian Communists have claimed that the ANL was their creation but some of the participating non-Communists have denied this. Its founders included Trifino Correia, a Communist, and João Cabanas, known as a Socialist. "The ANL," wrote its treasurer, "was an organization of sincere liberal democrats, and of elements of the medium and extreme left, and fought furiously against *integralismo.*"[6] Luís Carlos Prestes has described the ANL as a "united front which included Communists and non-Communists."[7]

The ANL, which had a warm supporter in Pedro Ernesto, inherited the Rio office of the defunct Clube 3 de Outubro. Then when Rio's mayor made a municipal theater available for the inauguration, so many workers showed up that some had to be turned away. There were Marxist pronouncements and descriptions of miserable conditions all over Brazil. Herculino Cascardo, who had led the naval revolt of 1924 and was not a Communist, was named ANL president, and Luís Carlos Prestes became "honorary president" after being nominated by Carlos Lacerda, son of writer-politician Maurício.[8]

Prestes was out of the country, having in 1931 accepted an invitation to visit the Soviet Union. Becoming a member of the Presidium of International Communism, he developed plans for overthrowing the Vargas Government.

Using false passports, Prestes and his wife, a German Communist he

[3] "Atualidades Mundiais" in Brazilian edition of *A Internacional Comunista,* September 1935, p. 54, quoted in Leoncio Basbaum, *História Sincera da Republica,* III, 84.

[4] Leoncio Basbaum, *História Sincera da República,* III, 85.

[5] From ANL program, quoted in Jorge Amado, *O Cavaleiro da Esperança: Vida de Luiz Carlos Prestes,* p. 237.

[6] Affonso Henriques, *Vargas, o Maquiavélico,* p. 289.

[7] Luís Carlos Prestes, interview, September 5, 1963.

[8] Carlos Castilho Cabral, *Tempos de Jânio e Outros Tempos,* pp. 21–22.

met in Russia, arrived in Brazil in April 1935. While Brazilian workers were becoming practiced at going on strike, and while the ANL prepared great public demonstrations for July 5, Prestes, having become a member of the Brazilian Communist Party's Central Committee and Political Bureau, joined other Party members in secretly preparing more sinister plans. They were aided by top-level international Communists. The most important among them were Harry Berger, a German, and Rodolfo Ghioldi, the Argentine Communist leader Prestes had known in Buenos Aires.

On July 5, anniversary of the rebellions of 1922 and 1924, the ANL displayed its strength by holding meetings all over the country. In Rio the demonstrators were handicapped by precautions taken by the military, but Luís Carlos Prestes was able to speak at the ANL headquarters. The "Cavalier of Hope," whose presence in the country had earlier been kept secret, said that "it is up to the initiative of the masses themselves to prepare actively for the moment of assault. The idea of assault ripens in the conscience of the great masses."[9]

Comment was considerable. Rio's *O Globo* condemned the ANL and warned of the Communist menace, whereupon its editor was challenged to a duel by ANL President Cascardo. But the duel never came off because the Navy Minister forbade Cascardo to go through with it and transferred him to an out-of-the-way post.

ANL statements of July 5, particularly Prestes' call on the masses to assault the Government, were contrary to the spirit of the new National Security Law. Rio Police Chief Filinto Müller made this clear when he analyzed the situation, revealing the Latin American plans of Communism's Third International and the use being made of the ANL. Müller's document went to the Justice Minister, who prepared a decree closing down the ANL. It was signed by Vargas on July 11, and neither a general strike called in São Paulo nor the ANL's appeal to the Supreme Court reversed the Government's action.

The ANL had stirred unrest to a greater extent than the Communist Party could have done. Now those who did not want to participate in a Communist rebellion dropped out and the preparations went forward secretly, Prestes relying heavily on his agents in various states. Among these was Silo Meireles, who had visited Russia with him. While Meireles organized the plot in the Northeast, Meireles' sister conspired in Rio with Pedro Ernesto.

[9] Affonso Henriques, *Vargas, o Maquiavélico*, p. 313.

3. Communist Rebellions in Natal and Recife

Prestes and Harry Berger hoped that the ANL's activities and the difficult economic situation would provide some backing for their conspiracy. But they knew that the important work would have to be done by trained military men.

Prestes had most of the money which Aranha had given him in 1930; also a transfer of $100,000 which the Russian Communists sent from Moscow via New York to Montevideo for use in Brazil and Argentina "on an experimental basis." The Brazilian experiment was set for December 1935.[1] Prestes and Berger, appreciating the importance of simultaneous outbreaks in different regions, had the directorate of the Brazilian Communist Party give strict orders that the general outbreak await its signal.[2]

But the Vargas Administration was immensely more alert than Washington Luís been in 1930, and the Rio police, assisted by members of the British Intelligence Service and the German Gestapo, had numerous spies at work. An agent of the Brazilian government was even passing as an adviser to the Brazilian Communist Party's Central Committee. Prestes, aware that the Rio police were intercepting communications, gave a good deal of authority to Silo Meireles in the Northeast.

If the Vargas Administration had any desire to precipitate events, it was assisted in November 1935 by the situations in the northeastern cities of Recife and Natal, where armed conspirators could hardly restrain themselves. In Recife the series of strikes put on by bakers, dockworkers, and streetcar workers had been followed by an alarming strike of the railroad workers. The Communist-backed strikers had been placing bombs on the tracks; and the police, trying to keep the railroad operating on a partial scale, had been firing on strikers.[3] While this was going on the conspirators consolidated their position in the important local Army infantry barracks.

At the Army barracks in Natal, north of Recife, corporals and sergeants were in danger of losing their jobs, re-enlistment not being permitted at the end of their five-year contracts. Backed by Communists, they agitated for tenure. Meanwhile the occupants of Natal's jail, who customarily had

---

[1] Carlos da Costa Leite and Meireles family, interview, September 6, 1963.
[2] Luís Carlos Prestes, interview, September 5, 1963.
[3] Malvino Reis, interview, September 2, 1963.

the privilege of spending their nights at home, were being armed by the warden for the future revolt.[4]

The Communist rebellion of 1935 broke out in Natal on the night of November 23 after a decision of the local military commander adverse to the sergeants and corporals. As Prestes has put it, this decision of the Vargas Government did the trick: the noncoms were good and ready and, with arms in their hands, were not disposed to wait.[5] Led by sergeants and assisted by some civilians, the men of the Natal battalion overpowered their superiors and then forced the state police to surrender. While state officials were fleeing, the rebels established a "popular national revolutionary government" headed by a musician in the battalion's band and made up of men who had participated in the local ANL.[6] Few had been killed in the revolt itself, but four lost their lives in the disturbances which accompanied the looting of banks and commercial houses.[7]

With news of the Natal outbreak, Silo Meireles' Revolutionary Secretariat of the Northeast unleashed a bloody struggle in Recife. The infantry battalion was dominated by the Communists, and most of its 1,200 men marched on the city to join the 2,000 railroad workers and other civilians the Communists had armed. The job of dislodging the rebels fell to the thoroughly anti-Communist Pernambuco state militia, directed by Public Safety Secretary Malvino Reis. Reis, who had barely missed death from Communist bullets during the railroad strike, decided that the only way to deal with Communist rebels was to shoot them without restraint. But he had little co-operation from the state Cabinet, at least one of whose members supported the revolt. He found it necessary to jail the Secretaries of Finance, Justice, and Agriculture.

Throughout November 24 and 25 the city was the scene of fighting quite unusual for Brazil, the number killed being estimated in the hundreds.[8] The battle went better for the state police after Army troops arrived from Paraíba and Alagoas. On the night of the 26th, by which time the rebels had dispersed in small groups, a depressed and hungry Silo Meireles was captured in the countryside.

The "popular" government of Natal had already been having trouble

[4] Carlos da Costa Leite and Meireles family, interview, September 6, 1963.
[5] Luís Carlos Prestes, interview, September 5, 1963.
[6] Despatch, U.S. Embassy, Rio, to U.S. Secretary of State, December 4, 1935.
[7] "A Revolta Comunista" in O Cruzeiro, August 29, 1964.
[8] Ibid.; also Luís Carlos Prestes, interview, September 5, 1963, and Malvino Reis, interview, September 2, 1963.

with armed groups from the interior, and it tumbled with news of the approach of the Paraíba and Alagoas Army battalions from Recife.

4. Communist Uprising in Rio

On November 25, Congress, on the recommendation of Vargas, voted a one-month "state of siege" for the whole country. The resolution was supported by Flôres da Cunha even though he had been insisting that his own state be exempted.

Prestes that day sent a note to his agent in Minas: "We are about to have the revolution. Here we cannot wait longer than two or three days. I count on your energy."[1] On the next day Prestes signed orders to be delivered to conspirators at military barracks in and around Rio, and a special edition of the Communist daily *Amanhã*, featuring Prestes and announcing uprisings throughout Brazil, was distributed in the barracks and elsewhere.

The men who received their orders from Prestes were badly outnumbered, and they had lost the element of surprise. Loyal commanders, already alerted by events in the Northeast, received additional warnings from Vargas' police who knew all about Prestes' orders of November 26 calling for a rebellion that night.[2]

It took, therefore, considerable ingenuity and boldness on the part of energetic little Captain Agildo Barata and his companion to dominate on behalf of Communism the Third Infantry Regiment at Praia Vermelha—the small beach bounded by two granite cliffs in Rio. Barata, himself a prisoner but not locked up, led 30 conspirators (officers and sergeants) in overpowering 1,700 men (including 300 officers and sergeants). But to maintain control throughout the early morning of November 27 was no easy matter, and it was utterly impossible to follow Prestes' order to take over police strongholds in the city and then march on Catete Palace.[3] The rebels of Praia Vermelha, boxed in between cliffs and the sea, were faced at the outset with a platoon of Government soldiers which had been placed at the street entrance of the regiment. General Eurico Gaspar Dutra, commander of the First Military

---

[1] Abguar Bastos, *Prestes e a Revolução Social*, p. 331.

[2] Sinval Castro e Silva Filho, interview, September 5, 1963; Castro Júnior quoted in Agildo Barata, *Vida de um Revolucionário*, p. 268.

[3] Agildo Barata, *Vida de um Revolucionário*, p. 261.

Region, had been in readiness, and quickly he brought against the regiment all manner of troops and artillery. Automatics were set up in nearby buildings. Góis had learned what was going on as early as 1:20 A.M. and was bristling with advice.

From the regiment the rebels sent word to Dutra that they would not surrender before the nation had been freed of Getúlio. Although they asked Dutra to join the "National Popular Revolution" headed by Prestes, Dutra had other ideas. The regiment's barracks, temporary two-story pavilions of wood and stucco erected for the Exposition of 1908, were hit by a formidable barrage, and casualties mounted. Exploding shrapnel started a serious fire, warships joined in the bombardment, and planes dropped bombs from overhead. Barata had been holding out in the hope that assistance would develop out of some disturbances at the Aviation School, reported earlier on the radio. But by noon the rebels of Praia Vermelha had had enough. Seeking to negotiate with Dutra outside the burning and battered barracks, they were disarmed and taken prisoner.

There had indeed been "disturbances" during the night at the Aviation School at Campo dos Afonsos, about fifteen miles west of Rio. The Communist leaning of seventy corporals studying mechanics there had not been considered a very serious matter, but great attention ought to have been given to the message which Police Chief Filinto Müller sent on the evening of November 26, warning of an outbreak scheduled at the school that night. In spite of this, a car drove in at the school's hospital entrance at 3:00 A.M. with five plotters led by an aviation captain who had been training himself by practicing tortures on animals. After a short skirmish in which two defenders of the Government were killed, the Communists dominated the school. Then they set forth from Campo dos Afonsos with thirty men to attack the nearby First Aviation Regiment, commanded by Colonel Eduardo Gomes, only surviving officer of the "Eighteen of the Fort."

The Communists, hoping to find active supporters in the regiment, were disappointed. They fired a shot at Gomes, hitting the hand in which he held his revolver,[4] whereupon the men of the regiment drove them back. Soon after, loyal troops arrived from Vila Militar. It was all over before the sun rose.

[4] Eduardo Gomes, interview, July 20, 1963.

5. Aftermath of the Communist Rebellion

During the short-lived Communist uprising of late 1935, Flôres da Cunha offered 20,000 soldiers to help the Vargas Government. Plínio Salgado outdid him by offering 100,000 green-shirts. Labor unions sent telegrams backing the government, and even the opposition press momentarily supported Vargas.

Getúlio himself was praised for his bravery after word spread that in the early morning hours of November 27 he had rushed from Guanabara Palace to the War Ministry and from there had gone to observe the situation at Campo dos Afonsos and at Praia Vermelha. He expressed his satisfaction with the conduct of Dutra and Eduardo Gomes and criticized War Minister João Gomes for his negligence.[1] Already in the 1932 fight against São Paulo, Dutra had highly impressed Getúlio's younger brother Benjamim.

The recent rebellion and fear of additional Communist activity were useful to Vargas as he pushed for modification of the Constitution. Góis, ever critical of an "old style" constitution of the 1891 variety, now prepared a long report to show that the 1934 Constitution was not appropriate for existing conditions. The War and Justice Ministers got to work with congressional leaders, and, in spite of a determined minority led by Deputado João Neves, the necessary two-thirds vote of both legislative houses was secured on behalf of three constitutional amendments. These made it easier for the legislature to authorize the President to establish a "state of war in any part of the national territory," and at long last permitted the President to fire military officers or government employees who had participated in subversive movements.

On December 20, 1935, with one month of martial law about to expire, Vargas asked Congress for an extension on the grounds that the uprisings had been part of a vast movement to undermine the Army and civilian institutions. Well enough impressed, Congress declared a "state of war" for the maximum period of ninety days and it did the same in March and June, 1936, thus allowing officials, if they wished, to continue press control, the search of homes, and the prohibition of public meetings.

The police, including the five hundred members of Rio's special force, were rounding up for investigation those considered to have supported the outbreaks. Full use was made of the prison ship *Pedro I*, anchored off Rio, and of the island prisons, such as Fernando de Noronha, in the

---

[1] Lourival Coutinho, *O General Góes Depõe,* p. 273.

Brazilian Northeast, and Ilha Grande, west of Rio. For a while Rio's jail alone held over 1,200 prisoners, although its ordinary capacity had been set at 400.[2] In the Recife jail the cells for two were being used for five.[3] The political prisoners wore their own clothes while the common prisoners, who generally did the most menial chores, wore striped uniforms. There was a certain amount of cardplaying, writing, and reading, but often the overcrowding and lack of hygiene made conditions horrible.[4]

While many political prisoners were released after investigation, writers hostile to Vargas complained that some were kept imprisoned for no apparent reason, that Filinto Müller's men overdid the rounding up of "Communists," and that the treatment administered was sometimes far from civilized. They felt, too, that politicians used the situation to charge opponents with being subversive. Alzira Vargas, concerned about the fate of some of the professors, discussed the situation with her father. He observed that "from all states there were being sent, without due process and without proof, hundreds of prisoners who were perhaps innocent." But he added that the Constitution was such that the matter was not in his hands. "I am not the police."[5]

Among those jailed was Rio's mayor Pedro Ernesto, who for a while had worked for the uprising; also ANL officials such as its president, Herculino Cascardo. Miguel Costa was found at his residence outside São Paulo and jailed.

Even legislators were not safe. After Police Chief Filinto Müller and Justice Minister Vicente Ráo had submitted their evidence to a special senatorial commission, one senator and four federal *deputados* were hauled off for investigation. Three of the *deputados* were given jail sentences after the Chamber in a 190-to-59 vote suspended their immunity to allow them to be sentenced by the newly created National Security Tribunal.

Of the foreigners who had come to foment the revolt, the first to be caught was a young American, the son of a former editor of *The Daily Worker*. By torturing him before his reported suicide in jail, the police learned a little to help them in the big search for Prestes.

The next to fall into the net was Harry Berger (real name Ernst Ewert), the hefty German who was generally considered top commander of Communist activities in South America. When the police seized him in Rio

[2] Abguar Bastos, *Prestes,* p. 342.
[3] Malvino Reis, interview, September 2, 1963.
[4] See Graciliano Ramos, *Memórias do Cárcere.*
[5] Alzira Vargas do Amaral Peixoto, *Getúlio Vargas, Meu Pai,* p. 140.

de Janeiro in January 1936 they disconnected the mechanical device which he had installed for destroying his files.[6] Thus they came into possession of over one thousand documents, including Berger's correspondence with Prestes, Meireles, and Cascardo. A safe-conduct dated November 26, 1935, was signed by Prestes and asked that "the greatest respect and consideration" be given Berger.

Berger got little of either. The Special Police, understanding him to say that he was a hardy veteran at enduring the severest tortures inflicted by the police of several countries, decided to test him.[7] What he suffered cut his weight from over two hundred pounds to about eighty. But by the time he went insane the police had learned little if anything from him.[8]

The search for Prestes provided an unexpected clue which yielded Ghioldi, the Argentine. Prestes himself was felt to be somewhere in Rio's poor and densely populated Méier District, but careful investigation there was producing no results. Early in March 1936, after some talk of giving up the search, the head of the Special Police got forty-eight more hours in which to comb an area which an intercepted message showed was promising. Fourteen members of his force, aided by patrolmen, invaded house after house, finally locating Prestes and his wife on March 5. The "Cavalier of Hope" at once assumed entire responsibility for the Communist rebellion.

For sixteen months Prestes was held "incommunicado" in a room at the headquarters of the Special Police in downtown Rio, with five guards on duty at all times. His reading material was limited to anti-Communist literature provided by the head of the Special Police, who once struck Prestes after the little prisoner had called him a "barbarian."[9]

While Prestes was being held the Vargas Administration asked Congress to authorize the establishment of the National Security Tribunal to try and punish subversives. Some prominent lawyers declared the idea unconstitutional. But in August 1936 a majority of congressmen decided otherwise, and in October the six members of the court, appointed by Vargas, started their work. In the words of Góis, the tribunal would learn how to "quiet recalcitrants."[10]

When Prestes was hauled before it, his face was bloody, the result of a blow which the police maintain he arranged to receive by getting

[6] Carlos da Costa Leite and Meireles family, interview, September 3, 1963.
[7] Eusébio de Queiroz Filho, interview, June 26, 1963.
[8] Affonso Henriques, *Vargas, o Maquiavélico*, p. 354.
[9] Eusébio de Queiroz Filho, interview, June 26, 1963.
[10] Lourival Coutinho, *O General Góes Depõe*, p. 355.

into a fight while he was being searched.[11] He assumed the position that the tribunal was illegal and was given a seventeen-year jail sentence. Already his pregnant wife, with Berger's girl friend, had been sent to Germany, where they were both to die in Nazi concentration camps.

[11] Eusébio de Queiroz Filho, interview, June 26, 1963.

6. Presidential Candidates Appear in 1936

In 1936, while the campaign was on to investigate Communists, politicians began preparing for the presidential election of January 3, 1938. Vargas thought it much too early. But the Constitution provided that candidates holding high office in Brazil had to resign their posts a year before the election and this made discussions in 1936 inevitable.

Antônio Carlos, the ambitious president of the Chamber of Deputies, found Vargas in the small upstairs office in Guanabara Palace, working over his pile of papers. When the Mineiro asked about the drops of water falling from leaks in the ceiling, Getúlio smiled and said: "I'm leaving the roof as it is so that you can repair it."[1]

The Integralistas looked to the campaign with an assurance born of the Communist rebellion. The "Council of 40," top political organ of the Green Shirt movement, included the director of the Government Mint and an important official of the Bank of Brazil. Serving on the "Council of 400" (to promote the spread of Integralismo throughout the country) were members of the Armed Forces and state police. The movement, encouraged by Police Chief Filinto Müller and a number of generals, seemed to have the blessing of Vargas himself. The President, speaking in May 1936 of the difficulty of containing Communism by ordinary legislation, said that the nation needed to strengthen the "bonds of family, religion, and State."[2] Mussolini's son-in-law Ciano began sending contributions to Integralismo,[3] which already had many sympathizers among Brazil's approximately 1,000,000 German descendants.

The monster parades of Integralistas, hailing "Order and Progress" and "God, Country, and Family," were no longer broken up by Communists. Impressive as never before were the marching and saluting Green Shirts, lifting stirring voices on public occasions to sing the first

[1] Benedicto Valladares, *Tempos Idos e Vividos: Memórias*, p. 110.
[2] Getúlio Vargas, *A Nova Política do Brasil*, IV, 156.
[3] Galeazzo Ciano, *Ciano's Diary, 1937–1938* (trans. Andreas Mayor), p. 30.

verse of the National Hymn and remaining silent during the last verse, to which they objected.

Radio and newspaper propaganda was stepped up on behalf of Plínio Salgado, the candidate for President who proposed to save democracy by means of "Integralista authority." Claiming to be inspired by Christ, he declared: "For Christ I want a great Brazil," "For Christ I lead you," and "For Christ I will do battle."[4] He could be threatening, too. He declared that punishment "in-ex-o-ra-bly" (*im-pla-cà-vel-men-te*) awaited not only the enemies of Integralismo, but also all who were indifferent.

For Flôres da Cunha, the ex-hopeful who doubted that Vargas would step aside in 1938, things went badly in 1936. To fight off the political work of Protásio and Benjamim Vargas in Rio Grande, he made peace with Borges and Pilla, but it was short-lived and, after it ended, his main support in his state consisted of his 20,000 *provisórios* and the state militia of 6,000.

Góis still wanted to disarm the *provisórios* and get all state militias to take orders from the Army. When he advanced this and other programs to Vargas as necessary for creating a respected government, Vargas asked him what they should do if Congress blocked reforms. Dissolve Congress, the Axis-admiring general replied. Vargas agreed.[5]

For the time being Góis was authorized to proceed against Flôres da Cunha, but he soon found himself obstructed by War Minister João Gomes, who declared Flôres incapable of taking "a hostile attitude."[6] Finally, in December 1936 Gomes was replaced by Dutra, a man who shared the ideas of Vargas and Góis. Flôres da Cunha's end was in sight as Góis set out to build up in the south the kind of military might Flôres would respect.

For politicians who were stronger than Plínio Salgado or Flôres da Cunha, the race for the Presidency began on November 20, 1936, with the inauguration of the Cacao Institute Building at Salvador, Bahia. The host, Bahia's Governor Juraci Magalhães, had some background information. Five months earlier Labor Minister Agamenon Magalhães, an anti-democrat known by his enemies as "the Chinaman," had approached him, suggesting the advisability of Vargas' continuing in office.[7] Agamenon was particularly close to Getúlio.

---

[4] Plínio Salgado, *O Integralismo perante a Nação*, pp. 97–98.
[5] Lourival Coutinho, *O General Góes Depõe*, p. 281.
[6] *Ibid.*, p. 283.
[7] Juraci Magalhães, interviews, October 1, 1964 and October 13, 1964.

Juraci replied at the Cacao Institute inauguration, giving a speech which emphasized the importance of the election and which distressed Getúlio, who was among those present. A few hours later Juraci was sitting under stars and coconut palms, describing to intimates Getúlio's reaction. "That man," said Juraci, "has monstrous thoughts. He doesn't want any presidential succession. We must form an alliance of São Paulo, Minas, Rio Grande, Pernambuco, and Bahia to force an election."[8]

Pernambuco's Lima Cavalcanti quickly agreed, and Juraci next tried to convert the governor of São Paulo. In a five-hour discussion Juraci explained to Armando de Sales that democracy could be preserved if the five states would agree on a list from which Vargas would be asked to choose an official candidate. Juraci even had a list ready: Armando de Sales, José Américo, and Medeiros Neto, the Bahian who had headed the Vargas forces in the Constitutional Assembly.

As a final inducement Juraci offered the São Paulo governor his support in case Getúlio refused to pick a name from this list.

But Armando rejected the proposal. His own candidacy, which had the support of Flôres da Cunha, was well advanced. Having built up a good administrative record, he was now speaking out on national issues and even lining up a successor to occupy Campos Elíseos. Yet if anything was clear it was that Vargas would never pick Armando's name.

Vargas had said that a candidacy representing the Paulista elite, coming so soon after the July 9, 1932, rebellion, would upset the country and be a disaster. Góis had added that the Armando candidacy would lack "goodwill" in the Army because of the Flôres backing.

At the end of 1936 Armando called on Getúlio to advise that he was resigning the governorship in order to run for President. Getúlio, who until then had got along well with the São Paulo governor, recalled with sadness that he had once had to exile Borges, and he reminded Armando that it might become necessary to turn São Paulo over to the old Republican Party, which had made a good showing in the last election.[9]

Immediately after Armando resigned his post Foreign Minister José Carlos de Macedo Soares did likewise. He was another Paulista and he thought he had Vargas' support—for the Presidency and not just for giving São Paulo two candidates. José Américo, his name on Juraci's list, prepared to take a leave from the federal Budget Tribunal, which he had served since leaving the Transport Ministry.

[8] Hélio Silva, Part 2 of "Lembrai-vos de 1937," *Tribuna da Imprensa*, Rio, October 3–4, 1959.
[9] *Ibid.*

7. The Nomination of José Américo

After the inter-American conference held in Buenos Aires in December 1936, Aranha was active politically on his own behalf. His chances were slim, but, undaunted, he had long conversations with Flôres da Cunha. Without Getúlio's blessing he even sought to effect a reconciliation between Flôres and the Administration. In April he took Flôres to Rio, and the Rio Grande governor, who had not called on the President for a year, hoped for some assistance in the Pôrto Alegre assembly, where he had been outvoted. But when the three leading Gaúchos gathered at Petrópolis, Getúlio was no help. Aranha, feeling let down, returned to Washington, and Flôres, feeling double-crossed, made a statement in favor of Armando de Sales.[1]

Soon after Aranha left Brazil, Antônio Carlos, the aristocratic "old Andrada," received the last of a series of stabs. After his latest unsuccessful bid for the Presidency had disturbed Minas politics and led him to cultivate Flôres da Cunha,[2] he had become a supporter of Armando de Sales. He was not the man Getúlio wanted presiding over Congress during the crucial days of 1937; and Benedito Valadares had come to view Antônio Carlos as a rival in Minas politics. In spite of attractive personal qualities, Antônio Carlos fell in a close vote, in which "class representatives" and Paulista Republicans helped give the congressional presidency to a younger Mineiro, Pedro Aleixo.

Juraci Magalhães, still pushing his list of three names, sent a fellow Bahian to discuss it in April 1937 with Vargas and Valadares. Vargas said it was too early to talk, and so Juraci's agent went to visit the Minas governor at Belo Horizonte. There Valadares and his visitor interrupted their discussions to listen to a radio speech in which Vargas announced that politicians were trying to upset the peace.[3] After Vargas went on to say that the Army and the "green" national flag[4] would defend the country against such disturbances, the opponents of Integralismo reminded the President that the Brazilian flag is both yellow and green.

In mid-May, Valadares too found Getúlio in no mood to help with the search for a "single candidate." The Minas governor was disturbed to have his political work thwarted by Agamenon Magalhães, who had

[1] Despatch, U.S. Embassy, Rio, to U.S. Secretary of State, April 15, 1937.
[2] Benedicto Valladares, *Tempos Idos e Vividos: Memórias*, pp. 109–112.
[3] Clemente Mariani, interview, August 22, 1963.
[4] Getúlio Vargas, *A Nova Política do Brasil*, IV, 226.

become acting Justice Minister as well as Labor Minister. But what most upset Valadares was Vargas' order that he put the Minas state militia at War Minister Dutra's disposal for possible use in São Paulo.[5] He feared that the federal government wanted at least to weaken his position, as it was doing in the case of other governors who displeased it with their political work.[6]

Returning from Rio to Belo Horizonte, Valadares considered breaking dramatically with the President. He told some friends that he would attack Vargas in a broadcast on May 19 at Belo Horizonte's new Inconfidência radio station, and he even tried out his bold oratory at the Palacio da Liberdade in the company of pleased representatives of Armando de Sales and Flôres da Cunha.[7] But influential Mineiros in Rio advised Valadares about the virtues of prudence in public, and they told him that Vargas wanted him to continue with his "co-ordinating work" if he would refrain from having any particular name in mind. Valadares could also reflect that Armando de Sales had the support of his local foes, Antônio Carlos and Bernardes. Instead of breaking with Vargas, Valadares reworded his speech, to the surprise and disappointment of some of his listeners. In it he announced that a convention would be held on May 25 to select the candidate in whom the nation had the greatest confidence.

After the Northeasterners, Juraci Magalhães and Lima Cavalcanti, threatened to support Armando de Sales if Valadares would not back José Américo, Vargas told Valadares that he should go ahead with the José Américo candidacy. Thus, over the objection of Agamenon Magalhães, the decision was reached. At the convention in Rio on May 25 representatives of the governors of all the states save Rio Grande and São Paulo nominated José Américo, with Valadares presiding. From Washington, Aranha wired his enthusiastic endorsement.

Getúlio, who could find faults with any candidate, had particular reservations about José Américo, "the candidate of the people," but he expressed his great pleasure at the news. Although he added that as President he had to remain impartial, the manner in which the nomination was made gave an appearance of Administration backing, especially

[5] Benedicto Valladares, *Tempos Idos e Vividos,* p. 122.

[6] Carlos Castello Branco, "Memórias do Senador Benedito Valadares," *Jornal do Brasil,* July 19, 1966.

[7] Hélio Silva, Parts 2 and 3 of "Lembrai-vos de 1937," *Tribuna da Imprensa,* Rio de Janeiro, October 3–4, 1957, and October 6, 1959. Hélio Silva, interview, September 3, 1963.

in comparison with the development of Armando de Sales' candidacy.
It was generally felt that Getúlio's command of the situation had suddenly collapsed with José Américo's nomination "thrust down his throat."

8. The Presidential Campaign

Late in February 1937, before José Américo's nomination, Getúlio spent
carnaval days relaxing with his family at a resort in Minas. Valadares,
noting the President's excellent spirits, was critical of Vargas' tendency
simply to let events unfold. Góis dropped in on the group hoping to
persuade Valadares to let him use the Minas state militia against Flôres
da Cunha. But the most significant thing Góis picked up from Valadares
was the news that Francisco Campos, the former khaki-shirt leader of
Minas, was drafting, at Getúlio's request, a new constitution for Brazil.[1]
Getúlio liked Campos' authoritarian ideas.

Agamenon Magalhães was eager to assume the governorship of Pernambuco, and he reflected Getúlio's displeasure at Lima Cavalcanti's
electoral work. Early in 1937 the governor's Secretary of Public Safety
was transferred from Pernambuco. Other key people were removed and
the governor even lost his palace guard.[2] On the basis that two of his state
Cabinet had been Marxists in 1935 and that he had "deliberately"
absented himself, Lima Cavalcanti was denounced for being involved in
the Communist insurrection. The Governor, who had put Agamenon
Magalhães in the federal Cabinet in 1934, learned from Getúlio that
"the revolt of creatures against their creators is traditional in Brazilian
political life."

Juraci also had troubles. As one of his brothers had backed the Communist rebellion, rumors pictured the governor of Bahia as pro-Communist. The Integralistas set out to bedevil him; he in turn sought to
ban their organization in Bahia.

Of help to Getúlio was a report from Montevideo early in May, 1937,
about plans for a rebellion in Brazil. Again use was made of a "state
of war" and a federal order was issued for disarming all the Gaúcho *provisórios*. Flôres da Cunha retorted that the state of war was "absurd" as
far as Rio Grande was concerned and he added that the real issue was
whether "Getúlio Vargas is to be allowed to succeed himself and estab-

[1] Lourival Coutinho, *O General Góes Depõe*, p. 292.
[2] Carlos de Lima Cavalcanti, interviews, August 1, 1963 and August 29, 1963.

lish a dictatorship." Getúlio then decided to make sure of the transfer of the *provisórios*' hundreds of machine guns and 16,000 rifles to the federal arsenals. When he did this by naming Góis to the powerful post of Chief of Staff, he satisfied War Minister Dutra. Leadership in the Army, now united, shared Getúlio's misgivings about democracy.

Nevertheless, for the moment democracy was given free rein. Censorship was removed and the "state of war" allowed to expire. José Carlos de Macedo Soares, whose candidacy did not catch on in spite of his own enthusiasm and his brother's *Diário Carioca*, rejoined the Cabinet as Justice Minister and freed hundreds who had been imprisoned as Communist sympathizers.

Shots were again fired at marching Integralistas. The leading presidential candidates, Armando de Sales and José Américo, opened their campaigns with rallies in Rio in July. At the earlier of these, a national coloration was added to the candidacy of Armando de Sales: he was nominated by the União Democrática Brasileira.

While Armando studiously criticized the mild inflation, José Américo sought leftist votes. A sincere liberal, this bespectacled writer unleashed a campaign which Getúlio described as shocking for its "demagoguery." When José Américo opened it in Rio he excitedly declared that he knew "where the money is." In making this dig at "monopolies" and the rich, he was pictured by some as trying to pose as the only honest politician in Brazil. Stressing his love for the masses and his hatred for Integralismo, he convinced many a leftist that he was no "official candidate," and this became clear when he attacked Vargas. "If Vargas wants to perpetuate himself in power," he said in Bahia, "the nation will fulfill its duty, go to the polls, and vote, even if this be in the face of bullets."[3]

In Minas, a predominantly conservative and Catholic state, José Américo's leftism was giving Armando de Sales so much strength that Valadares became frantic. Vargas told the Minas governor that José Américo was "crazy" and that they should "set aside the two candidates and choose a third." Even Lima Cavalcanti, noting alarm among Pernambuco conservatives and hearing that José Américo—if elected—planned to govern without the political forces which had been behind him, agreed with Valadares that it would be well if José Américo and Armando would both withdraw in favor of some other candidate. Valadares, with Ge-

[3] Hélio Silva, Part 4 of "Lembrai-vos de 1937," *Tribuna da Imprensa,* Rio, October 8, 1959.

túlio's blessing, sought to discuss this idea with Armando's successor in
the São Paulo governorship. But after the São Paulo governor kept postponing appointments to meet him, Valadares lost his patience and temper
and went to see the President.[4]

Vargas and Valadares then delegated Francisco Negrão de Lima, the
Mineiro who was supposed to be managing José Américo's campaign,
to call on governors and release them from any commitment to José
Américo. He was to suggest that the election be called off.[5]

Valadares, who had agreed to this new "revolution" after finding it
acceptable to the two military ministers, discussed strategy with Dutra
and rushed back to Minas to prepare and direct his state militia.[6] Dutra
sent him munitions.

[4] Benedicto Valladares, *Tempos Idos e Vividos: Memórias,* pp. 154–163.
[5] Hélio Silva, Part 7 of "Lembrai-vos de 1937," *Tribuna da Imprensa,* Rio de
Janeiro, October 17–18, 1959.
[6] Benedicto Valladares, *Tempos Idos e Vividos,* pp. 163–174.

9. The Cohen Plan

On September 30, 1937, the Brazilian press and radio alarmed the public
with details of the "Cohen Plan," discovered by the Army's General
Staff. Together with a grave message from War Minister Dutra, its text
filled the newspaper columns. For those who could not read, the "Hour
of Brazil" ("Hora do Brasil") broadcast the plot, a chapter each day.
The plan, simply signed "Cohen," called for a violent Communist take-
over of Brazil in the course of which newspapers were to be destroyed,
churches burned, and hundreds of people massacred. All this was to be
done "under the cloak of democracy."

An Integralista captain had been found typing a "Communist Plan" in
the office of the Chief of Staff.[1] Góis had taken it and later forwarded
copies to War Minister Dutra, Police Chief Müller, and the President's
chief military aide. The result was the publicity given to the "Cohen
Plan." (Years later the captain explained that, as a member of the Integralista "historical department," he had been giving attention to a
theoretical Communist attack in order to devise a counterattack; moreover

[1] Lourival Coutinho, *O General Góes Depõe,* p. 298.

he has pointed out that the publicized "Cohen Plan" differed in some respects from his original document.)[2]

Amid a wave of national concern Justice Minister Macedo Soares let the military prevail against his earlier views and suggested that Vargas ask Congress to declare a "state of war" again. Dutra explained that this would not affect political matters. But José Américo characterized the Communist threat as an invention for calling off the election, and Armando de Sales agreed.

The Cohen Plan, with its cold-blooded descriptions of atrocities, was so effective that on October 1, when the two chambers met to vote, even minority leader João Neves supported the appeal of the military. To the unhappy surprise of Armando de Sales, so did the governor he had recently installed in São Paulo. The Executive request was granted by wide margins in the Chamber of Deputies and in the Senate.

To counteract the popularity of Pedro Ernesto, freed after a little more than a year of illness in a prison hospital, Getúlio joined the military in a pilgrimage to the graves of men killed in 1935 by Communists. "Let this pilgrimage be a lesson and a warning," he said, adding that "the Armed Forces are on the alert in the country's defense."

As presiding officer of the "commission to execute the state of war," Justice Minister Macedo Soares had a difficult time with the other two members: an admiral, and General Newton Cavalcanti, Integralismo's friend. The Justice Minister objected to the rearrest of some Vila Militar officers who had recently been released by the Supreme Military Tribunal.

In most of the states the measures for executing the "state of war" were to be carried out by the governors. The exceptions were Bahia, Pernambuco, Rio Grande do Sul, and São Paulo, where the work was put into the hands of commanders of the Army military regions. The Vargas Cabinet decreed that the state militias of Rio Grande do Sul, São Paulo, and Pernambuco should forthwith be incorporated into the federal forces. Lima Cavalcanti could put up no opposition. In São Paulo the new governor again disappointed Armando de Sales by co-operating with Vargas;[3] his attitude was also a disappointment to some fiery Paulista Demo-

[2] Olbiano de Melo, *A Marcha da Revolução Social no Brasil,* pp. 104–109; José Loureiro Júnior and Plínio Salgado, interview, October 14, 1965. Olímpio Mourão Filho interview, November 29, 1966. The captain was Olímpio Mourão Filho.

[3] Despatch, U.S. Embassy, Rio, to U.S. Secretary of State, October 20, 1937.

crats who hoped that this time Flôres da Cunha would provide the assistance he had failed to deliver in 1932.[4]

Flôres da Cunha's opponents in the Rio Grande Assembly were one vote shy in their bid to impeach him. When he got his orders to turn the Gaúcho Military Brigade over to the Army, he asked for time and was given forty-eight hours. But his officers hesitated to resist the superior weapons the federals had been acquiring, and the head of the Brigade decided to accept "spontaneously" an opportunity to switch his allegiance to the federals.[5] With this decision strife was averted and Flôres was lost. On October 18 he chose voluntary exile and was wished good luck by some of his recent adversaries as he headed for the gambling tables of Montevideo. Getúlio, finding this more satisfactory than a Gaúcho civil war or even a jailed Flôres, named as *interventor* the Army regional commander who had been disarming *provisórios*.

[4] Júlio de Mesquita Filho, interview, August 7, 1963.
[5] Alzira Vargas do Amaral Peixoto, *Getúlio Vargas, Meu Pai*, p. 209.

10. Lining Up Support for a Change of Regime

Just as Flôres was falling, Dutra and Góis were admitting that for security reasons the 1934 Constitution needed drastic revision. Dutra persuaded most of the Rio generals to sign a statement supporting a change of regime. Coded telegrams then went from the War Ministry to the commanders of the military regions. The replies showed that they also agreed with their superiors. The Navy Minister adhered personally and gave assurances that Naval leaders would go along with the Army, as they had in 1889 and 1930.

To what were they all agreeing? Góis, familiar with a draft of Francisco Campos' new constitution, foresaw some kind of plebiscite followed by new elections; also a strong government which could put into effect the reforms he liked. But not until the week following the military adherences did Francisco Campos, scheduled to take over the Justice Ministry, read his "constitution" to the War and Navy Ministers.

The question arises as to whether this reading was entirely clarifying. Last-minute modifications were to change the document from what Góis, an intelligent man, expected.[1] But even if the War and Navy Ministers had listened attentively to a reading of the 187 articles which made up

[1] Lourival Coutinho, *O General Góes Depõe*, p. 314.

the final version, they might well have been confused about its effect on government organization.

At about the same time, Plínio Salgado was let in on the secret by Francisco Campos at meetings in the Rio home of an Integralista industrialist. The Green Shirt leader liked Campos' expressions about a "corporative" state, and agreed that there had been too much useless strife among political parties. But he told Campos that it would be better to amend the 1934 Constitution.

Campos, doing a selling job, assured Plínio that the Armed Forces were resolved to go along with the new plans, and he relieved Plínio of concern about the future of Integralismo. In fact he let Plínio understand that Integralismo might be the "base of the New State," although it was to become a civic association rather than a political party.

Plínio did feel that much in the proposed constitution was not in accord with the ideas of the Integralistas, who, he explained, were basically democratic. But the two men got along excellently. Campos, in a laughing aside to their host, said that he had not realized Plínio was so liberal. Plínio, considering the "fascist ideas" of "Chico" Campos, decided that he himself was closer than Campos to Vargas' thinking.

Plínio said that the Integralistas would not cause trouble. He appreciated that what the future would bring depended more on the goodwill of men than on printed words and he quickly got comfort from the police chief and the War Minister. Filinto Müller told him Integralismo had nothing to fear, and Dutra praised the Green Shirt movement.

After that, at the home of another Integralista industrialist, Plínio had a session with Getúlio.[2] The President opened up by remarking that if an election were held José Américo had a good chance of winning, in which case there would be an official policy antagonistic to the Integralistas. He went on to say that the Armed Forces had decided to "change the regime" and that he had agreed with them. Plínio, becoming highly animated, told of how much Integralismo had done and could do for Brazil. Vargas, properly enthusiastic, said that in reorganized Brazil the Education Ministry would be in the hands of the Integralistas and would be expected to assist the Integralista Youth Militia.

In the Army the Sigma had many advocates but none heartier than General Newton Cavalcanti, head of the troops at Vila Militar. From him Getúlio learned of Plínio's decision to put on a great demonstration of Green Shirt strength.

[2] Plínio Salgado, *O Integralismo perante a Nação*, pp. 117–123; Olbiano de Melo, *A Marcha da Revolução Social no Brasil*, p. 112.

The parade of "50,000 Green Shirts" on November 1 was decidedly impressive to Cariocas who watched. Starting from the customary point of origin for parades, Praça Mauá, the marchers demonstrated superb discipline and a great air of determination. After going down Avenida Rio Branco, they saluted the Integralista leader as he stood, Hitler-like, on the balcony of the Glória Hotel. Then they marched past Guanabara Palace, where Vargas viewed the parade in the company of General Cavalcanti, the Navy Minister, and the top presidential military aide.[3] Raised arms and three rousing shouts of *anauê* greeted the President. After the parade was over, the President's daughter (no admirer of the Integralistas) concluded that the strength of the Integralista movement was "much, much greater" than she had supposed. She noted that workers, industrialists, society women, soldiers, sailors, and officers of the Army and Navy were well represented.[4]

Although Getúlio's confidential "counters" found in the parade only 17,000 men, women, and children,[5] Plínio continued to refer to the march of the "50,000 Green Shirts." On November 1 he publicly declared that the 50,000 marchers were "taking this opportunity to affirm their solidarity with the President of the Republic and the Armed Forces in the fight against Communism and anarchical democracy, and to proclaim the principles of a new regime." The fight, he said, was also against "international capitalism, which acts against our economy, knifing us from time to time."[6] This speech marked Plínio's withdrawal from the presidential race. "What I desire is not to be President of the Republic, but simply the adviser of my country."

Getúlio was studying reports. Checking with his military ministers he learned that of the 4,000 Army officers, 1,200 were either registered Integralistas or sympathizers, as were half the Naval officers.[7]

On the day of the parade Negrão de Lima, Valadares' friend who had been general secretary of the Comitê Pró-José Américo, returned to Rio to report personally to Francisco Campos.

He had visited the states in the north and northeast, excepting—on Vargas' instructions—Bahia and Pernambuco. As Valadares and Vargas

[3] Despatch, U.S. Embassy, Rio, to U.S. Secretary of State, November 6, 1937; Affonso Henriques, *Vargas, o Maquiavélico,* p. 421; Olbiano de Melo, *A Marcha da Revolução Social no Brasil,* p. 115.

[4] Alzira Vargas do Amaral Peixoto, *Getúlio Vargas, Meu Pai,* p. 214.

[5] Despatch, Ambassador Caffery, Rio, to U.S. Secretary of State, March 28,

[6] Despatch, U.S. Embassy, Rio, to U.S. Secretary of State, November 6, 1937.

[7] *Ibid.*

already knew from his coded messages to Valadares, he could advise that all the governors he had seen were agreeable to dropping José Américo and accepting the Army's suggested change of regime.[8] In view of the "confused situation" they regarded the continuation of Vargas as the "easiest solution."[9] On November 5 the governor of São Paulo, feeling that Armando de Sales' position was hurting his state, accepted Negrão de Lima's suggestion that Vargas' term be extended.[10] With this, there appeared to be nothing to stop Getúlio, whose secret plans, shared by most of his Cabinet, called for the coup to occur on November 15, anniversary of the republicanization of Brazil.

[8] Hélio Silva, Part 7 of "Lembrai-vos de 1937," *Tribuna da Imprensa,* Rio de Janeiro, October 17–18, 1959. See also Benedicto Valladares, *Tempos e Vividos: Memórias,* pp. 180–181.

[9] Despatch, U.S. Embassy, Rio, to U.S. Secretary of State, November 6, 1937.

[10] Cardoso de Melo Neto, quoted by Hélio Silva in Part 9 of "Lembrai-vos de 1937," *Tribuna da Imprensa,* Rio, October 22, 1959.

11. The Secret Becomes Public

On November 3 Dutra and Góis agreed with General Cavalcanti that under the new regime Vargas should carry on provisionally, at least until the national plebiscite mentioned in Francisco Campos' constitution.[1] Góis then made a public declaration to advise that the military leaders were not seeking a military dictatorship, and, in case of a change of regime, sought nothing for themselves, but only substantial reforms to build a strong Brazil. This pronouncement aroused more comment than Plínio's words of November 1 about "a new regime."

José Américo already had an idea of what was being hatched when he heatedly asked Góis about the mission of Negrão de Lima. Góis was not helpful, but, soon after, the purpose of the mission was no longer a secret. Defying censors, the *Correio da Manhã* on November 5 described Negrão de Lima's proposal to the governors, although it erroneously reported that only two of them had reacted favorably.[2]

Justice Minister Macedo Soares, who had been trying to save the democratic regime, resigned on the eighth. By that time there were widespread

[1] Lourival Coutinho, *O General Góes Depõe,* pp. 320–321.

[2] Hélio Silva, Part 7 of "Lembrai-vos de 1937," *Tribuna da Imprensa,* Rio, October 17–18, 1959.

rumors that a new constitution, modeled on Portuguese and Polish lines, would be submitted to Congress.

As scheduled, Francisco Campos ("Chico Ciência") became Justice Minister on the ninth. But just as the brainy, antidemocratic author of the projected constitution was being sworn in, a storm broke in Congress. On the night of the eighth Armando de Sales had released a manifesto in the form of a handbill for immediate distribution in the Federal District barracks, and on the ninth it was read by his supporters in both legislative houses. Addressed to the military leaders, the manifesto noted that "the conviction is general that there will be no elections on January 3" and called on the Armed Forces to "protect the ballot boxes" and save Brazil from dictatorship. José Américo, like Armando, spent the ninth attacking the plot.

Vargas got in touch with São Paulo's governor and gathered that another uprising there was not imminent.[3] But Dutra was worried about the distribution of Armando's manifesto in the barracks, and both Francisco Campos and Agamenon Magalhães felt that the change of regime could not wait until the fifteenth. On the evening of the ninth these men joined Police Chief Müller and the commander of the Military Police in calling on Vargas in the small upstairs room of Guanabara Palace where he liked to work. His desk was piled high with the papers he wanted to handle before ushering in a new era for Brazil, but he agreed with his visitors. The necessary instructions were given at once.

[3] Alzira Vargas do Amaral Peixoto, *Getúlio Vargas, Meu Pai,* p. 218.

BOOK VI

EARLY YEARS OF THE ESTADO NÔVO, 1937–1938

"Old institutions which, up to now, were the bases of social and political organizations, are in bankruptcy. People are seeking new forms. . . . We are not concerned with the internal structures of other countries, just as we do not accept foreign interference with our organization."

1. November 10, 1937

EARLY ON THE rainy morning of November 10, 1937, troops guarded the doors of the Senate and Chamber of Deputies, preventing legislators from entering. The troops were those of the Federal District police force, Dutra preferring not to have the Army close Congress.[1]

There was no great national outcry. Eighty federal legislators signed messages congratulating Vargas. Only six, including congressional president Pedro Aleixo, sent messages opposing the coup, but the number would have been greater had not Armando de Sales *deputados* been confined incommunicado at their residences.

The Armed Forces, the military ministers maintained, had not assumed the initiative and were only backing a decision made by the head of the nation and the politicians.[2] Among the few objecting military men were Colonel Eduardo Gomes, who resigned his post at the First Aviation Regiment, and five generals, some of whom were relieved of their

[1] Hélio Silva, Part 11 of "Lembrai-vos de 1937," *Tribuna da Imprensa,* Rio, October 26, 1959.
[2] *Ibid.*

duties in accordance with an article of the new constitution which allowed the regime within its first sixty days to "retire" whomever it wished.

At a meeting of generals in the War Ministry on the morning of the tenth Dutra stated that the nation would get its constitution within ten minutes. He was right.[3] Presses had been at work turning out copies of the extraordinary brain child of Francisco Campos. The Constitution of 1937, which would have satisfied the most ambitious dictator, was decreed by Vargas as effective at once. It was signed at Catete Palace by all the Cabinet ministers except Agriculture Minister Odilon Braga, who resigned. As he was a Mineiro this gave Vargas the opportunity of satisfying the Partido Republicano Paulista and repairing the lack of balance which came about when Francisco Campos, a Mineiro, replaced Macedo Soares.

At Guanabara Palace early on the evening of the tenth Vargas addressed the nation by radio. He assailed the 1934 Constitution and described Congress as having been "inoperative." The method of electing Presidents every four years, including the use of defective political parties, was called a calamity; "universal suffrage becomes the instrument of the most audacious and a mask which only poorly disguises the connivance of personal appetites and schemes." In a hardly just reference to Armando de Sales, Vargas stated that "only yesterday, culminating demagogic intentions, one of the presidential candidates sent a frankly seditious document to be read in the Chamber of Deputies, and had it distributed in the barracks."

Mention was made of the recent "state of war," requested by the Armed Forces "on account of the fresh outbreak of Communist ambition, favored by the confused milieu of electioneering meetings." "When political contests threaten to degenerate into civil war it is a sign that the constitutional regime has lost its practical value."

"Backed by the confidence of the armed forces, and responding to the general appeals" of his fellow citizens, Vargas explained that he was agreeing to sacrifice the leisure he had earned. With moral and political "deceptions" eliminated, the nation could go forward under the new Constitution, which, he declared (without accurately indicating what lay ahead), "maintains the democratic form." "Let us," he concluded, "restore the nation . . . letting it freely construct its history and destiny."[4]

Having thus ushered in the Estado Nôvo (New State), Vargas went

---

[3] Lourival Coutinho, *O General Góes Depõe*, p. 317.
[4] Getúlio Vargas, *A Nova Política do Brasil*, V, 19–32.

to the Argentine Embassy to attend a dinner to which he had accepted an invitation before knowing that the tenth would be the day of the *golpe*. Someone recalled that back in 1933, ten minutes after the granite slab at Petrópolis had brought death and painful injury to the occupants of the presidential car, Getúlio's pulse had been found entirely normal. An observer, impressed now with Getúlio's calm on November 10, wrote that "of all the living statesmen of the world today, Vargas is without doubt the coldest, most rational and cynical. Emotion of any kind he does not know . . . For him loyalty and consideration have no meaning."

Getúlio turned to the problems of organizing his team and dealing with "friends" and "foes," especially the Integralistas.

Valadares in Minas continued to be "governor," but elsewhere the state chief executives became *interventores*. Two governors were promptly replaced: Juraci Magalhães, because he resigned and because Vargas no longer wanted him; and Lima Cavalcanti, because he was deposed in favor of Agamenon Magalhães, one of the many admirers of the growing Nazi strength.[5]

José Américo returned to the federal Budget Tribunal as though nothing had happened. But Getúlio, military commanders, and the police regarded Armando de Sales and his Constitutional friends in São Paulo as dangerous, particularly as Júlio de Mesquita Filho was entirely disposed to fight again and had been in touch with Flôres da Cunha. Armando de Sales was "exiled" under guard to a mining town in Minas and told he could go to Europe any time he wished.

Abroad the reactions were various. The German press was delighted with the Brazilian step and described it as displeasing to the Pan-Americanism advocated by the United States.[6] The president of the Italian Senate attributed the Brazilian change to the example of Italian fascism and the good work of Italian culture in Brazil. "The Integralista Green Shirts," he added, "are the sons or younger brothers of our glorious Black Shirts."[7] It was predicted that the Brazilian Mussolini would early adhere to the Italian-German-Japanese anti-Communist pact.

In Washington, Senator Borah expressed his belief that the new Brazilian regime had every characteristic of fascism;[8] and Senator Edward

[5] Gilberto Freyre, interview, September 29, 1964.

[6] Cable, Ambassador William Dodd, Berlin, to U.S. Secretary of State, November 12, 1937.

[7] Ambassador Phillips' message from Rome to U.S. Secretary of State, November 18, 1937.

[8] *Washington Post*, November 12, 1937.

Burke, recalling that Roosevelt had once praised Vargas as "one of the two people who invented the New Deal," hoped that F.D.R. would not follow the latest example set by his Brazilian friend. *The New York Times* editorially lamented Vargas' repeated suppression of political opposition and reported that in Washington there were "no cheers for the new regime."[9] Getúlio, hoping to do away with some of the misconceptions, had a private talk with the new American ambassador, Jefferson Caffery. "It is laughable," Getúlio said, "to think that the Germans, Italians, or Japanese had any connection whatever with the recent movement; nor had the Integralistas in any way."[10]

Osvaldo Aranha had been promising Roosevelt and Hull that a normal election would be carried out in Brazil. In a conversation with Sumner Welles the Brazilian ambassador had forecast with pleasure the election of José Américo and had added that if Vargas tried to serve beyond his elected term, he would be obliged to oppose him.[11] The coup, accompanied by Getúlio's announcement that Brazil was suspending all servicing on foreign debts, was such a shock to Aranha that he resigned. He was soon getting cables from Catete Palace asking him not to be precipitous and presently he received the letter which Vargas, planning the coup for the fifteenth, had written to forewarn him.[12]

But Aranha returned to Brazil, and Getúlio's choice of him for Foreign Minister in March 1938 was the clearest sign that the Estado Nôvo was not out to abandon friendship with the United States or sign up with the Berlin-Rome-Tokyo Axis. At the same time this appointment built up a balance against the influence of Francisco Campos and helped keep Aranha from becoming, as Campos had feared, a "center of the opposition."

"Chico" Campos, regarded by many as a new power behind the throne, had first opposed Aranha's presence in the country during the "transition" period, and then he had tried to keep him out of the Cabinet. He busied himself promoting a totalitarian and nationalistic philosophy in Brazil. In his speeches and writings the former Khaki Shirt was fond of saying that the 1930 revolution had been thwarted by politicians. "Cen-

---

[9] *The New York Times,* editorials, November 12, 14, and 22, 1937.

[10] Cable, Ambassador Caffery, Rio, to U.S. Secretary of State, November 13, 1937.

[11] Memorandum by Sumner Welles on conversation with Aranha, October 18, 1937.

[12] Hélio Silva, Part 12 of "Lembrai-vos de 1937," *Tribuna da Imprensa,* Rio, October 27, 1959.

turies of experience," he pointed out, "have demonstrated that the principle of liberty did not improve the lot of the average citizen or keep the strong from taking advantage of the weak. Only a strong state can guarantee to the individual the rights he ought to have."[13]

The old Partido Republicano Paulista (PRP) at last re-emerged after its seven-year eclipse. The new federal Agricultural Minister, Fernando Costa, had once worked with Washington Luís and Júlio Prestes. In São Paulo the Constitucionalista (Democratic) governor found his position untenable. His own party was furious with him for having supported Vargas in the events which preceded the coup of November 10, and the Republicans wanted a man of their own. Taking advantage of his shaky position, his own Secretary of Public Safety, with a good deal of backing in Rio, worked against him; and again the old cry went out for a "more legitimate" representative of the Paulista point of view.

Getúlio, listening to Rio Police Chief Müller and the São Paulo Public Safety Secretary, settled the matter in April 1938. The President was at São Lourenço in southern Minas on his fifty-fifth birthday when Müller brought the tall, dynamic Ademar de Barros of the PRP to call on him. Ademar, after completing his medical training in Germany, had participated in the Paulista rebellion of 1932, and in 1934 had shown his electioneering ability by trouncing a Democratic candidate in a race for a state assembly seat. Like Valadares in Minas, Ademar had not been a well-known figure, and his selection for the big job of São Paulo *interventor* came as a disappointment to the hopeful José Carlos de Macedo Soares.[14]

[13] See Francisco Campos, *O Estado Nacional e Suas Diretrizes* (Rio, 1937 edition).
[14] Despatch from U.S. Embassy, Rio, to Secretary of State, April 29, 1938.

2. The Constitution of 1937

Those who read the Preamble to the 1937 Constitution found it similar to Vargas' nationwide broadcast of November 10. They learned that the President, with the backing of the Armed Forces, was putting the Constitution into effect to bring an end to disorder. Threats to peace included ideological conflicts, and "party dissensions, which a notoriously demagogic propaganda seeks to pervert into a class struggle"; also "the state of apprehension created . . . by Communist infiltration, daily becoming more

extensive and more profound, requiring radical and permanent remedies." Perhaps it was in consideration of this description that the Constitution in its next-to-last article declared Brazil to be in a state of
emergency.

Although the Constitution's first article declared that political power
emanated from the people, the question of whether the people were to
have any voice at all depended on the President. It was up to him to
arrange for a plebiscite to approve the Constitution; after such approval
it was again up to the President to set a date for indirect elections for representatives to a National Parliament. The state of emergency, with or
without a parliament, gave the President dictatorial powers which could
not be touched by the judicial bodies.[1]

As it turned out, Vargas showed no interest in holding a plebiscite,
and so to look at the 1937 Constitution's provisions about elections and
legislative bodies serves no purpose except to get an idea of what Vargas
and Francisco Campos thought appropriate for the country in "normal"
times. Presidential re-elections (the term was set at six years) were not
ruled out. The contest for the Presidency was to be between only two
candidates: one chosen by the President; the other chosen, twenty days
before the expiration of the presidential term, by what political scientist
Karl Loewenstein has called "an Electoral College of six hundred hand-
picked men."[2]

In the Chamber of Deputies, made up of individuals chosen for four
years by municipal leaders, no state was to have more than ten representatives or fewer than three. As Júlio de Castilhos might have wished,
the chief function of the *deputados* was to initiate discussion of, and
vote on, taxes and budget increases.

In addition, there was to be a Federal Council (made up of two representatives from each of the twenty states plus ten chosen by the President) to consider such matters as trade and international treaties. A National Economic Council (made up of representatives of the different
occupations) was to push for the "corporative organization of the national economy."

The Constitution enumerated provisions about working hours, minimum wages, vacations, and other similar matters which had been drawn
up by the Provisional Government. At the same time it prohibited strikes

[1] 1937 Constitution, Art. 170.
[2] *Ibid.*, Arts 82–84; Karl Loewenstein, *Brazil under Vargas*, p. 54.

and lockouts, calling them "antisocial and harmful to labor and capital, and incompatible with the highest interests of national production."[3]

The nationalization of mines, sources of energy, banks, insurance companies, and basic and essential industries was to be regulated by law.[4] Vargas, however, chose to be flexible. The president of the Canadian-owned "Light & Power"—the largest foreign company in Brazil—praised him for "statesmanlike vision" when he modified some of the provisions about waters and mines so as not to stifle foreign capital.[5] Further "statesmanlike vision" was demonstrated with the repeal in October 1941 of a decree which provided that the capital of banks should by August 1946 be entirely in Brazilian hands.[6]

Under the new Constitution the oral as well as the written word became censorable during a state of emergency. The recent "state of war" had already added censorship to the functions of the Justice Ministry's Propaganda Department. Now, its activities enlarged by the Estado Nôvo, the Department moved into Tiradentes Palace, from which the lawmakers had been expelled. Propaganda included the Hora do Brasil, the nightly government broadcast which all radio stations had to carry and which Vargas critics called "the silent hour." Censorship and propaganda were directed by the intellectual-looking Lourival Fontes, an admirer of Italian fascism whose hair was usually in disarray.

Even if in some way a constitutional amendment were to end the national emergency, there still remained the Constitution's articles calling for a sweeping censorship law "to guarantee peace, order, and public safety."[7] One of the many provisions of the December 1937 Press Code made it illegal to publish any remark which might provoke disrespect for the public authorities.

Photographs of Vargas, who liked to be known as the "President" and not "dictator," had to be displayed in all shops, restaurants and places of business. At the same time the great man liked to be known for benign, human qualities. He took up golf, playing often with financial adviser Valentim Bouças, and joined in jokes about his poor scores. After a good day on the links, Getúlio told a reporter: "My luck at golf . . . and other things . . . has been very good."

[3] 1937 Constitution, Art. 139.
[4] *Ibid.*, Art. 144.
[5] Paul Frischauer, *Presidente Vargas*, p. 360.
[6] Karl Loewenstein, *Brazil under Vargas*, pp. 208–209.
[7] 1937 Constitution, Art. 122, Par. 15 a.

3. The Woes of Plínio

Getúlio's first public appearance after installing the Estado Nôvo was on November 15, 1937, at the inauguration of an ornate statue of Brazil's first President, Marshal Deodoro da Fonseca. At the ceremony the Green Shirts made another great show of force as they saluted Brazil's new strong man.

But all was far from cordial between Integralismo and Vargas. Plínio Salgado, hearing in Vargas' broadcast of November 10 no word of appreciation, felt that the Integralistas had been betrayed.[1]

Vargas was in no mood to see many thousands—Plínio spoke of one and a half million—proclaiming their allegiance to the Sigma and its leader. As to Plínio's claims, Getúlio had the reports of his "counters" at the November 1 parade, and, as to Plínio's purposes, these seemed apparent from his past militant declarations about dominating Brazil. Having no intention of letting Plínio follow the example of party leader Hitler in shoving aside the official head of state, Getúlio remarked more than once that the Integralistas had in mind "Hindenburgizing" him.

In addition to that compelling consideration, there was Getúlio's resolution to build up a strong loyalty to a united Brazil; not to groups with their own slogans, and not to a Brazil as interpreted by the penmanship and oratory of Plínio Salgado. Broadcasting at midnight on December 31, 1937, Vargas said that "political intermediaries" between his office and the people had been eliminated with the suppression of "cliquish interests," and he likened a new law code, to "a single flag" which would protect all Brazilians and provide uniformity.[2]

The flags and songs devoted to the Sigma were not the only trappings to be outlawed. Article 2 of the new Constitution permitted only the national flag, anthem, and coat of arms. This meant abolishing the insignia and anthems of the twenty states, for which, in Getúlio's opinion, too much devotion had too long been shown, resulting in the neglect of Brazil as a whole. To help bring this message home to the people, an unusual Flag Day ceremony was held in Rio on November 27, 1937. The flags of all the states were publicly burned. Francisco Campos, in excellent form, glorified the Estado Nôvo.

Some disgusted Integralistas wanted to break with the Estado Nôvo, but Plínio prepared to abide by the new rules and turn Integralismo into a "cultural association." Asking Campos about the requirements for

[1] Plínio Salgado, *O Integralismo perante a Nação*, p. 125.
[2] Getúlio Vargas, *A Nova Política do Brasil*, V, 123.

registering, he was surprised to learn that Vargas had decided to make his appointment as Education Minister dependent on the complete suppression of Integralismo.

Through such Army friends as Newton Cavalcanti, Góis, and Dutra, Plínio arranged to see Vargas. The President was in a cheerful mood as he advised of a new decree which Campos was preparing. Besides proscribing political parties, it would outlaw distinctive uniforms and salutes such as characterized Integralismo, and would require the Integralistas, if they wanted to be a cultural, sporting, or educational society, to change everything, their name included. An appeal from the dejected Plínio brought the President's promise to speak once more with his Justice Minister.

With Integralista publications banned, and the censored press downgrading the Green Shirt chief and his movement, it was not an encouraging promise. Soon after it was made Góis brought Plínio bad news: it had been impossible to persuade Vargas and Campos to let Integralismo continue. This so upset General Newton Cavalcanti that he resigned early in December 1937 as commander at Vila Militar in a letter which accused the Government of breaking its agreement with Plínio.[3]

Plínio got more rebuffs. On his authorization some of his followers proposed that the Education Minister be the Integralista "military chieftain," a part-German, pro-Nazi history professor. The Government ignored the suggestion.[4] Plínio could not even register Ação Brasileira de Cultura, the organization which he hoped would promote Christian virtues and the study of cultural problems. Campos refused to believe that it really included as many as the four thousand "technical schools" which Plínio claimed for it. When Vargas asked his Ministers of War, Navy, and Justice whether the new society should be allowed to register, Dutra alone voted in the affirmative. Campos, who liked to be finicky, abstained on the ground that Plínio had appealed to Vargas after he, Campos, had refused registration.[5]

Late in January 1938, after these many reversals, Integralismo's "Inner Council of 40" voted thirty-eight to two against collaborating with Vargas.[6] Already there had been Integralista flare-ups, the seizure of Integralista literature, and the arrest of Integralista plotters.

[3] Newton Cavalcanti, letter, December 2, 1937, quoted in Olbiano de Melo, *A Marcha da Revolução Social no Brasil*, pp. 119–123.

[4] Olbiano de Melo, *A Marcha da Revolução Social no Brasil*, p. 124.

[5] Francisco Campos, interview, September 3, 1963.

[6] U.S. Embassy, Rio, despatch to Secretary of State, January 28, 1938.

4. For Brazil and the Estado Nôvo

The decree which made Integralismo illegal, and the efforts of the President and his Justice Minister on behalf of nationalism, affected "colonies" of foreigners and their native-born descendants in Brazil. Of the three Axis communities, the Italian, strong in São Paulo, was by far the largest, numbering over 4,000,000. The 200,000 Japanese generally lived in agricultural communities. The Germans, numbering over 800,000 in the south, were proud of their schools and "superiority," and co-operated the least with the Vargas regime's drive to Brazilianize Brazil. Resistance was encouraged by the big German Embassy, which considered the drive a great inconvenience to German colonists and saw in it a wish to reduce the prestige of the Hitler-run Fatherland.

The inauguration of a bridge connecting Brazil with Argentina brought Getúlio to Rio Grande in January, 1938. There Colonel Osvaldo Cordeiro de Farias warned him of the extensive Nazi activities in the south. On his return to Rio, Vargas conferred with Góis and Campos, and the "big three" decided on energetic measures. Cordeiro de Farias, a Gaúcho, was named *interventor*; he closed all Nazi Party centers in the state and deported the chief Nazi agent. Editors of German-language newspapers in Rio Grande were told to stop inviting readers to support Hitler. Finding in Rio Grande over 2,800 private German schools, only twenty of which made use of Portuguese, Cordeiro put all private schools under state jurisdiction. In Santa Catarina, where 25 per cent of the inhabitants were German-speaking, laws specified that teaching in all primary schools had to be in Portuguese and that all schools had to bear Luso-Brazilian names.

The German and Italian amabassadors protested the Brazilianization of education, the closing down of foreign political parties, and the outlawing of insignia. But, as German Ambassador Karl Ritter pointed out, the Italians in Brazil retained "their language, culture, and racial consciousness" less than the Volksdeutsche in the three southern states.[1] Although Italian Foreign Minister Ciano advised Vargas that Italy would have liked to see more fascist courage in Brazil, the Italians obeyed Brazil's decrees. In April 1938 the Italian ambassador and his retinue appeared for the first time at a public function without black shirts and Fascist emblems.

On the other hand, the corpulent German ambassador was determined

[1] Department of State, *Documents on German Foreign Policy, 1918–1945,* Series D, Vol. V, p. 825.

to apply the "plain speaking" which Berlin recommended on behalf of "the prestige and preservation of the German community in Brazil."[2] Ritter, leaving the Justice Ministry without having obtained permission to register all sorts of pro-German cultural societies, was likened to a "mad lion" by Campos.[3] In Washington, Undersecretary Sumner Welles was soon chiding Americans who passed judgment on the new Brazilian regime as fascist; and Lord Marley, opposition whip in the British House of Lords, declared that the Brazilian dictatorship had been established precisely to halt inroads by Nazis and Fascists.

[2] *Ibid.,* p. 840.
[3] Francisco Campos, interview, September 3, 1963.

5. Early Plots against the Estado Nôvo

Although Armando de Sales continued in exile near Belo Horizonte, his backers were released from their "confinements at home" late in 1937. Pedro Ernesto received his back salary and quit politics and plotting to return to medical activities. But others, notably Otávio Mangabeira, Washington Luís' Foreign Minister, lost no time in conspiring against the Estado Nôvo. Plotting at Rio's Glória Hotel, Mangabeira was joined by Euclides Figueiredo, of the Paulista 1932 uprising. Offers of support came from São Paulo, where Júlio de Mesquita Filho was arrested in January 1938 for hatching subversive plans.

An agent of the conspiracy visited exiles in Argentina and Uruguay. Although the Communist exiles were unco-operative,[1] Rio Grande's Ex-Governor Flôres da Cunha gave him money. Flôres also visited the American Embassy in Montevideo to explain that the Estado Nôvo was bad for the continent and for foreign investors.

Even before Integralismo was officially dissolved by the Government decree of December 3 forbidding political parties, numerous Green Shirts spoke of using force. More optimistic than they might have been had they seen Vargas' intelligence reports, they counted on "70 per cent of the Navy and 2,000 Army officers."[2] Early in January 1938 a naval commander told the secretary of Integralismo's "Council of 40" that Navy men would march on Guanabara Palace whether or not Integralista ci-

[1] Carlos da Costa Leite and Meireles family, interview, September 6, 1963.
[2] Hélio Silva, "Rapsódia Verde" (MS), Ato II, 47, and Ato I, 31.

vilian chieftains supported them.[3] After this, Plínio picked Belmiro Valverde, fifty-four–year–old physician from Bahia, to lead the Green Shirts in Rio. Plínio would maintain relations with Mangabeira's non-Integralista group at the Glória Hotel. It had found a military chief in General José Maria Castro Júnior, the meticulous head of the Army's War Material Division.

The authorities had been seizing ammunition in raids on Integralista centers in Santa Catarina, Paraná, and Paraíba. In the Rio area they were so alert that the conspiring Navy lieutenants decided to suspend their revolt, originally planned for March 10, 1938. Confusion among the rebels began because some of the conspirators received the postponement orders only after they had started making prisoners of loyal sailors, and it became complete during the following days when messages for starting and stopping the "rebellion" were issued in rapid succession. The Rio police found a large supply of machine guns and arms at the home of Integralista Belmiro Valverde; also a list of Government officials to be "eliminated."

The plot was given wide publicity. German and Italian subversives were rounded up, and there were dismissals from the Integralismo-infused Bank of Brazil. Otávio Mangabeira and Euclides Figueiredo were arrested while Plínio Salgado was on his way from Rio to a hiding place in São Paulo. Vargas and Campos told Góis and the others who wanted a plebiscite on the Estado Nôvo that the moment was inopportune.

Mangabeira and Figueiredo remained under arrest, but few others were held long. Police Chief Müller said that Plínio Salgado bore no responsibility and would not be disturbed. Castro Júnior, chief of the rebellion, was quickly released and returned to his Army post. He became careful to limit his contacts with conspirators to whispered words in church.[4]

Integralista Belmiro Valverde was much more active. He attracted so many bomb-fabricating followers that the conspirators' two Rio houses became inadequate, and Flôres da Cunha money had to be used to rent a third on isolated Niemeyer Avenue. This became the headquarters where Belmiro and his cohorts, cheered by the German-Austrian *Anschluss*, prepared a plot which had similarities to the *Putsch* which eliminated Dollfuss in Austria in 1934.[5] General Newton Cavalcanti and Colonel Eduardo Gomes disappointed the conspirators, but Integralismo was

[3] Olbiano de Melo, *A Marcha da Revolução,* p. 125.
[4] Hélio Silva, "Rapsódia Verde," Ato II, 54.
[5] Alzira Vargas do Amaral Peixoto, Ch. 7 of "A Vida de Getúlio . . .," *Fatos & Fotos,* July 27, 1963.

known to be strong in the local Military Police, the Navy, and some Army barracks.[6]

Valverde's advisers believed that 600 well-disciplined men could overthrow the regime, and they had a carefully developed plan. At night communication centers would be seized, phones cut, and fires started to produce general panic. While assault groups were capturing the top men of the Estado Nôvo, sailors, assisted by Integralistas dressed as Marines (in uniforms supplied by Plínio's son-in-law),[7] would seize Vargas at Guanabara Palace and put him aboard the cruiser *Bahia*. "The man must not escape," prisoner Figueiredo wrote on a copy of the detailed plan when it was submitted to him at the military hospital.

One of the conspirators, Júlio Nascimento, belonged to the group of Marines which had the responsibility of guarding Guanabara Palace. Learning on May 8 that he would take his turn as head of the Guard on the night of the tenth, he argued that Vargas should be overthrown at 1:00 A.M. on the eleventh.[8] There were some objections because the next arms shipment, to be provided by Flôres da Cunha or São Paulo friends of Armando de Sales, was due in a week, but Nascimento countered that sufficient arms would be commandeered from the Guanabara Palace Guard. General Castro Júnior finally acquiesced and sent word to Mangabeira and Figueiredo that they would be freed on the night of the tenth.

[6] David Nasser, *A Revolução dos Covardes*, pp. 45–46.
[7] Manoel Pereira Lima in Hélio Silva, "Rapsódia Verde," Ato V, 4.
[8] Manoel Pereira Lima in Hélio Silva, "Rapsódia Verde," Ato IV, 82; Júlio Nascimento in Hélio Silva, "Rapsódia Verde," Ato III, 57.

6. Fournier's Attack on Guanabara Palace

On the evening of May 10, with the Estado Nôvo six months old, Cabinet ministers and other dignitaries of the dictatorship went to the former Senate building to hear Francisco Campos broadcast the merits of the new regime and speak of the tranquillity the nation could expect. Then a few of them joined Campos at his residence to sip champagne.

While groups of conspirators gathered outside the homes of the regime's top figures, a non-Integralista plotter, Lieutenant Severo Fournier, waited in vain at the Niemeyer Avenue headquarters for the officers and sergeants who had enthusiastically agreed to be present for their appointment with destiny. Although in 1932, fighting under Euclides Figueiredo, he had become acquainted with the "failings" of volunteer "patriots,"[1] Fournier vowed to "fulfill his mission" with the forty-five inexperienced Green Shirts who showed up. Many had marched for God, Country, and Family at Niterói but were untrained at using rifles and had to be given a last-minute lesson while donning Navy uniforms. Then by truck they were despatched to Guanabara Palace, followed closely by a car bearing Fournier and several other conspirators.

Júlio Nascimento visualized his job at Guanabara Palace as limited to immobilizing the thirty guards. He told them that "reinforcements" would arrive (as the Communists might attack), but he was almost as surprised as the other guards when the truck brought men whose mannerisms, and civilian shoes and socks, marked them as impostors. After some arguing and scuffling four guards were killed. The other loyal Marines were then put in a room with one Integralista sentry, and Fournier set out to direct the attack on the Palace.

Inside the Palace, which had been awakened by the shooting, two defective machine guns were found. One was beyond repair and the other jammed hopelessly after being used to fire a few shots from a window.

Fournier fired back at the Palace. But he discovered that hatchets, bombs, and two machine guns, brought for the occasion from Niemeyer Avenue, had been left behind in the truck, and it had been driven away against his orders. Integralistas seemed either unwilling or unable to fire the large machine gun taken from the guard house.[2] Those who showed willingness soon put it out of order and it had to be abandoned in the nearby wooded grounds to which some of the more frightened Integralistas were repairing. The only machine gun which functioned was a light one Fournier used while he directed operations; no one else would fire it.

After a presidential car drove up to the Palace, bringing Benjamim Vargas, Fournier irately commanded his men not to let anyone escape; but the car soon drove off with two men sent by Benjamim to get help. It was hit by two bullets but no one was injured.[3]

Benjamim, who had been dining out, found the Palace practically defenseless. Getúlio was pacing his study floor with a revolver in hand. A few other revolvers had been distributed, but there was little ammunition.

The official presidential telephone line had not been cut and was used by Alzira Vargas and others to send out pleas to Filinto Müller, Dutra,

[1] David Nasser, *A Revolução dos Covardes*, pp. 120–123.

[2] *Ibid.*, p. 128; Júlio Nascimento in Hélio Silva, "Rapsódia Verde" (MS), Ato III, 60.

[3] Alzira Vargas do Amaral Peixoto, *Getúlio Vargas, Meu Pai*, p. 124.

Góis, Francisco Campos, Copacabana Fort, and the Special Police. Müller said that policemen were on their way, and, after these failed to show up, he promised a troop led by Rio Grande *interventor* Osvaldo Cordeiro de Farias. There were more phone calls, more promises, and hours of waiting. Those who had been reached by phone were having their own adventures.

7. More about the Integralista *Putsch*

One of Rio's radio stations had been seized by Integralistas and was broadcasting messages which brought Plínio Salgado to his feet in São Paulo. Surrounded by supporters, he cavorted and danced with joy at the news that Vargas and his ministers were about to become prisoners and that the Navy Ministry building was already in Integralista hands.[1]

In Rio a submarine commander waited in a hotel bar for word which never came from General Castro Júnior that sailors should go ashore to assist Fournier in getting Vargas aboard the *Bahia*. More disposed to act, Navy Lieutenant Arnoldo Hasselmann Fairbairn and thirty poorly armed sailors took control of the Navy Ministry on the downtown waterfront and spent the hours before daybreak defending themselves against loyalist gunfire.[2]

Police Chief Müller, who had once celebrated his birthday by marching between the saluting arms of Green Shirts, was surprised by news of the Integralista outbreak. He rushed to the police headquarters but, as he had let most of the men off duty "in honor of the commemoration of the Estado Nôvo," he found only four policemen.[3] One of them was a conspirator, vainly awaiting the arrival of the Integralista group assigned to attack the police headquarters.

Fifteen pillars of the regime, among them men who returned to their homes at midnight after drinking champagne with Campos, were on the list to be captured.[4] A member of the War Minister's staff was taken on a wild ride which ended when his captors, fearing pursuit, abandoned the pajama-clad colonel and the car. Góis was held for several hours in his apartment by twenty noisy men, directed by "Nathan," the revolt's "General Organizer of Assaults." But the leaders of most of the assault groups were not much inspired by the motto *Avante* (Forward) written in green

[1] Hélio Silva, "Rapsódia Verde" (MS), Ato V, 5.
[2] Ambassador Caffery, Rio, despatch, to Secretary of State, May 12, 1938.
[3] Hélio Silva, "Rapsódia Verde," Ato V, 8.
[4] National Security Tribunal testimony in National Archives, Rio.

letters on the white neckerchiefs distributed to conspirators. Those in charge of bringing Campos and Dutra to the Niemeyer Avenue head-quarters decided at the last minute to do nothing. Dutra, who received urgent calls at his home at 1:00 A.M., made his way on foot to nearby Leme Fort, passing a bar where a dozen leaderless members of an assault group had gathered.

Finding twelve soldiers and one truck at Leme Fort, Dutra drove off to defend the Estado Nôvo. When he announced his presence at the principal gate of Guanabara Palace bullets wounded two of his soldiers and Dutra was nicked on the ear. He rode away in a motorcycle sidecar to get reinforcements, but the presence of his men in front of the Palace was enough to send most of the Integralistas fleeing into the wooded Palace grounds.[5]

When Dutra reached the police headquarters he found Cordeiro de Farias helping to organize a truckload of police in civilian attire. Dutra told Cordeiro to take command of available men and proceed to Guana-bara Palace.

The center of attention became a locked underground door connecting Guanabara Palace with the grounds of the Fluminense Football Club. As 5:00 A.M. approached, the rescuers on the Club side of the door were try-ing to get it open and even considering breaking it down. But inside the Palace the President's secretary at length located a porter with the key.[6] In came Cordeiro de Farias and the head of the Special Police and their men. For the besieged the ordeal was over.

Dutra arrived with Góis after a painfully wounded Hasselmann, four of whose men had been killed, surrendered in the Navy Ministry build-ing. By that time the unrest stirred up downtown had subsided, and hun-dreds of conspirators—most of whom had done more conspiring than fighting—deserted their various headquarters.

Guanabara Palace was now filled with officials, politicians, and friends of the dictator, all with stories to tell. Vargas, however, spoke little, and several hours later he took his usual walk with one aide to Catete Palace.

Góis' nap in a Palace armchair was broken by the shooting with which Government men went after Integralistas caught in the Palace grounds. Fournier and Nascimento had long ago fled, but most of Fournier's fol-lowers, having abandoned their *avante* neckerchiefs and the "uniforms" which had covered their ordinary clothing, were captured and seven

[5] Dutra quoted in Hélio Silva, "Rapsódia Verde," Ato IV, 87.
[6] Alzira Vargas do Amaral Peixoto, interview, July 11, 1963.

killed. Plínio, still close to his radio in São Paulo, was no longer jubilant.

The Italian Embassy, recommended by Fournier to a companion fleeing from Guanabara Palace,[7] became a popular haven, and among its new occupants was "Nathan," the "General Organizer of Assaults." Finally Filinto Müller's men surrounded the Embassy building, and a price of 100,000 milreis was put on Fournier's head.

[7] David Nasser, *A Revolução dos Covardes,* p. 142.

8. Fournier Reaches the Italian Embassy

Fournier was hidden by nervous friends until June 25. Then some Army officers drove past Müller's guards outside the Italian Embassy, unloaded him from the car trunk, and drove away.

Ambassador Lojacono let out a wail and hurriedly cabled Rome, where Mussolini, concerned about Italian funds frozen in Brazil, decided that "the man should be exchanged for money."[1] The Brazilian Government brought all sorts of pressure to bear on the distraught ambassador, who was determined not to violate the principle of political asylum. Dutra's Army officers found Lojacono "arrogant and unco-operative,"[2] and a special Vargas troubleshooter heard the Ambassador declare in Italian that it was not his fault that Brazil had an "army infested with gangrene."[3]

Italian Foreign Minister Ciano, after cabling Lojacono to settle the matter at once, explained privately to the Brazilian ambassador in Rome that if Lojacono resigned, his successor would turn Fournier over to the Brazilian authorities. But Ciano asked that this new demonstration of Italian friendship for Brazil be kept secret.[4]

Lojacono yielded. Fournier was persuaded to sign a flowery letter thanking the Ambassador for his kind hospitality and declaring that he was leaving voluntarily. Lojacono wrote an equally fine letter thanking Dutra for all the understanding he had shown for the Ambassador's "moral position." Fournier was given a ten-year jail sentence but he died of tuberculosis before completing it.

For Vargas the main repercussion of the affair at the Italian Embassy

[1] David Nasser quoted in Hélio Silva, "Rapsódia Verde," Ato V, 13.

[2] Report of Ângelo Mendes de Morais (then a lieutenant colonel) to Dutra, given in Hélio Silva, "Rapsódia Verde," Ato V, 14–21.

[3] Lourival Coutinho, *O General Góes Depõe,* p. 354.

[4] Hélio Silva, "Rapsódia Verde," Ato V, 14.

stemmed from the participation of Foreign Minister Aranha's brother, an Army captain, in smuggling Fournier into the Embassy. Relations between Aranha and Dutra, already poor,[5] became worse when the furious War Minister demanded that all the officers involved in the Embassy incident be fired. Vargas hesitated to act but Dutra resigned "irrevocably," and only withdrew his resignation when he got his way. Then Aranha resigned, remarking that Vargas had acted against his brother without enough study and without consulting him.[6] On the side he complained that Brazil ought to have the plebiscite mentioned in the Constitution, and that Vargas had denied him any voice in political affairs.[7]

Again there was the possibility that Aranha might become a focus of opposition to the dictatorship. Vargas' wife called on Aranha's mother, who had much influence over Osvaldo and who presided over the councils of the large, united family.[8] The pressure put on her, and Getúlio's appeal that the Gaúchos stick together, finally prevailed in July 1938.

[5] Lourival Coutinho, *O General Góes Depõe*, p. 353.
[6] Cable, Ambassador Caffery, Rio, to U.S. Secretary of State, June 29, 1938.
[7] Cable, Ambassador Caffery, Rio, to U.S. Secretary of State, July 7 and 14, 1938.
[8] Messages, Ambassador Caffery, Rio, to U.S. Secretary of State, July 4 and 15, 1938.

9. Dealing with the Troublemakers

At a Cabinet meeting held on May 16, the Constitution received two amendments after Francisco Campos disclosed that the President's legislative power allowed him to change it whenever he saw fit. One of these listed offenses, including an attack against the President's life or liberty, for which punishment could be the death penalty. Prevailing sentiment was strongly against the death penalty, and it was generally felt that the amendment was promulgated in the hope of deterring future attempts to overthrow the Government.[1] Vargas declared that the new amendment would not be retroactive.[2] The second amendment, which came to be used against the Foreign Minister's brother, extended for an indefinite period the constitutional article allowing the Government to fire civilian or military personnel "in the interest of public service or as felt desirable for the regime."[3]

[1] Despatch, Ambassador Caffery, Rio, to U.S. Secretary of State, May 19, 1938.
[2] Severo Fournier in David Nasser, *A Revolução dos Covardes*, p. 147.
[3] 1937 Constitution, Art. 177.

To the members of the Vargas family it seemed inconceivable that troops and police should have taken so long to end the siege on the Palace. More than one "defender" of the regime attributed a dubious attitude to fellow "defenders," and implied that the truth had been stretched in justifying delays. Filinto Müller explained that the authorities had hesitated to order out troops without knowing on which side they stood, and felt safe in doing so only after a reasonable period had passed without their joining the rebellion.

Reflecting on the performance of the police and the presidential guard, Benjamim Vargas decided that his brother needed a "personal" guard, one on which the Vargas family could always rely and which would report directly to Benjamim. The Gaúchos from the São Borja district with whom he had served in 1932, Benjamim told Getúlio, were "real men." "They will be loyal to you, guard the Palace while you sleep or work, and accompany you wherever you go."[4] Alzira has described them, "trusting no one and armed to the teeth, the custom of their birthplace." Some time was spent trying to civilize them a little for their new role.

In Rio, Müller's men made up for their somewhat sorry showing on the night of May 10. Assisted by a detailed plan of attack found by the Traffic Department in the car used by Fournier, the Rio police arrested 1,167 civilians and 437 military men (mostly sailors).[5] With trials still pending for many suspected of involvement in the 1935 rebellion, Vargas and his Cabinet at their May 16 meeting signed a decree-law which allowed the National Security Tribunal to deal with the new prisoners by limiting each testimony to five minutes and pronouncing sentences within thirty minutes. By early June about 600 Cariocas, mostly civilians, had been released. Among them was the Bank of Brazil exchange director, who had been held merely because he had belonged to the Council of 40; also an industrialist who indignantly explained that he had joined the Integralista Party some years earlier at the request of Vargas.[6]

The slow-moving wheels of justice of the 1934 Constitution had not impressed Vargas well, and he had no desire to have the Estado Nôvo associated with cells full of innocent persons awaiting trial. In August 1938, over three hundred still being held in connection with the Natal rebellion of 1935 were judged, and most of them were found innocent.

[4] Alzira Vargas do Amaral Peixoto, Ch. 7 of "A Vida de Getúlio . . .," in *Fatos & Fotos,* July 27, 1963.

[5] Despatch, Ambassador Caffery, Rio, to U.S. Secretary of State, June 10, 1938.

[6] *Ibid.*

By September 1938, the Security Council and the Rio police had gathered up reams of testimony about the Integralista rebellion, put the pieces together, and concluded the trials of everyone involved.

Hundreds were convicted and sentenced to a few years in jail. Like Fournier, Palace Guard Nascimento got the ten-year maximum for a political crime. (One of the other traitors in the Palace Guard, a man who had killed two companions, got the stiffest sentence: ten years plus thirty more for murder.) General Castro Júnior, who had spent the night at home although he nominally headed the uprising, was retired from the Army. Flôres da Cunha was absolved. Ex-Labor Minister Lindolfo Collor, scheduled to get a Cabinet post in Castro Júnior's junta if the revolt had succeeded, was released from a Rio jail, and so was Otávio Mangabeira, but they were instructed to get back to their home states.

At his São Paulo residence of hiding (known to the government) Plínio Salgado advised that he had first learned about the rebellion on the evening of May 10. Plínio could also point to a "directive" he had issued in April, 1938, advising his followers against violence.[7] He remained in half hiding.

Bernardes' son concluded that although everything possible had been done to overthrow Vargas the dictator's position was secure, and that there was "no use in our continuing to play a losing game."[8] But after one important prisoner escaped and was recaptured, the papers on him confirmed the government's belief that a few prominent individuals would continue plotting.

For Vargas the most troublesome group was made up of Armando de Sales supporters who called Júlio de Mesquita Filho "the Captain" because of his role in 1932. As editor of *O Estado de S. Paulo*, Mesquita enjoyed being rude to the dictatorship's censors, and his feelings were shared by equally strong-minded followers. Friendly to Otávio Mangabeira, Euclides Figueiredo, and Fournier, these Paulistas had a low opinion of Integralismo. When Mesquita prepared to support the May 11 Rio uprising with a Paulista revolt (which never materialized because Castro Júnior told Mesquita to wait[9]), it was with the understanding that the movement was inspired not by Integralistas but by the whole antidictatorship current.

The Estado Nôvo tried to induce these "unreconstructible" democrats

[7] Plínio Salgado, *O Integralismo perante a Nação*, p. 141 n.

[8] Despatch, U.S. Embassy, Rio, to U.S. Secretary of State, September 16, 1938.

[9] Júlio de Mesquita Filho, interview, August 7, 1963.

to leave Brazil. Armando de Sales, who had been released from Minas just before May 11 and had no connection with the *Putsch*, was put under house arrest again, in Rio and São Paulo. On one complaint after another, and at inconvenient hours, Mesquita and his followers were hauled off for short stays in jail. The São Paulo Secretary of Public Safety admitted that the purpose of it all was so to "upset their lives" that they would decide to go abroad.[10]

Finally the federal government bluntly told these foes, condemned by the National Security Council, to leave the country. In October 1938 a wire from Filinto Müller advised Otávio Mangabeira in Bahia that a shipload of Integralistas was on its way to Fernando de Noronha and that he would be put aboard if, by the time the ship reached Salvador, he were not on his way to exile.[11] Mesquita was in the famous "Chapel" jailroom of Rio's Casa de Correção when he got his shipping instructions, and he left in November for France with Armando de Sales, who was told to get out of the entire continent.[12] Artur Bernardes and Lindolfo Collor were also sent abroad.

Plínio Salgado, a frail "religious mystic" writing a life of Christ at a ranch in the interior of São Paulo,[13] was less troublesome. But, in May 1939, he received the suggestion that he, too, leave Brazil. Thereupon he released a manifesto to the Integralistas, reminding them that he had taught them "faith in God, love of country, the ideal of national unity, the practice of Christian virtues," and the merit of personal sacrifice. After referring to the serious international situation, he urged his followers to respect the constituted authorities.

The Green Shirt also addressed a farewell note to Dutra. "In this hour," Plínio wrote, "I turn over to the Army's vigilant watchfulness, intelligence, and defense the work which I spent six years constructing."[14] Offered a professorship at Coimbra University, he left for Salazar's Portugal in June 1939. Plínio considered himself a democrat who opposed the suppression of liberties. But he was not a loud critic of the Estado Nôvo and received much better treatment in Portugal than non-Integralista exiles who condemned the Estado Nôvo whenever possible.

As long as they could, Armando de Sales and his supporters stayed in

---

[10] Paulo Duarte, *Prisão, Exílio, Luta*, p. 8.

[11] Biographical sketch of Otávio Mangabeira in files of *O Estado de S. Paulo*.

[12] Biographical sketch of Armando de Sales Oliveira in files of *O Estado de S. Paulo*; Affonso Henriques, *Vargas, o Maquiavélico*, p. 434.

[13] Despatch, U.S. Embassy, Rio, to U.S. Secretary of State, February 16, 1939.

[14] Plínio Salgado, *O Integralismo perante a Nação*, p. 147.

France. From Paris they wired President Roosevelt their congratulations for the reference to freedom in his January 1, 1939, message to Congress, and they went on to denounce Vargas.[15] Telegrams from Mesquita to Hull and Welles called Aranha's speech before the Washington Press Club an "insult." At a time when Brazil "is under a tyranny which has abolished all public liberties and is exiling or arresting all who fight for liberty, including one of the most illustrious statesmen of Brazil for the sole reason that he was a candidate for the Presidency," Aranha, they said, had no right to extol American democracy or denounce Nazi and fascist dictatorships.[16]

Paulo Duarte, a Paulista exile who went with Mangabeira to the United States after France fell to Hitler, blamed the State Department when the New York daily *PM* failed to publish Mangabeira's story on the Brazilian situation. Duarte has written that he himself encountered "all the ill-will of the State Department, for which the dictators of Latin America and the rest of the world are the raw material most suitable to its reactionary policy."[17]

Armando de Sales and Mesquita went to Argentina. But even in Buenos Aires there were frustrations which Mesquita attributed to the Vargas-Roosevelt alliance. "In Buenos Aires, Americans kept people away from me. Roosevelt upheld Vargas, finding it more convenient to deal with one dictator than three hundred *deputados*."[18]

In Brazil, Mesquita's newspaper, *O Estado de S. Paulo,* tried under censorship to continue the policy of its lost "Captain" (and managed to print *interventor federal* without using capital letters.) The result was that in March 1940 the newspaper was seized and made a mouthpiece of the Vargas regime.

Duarte was not alone in complaining that the State Department was trying to influence press reports about Brazil. Thus Carleton Beals wrote in 1938:

Sumner Welles of our State Department has taken American journalists to task for calling Brazil Fascist and thus endangering American friendship in that quarter. It is a sad day when a high member of the State Department converts himself into a voluntary propagandist for a regime as brutal, as anti-American, as that of Vargas in Brazil.[19]

[15] Paulo Duarte, *Prisão, Exílio, Luta,* p. 9.
[16] Letters dated February 19, 1939, in National Archives, Washington.
[17] Paulo Duarte, *Prisão, Exílio, Luta,* p. 9.
[18] Júlio de Mesquita Filho, interview, August 7, 1963.
[19] Carleton Beals, *The Coming Struggle for Latin America,* p. 169.

Beals spoke of the "thousands" who had been murdered in Brazil, and he attacked Roosevelt and Hull for professing friendship for Vargas.[20] He felt that Vargas, although "for the moment" more powerful than Mussolini or Stalin, was in a really "shaky" and "unstable" position, with the masses all against him.

[20] *Ibid.*, p. 249.

10. A Short Break in Relations with Germany

Thousands were not being murdered in Brazil; the regime was not anti-American; nor did Vargas have the masses against him. Never forgetful of labor, Vargas signed a decree on May Day 1938 calling for studies which would bring about minimum wages, and he exempted from taxes property purchased by members of the working classes through the Pension and Retirement Institutes.

After Fournier fired on Getúlio and his family at night in an act contrary to Brazilian ways, indignation was almost universal and the reaction in Getúlio's favor was strong. Getúlio was well received in July 1938 when he extolled the Estado Nôvo in three speeches in Minas. Then he visited São Paulo for the first time since 1930 and was given a surprisingly enthusiastic reception. Throughout Brazil the controlled press made the most of the Integralista fiasco. Rio's *Correio da Manhã* reproduced a letter to show that Plínio wanted "all the Fascists of the world to close ranks against Jewish influence."[1]

Ambassador Ritter felt that the May 11 *Putsch* confirmed the unpopularity of a regime whose chief had broken his word with the Integralistas, and in his despatches to Berlin he predicted new revolts. Concluding on May 12, 1938, that the regime had become "even more unpopular" than before, he recommended that the "insurrection" be handled sensationally by the press in Germany, and if possible elsewhere in Europe. "This would bring home to the present Government that it might become impractical for them to continue to show so little understanding for German interests."[2] In Germany, Vargas was pictured as causing the Brazilian press to spread slanders against Germany and much was written about "our duty to protect our German citizens against the anti-German course on

[1] *Correio da Manhã*, Rio, May 17, 1938.
[2] Department of State, *Documents on German Foreign Policy*, Series D, Vol. V, p. 838.

which Brazil, with the support of the United States, has embarked."[3]
"No longer will great Germany tolerate further annoyances and chicanery
in connection with Germans, German business, and the German press in
Brazil."[4]

Getúlio, in thanking President Roosevelt for congratulating him on
his "fortunate escape," expressed the view that "advocates of foreign
doctrine attempted a coup against Brazilian democracy."[5] When he addressed a huge crowd outside Catete Palace on May 13 ("I expected a
demonstration from the working class and I have received a demonstration from the whole of the Brazilian people"), Getúlio blamed the assault
on a group of fanatics "with help received from abroad."[6] This remark,
upsetting to Ritter, was considered by the Brazilian press to be applicable
to Germany; and Aranha observed that, while he had no proof, he felt
there had been some German connection with the *Putsch.*[7]

The stepped-up attacks on Vargas in the German newspapers lasted
about a week, at the end of which the Brazilian ambassador in Berlin
gave the German Foreign Ministry his personal view that Vargas had not
meant Germany in his reference to "help received from abroad," but
probably had in mind Brazilian political opponents in Argentina and
Uruguay.[8] A few days later the Brazilian government asserted that it had
no evidence sustaining Brazilian press reports that "German firms and
German nationals participated in or lent support to the events of May 11
in Rio de Janeiro."[9] The German press then made an about-face and spoke
of Vargas' "farsightedness."[10]

Diplomatic relations, nevertheless, deteriorated. One cause was Ritter.
Late in May 1938 he refused Aranha's invitation to a diplomatic ball and
shocked him by stating that as long as the Nazi Party was outlawed in
Brazil the Brazilian ambassador in Berlin would receive no more social
invitations from the German government (a threat which the German
Foreign Office refused to back). Particularly damaging to relations was the

[3] *The New York Times,* May 15, 1938.

[4] *Ibid.,* May 17, 1938.

[5] Cables of Franklin Delano Roosevelt (May 12) and of Vargas (May 16) in
National Archives, Washington.

[6] Getúlio Vargas, *A Nova Política do Brasil,* V, 211–213.

[7] Cable, Ambassador Caffery, Rio, to U.S. Secretary of State, May 13, 1963.

[8] Department of State, *Documents on German Foreign Policy,* Series D, Vol. V,
p. 845.

[9] *Ibid.*

[10] Cable from Ambassador Wilson, Berlin, to U.S. Secretary of State, May 27,
1938.

Brazilian government's discovery in June of plans for a revolt in the south, drawn up by German-Brazilians and German nationals. Without Ritter's knowledge, the plans mentioned his name. After it was reported that one arrested plotter had committed suicide, two others, German nationals, received asylum in the German Embassy.[11] Getúlio, in a speech in July, fortified nationalistic feeling by referring to foreign elements who incited green or red extremisms and who, through qualified emissaries, were in touch with those who greedily sought to grab Brazil.[12]

As far as Aranha and the United States were concerned, the growing Brazilian-German trade, based on "compensation" or "barter" marks and stimulated by the Bank of Brazil exchange director,[13] was in conflict with the spirit of the United States-Brazilian Reciprocal Trade Agreement. Between 1933 and 1938 Germany doubled her share of Brazilian exports, becoming the largest buyer of Brazilian cotton and the second largest of Brazilian coffee and cacao. Although Brazil had been placing orders in Germany for coal and for military and railway equipment, Rio's surplus of blocked "compensation" marks grew. In June, 1938, when this surplus reached 40 or 50 million marks, Brazil refused to accept any more. Germany was accused of purchasing Brazilian goods on credit merely to resell them at lower prices and for stronger currencies on the world market. Retaliating, early in July the German government suspended all trade with Brazil and annouced a large coffee purchase from Colombia.

Both countries had been finding the trade useful and they kept this matter apart from the squabble which centered on Ritter's attitude about German colonists and organizations. With the "trade war" of June and July 1938, Brazilian exporters, particularly of cotton, were hard hit. Neither their pleas nor the Vargas policy of increasing trade allowed Brazil to maintain its position long. Rio submitted, agreeing on July 20 to accept "barter" marks again, and trade was resumed.

Late in July, Ritter met in Montevideo with the chief German representatives to Argentina, Chile, and Uruguay to discuss steps to be taken against the anti-German attitude found in "most of the South American countries."[14] But he was already so unwelcome in Brazil that it was too late for him to put into effect the recommendations reached in Monte-

[11] Department of State, *Documents on German Foreign Policy,* Series D, Vol. V, pp. 860–863.

[12] Getúlio Vargas, *A Nova Política do Brasil,* V, 243.

[13] Despatch, Ambassador Caffery, Rio, to U.S. Secretary of State, May 27, 1938.

[14] Department of State, *Documents on German Foreign Policy,* Series D, Vol. V, p. 863.

video. There was dismay in the Brazilian Foreign Office in September 1938, when it was learned that he planned to return to his Rio post after attending a Nazi Party rally in Nuremberg. Finally, on September 30, the day of the Munich Pact, the Brazilian government declared Ritter *persona non grata,* since he "had not complied with the usual formalities of courtesy."[15] Germany therefore asked for the recall of the Brazilian ambassador in Berlin.

The stationing of a Brazilian artillery unit in the heart of a German area in Santa Catarina did not mean that Vargas wished to have poor relations with an expanding Germany. Neither did the campaign against the Nazi Party in Brazil. Nor, for that matter, did the step taken against Ritter, and relations vastly improved after it was taken. Brazilian Air Force officers left in January 1939 for a visit to German aircraft factories and were feted by Goering. Hitler gratified the admiring Brazilian military by inviting Chief of Staff Góis to visit Germany and to command a German division in maneuvers.

In March 1939, after Hitler violated the Munich Pact by invading Czechoslovakia, Vargas went to the Arsenal to inspect some artillery just received from Germany and to comment on the world situation. Observing that the old foundations of social and political organization were proving to be bankrupt, he noted that great peoples were trying new forms and were getting rid of forces which contributed to disunity and negativism. Brazil, he said, would not partake of foreign ideologies, but neither should it isolate itself from other peoples. "We are not concerned with the internal structures of other countries, just as we do not accept any foreign interference with our organization. We shall be united by the spirit of defending the American continent, without being hostile to any who recognize our sovereignty and respect our laws."[16]

The American Embassy interpreted these sentiments as meaning that Brazil should not place her eggs in one basket until definitely obliged to commit herself in the event of a world war, and in the meantime should squeeze the maximum out of the United States on the one hand and the fascist powers on the other.[17] Aranha, under a veritable barrage from his foes because of agreements he had reached in Washington, kept silent. By early June 1939 Germany and Brazil had agreed to exchange ambassadors.

[15] Woermann in *Documents on German Foreign Policy,* Series D, Vol. V, p. 873.
[16] Getúlio Vargas, *A Nova Política do Brasil,* VI, 192.
[17] Despatch, U.S. Embassy, Rio, to U.S. Secretary of State, April 22, 1939.

Internally the situation was so favorable to the Vargas regime that in February 1939 Góis said he would be able to take his first vacation in years.[18] The Deputy Minister of Justice noted that Vargas was enjoying a period of tranquillity unmatched since he had taken over the government in 1930. Such was the attention given to what Vargas called "the spectacle of a world tormented by uncertainty"[19] that Brazilian interest in a plebiscite diminished.

[18] Despatch, U.S. Embassy, Rio, to U.S. Secretary of State, February 16, 1939.
[19] Getúlio Vargas, *A Nova Política do Brasil,* VI, 192.

BOOK VII

THE ESTADO NÔVO AND A
WARRING WORLD, 1939–1942

"Sometimes our friends want
me to move a little fast;
then I must defend myself."

1. Conversations in Washington, 1939

AT THE TIME Hitler invited Góis to visit Germany, Vargas and Foreign Minister Aranha were considering Roosevelt's telegram asking that Aranha come to Washington to discuss important matters. Roosevelt's suggestion was quickly accepted. Aranha (described by the German chargé in Rio as "a hireling of North America"[1]) sailed on January 29, 1939, accompanied by financial experts.

Brazil's decision in November 1937 to go into complete default on its foreign-debt service, thus abandoning the Aranha Plan of 1934, was dictated by insufficient foreign exchange. Early in 1938 the exchange shortage became so acute that Brazil froze all foreign balances. The principal causes were the low coffee prices and the growing trade with Germany (which produced only "barter" marks).

To the enormous Brazilian coffee stock of 1930 was added the thirty-million-bag all-time peak crop of 1933. The Provisional Government imposed coffee export taxes and a tax on each new bush planted. Its most dramatic step on behalf of the price, however, was the inauguration of the

---

[1] Department of State, *Documents on German Foreign Policy*, Series D, Vol. V, p. 881.

great coffee-burning program, which from 1932 to 1938 destroyed sixty million bags, the equivalent of four years of exports. Yet the spot price for Santos coffee in New York averaged only 9.8 cents per pound from 1931 to 1937, compared with 13.1 cents in 1930 and 21.7 cents in 1929.[2]

After Brazil's share of the world market dropped from around 60 per cent before 1932 to less than 50 per cent in 1937, the Estado Nôvo decided that Brazil was tired of playing a price-support game alone. An export-tax reduction combined with aggressive sales efforts sent Brazil's share of the market to over 57 per cent in 1939. But the price fell so low that, even with increased sales, exchange earnings declined. As Aranha sailed for Washington in January, 1939, the price was only 7.5 cents.

Germany, wanting to combat "United States Pan-Americanism" by a "peaceful invasion" of Latin America undertaken by linguists, educators, and scientists, commented on Aranha's trip. He was being called to Washington, Germans proclaimed, so that Roosevelt could "read him the riot act." They added that unless Brazil ceased producing cotton, the United States planned to engage in a cotton-dumping program "as it does with wheat."[3] Aranha, greeted in Washington by Hull and Welles, declared that "all friendly people have to fear Germany."

During his month of negotiating, Aranha cabled Vargas that it would be helpful to his mission if Brazil would co-operate militarily with the United States. Aranha added that General George C. Marshall, as United States Army Chief of Staff, was ready to visit Brazil provided his opposite number, Góis, would quickly reciprocate.

At Petrópolis, Vargas called in Dutra, who was not enthusiastic about the cable, and Góis, who was planning to visit Europe. Dutra pointed out that it was the French Military Mission which had been giving training to the Brazilian Army. The Americans, he felt, could teach Brazil nothing about military preparation, but he conceded that they might have some useful ideas about coastal defense.[4] Vargas' reply to Aranha, composed by Góis with Dutra's approval, reflected much more caution than Aranha liked, but it allowed him to arrange Marshall's visit. After it had been decided to follow Aranha's suggestion about Góis, the Germans were told that Góis would visit Germany and other European countries after his United States trip.

---

[2] For coffee information, see João Oliveira Santos, *Análise das Tendências do Mercado Internacional do Café,* and Winfield C. King, *Brazil's Coffee Industry.*
[3] *The New York Times,* January 28, 1939.
[4] Lourival Coutinho, *O General Góes Depõe,* p. 359.

The Hull-Aranha understandings were concluded with much ceremony in Washington on March 9. Brazil agreed to resume servicing the foreign dollar debts on July 1, 1939, encourage American investments, free the exchange market, and create a Central Reserve Bank (free of government interference).[5] The Export-Import Bank, in touch with Wall Street banks, agreed that Brazil would be loaned $19,200,000 which would go to unpaid United States exporters. It also agreed to help Brazil purchase ships for its government-owned Lloyd Brasileiro and equipment for railways. Washington would provide technical assistance, and Congress would be asked to authorize a loan of $50 million in gold to help establish the oft-discussed Brazilian Central Reserve Bank.

Roosevelt opponents in the United States Senate attacked the understandings and pointed out that Brazil might altogether get credits of as much as $120 million. Senator Reynolds called Aranha "the greatest drycleaner and finest salesman the world has ever known."[6]

But in Brazil the arrangements were seen as helpful principally to United States exporters. Where were all those planes, cruisers, and coastal artillery pieces? When the agreements were made public there was general disappointment, especially in military circles, and when Aranha docked, neither military minister was on hand to greet him. Chief of Staff Góis was out of town. Education Minister Gustavo Capanema, who sided with Dutra,[7] belittled the Foreign Minister, and Justice Minister Francisco Campos made a particularly sarcastic remark about his sojourn in the United States.[8] The São Paulo correspondent of the *Correio da Manhã* reported: "Today we have a very real commercial relationship with certain European countries, and we cannot abandon it in exchange for vague promises."[9]

Aranha, a less hesitant man than Finance Minister Artur de Souza Costa, had agreed to the resumption of servicing foreign debts without being convinced that his government would carry it out.[10] The Army, which Vargas was careful to see get first call on the budget, felt this must mean a reduction of its expenditures. The Finance Minister, who could not have missed hearing rumors that Aranha was interested in assuming the Finance post and organizing the Central Reserve Bank, called the

[5] Department of State, *Foreign Relations of the United States, 1939*, V, 352–354.
[6] *The New York Times,* March 14, 1939 (dateline Washington, March 13).
[7] Gilberto Freyre, interview, September 29, 1964.
[8] Despatch, U.S. Embassy, Rio, to U.S. Secretary of State, April 22, 1939.
[9] *Correio da Manhã,* Rio, April 9, 1939.
[10] Department of State, *Foreign Relations of the United States, 1939,* V, 357.

Washington agreements pure "literature" and said the foreign debt payments simply could not be made. After Vargas held a full Cabinet meeting to afford Aranha the opportunity of reporting, Valentim Bouças, the President's golf partner and financial adviser, told Ambassador Caffery: "This Government will not resume payment of the foreign debt on July 1."[11]

So bitterly was Aranha attacked that he had to leave Rio for a month to recuperate from a near-breakdown. But he was back at work in June, threatening to resign if Vargas asked him to sign a letter on the debt matter drafted by the Finance Minister.[12] Finally Vargas ordered the Finance Minister to make $1 million available, an amount so insignificant compared with the smallest sum of $9 million mentioned by Aranha in Washington that it was rejected by the indignant United States Foreign Bondholders Protective Committee.

Vargas did sign a decree "freeing" foreign exchange transactions, but the new regulations differed from understandings reached in Washington. It was now decided that the Bank of Brazil would take 30 per cent (instead of 10 per cent) of export drafts at the official rate of 16.5 milreis per dollar, leaving only 70 per cent to get the free rate of 18.4. Nonetheless, the Export-Import Bank furnished the promised credits for overdue payments to American exporters. The Brazilian Central Reserve Bank was never established.

While Aranha was having his troubles, General Marshall reached Brazil on a warship. This was one day after the arrival of Mussolini's daughter, Edda Ciano, who gained as much of a reputation for being late to appointments as Marshall did for always wanting things to start on time. Marshall in Rio could only broach the subject of military co-operation, but he had the chance to explore it more thoroughly after he took Góis north with him on the *Nashville*.

Góis received royal treatment in Washington and was impressed with the industrial and military establishments he saw. The only faults he could find with United States society concerned "the racial question and capitalist domination."[13] When Góis called attention to United States military unpreparedness, Roosevelt blamed isolationists.

After two months Góis returned, bringing the ideas he had suggested

[11] Despatch, U.S. Embassy, Rio, to U.S. Secretary of State, April 22, 1939.

[12] Department of State, *Foreign Relations of the United States, 1939*, V, 357 and 360.

[13] Lourival Coutinho, *O General Góes Depõe*, p. 362.

for military co-operation. They were not mentioned in the controlled Brazilian press, and they were approved by Vargas when he studied them in August. Brazil would continue with its concentration of armed forces in the south. Defense of the Northeast would be provided by air and naval bases to be constructed with United States technical and financial assistance; also by a formidable supply of United States weapons to be paid for by the shipment of Brazilian raw materials and to be used by newly organized Brazilian Army units.[14]

As Roosevelt had predicted, Góis' plans for visiting Europe had to be canceled, war breaking out there early in September, 1939. This development, placing in jeopardy arms shipments from Germany, resulted in further Brazilian Army appeals for United States weapons. But the surplus which could be offered for sale—not, as Brazil wished, for barter—was a great disappointment to the Brazilian Army.

[14] Stetson Conn and Byron Fairchild, *The Framework of Hemisphere Defense,* p. 268.

2. Plans for a Stronger Brazil, 1940

Nostalgic members of Rio and São Paulo society continued to speak disparagingly of "the mannerless Gaúcho usurpers." But these commentators were politically unimportant. By late 1939 even Afrânio de Melo Franco, who had broken with Vargas in 1933 and who in principle opposed dictatorship, was stating privately that the Estado Nôvo was rendering good service.[1]

Getúlio, the embodiment of the tranquillity he had promised Brazil, occasionally found time to relax with his crossword puzzles. Usually he was keeping up with his paper work, and at night until 1:00 A.M. could be found alone in his Guanabara Palace office, reading and signing documents. To reach him by phone was practically impossible. He detested the instrument, preferring to observe the people with whom he conversed.

Many criticized Vargas for having devoted his attention almost exclusively to political affairs. But that he had done so allowed him now to turn his attention to other matters. Using different-colored pencils when handling different subjects in the papers on his desk, he methodically drew up plans for the development of Brazil.

When he opened the Rio-Bahia highway in April 1939, he spoke not

[1] Despatch, U.S. Embassy, Rio, to U.S. Secretary of State, December 15, 1939.

only of other road-building projects but also of a forthcoming steel plant and a projected airplane factory.[2] In December 1939 he called the *interventores* to Rio to review recommendations on health, education, agriculture, minerals, public works, transportation, and social legislation.

During much of 1939 Getúlio, with the help of Finance Minister Souza Costa and Army people, had been working on a Five-Year Plan which would identify the Estado Nôvo with grand designs. Unveiled in January, 1940, it allowed Brazil's citizenry to bask in the satisfying assumption that basic industries, particularly steel, would be built. It looked to the realization of the old idea of establishing a hydroelectric power plant at the vast Paulo Afonso Falls on the São Francisco River in the Northeast, and of controlling the river's flood waters. Railways and highways were to be constructed and Lloyd Brasileiro was to get twelve new ships from Europe.

Most of the military requirements were to come from the £7,500,000 balance of the £8,280,000 contract signed in 1938 with Krupp of Germany.[3] Airplanes and three destroyers were to be purchased in the United States. Six more destroyers were to be built in England, but the European war soon forced the British to cancel this agreement.

The war made it difficult for Brazil to acquire the fighting equipment visualized by the Five-Year Plan, and it played havoc with the plan in other ways. The estimated cost of the Plan, $30 million per year, was to be derived mainly from the Bank of Brazil's exchange operations, with an assist from 7-per-cent ten-year bonds to be sold in Brazil. But the exchange operations dwindled with the wartime collapse of foreign trade, and by mid-1940 Vargas had to decree advances to the producers of traditional exports piling up in Brazilian warehouses.

The proposed steel plant, close to Getúlio's heart, had been mentioned in the speech which ushered in the Estado Nôvo. Brazil has no lack of iron ore. Although Santa Catarina coal is low grade, the United States Steel Corporation considered the steel project feasible; its own interest, however, was negligible. Brazil, it pointed out, could acquire steel more cheaply by importation.[4] Vargas' negotiators, Major Edmundo de Macedo Soares and millionaire Guilherme Guinle, felt that a steel plant would save foreign exchange, besides being a big step forward in industrializa-

---

[2] Getúlio Vargas, *A Nova Política do Brasil*, VI, 198.
[3] Department of State, *Foreign Relations of the United States, 1940*, V, 634–635.
[4] Adolf A. Berle, interview, March 8, 1963.

tion and a source of national pride. The Brazilian military strongly favored the plant.

Brazil's popular ambassador in Washington, gourmet Carlos Martins, let the State Department know that Vargas considered the plant "a most important test of the Good-Neighbor policy." If the Ambassador was worried about a rumor that assistance for the project was tied to payments on Brazil's foreign debt, he could breathe more easily in March, 1940. Brazil agreed to disburse over a four-year period between 40 per cent and 50 per cent of the payments called for in the Aranha Plan of 1934. This required about $17,000,000 yearly on eighty-two federal and local issues having a principal of $996,000,000.[5]

In May, 1940, after word reached Washington that Krupp wanted to build the Brazilian steel plant, Vargas let the State Department know that an Export-Import Bank loan of $15 or $20 million would be welcome so that Brazil could build its plant independently of any foreign corporation. Ambassador Martins stressed Vargas' need "to demonstrate that Brazilian-American relations were based on reciprocity."

During the next months everything indicated that Getúlio's great hope for Brazil would be realized. Late in May, Federal Loan Administrator Jesse Jones agreed to advance funds on the condition that his agency and the Brazilians could agree on construction plans. In July, after Germany had overwhelmed the Low Countries and France, the American foreign ministers met at Havana and heard Hull pledge economic and financial co-operation. Roosevelt requested Congress to authorize the Export-Import Bank to lend up to half a billion dollars to assist Western Hemisphere countries. Undersecretary Sumner Welles reminded Jesse Jones in August that if Brazil accepted the "liberal" German offer "Germany's predominance in Brazilian economic and military life would thereby be assured for many years."[6]

Alzira Vargas, decoding cables in the presidential office, had good news for her father in September 1940. With the announcement of the $20-million deal, Aranha and Welles were exchanging happy messages, and Getúlio was receiving congratulatory telegrams from all over Brazil. Ramifications included ocean shipping of coal from southern Brazil, and equipping the Central do Brasil Railroad to carry rich iron ore from

[5] Department of State, *Foreign Relations of the United States, 1940*, V, 575, 600–601.
[6] *Ibid.*, V, 606–610.

Minas. About a year and a half after work began in 1941 at the Volta Redonda site in the state of Rio, ninety miles from the federal capital, the initial Export-Import Bank loan was increased to $45 million. It was estimated that the cost of constructing the 300,000-ton-per-year steel plant of the Companhia Siderúrgica Nacional would be $70 million. Local currency costs equivalent to $25 million were supplied by the sale of shares to the Brazilian government, the Social Security Institutes, and Brazilian investors.

As a planner Getúlio traveled much by plane in the Brazilian interior in 1940. The first Brazilian President to visit the jungle and confer there with Indians, he distributed machetes and hoes and took a canoe ride with local tribesmen. Smoking a cigar with a chief, he watched Indian dancers. Back in Rio, he approved a plan which was to colonize Goiás by furnishing each settling family a house and fifty acres.

It was good to get out of the capital and speak to long-neglected audiences about the Estado Nôvo. Between October 5 and 21 Getúlio flew ten thousand miles on a trip through the north. Making it clear that he was no "tourist," but the maker of sound plans, he suggested a cure for the depressed economies of backward Pará and Amazonas: agricultural colonies, systematic planting, scientific methods, and technical steps to improve health conditions. The Instituto Agronômico do Norte was to help.

The Ford rubber operation, visited by Vargas on this trip, seemed to confirm ideas he had been preaching for ten years. All was cleanliness and order; not a mosquito or housefly.[7] A few days later, at Manaus and Pôrto Velho, the dictator again stressed "planned," "systematic," and "rational" exploitation of the Amazon's riches. "Contrary to the belief of many, the climate of Amazônia is generally possessed of conditions favorable for a healthy life and productive work."

Vargas may not have known how many millions of Ford dollars it had taken to create the conditions which impressed him at Belterra, Amazonas. He would have joined Henry Ford in berating those who doubted the economic possibilities of plantation rubber in Brazil. But a little over a year later an onset of leaf blight, swarming caterpillars, and bugs would doom Ford's rubber venture and suggest that all was not as simple as Vargas' words implied. Amazon rubber trees seemed to thrive only when scattered through a forest, not on plantations where diseases spread.

[7] Mira Wilkins and Frank Ernest Hill, *American Business Abroad,* p. 180.

3. Neutrality under Trying Circumstances, 1940

Although Aranha had initiated discussions with the Export-Import Bank about credits for ships, the matter was placed in the hands of the Communications Ministry, leading Aranha to remark that in the future he would limit himself to being Foreign Minister.

Some of the international incidents he handled sprang from the Declaration of Panama, signed by the American republics in October 1939. This embodied Roosevelt's idea that belligerents should keep their warships and submarines three hundred miles from American coasts. A whole series of violations ensued, the most publicized being the battle between three British warships and the German pocket battleship *Graf von Spee*, ending with the destruction of the German ship off Montevideo. Relations between Brazil and Britain, hurt by the British blockade, deteriorated further in February 1940 when the British sank a German freighter fifteen miles off the Brazilian coast.

After accepting Aranha's choice of old Afrânio de Melo Franco to represent Brazil on the Inter-American Neutrality Commission, Vargas in January opened the Commission's deliberations in Rio. He stressed that "the twenty-one American states have resolved to keep out of the Old World's struggle."[1] In speeches made on a trip to southern Brazil in March, Vargas told German descendants that they owed their allegiance only to Brazil, which, he declared, "is not pro-German or pro-British." Laying emphasis on a strict neutrality, he added that if Brazil became involved in any controversy, it would act jointly with the other American nations.

Vargas was back in Rio when the inactive phase of the European war gave way to striking German victories, hardly surprising to German-decorated generals in the Brazilian Army. Brazilian trade with Europe suffered a complete collapse when Denmark and Norway fell to Hitler.

After Germany unleashed its *Blitzkrieg*, invading the neutral Low Countries and battering France's defenses, the Vargas brand of neutralism, fashionable earlier in the year, was criticized. In New York former diplomat James W. Gerard told Brazil to "wake up." A victorious Germany, he said, would quickly dominate the "virtually German" Brazilian south. On June 10, with France falling and Italy entering the war on

---

[1] Afonso Arinos de Melo Franco, *Um Estadista da República*, III, 1591.

Germany's side, Roosevelt spoke at the University of Virginia, making his sympathy for the foes of the Axis unmistakably clear. "The hand that held the dagger has struck it into the back of its neighbor," he exclaimed.

Washington and Aranha were dismayed to learn of Vargas' speech of June 11 to officers aboard the *Minas Gerais*. Expanding on ideas expressed over a year earlier when he inspected Krupp-made artillery, Getúlio said:

We and all humanity are passing through a historical moment of great repercussions, resulting from a violent shifting of values. We are marching to a future different from the one we knew in the realm of economic, social, and political organization, and we feel that old systems and antiquated formulae have entered into decline. It is not, however, as die-hard pessimists and conservatives maintain, the end of civilization, but the tumultuous and fruitful beginning of a new era. Vigorous peoples, fit for life, need to follow the direction of their aspirations, instead of pausing to contemplate what has crumbled and fallen into ruins. . . . Balanced economy no longer allows privileged classes to enjoy a monopoly of comfort and benefits. . . . The State, therefore, should assume the obligation of organizing the productive forces, to provide the people with all that is necessary for the collective welfare. . . . The era of improvident liberalism, sterile demagoguery, useless individualism, and disorder has passed.[2]

Getúlio had discussed the speech with Góis before delivering it and had commented that "one has to shake the tree vigorously to get the dead leaves to fall."[3] After the speech had been given, Getúlio let it be published in its entirety by the Brazilian press. Phrases were quickly picked up by the press in the United States and elsewhere and presented under sensational headlines such as that in Buenos Aires' *Crítica*: "Vargas, with Fascist language, justifies the aggression of barbarians."

In spite of Getúlio's recent plain speaking to German-Brazilians, Ambassador Caffery chose to interpret the controversial parts of the speech as "sops" to Brazil's large German and Italian populations.[4] Alzira writes that her father's words were intended to help prod the United States into finalizing the steel mill arrangements.[5] What seems clear is that Vargas, unaware of F.D.R.'s University of Virginia speech, saw events dramatically confirming the concept of the Estado Nôvo. He did not feel that his

[2] Getúlio Vargas, *A Nova Política do Brasil,* VII, 331–333.

[3] Lourival Coutinho, *O General Góes Depõe,* p. 367.

[4] Department of State, *Foreign Relations of the United States, 1940,* V, 616.

[5] Alzira Vargas do Amaral Peixoto, Ch. 9 of "A Vida de Getúlio . . .," in *Fatos & Fotos,* September 7, 1963.

dedication to neutrality required that he cease assailing "improvident liberalism" or "sterile demagoguery."

In Aranha's office Góis tried to explain to Ambassador Caffery that Vargas had in mind making social and economic reforms similar to those of Roosevelt's New Deal. But the vexed Ambassador had other observations to make about Vargas' words: United States citizens held Brazil in highest esteem and therefore were filled with "consternation."[6]

Guided by Aranha and propaganda boss Lourival Fontes, the Brazilian press reported that relations with the United States had never been better. The speech was described as calling the Brazilian people's attention "to the transformation the world is undergoing, thus justifying the necessity of strengthening the state both economically and militarily."[7] Vargas, having shaken the tree and noted some resulting activity by Brazilian democrats who opposed him,[8] cabled Washington that his words were

a warning, a call to reality, addressed to Brazilians and which might cause surprise only to persons devoted to routine, not to a far-seeing mind like that of Roosevelt, who is liberal-minded, progressive, and forward looking, crying out as the voice of the whole continent regarding perils which threaten America and who knows that Brazil will not fail him in loyalty.[9]

Getúlio was highly provoked by the treatment which the foreign press gave to "his sincere words and patriotic foresight." Addressing a group of maritime workers on June 29, he assailed those who had interpreted his recent speech "with false commentary and tendentious publication of isolated phrases."[10] A bit later, after someone sent Dutra a collection of United States press clippings attacking the Brazilian dictator and Armed Forces, Getúlio observed that in Brazil he prohibited the press from criticizing Roosevelt or the United States. Aranha tried to explain United States press freedom, but incensed Brazilian generals discussed suing the offending United States newspapers.[11]

Washington was worried about the Latin American reaction to German successes in Europe. With the Uruguayans "climbing on the Nazi band wagon,"[12] United States observers were convinced that there was danger

[6] Lourival Coutinho, *O General Góes Depõe*, p. 368.
[7] Department of State, *Foreign Relations of the United States, 1940*, V, 623.
[8] Cable, Ambassador Caffery, Rio, to U.S. Secretary of State, June 17, 1940.
[9] Department of State, *Foreign Relations of the United States, 1940*, V, 622.
[10] *Ibid.*, p. 625; Getúlio Vargas, *A Nova Política do Brasil*, VII, 348.
[11] Cable, Ambassador Caffery, Rio, to U.S. Secretary of State, September 23, 1940.
[12] Department of State, *Foreign Relations of the United States, 1940*, V, 1151.

also in Brazil. Late in May, Ambassador Caffery described the public and the Government, including Aranha, as getting panicky.[13] Although Caffery felt that most thoughtful Brazilians favored the Allies, he considered the pro-Axis elements better organized.

Hans von Cossel had the title of German Embassy counselor and press attaché. But his prestige among Germans exceeded that of their ambassador, for Cossel was the personal representative of Adolf Hitler. At his well-financed headquarters in São Paulo he directed a staff of over a hundred in disseminating anti-United States propaganda in pro-German newspapers, over the radio, and in pamphlets.[14]

The Germans were well entrenched in commercial aviation and were felt to have done an excellent job in this field. Condor, handsomely subsidized by its parent, Deutsche Lufthansa, had over twenty-five German aircraft piloted by Germans. Its routes, many of them of dubious commercial value, covered the strategic Northeast. Brazilian airlines (VASP and VARIG) used German equipment and Condor's shops, and had working agreements with Lufthansa.

The only direct air service between South America and Europe was carried out by LATI, the Italian airline. Its usefulness was defended by Aranha, but it was also very useful to Germans. Called by a British spy "the biggest gap in the British economic blockade," it carried German and Italian diplomatic pouches, propaganda, mica, diamonds, platinum, and chemicals; also Axis officials and agents.[15] As was suspected at the time, LATI passed shipping information on to Nazi raiders and submarines, and both LATI and Condor helped Axis merchantmen run the British blockade.[16]

In October 1940, Vargas decreed that all pilots of aircraft of Brazilian registry should be native-born Brazilians, but in special cases temporary exceptions to this ruling were granted. Washington sought to have Panair do Brasil, then wholly owned by Pan American Airways, expand in Brazil. After VASP suffered a plane crash Washington offered to sell it planes in return for its de-Germanization.

Rio authorities discounted Allied press reports of "almost unbelievable

[13] Cable to U.S. Secretary of State, from Ambassador Caffery, May 27, 1940.
[14] Russell B. Porter article in *The New York Times,* dateline Buenos Aires, June 25, 1940.
[15] H. Montgomery Hyde, *Room 3603,* p. 145.
[16] William A. M. Burden, *The Struggle for Airways in Latin America,* p. 69.

Nazi penetration" and "Fifth Column peril" in Brazil. As Rio Police Chief Filinto Müller saw his job, it was to round up people suspected of wanting to overthrow the Estado Nôvo. These turned out to be Communists; not the Nazi spies who radioed information about ship departures to German submarines.[17] One hundred "Communists" were seized in December 1939, and fifty more in April 1940. In November 1940, Luís Carlos Prestes went on trial again. This time he was accused, with five others, of being responsible early in 1936 for the brutal slaying of Elza Fernandes, a teen-age beauty whose informing to the police had imperiled Communist conspirators. Prestes, in hiding before his capture, had sent a harsh letter to some of his followers, scolding them for letting sentiment stand in the way of their duty, which was to kill the girl.[18] Elza's death had followed. To Prestes' original sentence of seventeen years were added thirty more.

A big part of the job of combating the activities of men like Cossel fell to Lourival Fontes. Right after the outbreak of the war in Europe, Fontes' Propaganda Department was expanded into a more impressive Department of Press and Propaganda—the much-disliked DIP. This reported directly to Vargas, and its transfer from the Justice Ministry annoyed Francisco Campos.

At least until January 1941, when Fontes clearly forbade attacks on the United States, it was hardly true that Roosevelt and the United States went unscathed in the Brazilian press. But the English, because of naval incidents and their blockade of Hitler's "Fortress Europe," suffered much worse. Brazil had numerous pro-German newspapers, three of which were in Rio, and they were particularly vociferous after the Nazi military successes of 1940. The DIP cracked down in September 1940, suspending for five days Rio's noisy pro-German *Meio Dia* for "disturbing the interest of continental peace."[19] For a while publication of the sixty foreign-language newspapers, mostly German and Italian, was allowed as long as Portuguese translations accompanied the texts. But finally in August 1941 all of them were closed, the censors' wishes harmonizing perfectly with the Brazilianization campaign.

---

[17] Tad Szulc, *Twilight of the Tyrants*, p. 84.
[18] Pedro Lafayette, *Os Crimes do Partido Comunista*, pp. 41–72. Heitor Moniz, *Communismo*, pp. 115–118.
[19] *The New York Times*, October 1, 1940.

4. The Drive for Arms Which Shook the Cabinet

During the latter part of 1940 Brazil-United States military co-operation discussions usually ended with the Brazilians insisting that the United States provide them with arms. The United States was equally insistent that more should be done to protect the Brazilian Northeast; it felt that a United States Army force should be placed there.

Brazilian generals considered Germany their best source of modern combat equipment.[1] They presented the United States Army a $180-million list of needed armaments, but the United States, with its own preparedness program and all-out aid to England, had nothing to spare. Góis and his Army friends expressed their appreciation of gifts received from the United States in the form of cases of whiskey and cartons of Lucky Strikes,[2] but said that neither these nor fine words equaled the arms which Germany was placing at Brazil's disposal in Europe.

For a while the Brazilian military wanted assurances of United States arms before agreeing even to discuss mutual defense. But the steel-plant agreement improved the atmosphere, and so Góis, in Washington for a meeting of Army Chiefs of Staff of the American republics, conceded that arms and defense might be discussed together. The Góis draft of October 29, 1940, which became in essence the agreement between the Brazilian and the United States Armies, provided that United States forces should join Brazilian forces in defending Brazil only if Brazil should be attacked before having adequately prepared her defenses. Brazil agreed to end Axis subversion; Washington agreed to furnish Brazil what arms she could in exchange for raw materials.[3] In case of an attack on an American republic by a non-American nation, Brazil would "extend the use of its naval and air bases."[4]

With a subsidiary of Pan American Airways preparing to build and improve airfields in the Brazilian Northeast, the United States military tried to get diplomats to appreciate the urgency of stationing United States troops in the Brazilian bulge. One Washington representative declared that Brazil was less alarmed than she should be and "seemed more concerned over future economic independence than immediate prepared-

---

[1] Conn and Fairchild, *The Framework of Hemisphere Defense*, p. 275.

[2] Cable, Ambassador Caffery, Rio, to U.S. Secretary of State, October 10, 1940.

[3] For additional details, see Conn and Fairchild, *The Framework of Hemisphere Defense*, p. 277.

[4] Department of State, *Foreign Relations of the United States, 1941*, VI, 490.

ness."[5] But the stationing of United States troops on Brazilian soil was a touchy matter, especially with Brazil maintaining that it could organize its own defense if it had arms. Both Caffery and Aranha thought it would be a mistake to ask Vargas for permission.

British naval activity continued to upset the Brazilian military. Late in November the British took merchandise from a Brazilian ship at Trinidad, and early in December they seized twenty-two German passengers from another Brazilian ship, this time right off Rio de Janeiro. Next, they captured a French ship off Santa Catarina.[6]

What most angered Góis and Dutra was British reaction to their attempt to violate the blockade and transport German arms from Portugal. Early in November 1940, after the *Siqueira Campos* had been loaded with guns and ammunition, as well as four hundred passengers, it was seized by the British at Lisbon and taken to Gibraltar. In the face of pressure from United States and Brazilian diplomats, the English insisted that the arms shipment would provide Germany with Brazilian currency to be used for subversive purposes and that any break in the blockade would help German propaganda, strengthen the pro-German element of the Brazilian Army, and be a precedent leading to other Latin American requests.

At length the British agreed that the *Siqueira Campos* would be released if certain demands were met, such as the immobilization of all "enemy" ships in Brazilian ports, and the hope was expressed that Brazil would also stop LATI from flying to Brazil. These demands stirred up more resentment, and the Vargas Cabinet, its eye on British properties in Brazil, met to consider retaliatory measures. Aranha found the pressure from the military so great that he did not exclude the possibility of a break in diplomatic relations with England.[7] In Washington the State Department was thoroughly alarmed. Finally, on December 15, after much anti-British feeling had been provoked in Brazil and after officials in Washington had done their best on Brazil's behalf, the *Siqueira Campos* was released. Vargas, addressing military leaders on December 31, 1940, stated that Brazilian purchases, the minimum necessary, were made with funds "produced by our labor." "To impede delivery to us would be a violation of our rights."[8]

But one assurance the Brazilians had given, and this was that the *Siqueira Campos* shipment would be the last. Thus a new crisis arose in

[5] *Ibid.*, p. 492.

[6] Hélio Vianna, *História da República: História Diplomática do Brasil*, p. 272.

[7] Department of State, *Foreign Relations of the United States*, 1940, V, 654.

[8] Despatch, U.S. Embassy, Rio, to U.S. Secretary of State, January 17, 1941.

January 1941, when the British forced the *Bagé* to unload at Lisbon a new lot of Krupp arms about to leave for Brazil. As in the *Siqueira Campos* case, Brazilian military leaders pointed out that the material included parts necessary for artillery received in former shipments.

Aranha, arguing that he had already given his word with the approval of Vargas, Góis, and Dutra, refused to heed the demand of the military that he reopen the matter with the British. According to Aranha, who insisted he would resign rather than submit to the Army's wish, Dutra and Góis had been pushed into the situation by the Germans. Dutra, denying he had backed Aranha's pledge that the *Siqueira Campos* shipment would be the last, submitted his resignation.[9] Góis excitedly threatened reprisals against British companies in Brazil and branded Aranha as pro-British. While Aranha hoped for a victory by having his Washington connections get the arms released, Góis secretly asked General Marshall to arrange a satisfactory resolution of the *Bagé* case. Nothing could secure the arms, and after Rio Grande *interventor* Cordeiro de Farias tried to smooth ruffled feathers in Rio, Vargas told Dutra he could not accept his resignation.

Aranha and Dutra, long at odds, would not make peace. Even the long-standing personal friendship between Aranha and Góis was strained to the limit as the result of the leading role played by Góis among Army men who provoked vicious press attacks against the British. So strong was the press campaign that Aranha spoke with Lourival Fontes and persuaded him to ask editors and publishers to tone down the *Bagé* affair. If war reached the Americas, Fontes explained to the newspapermen, Brazil would hardly side with Germany.

Góis exploded. He sent an official message to Fontes instructing him to call in all Rio newspaper owners and ask them if they were pro-Brazil or pro-Britain; he added that the Army had to know who were Fifth Columnists of whatever color. Feeling that Góis had become unbalanced, Fontes refused to comply.

In defiance of Góis' demands, which were backed by Dutra, Paulo Bittencourt's *Correio da Manhã*, on January 19, 1941, carried a paid advertisement of the Commission of British Industries which included a pro-British remark that Aranha had made in November. The editorial in José Eduardo de Macedo Soares' *Diário Carioca* urging civil unity behind Vargas was regarded as a warning to the military to keep its hands off civilian affairs.

⁹ Cable, U.S. Embassy, Rio, to U.S. Secretary of State, January 13, 1941.

Góis got in touch with Dutra, who agreed that the *Correio* should be closed indefinitely; it was felt that the *Diário Carioca*, whose management had often been friendly to Góis, should be suspended temporarily. But when the matter went to Vargas he told Fontes to take no step against the *Correio* and to apply a short suspension against the *Diário Carioca* on the ground that its editorial might be interpreted as creating dissension between the President and the Armed Forces.[10] Soldiers unnecessarily descended on the *Diário Carioca* until Góis, who disclaimed responsibility for this, got the War Minister to call them off.

All in all it was a victory for Aranha over the military. Góis remarked: "We went hunting for a lion and all we got was an alley cat." Dutra became determined to get Fontes out of the DIP and had in mind installing as his successor an Army major who had been an Integralista and was reportedly pro-German.

The military revised the list of arms needed from the United States; by now including the material which could not be delivered from Germany, it upped the figure to $250 million. The United States Army listed some items valued at $80 million which it said it could furnish over the following 2½ years, and it recommended extending the necessary credits, of which $12 million was to be the first installment.[11]

Before visiting Washington in October 1940, Góis had left Vargas a draft of a decree which would bring all aviation matters, except naval aviation, into a subministry of Aeronautics, reporting to the War Minister. But during Góis' absence Getúlio had decided to do just what Góis opposed; he would create an Air Ministry. This prompted Góis to grumble that Getúlio found satisfaction in "weakening the Armed Forces" by dividing them up.[12]

Early in February 1941, while political and military circles were buzzing about the *Bagé* affair, the Army was advocating that the new ministry be headed by an Army man. The Navy felt otherwise. The decision of Vargas was revealed to Ambassador Caffery by Valentim Bouças in more or less these words:

I was playing golf with the President on Sunday morning. To our surprise we were interrupted in the middle of the game by General Pinto [chief presidential military aide]. Pinto was very agitated. I withdrew. Pinto became more and more agitated. After this interview, Vargas' golf was worse than usual. After

[10] Despatch, U.S. Embassy, Rio, to U.S. Secretary of State, January 22, 1941.
[11] Conn and Fairchild, *The Framework of Hemisphere Defense*, pp. 279–280.
[12] Lourival Coutinho, *O General Góes Depõe,* p. 372.

the game we had lunch and Vargas went off by himself at the end of the veranda for an hour and spoke to no one. At the end of the hour he said to me: "I will give you some news: a decree will appear tomorrow morning creating the Air Ministry, and Joaquim Pedro Salgado Filho, an intimate friend of Osvaldo Aranha, will be the new minister."[13]

Aranha was pleased with the choice of his fellow Gaúcho, a civilian who had served as Labor Minister in the mid-1930's.

Later in February, Caffery was at Petrópolis hearing Vargas express his pleasure about the promised United States arms, and urge that the necessary credits be extended. "As long as I am in office," Vargas said encouragingly, "the United States can count on my sympathy and cooperation. I have entire confidence in the goodwill and good intentions of President Roosevelt. I know that Brazil will get a fair deal at his hands. If the United States declares war on any non-American country Brazil will not declare war too but the United States can count on our full cooperation and help short of a declaration of war: the use of our ports, the acquiring of materials here, etc., etc. If war is declared by any non-American country on the United States, Brazil will enter the war at once on the side of the United States." Vargas criticized England for the *Siqueira Campos* incident, but expressed appreciation for what the United States had done to get the vessel released.[14]

[13] Cable, Ambassador Caffery, Rio, to U.S. Secretary of State, February 10, 1941.
[14] Cable, Ambassador Caffery, Rio, to U.S. Secretary of State, February 18, 1941.

5. On the Eve of Pearl Harbor

United States attention to Brazil increased sharply. "What is Vargas like and where does he stand?" people were asking. North Americans found the Brazilian dictator highly respected; one of them reported that he was "almost loved by an overwhelming majority throughout the country."[1] Although visitors from the United States noted that Getúlio was taking care of a fantastic amount of detail work, he seemed invariably calm and in good spirits. As he walked with a slow step, the odd way in which the little man's head jerked from right to left suggested alertness.[2] Posing for a bust by Jo Davidson, he would pace the floor and exchange good-

[1] Report (Buenos Aires, November 25, 1941) sent to U.S. State Department by a Mr. Simpson (of New York).
[2] Harold Callender in *The New York Times,* August 1, 1941.

humored remarks in French. Inclined not to take sides, and apparently excited by nothing, Vargas, his visitors found, was a sharp contrast to the tall, restless, nervous, talkative, imaginative Aranha, who loved to argue and engage in difficult abstractions.[3] Getúlio knows, Aranha once said, "that I am a sincere Brazilian patriot, but he knows that I am enthusiastic and sometimes my enthusiasm gets the better of me."[4]

Vargas' prestige had soared with the development of plans for the steel plant, coal mines in the south, railway improvements, and an airplane engine factory near Rio, which was being discussed with the United States. Another booster was a paper industry in the pine forests of Paraná. Concerned with the difficulty of importing newsprint, Getúlio turned to Assis Chateaubriand, owner of the largest newspaper chain, suggesting that he establish such an industry. Declining for himself, Chateaubriand suggested the firm run by the Jewish Klabin family. When the Klabins were hesitant the dictator insisted. He offered a Bank of Brazil loan and gave the Klabins eight days to draw up plans.[5] After the first shipload of machinery for the plant had been torpedoed by the Germans, Adolf A. Berle and others in the State Department helped arrange a second shipment, which reached its destination.[6]

On May Day 1941, Vargas sent greetings to Hitler: "Felicitations of the Brazilian government and people, as well as my wishes for your personal happiness and the prosperity of the German nation." This message and Hitler's similar reply were announced officially by the Brazilian government.[7] Late in May, Caffery found Vargas "a little more cautious than usual" and weighing his words "more carefully than he usually does with me." Aranha told the Ambassador that he was not surprised, as Vargas was "obviously worried about the continued German advance in Crete as well as the budding conspiracy in military circles."[8] Furthermore, Vargas felt that Washington showed more interest if there was some doubt about his position.[9]

[3] *Ibid.*

[4] Despatch, Ambassador Caffery, Rio, to U.S. Secretary of State, October 10, 1941.

[5] Horácio Lafer, interview, August 7, 1963; Napoleão de Carvalho, interview, August 6, 1963.

[6] Adolf A. Berle, interview, March 8, 1963; Horácio Lafer, interview, August 7, 1963.

[7] *The New York Times,* May 10, 1941 (dateline Rio, May 9).

[8] Cable, Ambassador Caffery, Rio, to U.S. Secretary of State, May 29, 1941.

[9] Merwin Bohan, interview (recalling conversation with Alzira Vargas do Amaral Peixoto), August 20, 1964.

Vargas' good wishes to Hitler were sent while the United States and Brazil were discussing an agreement on strategic materials. Concluded in mid-May, it gave the United States for two years preclusive rights on specified amounts of rubber and strategic minerals. The United States Government's Metals Reserve Company and Rubber Reserve Company would buy what private United States companies did not absorb.[10] Brazilian mineral exports to the United States, valued at $3 million in 1938, rose to $44 million in 1942,[11] but some of the amounts mentioned in the 1941 agreement bore little relation to what conditions were to make possible. The agreement was amended in 1942 by separate arrangements on individual products. In June 1941 Brazil took steps to prevent strategic materials from being exported to Axis nations.[12]

By mid-1941 German occupation of Dakar, in French West Africa, appeared imminent, and the United States Army was determined to rush thousands of soldiers to the Brazilian bulge. However, Aranha "literally threw up his hands in consternation," and agreed with Góis that acceptance of the American proposals would mean the downfall of any Brazilian government.[13] Although Hitler's invasion of Russia late in June 1941 reduced the threat to the Brazilian Northeast, Roosevelt's long letter to Vargas about the world situation included a reference to the danger to Natal.

The Brazilians stuck to their position. Before they agreed to hold a military conference with United States officers in Rio in August 1941 they again stipulated that United States forces should be used in Brazil only if Brazil, being threatened, should ask for them. The conference's accomplishments were minor. In spite of the troubles which Góis gave the United States mission, he was criticized by Brazilian "patriots",[14] who spread rumors that Brazil was losing its sovereignty in the Northeast.

As for arms, Brazil had received from the United States little more than a few searchlights. The Lend-Lease Agreement of October 1941 covered $100 million worth of future arms, for which Brazil was to pay $35 mil-

[10] Department of State, *Foreign Relations of the United States, 1941*, VI, 538–541.

[11] Frederic W. Ganzert, "Wartime Economic Conditions," in *Brazil* (Lawrence F. Hill, ed.), p. 312.

[12] William L. Langer and S. Everett Gleason, *The Undeclared War*, p. 600.

[13] Conn and Fairchild, *The Framework of Hemisphere Defense*, pp. 288–290.

[14] Langer and Gleason, *The Undeclared War*, p. 603; Lourival Coutinho, *O General Góes Depõe*, p. 378.

lion between 1942 and 1947.[15] The shipment of $16 million worth was promised within a year, but Brazilians remained skeptical.

Brazilians, Caffery pointed out, were no less blind to dangers than some North Americans late in 1941, and they "had precious little interest in implementing aid to Britain, much less succor to Red Russia."[16] Caffery, asked by the State Department to work out with Brazil one agreement after another, had to notify Washington that even Aranha looked unfavorably on the United States List of Blocked Nationals ("The Americans are interfering in the internal affairs of Brazil") and was unhappy about the spread of unpopular Panair do Brasil at the expense of Condor. Air Minister Salgado Filho observed that "Condor is the oldest airline in Brazil and has rendered excellent services to this country."[17]

When the United States suggested the elimination of LATI by cutting its fuel supply, the Air Minister insisted that such a step should await the inauguration of service to Lisbon and Portuguese West Africa by Pan American Airways. The British Intelligence Service meanwhile worked on its own scheme, forging a letter apparently signed by LATI's president in Rome. So carefully was the letter's "discovery" arranged, and so skillful was the forgery, that it was pronounced authentic at the American Embassy and found its way to Vargas. Dated October 30, 1941, it said in part:

There can be no doubt but that the fat little man is falling into the pocket of the Americans and that only violent action on the part of our green friends can save the country. . . . The Brazilians may be, as you have said, a nation of monkeys but they are monkeys who will dance for anyone who will pull the string.[18]

[15] Department of State, *Foreign Relations of the United States, 1941*, VI, 534–537.
[16] Caffery quoted in Conn and Fairchild, *The Framework of Hemisphere Defense*, p. 298.
[17] Department of State, *Foreign Relations of the United States, 1941*, VI, 526.
[18] H. Montgomery Hyde, *Room 3603*, pp. 145–146.

6. Rio Foreign Ministers' Conference, January 1942

In a Cabinet meeting called by Vargas after Japan's attack on Pearl Harbor it was unanimously resolved that Brazil declare its solidarity with the United States in accordance with its tradition and obligations.

The United States Army was more determined than ever to get a large force to northeast Brazil, but it made no headway. Roosevelt remarked that Vargas had "to feel his way—be sure of his ground."[1] Getúlio confided to an associate: "Sometimes our friends want me to move a little fast; then I must defend myself; I hope to be completely out of the woods by the time the Foreign Ministers arrive here next month."[2]

United States diplomats prepared for the Rio meeting of American Foreign Ministers by lining up republics to break relations with the Axis. Chile, run by a provisional government and about to hold a presidential election, was concerned about the vulnerability of its long coastline. Argentina's new President, Ramón Castillo, had a pro-Axis complex. Although in 1940 the signers of the Act of Havana had agreed that an Axis attack on any one of them should be considered an act of aggression against them all, Argentina's Foreign Minister argued that an attack in the mid-Pacific was not an attack on the Americas. "Do not forget," said an Argentine admiral, "that one fifth of our population is of 'totalitarian' origin, principally Italian."[3]

In Brazil, Aranha advised Caffery: "You can tell Welles that I shall be wholeheartedly with him at the Conference on every question except one; and that is the blacklist."[4] Dutra, on the other hand, asked Góis for a letter stating that Brazil was unprepared for war.[5] Góis went further and wrote that a break in relations would "immediately and inevitably" mean war and that he found it his conscientious duty to reiterate that the Armed Forces were not sufficiently equipped to defend Brazil. Armed with this, Dutra prepared a memorandum urging that Brazil postpone breaking relations until "we are in a position to provide loyal co-operation with the United States." In the absence of modern coastal and antiaircraft artillery, he predicted assaults on vulnerable areas and on Brazilian shipping, disrupting communications between the south and the Northeast.[6]

Nevertheless, on January 12 Vargas told a meeting of his Cabinet and top military authorities that he had decided that Brazil's highest interests and commitments dictated that it "must stand or fall with the United States." When Dutra and Góis stressed the uselessness of the token United States shipments of a few small unarmed tanks, Getúlio explained

---

[1] Conn and Fairchild, *The Framework of Hemisphere Defense*, p. 309.

[2] Ambassador Caffery, Rio, Message 2090 to U.S. Secretary of State, December 17, 1941.

[3] Department of State, *Foreign Relations of the United States, 1942*, V, 17.

[4] *Ibid.*, p. 7.

[5] Lourival Coutinho, *O General Góes Depõe*, p. 378.

[6] José Caó, *Dutra*, pp. 127–131.

that he did not have to rely on the Armed Forces to control subversive activities. They could, he said, be handled by the Brazilian people, who were wholly in agreement with his decision.[7] Dutra and Góis offered their resignations, but Vargas did not act on them.[8] A State Department man commented that "loose talk by members of our Embassy about the desirability of replacing Góis made it difficult for Vargas to remove him."[9]

By the time the Foreign Ministers gathered in Rio the republics in the Caribbean Islands had declared war. The United States, its hands full, was discouraging further war declarations and pushing for all to follow the example of Mexico, Colombia, and Venezuela, which had broken relations with the Axis. But Vargas, opening the Conference in Tiradentes Palace, carefully avoided mentioning this subject. He praised Roosevelt, expressed Brazil's determination to defend its territory, and stressed the importance of economic collaboration, one of the matters to be discussed by the Foreign Ministers.

For his cautious speech Vargas received praise in a letter the Italian ambassador addressed to Aranha. In this, and in letters from the German and Japanese ambassadors, Aranha was reminded that a break in relations would lead to all-out war.[10]

Getúlio sent for Sumner Welles, chief of the United States delegation. Referring to the "veiled threats"[11] from the Axis ambassadors, he agreed that a break in relations would soon bring Brazil into the war. His responsibility was particularly great, he told Welles, because, in spite of his efforts during the past eighteen months, the United States had not furnished even the minimum of war supplies. Brazil, he went on, should not be treated "as a small Central American power which would be satisfied with the stationing of American troops upon its territory," but should be regarded as a friend and ally to be furnished equipment so that its own Army could defend areas vital to the United States and Brazil.[12] Welles in Washington had agreed to ask Vargas to permit the stationing of

[7] Sumner Welles in Department of State, *Foreign Relations of the United States, 1942*, V, 633.

[8] Despatch, Ambassador Caffery, Rio, to U.S. Secretary of State, January 16, 1942.

[9] Division of the American Republics, U.S. State Department memorandum, February 6, 1942.

[10] The letters are given in Ministério das Relações Exteriores (Ministry of Foreign Relations), *Relatório de 1942*, pp. 120–123.

[11] *Ibid.*, p. 6.

[12] Department of State, *Foreign Relations of the United States, 1942*, V, 635.

United States troops in northeast Brazil, but he quickly decided it would be "inexpedient" to make the request. It seemed evident he would be doing well to get Vargas to overrule the military on the single point of breaking relations with the Axis. Although Welles had just delivered a personal letter in which Roosevelt assured Vargas that "before long we shall be able to supply you with the equipment,"[13] cables were soon humming with new promises.

Upon reaching Rio, Welles had cabled Secretary Hull agreeing that "if the Argentine government is unwilling to join in a continental declaration for a severence of relations with the Axis powers, Argentina should be allowed to proceed alone." While the Argentines gave Welles trouble, Vargas, Aranha, and the Foreign Ministers of Uruguay and Bolivia pleaded against a rupture in the American family of nations which would antagonize Argentina and leave Argentina and Chile "the foci of Axis agents and of subversive activities directed primarily against neighboring countries."[14]

Needing a clear understanding with influential Brazil, Welles arranged to see Getúlio. As was his way with United States diplomats, Getúlio came to the point quickly, appeared reasonable and frank, and left little doubt that he made the decisions in Brazil. The Brazilian military, he said, had called his attention to the problem Brazil would have in defending the south in case it got into war with the Axis and had to contend with an ambitious, pro-Axis Argentina. Vargas said he wanted three things: the weapons and mechanized equipment on which the Army was insisting, a commitment of the United States to defend Brazil should the need arise, and, lastly, a Rio Conference formula which the Argentine government would support. After Welles assured Vargas on the first two points, Vargas told him that if the foreign ministers arrived at the formula he had mentioned, Brazil would break relations with the Axis before the Conference ended.[15]

The formula adopted unanimously at Itamarati Palace on the evening of January 23 satisfied the Argentines and Chileans because it "recommended," rather than "required," the break in relations. When Secretary Hull heard about it in Washington, he considered it so serious a "surrender" to Argentina that he spoke by phone to Welles more sharply than

[13] Conn and Fairchild, *The Framework of Hemisphere Defense*, p. 313.

[14] Department of State, *Foreign Relations of the United States, 1942*, V, 37 and 42.

[15] Sumner Welles, *Seven Decisions That Shaped History*, pp. 110–111.

he had "ever spoken to anyone in the Department."[16] But Welles, told by Hull to repudiate the arrangement he had just made, appealed to Roosevelt, who decided that "the judgment of the man on the spot" should prevail. This settled, during the next few days Peru, Uruguay, Bolivia, and Paraguay broke with the Axis in spite of Hull's gloomy prediction that Welles had been "taken in" by promises.[17]

Finally, at the closing session on the evening of January 28, Aranha spoke. He praised democracy and announced that a few hours earlier Vargas had ordered the break in diplomatic and commercial relations with the Axis powers.

[16] Cordell Hull, *The Memoirs of Cordell Hull*, p. 1148.
[17] Sumner Welles, *Seven Decisions That Shaped History*, pp. 116–117.

7. The Roosevelt-Vargas Alliance in Early 1942

At the Rio Conference the discussions about economic co-operation went well for the Brazilians. Vargas decided to send Finance Minister Souza Costa to Washington to conclude arrangements for United States help for the Itabira iron mines, Brazilian rubber production, and the development of Brazilian natural resources, strategic and otherwise.[1]

On leaving Brazil, Souza Costa remarked to Caffery that the principal object of his trip was the "procurement of necessary armaments." But he and the Brazilian Army's representative in Washington had poor luck at first. When Aranha, in Rio, saw a cable listing the equipment available to Brazil, he called it "the old run-around." "You are dumping a lot of trucks on us," he said to Caffery. "Tell Welles he had better just file this away and forget it."[2]

After Souza Costa had expressed his complete dissatisfaction and Welles had indicated that he would support the Brazilian position, the argument was settled by a decision of Harry Hopkins,[3] head of the new Munitions Allocations Board. Planes were to be turned over quickly, and tanks and antiaircraft guns (some of them taken from the defenses of New York harbor) were to be furnished. The Lend-Lease Agreement of October 1941 was replaced by a new one which raised to $200 million

[1] Ministério das Relações Exteriores, *Relatório de 1942*, pp. 33–36.
[2] Department of State, *Foreign Relations of the United States, 1942*, V, 641.
[3] Conn and Fairchild, *The Framework of Hemisphere Defense*, p. 315.

the value of weapons which Brazil was to receive by paying, between 1943 and 1948, 35 per cent of the value.[4] After Vargas discussed these new developments with Dutra, he was able to wire Souza Costa that he was fully satisfied.

In the case of the rich iron ore at Itabira, Minas Gerais, the Washington Accords of March 3 doomed the effort of an American entrepreneur, Percival Farquhar, who for twenty-three years had struggled to overcome nationalistic opposition to large-scale exportation by foreign private enterprise.[5] Under the Washington Accords, the British, using wartime powers, were to expropriate the Itabira Iron Company and present the mines to the Brazilian government; Brazil would expropriate the creaky narrow-gauge railway used for moving the ore to Vitória, Espírito Santo; and the Export-Import Bank would lend Brazil $14 million to improve the rail line and ore-loading facilities.[6] Britain and the United States Metals Reserve, short of rich, low-phosphorus iron ore, overoptimistically agreed to purchase 750,000 tons of it annually for three years from the newly formed Brazilian government-controlled Companhia Vale do Rio Doce. Vargas, speaking at the uncompleted Volta Redonda steel plant in May, 1943, reminded his hearers that the 1930 revolution had been a nationalistic one, and he pointed with pride to the steel company and to the way his Administration had prevented an "international monopoly" from controlling the potentially important Itabira iron-ore exports.[7]

The Souza Costa mission to Washington covered itself with glory. The Export-Import Bank offered up to $100 million to develop raw materials in Brazil, and the Rubber Reserve Company raised its buying price and put up $5 million to increase rubber output in the Amazon Valley. Brazil visualized itself producing airplane engines at the government-owned Fábrica Nacional de Motores, near Rio, with the help of Wright Aeronautical Corporation.

Most of the financial assistance and Lend-Lease deliveries allocated by Washington to Latin America during the war years went to Brazil.[8] As a result of the Washington Accords of March 3 and the further agreements negotiated in 1942. Brazil was assured sales of coffee and cacao even when

[4] Department of State, *Foreign Relations of the United States, 1942*, V, 815–818.

[5] Charles A. Gauld, *The Last Titan: Percival Farquhar*, pp. 281–324.

[6] Ministério das Relações Exteriores, *Relatório de 1942*, p. 34.

[7] Getúlio Vargas, *A Nova Política do Brasil*, X, 54.

[8] Regarding Lend-Lease, see Conn and Fairchild, *The Framework of Hemisphere Defense*, p. 329.

they could not be shipped. Scarce United States chemicals, farm equipment, rayon, and steel products were allocated to Brazil.[9]

Soon after the Washington Accords were signed Vargas allowed the United States to station several hundred Army maintenance personnel in the Northeast, improve airports, construct buildings and roads, and engage in unrestricted flights in certain areas.[10] By that time LATI no longer flew to Brazil, and Condor was in the process of becoming a Brazilian company.

Brazil still opposed having a large United States force in the Northeast. It made this clear again in May 1942, when a military co-operation agreement was signed setting up Mixed Commissions in Washington and Rio. But by then the United States Army was coming around to the Brazilian view that the burden of defense should rest with Lend-Lease-armed Brazilian troops.

The Germans protested that the use of Brazilian air bases for flying United States military to Africa was a violation of Brazil's neutrality. But their objections were ignored. More and more attention was being given to making the Brazilian bulge a great link in the air route across the Atlantic. While Recife became a large base used by the United States Navy, there was tremendous activity at the air bases of Belém, Fortaleza, Recife, Salvador, and particularly Natal.

[9] Frederic W. Ganzert, "Wartime Economic Conditions," in *Brazil* (Lawrence F. Hill, ed.), p. 313.
[10] Conn and Fairchild, *The Framework of Hemisphere Defense,* p. 317.

8. Alterations in the Administrative Team

The June 1941 modification of the Cabinet, which had remained unchanged since Aranha joined it in March 1938, resulted from differences between Vargas and São Paulo *interventor* Ademar de Barros. The ambitious Ademar turned out to have a strong mind of his own and a flair for using bulldozing tactics to get things done. He was opposed not only by state Democratic leaders but also by some of the Republicans. He dismissed his state Finance Secretary, who then went to Vargas with a great dossier of accusations, describing the *interventor* as guilty of graft and recalling a vitriolic speech made by Ademar against Vargas in 1934.[1]

[1] Viriato de Castro, *O Ex-Leão de São Manoel: Adhemar,* Ch. 2; Carlos Castilho Cabral, *Tempos de Jânio e Outros Tempos,* p. 33.

The appointment of Agriculture Minister Fernando Costa to replace Ademar called for other Cabinet changes. The Paulista Republicans this time got the Labor Ministry, but the lawyer who filled the post, Alexandre Marcondes Filho, showed few of the conservative characteristics of pre-1930 Paulista Republicanism. Getúlio, who appreciated the political importance of the industrial workers of São Paulo, told Marcondes that the country needed a Labor Minister familiar with São Paulo because so much of São Paulo's labor force originated in Axis countries.[2] The Estado Nôvo's first Labor Minister, from the Northeast, was named to the Supreme Court but the Northeast continued with Cabinet representation when it got the Agriculture post vacated by Fernando Costa.

Justice Minister Francisco Campos had lost major battles when Aranha entered the Cabinet and when censorship and propaganda were removed from his supervision. His book *O Estado Nacional*, published in 1940, had created a furor in the Americas,[3] to the dismay of Aranha. It had pictured democracy as a fantasy, a negative concept of the nineteenth century which was incapable of solving current problems and was useful only to reactionaries. And it had praised Hitler for his leadership of the masses,[4] who, Campos had observed, should be kept in a permanent state of excitement. "The only people who have any doubts about the advance of the totalitarian system are those who live in a fairyland of wishful thinking." "For political decisions, a legislative chamber has today the same importance as a room in a museum."[5]

"Every people," Campos had written, "clamors for a Caesar."[6] But the Vargas technique never seemed Caesar-like to Campos, who resigned due to ill health late in 1941. When the resignation was not accepted, he took an extended sick leave, and his top aide, Vasco Leitão da Cunha, became Acting Justice Minister.

Down from Petrópolis on May 1, 1942, for his annual pronouncement to labor at Vasco da Gama Stadium, Getúlio suffered an automobile accident, which fractured his jawbone, hand, and thighbone. The repair work on the jawbone was temporarily disfiguring, making him reluctant to re-

---

[2] Alexandre Marcondes Filho, interview, August 8, 1963 (written up in Marcondes Filho's memorandum of September 3, 1963).

[3] *The New York Times,* dateline Buenos Aires, October 5, 1940.

[4] Francisco Campos, *O Estado Nacional, Sua Estructura, Seu Conteudo Ideologico*, p. 29.

[5] *Ibid.,* p. 28.

[6] *Ibid.,* p. 17.

ceive visitors, and the broken hip kept him in bed into the month of July with his leg suspended.[7]

Getúlio was convalescing when he had to settle the dispute between Acting Justice Minister Leitão da Cunha and Police Chief Filinto Müller. Müller, who did not like taking instructions from the Justice Ministry, had opposed the holding of a pro-United States Fourth of July parade by students. He had been put under forty-eight–hour house arrest by Leitão da Cunha,[8] a supporter of the parade. The parade, held in the pouring rain, had produced lusty cheers for Vargas, Roosevelt, Aranha, and Leitão da Cunha.

Partisans lined up behind Müller or Leitão da Cunha, turning the contest into one between "the two camps which at the beginning of May 1942 struggled for the succession to Vargas."[9]

Dutra led the camp which supported the Police Chief. It included the anti-Vargas press, which liked the War Minister's opposition to DIP Director Lourival Fontes. The *Diário Carioca*'s José Eduardo de Macedo Soares got no satisfaction from Ambassador Caffery, who was accomplishing his job by giving no encouragement to Vargas foes. In its quest for freedom the anti-Vargas press turned to the British Embassy.

Aranha led the camp which supported Acting Justice Minister Leitão da Cunha, and Justice Minister Campos wired his support. This group included Lourival Fontes; also Rio state *interventor* Ernâni do Amaral Peixoto, husband of Alzira Vargas. The American ambassador, seldom kind in his remarks about José Eduardo de Macedo Soares, saw the newspaper publisher less interested in press freedom than in replacing Amaral Peixoto as head of Rio state. As for the honeymoon between the press and the British Embassy, Caffery attributed it to lavish British subsidies.[10]

After careful study Getúlio handled the Leitão da Cunha-Filinto Müller squabble by accepting the resignations of Justice Minister Campos, Acting Justice Minister Leitão da Cunha, Police Chief Müller, and DIP Director Fontes. Aranha was delighted when a close Gaúcho friend became police chief. Dutra was equally pleased to be able to name an Army

---

[7] Alzira Vargas do Amaral Peixoto, Ch. 8 of "A Vida de Getúlio . . .," in *Fatos & Fotos*, August 3, 1963; cable, Ambassador Caffery to U.S. Secretary of State, July 15, 1942.

[8] Vasco Leitão da Cunha, interview, June 24, 1966.

[9] Alzira Vargas do Amaral Peixoto, Ch. 8 of "A Vida de Getúlio . . .," in *Fatos & Fotos*, August 3, 1963.

[10] Cable, Ambassador Caffery to U.S. Secretary of State, July 20, 1942.

man to head press censorship. Labor Minister Marcondes Filho, the new star in the Cabinet, added the Justice post to his responsibilities.

Neither the new DIP director nor the new police chief was effective in his post. Müller's successor, preparing to step up action against a spy ring reported by the American Embassy, complained that he could trust no one in the Police Department, and he added that Müller's people had burned up all the papers and "wrecked the place."[11]

A Hamburg radio broadcast lamented the removal of Müller, Campos, and Fontes,[12] perhaps not appreciating that the ex-head of the DIP had for a year and a half worked with Aranha against Dutra. The round had really ended in a draw between the two camps, neither of which considered itself anti-United States. Dutra, while claiming to be just as pro-United States as Aranha, kept making the point that Brazil was in no condition to be pushed into war.

Both Aranha and Dutra scolded the United States for the gasoline shortage. The lack of tankers was given as the reason for the regulation of July 1942 rationing fuel for delivery vehicles and banning its use for all private automobiles except those of high government officials and top diplomats. But the regulations were announced when food shortages and inflation were becoming noticeable and just when Brazilians were discussing a United States gasoline shipment to Argentina. Brazil, Aranha said, was doing everything the United States asked; he inaccurately added that Brazil was often penalized and Argentina often rewarded.

[11] Cable, Ambassador Caffery to U.S. Secretary of State, July 23, 1942.
[12] Cable, Ambassador Caffery to U.S. Secretary of State, July 22, 1942.

BOOK VIII

BRAZIL AT WAR,
1942–1945

1. Brazil Declares War on Germany and Italy

 SOON AFTER Brazil broke relations with the Axis several Brazilian ships were torpedoed as they carried merchandise to and from the United States.

There was a violent reaction in March 1942, when it was learned that fifty-three lives had been lost aboard the *Cairu*, sunk between Norfolk and New York.[1] Cariocas swarmed through Rio's streets, intent on attacking German-owned stores, most of which were saved when their owners pulled down the steel shutters. In the south, too, anti-German groups wanted to be heard. There were protests in Rio Grande, and Hitler's effigy was buried in Santa Catarina. Vargas on March 12 ordered the confiscation of 30 per cent of the funds of Axis subjects in Brazil. Total Axis property in the country, including large Japanese land concessions in the interior, was estimated to be worth half a billion dollars. German, Italian, and Japanese credits with the Bank of Brazil, frozen immediately after Brazil broke with the Axis, did not form a part of this estimate.

During May, June, and July 1942 twenty-six persons perished on eight

[1] Manoel Thomaz Castello Branco, *O Brasil na II Grande Guerra*, pp. 54–58.

Brazilian ships sunk in the Atlantic off northern South America.[2] Then suddenly in three days, August 15–17, there was a massive attack designed to fill Brazil with fear. Within twenty miles of the northeastern states of Bahia and Sergipe, over six hundred lives were lost as five Brazilian ships went down, one of them carrying pilgrims to the São Paulo Eucharistic Congress, another carrying 120 soldiers. The atrocities brought Vice-Admiral Jonas H. Ingram, based at Trinidad, in pursuit of the Germans. Roosevelt declared: "This despicable and barbarous act, in complete disregard of all civilized and chivalrous conduct, is absolutely useless in its desperate effort to coerce and intimidate the free people of Brazil . . ."

Demonstrations occurred throughout Brazil. In Vitória, where mobs paraded behind a picture of Vargas, a German bar and the Bayer agency were stoned. In the capital of Santa Catarina, crowds destroyed the furnishings of some Germans and then, cheering the American Consulate, forced German shop-owners to shout "Viva o Brasil!" The demonstrations in Pernambuco on the eighteenth began in fairly orderly fashion. After gathering at the dock section, crowds of students and office workers moved from one German firm to another, tearing down signs and carrying them to the deposit of the Metal Campaign for the Brazilian Navy. Then laborers and vagrants jointed the activities, breaking down the steel shutters of about twenty stores and looting them completely before the police decided to appear.

In Pôrto Alegre, Luso-Brazilians, long resenting the more prosperous German-Brazilians who were inclined to hold themselves superior to their environment, went far beyond what authorities thought a proper "safety valve" display. The depredations, which began on the eighteenth, showed advance planning and private vengeance on the nineteenth. The authorities stepped in.[3]

In Rio on the eighteenth crowds demonstrated in front of the gates of Guanabara Palace, calling for "war" and "revenge." Getúlio, who had not been seen in public since May 1, was in the Palace, experimenting at walking with a cane. After ordering the Personal Guard to open the gates, he dressed to make an appearance.[4]

In his customary serious tone Vargas praised the sentiments of the

[2] Ibid.

[3] U.S. Consulate, Pôrto Alegre, report, August 29, 1942.

[4] Alzira Vargas do Amaral Peixoto, Ch. 8 of "A Vida de Getúlio . . .," in Fatos & Fotos, August 3, 1963.

demonstrators. He did not promise war, but said that Brazil would confiscate aggressor nation ships in Brazilian ports and make further use of assets of Axis subjects. Spies, fifth columnists, those who had informed about the movements of the ships which had been sunk, all who had worked against Brazil, would be sent with picks and shovels to open roads in the Brazilian interior. Vargas told his listeners to return to their homes, holding their heads high. The flag of Brazil would not be humiliated, for "Brazil is immortal."[5]

Dutra issued a statement condemning the "monstrously criminal" act which had killed so many defenseless Brazilians.

Vargas communicated with Roosevelt and then, on August 21, authorized Aranha to send off notes telling the governments of Germany and Italy that the acts of war practiced against Brazil had created a state of belligerency. After a full Cabinet meeting on the twenty-second, a public announcement disclosed that Brazil was at war with Germany and Italy. Japan, it was "unofficially" reported, had committed no aggression.

The war declaration transformed the people's anger into a sober contemplation of what lay ahead.[6] It solidified the position of Vargas, honored by labor-union parades.[7] Caffery reported: "The ex-office holders, whose hopes were so high a few weeks ago, are very sad again: Vargas' recent actions and especially his declaration of war have put him completely on top, to their discomfort."[8] Virgílio de Melo Franco asked Vargas for a position where he could serve the nation and was put in charge of the confiscated German Transatlantic Bank. Communists who had worked for the 1935 rebellion came from Uruguay and Argentina to offer their services to the armed forces, but they were jailed.[9]

The question of administrative organization of forces in the Northeast was finally worked out in November 1942, following the recommendations of the Joint Brazil-United States Defense Commission. Brazil would be responsible for the defense of her territory and the protection of military establishments there; coastal-area defense would be the joint responsibility of the Brazilian and the United States forces. But the authority and responsibility for co-ordinating all the work by all the forces, and for protecting navigation, would be in the hands of Admiral Ingram, whose

[5] Getúlio Vargas, *A Nova Política do Brasil,* IX, 227–228.
[6] U.S. Consulate, Pôrto Alegre, report, August 29, 1942.
[7] U.S. Consulate, Pará, report, September 8, 1942.
[8] Cable, Ambassador Caffery to U.S. Secretary of State, August 27, 1942.
[9] Carlos da Costa Leite and Meireles family, interview, September 6, 1963.

declaration that he was "Chief of the Allied Forces in the South Atlantic" was accepted by the Brazilians and the United States Army. He was, however, not to control the administration or discipline of the Brazilian forces.[10] Ingram's headquarters were in Recife, as were those of the Brazilian Army, Navy, and Air Force commanders in the area.

Also in Recife, General Robert L. Walsh established the headquarters of the United States Army Forces South Atlantic, but the 2,000 men under its command were on Britain's Ascension Island in the mid-Atlantic. Walsh's supremely important task was to direct a separate entity, the South Atlantic Wing of the United States Air Transport Command, headquartered in Natal. Natal was soon to become the world's busiest airport, with planes often landing at the rate of one every three minutes.[11] Four-engine planes, after loading up at Natal with high octane gasoline, made the hop directly to Africa; two-engine planes, a majority, refueled at Ascension Island.[12]

General Walsh, who had pushed for United States aid in setting up the airplane motor factory near Rio, was well regarded by Brigadeiro Eduardo Gomes, in charge of Brazilian air activity in the Northeast. Relations between Brazilian and United States forces were generally good, but there were occasional disagreements between men under pressure to get a great deal done quickly. When the United States Air Transport Company bought some land for an air base, Gomes had the Brazilian government expropriate the land so that it would not be in foreign hands. Not all the decisions of straight-laced Gomes seemed as reasonable as this one to some of the air-base people from the United States.[13]

[10] Manoel Thomaz Castello Branco, *O Brasil na II Grande Guerra*, p. 88.
[11] Vincent de Vicq de Cumptich, interview, July 9, 1963.
[12] Bascombe W. James, interview, June 17, 1963.
[13] Vincent de Vicq de Cumptich, interview, July 9, 1963.

2. Some Problems for João Alberto

In August 1942, Vargas accepted the suggestion of Luís Simões Lopes, civil service administrator, for the creation of a new organization with authority to co-ordinate economic mobilization. Thus in September, ex-Police Chief João Alberto, who had recently been head of a Council on Foreign Trade and minister to Canada, became Co-ordinator of Economic Mobilization. A sort of "economic czar," he was assigned powers over production, exports, imports, transportation, distribution, prices, and rationing.[1]

Besides running into complaints from those unfavorably affected by his decrees, the tall, genial Army-man-turned-diplomat had to contend with Finance Minister Souza Costa, who hesitated to appropriate funds for the new office, feeling that João Alberto was encroaching on his prerogatives. João Alberto, reporting to Vargas that the "liberal economic machine is absolutely incapable of meeting the exigencies of war," added that the Finance Minister had fallen down on his job.[2]

The Co-ordinator's severest problems were due to the scarcity of imports. Even though half the space on the limited number of freighters reaching Brazil was used for petroleum and coal, these fuel imports were down to 40 per cent of normal.[3] The sudden upsurge in usage of high-ash national coal, whose annual production went from one to two million tons during the war, contributed to the transportation strain. The railroads entered the war in poor condition and came out of it in great need of new equipment and repair.

The discovery of petroleum in Brazil—made in January 1939 outside Salvador, Bahia, by drillers contracted by the Agriculture Ministry's Department of Minerals—was a notable achievement of the Estado Nôvo. But as much development work was needed, the discovery came too late to help in the emergency. Morris L. Cooke, head of a Washington-appointed commission to deal with the economic impact of the war on Brazil, wrote that "the scarcity of petroleum products in Brazil has brought the effects of the war home to more people than anything else."[4] Some got their cars to go by using contraptions known as *gasogênios*, which produced gas from charcoal. Trucks and taxis were limited to 70 per cent of the fuel they had used in 1941.[5] Mixing alcohol with motor fuel had been required since 1931 to reduce imports and help sugar growers, and now the proportion of alcohol exceeded 75 per cent.[6] Diesel oil was replaced by expensive cottonseed oil.

[1] Manoel Thomaz Castello Branco, *O Brasil na II Grande Guerra*, pp. 67–77.

[2] Despatch from Walter Donnelly (counselor of Embassy for Economic Affairs) to U.S. Secretary of State, June 8, 1943.

[3] Morris Llewellyn Cooke, *Brazil on the March: A Study in International Cooperation*, Ch. 8.

[4] *Ibid.*, p. 164.

[5] Frederic W. Ganzert, "Wartime Economic Conditions," in *Brazil* (Lawrence F. Hill, ed.), p. 317.

[6] George Wythe, *Brazil: An Expanding Economy*, p. 149; Morris L. Cooke, *Brazil on the March*, p. 176.

Almost every product was in demand at what seemed good prices. Brazil was buzzing with men battling fuel and equipment shortages to establish new industries and get strategic minerals from the ground. Quartz crystals for radar were all the rage and for a while were the favorite of speculators.

The "Battle of Rubber" was under way. With ample United States funds, João Alberto was supposed to move 50,000 men from the impoverished Northeast to Amazônia so that they could tap some of the millions of wild hevea trees scattered about roughly one per acre.[7] Remote rubber-producing areas were to be opened along the lonely headwaters and creeks; barracks and airfields were to be constructed; tools, foods, and medicines were to be made available.

Brazilian rubber had long been fascinating to discuss but anything but fascinating to gather.[8] Manaus' $2-million opera house was a reminder of the days before 1912, when Amazônia had dominated the world rubber market, importing luxuries and exporting as much as thirty-nine thousand tons of rubber per year at prices which went over two dollars a pound. Ever since Far Eastern plantations had killed the brief boom, there had been dreams, frequently mentioned by Vargas, of reviving the region, from which only eighteen thousand tons of rubber were shipped in 1941.[9]

Under the five-year rubber agreement signed on March 3, 1942, the United States Rubber Reserve Company was to get all rubber not needed for Brazilian domestic purposes, paying at Belém thirty-nine cents per pound for top grade. In spite of price increases and premiums for any excess over five thousand tons delivered, the Rubber Reserve Company found it impossible to enforce the clause giving it exclusive right to amounts above ten thousand tons, the maximum felt necessary for Brazil's annual needs. Suddenly the Brazilian rubber-products industry came to life. Crude rubber and rubber goods, particularly tires, found their way to other South American countries in violation of quotas established by the United States.[10]

The rubber program's main difficulty lay in obstacles to increasing production. The first rural workers from Ceará had as bad an experience

[7] Note from Charles A. Gauld, April, 1965. Conversation with Charles H. T. Townsend, Jr., December 23, 1966.

[8] See Vicki Baum, *The Weeping Wood.*

[9] U.S. Consulate, Belém, report, January 5, 1942.

[10] Department of State, *Foreign Relations of the United States, 1942,* V, 698–729.

as their predecessors forty years earlier. They were stuffed in the hold of a ship with a little advance travel money, and when they reached Amazonas they found both man and nature hostile.[11] João Alberto was able to move only 12,000 men—not the 50,000 originally contemplated. Considered "barbarians" in their host areas, they were soon furnished barracks by the United States government, which even sent troupes of entertainers to brighten their lives.[12] But few ended tapping rubber. Some died; most returned to their homes, many of them sick.[13]

The men who held the key to reaching the overburdened experienced tappers were the old-time traders with their river boats. Sullen about the invasion, they were described by the armies of United States technicians as corrupt exploiters.[14] But it was to them that the program finally turned, with offers for rubber as high as a dollar a pound at some points of the interior.[15] Production reached twenty-nine thousand tons in 1944 (compared with the United States hope of forty thousand), a little of this, as was traditional, finding its way from Bolivia.

One of the largest factors adding to Brazil's contribution of rubber to the Allied cause came when a cargo ship, on its way to Germany from the Far East, was sunk in in Brazilian waters, yielding a sizable amount of baled rubber.[16] As for the high-cost roads built in the interior by the Rubber Development Corporation, it was felt they would be useful in case war developments should make it necessary to build air bases there.

[11] U.S. Consulate, Manaus, report, July 14, 1942; U.S. Consulate, Belém, report, March 9, 1942.

[12] Jefferson Caffery, interview, August 4, 1964.

[13] Conversation with Estanislau Fischlowitz, April 12, 1965.

[14] Department of State, *Foreign Relations of the United States, 1943*, V, 680–683.

[15] S. Maurice McAshan, Jr., interview, May 27, 1963.

[16] *Ibid.*

3. The Brazilian Expeditionary Force

The ailing Góis became critical of the Brazilian military. It was doing nothing, he said privately, to carry out its part of a program he had presented to Navy Secretary Frank Knox in Rio in September, 1942.[1]

Getúlio, lunching with members of the Armed Forces on the last day of 1942, was less pessimistic: "Since the sorrowful days of August our

[1] Lourival Coutinho, *O General Góes Depõe*, p. 386.

collaboration with allied nations has been continuous and efficient. We have not limited ourselves to furnishing strategic materials. The use of our shoreline, the base of operations for transporting arms and men to the theaters of war, has made possible the magnificent achievements in North Africa, the first step of the great victory." Vargas referred to the accomplishments of the Merchant Marine, the Navy, and the Air Force. After speaking of the good work of the Army, he said: "We must consider the responsibilities of action outside the continent." Such an action, he added, should not be "restricted to a simple expedition of symbolic contingents."[2]

These words surprised Dutra and Góis. Vargas had high ideals for Brazil, but he dwelt on practical considerations when Góis, sent by Dutra to find out what it was all about, visited the summer palace at Petrópolis. Washington, Vargas explained, was making it clear that nations whose troops were fighting had priority in getting United States arms. "In view of Dutra's insistence" about arms, Vargas had authorized Brazil's top Army men in Washington to say that Brazil was prepared to send soldiers overseas.[3]

Dutra started planning with eagerness, and, within six days of Vargas' year-end talk, he had a memorandum for his chief, stating that the expeditionary force should be a large one.[4]

In February 1943, Vargas left the bedside of his dying youngest child, Getúlio Filho, to take a plane to Natal. Roosevelt, flying home from the Casablanca conference with Churchill, was making an unexpected stop at "the air funnel to the battlefields of the world."[5]

As the Natal meeting had been kept secret, there was no end of surprise when United States and Brazilian personnel at the bases saw the two Presidents riding around in a jeep to inspect military installations. Roosevelt, Vargas, Harry Hopkins, and Caffery then dined on a destroyer. As at an earlier meeting, when Roosevelt had stopped at Rio on his way to the Buenos Aires conference late in 1936, the two Presidents conversed in French.[6] Roosevelt discussed developments in Africa and suggested that Brazil become a member of the United Nations. Vargas agreed, adding: "However, this might be an opportune moment to say again that we

  [2] Getúlio Vargas, *A Nova Política do Brasil,* IX, 325.
  [3] Lourival Coutinho, *O General Góes Depõe,* pp. 387–388.
  [4] José Caó, *Dutra,* pp. 145–146.
  [5] Conn and Fairchild, *The Framework of Hemisphere Defense,* p. 326.
  [6] Jefferson Caffery, interview, August 4, 1964.

need equipment from you for our military, naval and air force."[7] When the Americans spoke of the possibility of Brazil's sending troops to the Azores and Madeira, Vargas spoke of the need of equipping them.

Although Roosevelt offered to provide medical help for Vargas' son, it was too late to arrest the fatal paralysis. The death of the attractive "Getulinho" in his early twenties had a profound effect on his parents. Darci, Vargas' trim, chic wife, was never the same after the tragedy and devoted herself from that time almost exclusively to charitable works. As for the boy's father, Alzira writes that "his assurance and self-confidence were destroyed."[8] In his work he was aided less than formerly by the cheerful word of Darci.

On March 15, 1943, the President got around to approving Dutra's memorandum about an expeditionary force. "This operation," Vargas wrote, "is dependent on the receipt of war material we need both for outfitting the expeditionary force and for the troops which must remain to protect our own territory."[9]

Aside from the military contribution, the use of Brazilian troops in the fighting theater would give a great lift to the prestige of the Good Neighbor Policy and Brazil. There were some reservations in the United States Army, but they were overcome in April 1943 when General Marshall gave his approval.[10] Half the equipment necessary for one division would be sent to Brazil for training purposes, and the Brazilian divisions, once overseas, would be re-equipped by the United States.

Dutra at first had in mind a force of 100,000 men distributed among five divisions. Early in August he invited João Batista Mascarenhas de Morais, the quiet general who headed the Second Military Region, to command one division. Then Dutra sped to the United States with a letter from Vargas to Roosevelt telling of the "desire of the Brazilian Army to take an active part in the war."[11] In Washington it was decided that the Brazilians would send 60,000 men to North Africa starting in mid-1944.

Back in Rio, Dutra requested and received an appointment from Vargas to head the Fôrça Expedicionária Brasileira (FEB). Almost everything

[7] Department of State, *Foreign Relations of the United States, 1943*, V, 656.
[8] Alzira Vargas do Amaral Peixoto, Ch. 8 of "A Vida de Getúlio . . .," in *Fatos & Fotos*, August 3, 1963.
[9] José Caó, *Dutra*, p. 146.
[10] Conn and Fairchild, *The Framework of Hemisphere Defense*, p. 328.
[11] Telegram, Ambassador Caffery, Rio, to U.S. Secretary of State, August 9, 1943.

about Dutra's plans, including the men being considered for division and regiment commanders, seemed mediocre to the critical Góis. Bitter at "the errors of the regime" and citing his failing health, Góis resigned as Army Chief of Staff and accepted an appointment from Aranha to go to Montevideo as a special ambassador to the Committee of Emergency and Political Defense of the Americas.[12]

As he had a year earlier, Vargas lunched with military officers on December 31, 1943. Stressing his favorite theme, the unification of Brazil, he pointed out that the Expeditionary Force was made up of contingents from every state.

First Division Commander Mascarenhas de Morais returned in January 1944 from an inspection tour of the Mediterranean area, and then his division engaged in long marches in the Rio district. Reflecting the pride of all Brazilians, Vargas in May 1944 attended the maneuvers at one of the camps. By then the Axis had been forced out of North Africa; Italy, where the Brazilians were to go, had been taken over by hard-fighting Germans. After watching Osvaldo Cordeiro de Farias' divisional artillery display its skill, Vargas anounced: "We are certain to come out victorious very soon." The scales of victory, he said, had been tipped in favor of the Allies when the vast United States industrial potential had been thrown in. "Only nations sufficiently industrialized, and able to produce necessary war materials within their own borders, can really be considered military powers." Brazil, Vargas said, was making a start in that direction, and the completion after the war would be easy.[13]

Four days later, Vargas appeared in a pavilion constructed near the Rio obelisk to which some Gaúchos in 1930 had tied their horses. Getúlio watched the parade of the entire 25,000-strong First Division. He heard the cheers of the public . . . a public which was putting up with blackouts, gasoline shortages, and inflation. Dramatically he bade farewell to the Expeditionary soldiers. The hour had come for vengeance against those who in 1942 had used "pirate ships barbarously to massacre Brazilian lives." "Our Army, which has covered itself with honors in memorable deeds . . . will demonstrate its new arms and its traditional bravery on the battlefields of Europe." Vargas assured the soldiers that everything had been done to make sure they lacked nothing. "Your wives, mothers, sweethearts, and children confidently await your return. . . . The Nation is proud of your courage, your dedication. May God's blessings accompany

[12] Lourival Coutinho, *O General Góes Depõe*, p. 392.
[13] Getúlio Vargas, *A Nova Política do Brasil*, X, 299–301.

you, as our spirits and hearts accompany you until you return with victory."

Sea transport was supplied by the United States. Vargas, accompanied by Dutra, went aboard the *General Mann* on the night of June 30 to wish a good trip to General Euclides Zenóbio da Costa's first contingent of 5,400 men. But the fourteen-day voyage to Naples was a dull, melancholy affair.[14]

Two more contingents left in September 1944. The fourth and fifth echelons, sailing in November 1944 and February 1945, brought the remainder of Mascarenhas' First Division to Italy. With the decision not to train and transport the additional divisions which Dutra had contemplated, Mascarenhas became commander of the whole FEB.

The Brazilian Air Force (FAB) was represented in Italy by more than 400 men, including Getúlio's oldest son, Lieutenant Lutero Vargas. After training in Panama and the United States, the FAB sailed for Italy early in October 1944. As members of the First Pursuit Group, commanded by Major Nero Moura, these men became a part of the United States 350th Fighter Group and supported Allied ground activities magnificently with telling air attacks against German communications systems and defenses. Eight Brazilian pilots lost their lives.

In September 1944, the first FEB contingent joined General Willis D. Crittenberger's Fourth Corps, which was a part of General Mark Clark's Fifth Army. The Germans had retreated behind the formidable "Gothic Line," a mountainous defense across northern Italy. The Brazilians, their spirits high, devised a banner and slogan ("The snake is smoking"), and prepared to participate in difficult actions against Castelnuovo and Monte Castello. Before winter came on, attacks on both these strongholds had been rudely repelled, the Brazilians suffering over 300 casualties at Monte Castello.[15] By this time the second and third contingents from Rio had joined the first and all were under the direct command of Mascarenhas.

Winter was not an agreeable pause. FEB members, doing patrol work, suffered from unfamiliar cold and snow. In February 1945, after the Fourth Corps had been strengthened by the arrival of the United States Tenth Mountain Division, well trained for the difficult weather and terrain, Operation Encore got under way as a prelude to the big spring offensive. While United States forces were locked in furious combat at Monte della Torraccia, the Brazilians battled for Monte Castello. In Feb-

---

[14] Manoel Thomaz Castello Branco, *O Brasil na II Grande Guerra*, pp. 162–163.
[15] José Caó, *Dutra*, pp. 166–168.

ruary and March, when both Monte Castello and Castelnuovo fell, the victorious Brazilian regiments could reflect that storming these strongholds had cost, over the months, hundreds of Brazilian lives.

Then, along with their allies, the Brazilians pushed ahead.[16] In the toughest job done by the FEB,[17] the town of Montese was taken in April at a cost of 426 Brazilian casualties.

Later in April, when the Germans were in retreat, General Mascarenhas de Morais received the unconditional surrender of a German division— the first German division to surrender in Italy.[18] Soon afterwards the troops of Crittenberger's Fourth Corps entered Milan, where the corpses of Mussolini, his mistress, and others were hanging by their heels from a filling station girder. All the German forces in Italy surrendered on May 2.

Clark and Crittenberger had high praise for the Brazilian contribution in Italy and the Brazilians felt great admiration for these Americans. Of the 25,300 men sent to Italy by the FEB, 15,000 had participated in the fighting. Four hundred fifty-one had lost their lives and about 2,000 had been wounded in combat.

[16] See Headquarters IV Corps, U.S. Army, *The Final Campaign across Northwest Italy.*

[17] J. B. Mascarenhas de Moraes, *A F.E.B. pelo Seu Comandante*, p. 297; Vernon Walters, interview, May 14, 1965.

[18] Vernon Walters, "Why Brazil is Different" (MS).

4. "Father of the Brazilians"

Vargas usually skipped the state dinners which Foreign Minister Aranha staged so handsomely at Itamarati Palace. After a day's work at Catete, he liked to relax with a whiskey at Guanabara Palace in the company of family and close friends. After dining with them he would make his way to his workroom, often for conferences.

More and more he found it good to turn to his daughter Alzira and his younger brother Benjamim. Benjamim, who headed the Personal Guard and resided at Guanabara Palace, had business interests which excited little admiration, and he kept late hours. But his advice when Getúlio sought it seemed helpful, and around the end of 1942 Getúlio called on him, as he had before, to help iron out frictions in the São Paulo state government. Alzira, sparkling with intelligence, wit, and youthful charm, delighted any English-speaking visitor for whom she might be called in to translate. A valuable member of the presidential staff, she resided at Niterói, where her husband presided over the affairs of Rio state.

An almost endless list of decrees flowed from Vargas' desk. One required employers to pay half the normal wages to employees engaged in military service. Another forbade industrial workers to leave their jobs. In 1944, to step up output, a ten-hour workday was decreed with what it was hoped was fair pay for the excess over eight hours.

A host of complaints reached the Presidency. Cariocas, going meatless four days a week, objected that apparently ample supplies were available for hotels and restaurants. The invasion by all sorts of United States missions led one prominent Brazilian to warn Washington about the effects of "so many people knowing so much" and telling all to Brazilians with a patronizing air which assumed that Brazil could do nothing for herself.[1] Another Brazilian adviser to Washington declared in the United States that many of the Americans who "flaunted their own mannerisms" in Brazil, were "not mentally equipped" to be there.[2]

Aranha, determined to ship rubber to Chile, told Finance Minister Souza Costa that he would resign before breaking an agreement made between governments. After the United States called the shipment a breach of the rubber deal,[3] Aranha complained that the United States sought to treat Brazil like a "banana republic." Caffery had to report that since Brazil had declared war he was finding Aranha "harder and harder to handle" in economic matters.[4]

The Aranha-Dutra feud seemed to be simmering down. Early in 1943 Aranha advised Caffery that Dutra was co-operating wholeheartedly in the war effort. He added that Vargas had been right in retaining Dutra as War Minister. "I entirely agree with President Vargas that we do not want a popular War Minister. A popular War Minister might get ambitious and cause us no end of trouble."[5]

[1] Memorandum, Division of American Republics, State Department, November 9, 1942, re conversation with José Nabuco.

[2] Address of Hernane Tavares de Sá before the International Education Assembly at Frederick, Maryland, June 9, 1944 (as reported in *The New York Times,* June 10, 1944).

[3] Department of State, *Foreign Relations of the United States, 1942,* V, 722–729.

[4] Airgram, Ambassador Caffery, Rio, to U.S. Secretary of State, September 28, 1942.

[5] Despatch, Ambassador Caffery, Rio, to U.S. Secretary of State, February 23, 1943.

A frequent visitor to Getúlio's office was Finance Minister Souza Costa. A new arrangement was due for servicing the foreign debt and he wanted to settle the matter permanently. Reduced imports had built up Brazil's foreign exchange and the Finance Minister proposed applying $83 million to cut the face value of the principal by $340 million; he offered $33 million annually to pay interest on, and amortize, the remainder.[6] Although most of the Cabinet was apathetic, and Aranha said that Souza Costa was too liberal, discussions were carried on with British and United States bondholders late in 1943. After the usual tussle between the British and the Americans, whose holdings were largely in different issues, Vargas in November 1943 signed the decree which permanently took care of the foreign debt of the federal, state, and municipal governments. The holders of the indebtedness (two thirds of it sterling) had the choice of retaining the face value of their securities or accepting some cash in return for a reduction. Interest rates were revised downward from those originally contracted, particularly on issues where the holders chose to retain the original face values.

The most serious financial problem was dealing with wartime inflation.

Bolstering the value of the Brazilian currency had ceased being a fetish since Whitaker had left the Finance Ministry in 1931. Much of the world in the mid-1930's was concluding that a little inflation was preferable to austerity during depression. Attention to the Brazilian Northeast, and sizable public works (such as a start on broad President Vargas Avenue cutting through Rio) contributed to continuous federal-budget deficits. Living costs between 1934 and 1940 increased by about 6 per cent annually. The milreis, which depreciated in terms of the dollar in the 1930's, was renamed the "cruzeiro" late in 1942, and it had a value of between 5 cents and five and a half cents during the war years.

Every kind of inflationary pressure struck Brazil during the war, and by previous standards the cost of living soared. The federal budget continued unbalanced, but more serious were the effects of heavy United States spending in Brazil and the large favorable trade balances. By the end of 1946 Brazil had $800 million in gold and foreign exchange. The purchase of all this exchange meant the issuance of many billions of cruzeiros. Between the end of 1941 and the end of 1946 bank deposits and currency in circulation more than tripled, with living costs showing an increase averaging about 18 per cent per year.[7]

---

[6] Department of State, *Foreign Relations of the United States, 1943,* V, 722.
[7] See Oliver Ónody, *A Inflação Brasileira, 1820–1958,* p. 25.

Anti-inflationary measures included attempts to freeze prices and rents. Other steps sought to slow the growth in purchasing power by imposing new taxes and offering six billion cruzeiros worth of war bonds. The new taxes caused an outbreak of criticism of the Finance Minister, who was charged with "neglecting his responsibilities."[8] Unsuccessfully he tried to persuade wealthy Paulistas to buy the war bonds.[9] To dispose of them it was decreed that government employees had to take 3 per cent of their salaries in bonds, and income-tax payers had to purchase amounts equal to their income-tax payments in the preceding year.[10] With the auctioning to Brazilians of property belonging to Axis private citizens, bonds were set aside for the "Axis sellers."[11] An emergency excess-profits tax was enacted in January 1944, but concerns were exempt if they would buy certain amounts of "equipment certificates" to be used for importing machinery on a priority basis when the war ended.

Living costs, up 10 per cent in 1941 and 12 per cent in 1942, rose more steeply in 1943 in spite of anything Vargas, Souza Costa, or João Alberto could do. Getúlio, who was seeking to balance things fairly, had no alternative but to turn to wage increases, inflationary though they might be.

A call for decreed minimum wages had been enacted by Congress in 1937 and was included in the 1937 Constitution. Valdemar Falcão, the first Labor Minister of the Estado Nôvo, sent teams to discuss wage conditions with management and labor all over Brazil. The resulting decree of May 1, 1940, establishing different minima for different regions, was celebrated by Cariocas in Vasco da Gama Stadium. As he did annually, the President opened his speech there with the salutation "Workers of Brazil!" He stated that the minimum wage, a promise made in 1930, had been achieved after accurate studies, and would contribute to better health and productivity.[12] Three months later the Labor Ministry created the SAPS (Serviço de Alimentação da Previdência Social) to serve workers "nourishing food" at "reasonable" prices.[13]

The dictatorship's gift to labor, announced at the Stadium celebration

---

[8] Despatch from Counselor of Embassy for Economic Affairs, Rio, to U.S. Secretary of State, May 8, 1943.

[9] Cable, Ambassador Caffery, Rio, to U.S. Secretary of State, May 17, 1943.

[10] Frederic W. Ganzert, "Wartime Economic Conditions," in *Brazil*, p. 320; Bureau of Latin American Research (Washington), report, October 26, 1942.

[11] Enclosure sent with Despatch, Rio Embassy, to U.S. Secretary of State, July 13, 1943.

[12] Getúlio Vargas, *A Nova Política do Brasil*, VII, 293.

[13] *Brazil, 1946* (Ministry of Foreign Affairs), p. 230.

on May Day 1941, was a revised system of handling grievances and disputes. Soon after that, Paulista Marcondes Filho took over the Ministry. Finding over five hundred edicts on labor matters, he and his staff spent almost two years compiling them into a thick volume, one of the world's longest labor codes. Getúlio, who mentioned it in his annual address of of May 1, 1943, ordered Marcondes to get suggestions from representatives of employers and employees before making it official.[14] The Consolidação which Vargas gave Brazil in 1943 is largely still in force.

By 1943 inflation made the minimum wages of 1940 entirely inappropriate. Again the Labor Ministry made studies, and on November 10, 1943, Getúlio decreed the first nationwide increases. The new standards, particularly in Rio, more than covered the rise in living costs for those in the lowest bracket. Other decrees helped wage earners in all brackets, with increases ranging from 85 per cent for the poorest-paid to 10 per cent for those in the top bracket. After thus celebrating the sixth anniversary of the Estado Nôvo, Vargas inaugurated the magnificent new Finance Ministry building in Rio.

[14] Alexandre Marcondes Filho, interview, August 8, 1963, and his memorandum, September 3, 1963.

BOOK IX

THE FALL OF THE
DICTATOR

"The fashionable word
has become 'democracy'."

1. Forces for Democracy in Brazil

Not LONG BEFORE Brazil declared war Washington's director
of the Office of War Information, Archibald MacLeish, was
well impressed with a "Declaration of Principles" which had
appeared in Rio newspapers. What surprised MacLeish was that Lourival
Fontes forbade editorial discussion of this eulogy of the Atlantic Charter
and of the fight for freedom.[1] From the State Department, MacLeish
later learned that the signers of the declaration were mostly Vargas foes.

Brazil's entry into the fight on the side of the Allies gave opponents of
the regime further opportunity to manifest support for antidictatorial
concepts. On January 1, 1943, the Society of the Friends of America was
launched at a meeting in Rio's Municipal Theater amid speeches glori-
fying men who had brought liberty to the continent. There was praise for
Aranha; also for Afrânio de Melo Franco, who had died a few hours before the Society held its inauguration and had been replaced as a director
of the Society by his son Virgílio.

For their president the "Friends of America" chose General Manoel
Rabelo, who had served as *interventor* of São Paulo in 1931. In visiting

[1] Archibald MacLeish, letter, July 9, 1942, to L. Duggan, re declaration appearing in Brazilian press on June 10, 1942.

chapters of the new society, which was attracting hordes of Communists, Rabelo incurred the wrath of Dutra. The Army commander in Recife asked Dutra not to allow Rabelo to visit his area because so many Communists were agitating under the cloak of the Friends of America.[2] The society organized an "Anti-Fascist Week" in May, 1943, and declared that liberty would be the theme of the discussions. Those who celebrated antifascism in Belo Horizonte had the inspiration of a message from Virgílio de Melo Franco.

In August, 1943, Mineiros and Cariocas withdrew from the National Juridical Congress on the ground that the Government interfered with free discussion. Soon after, Afonso Arinos de Melo Franco, Virgílio's younger brother, was having discussions with Odilon Braga, the Mineiro who quit as Agriculture Minister when the Estado Nôvo was born. They felt that Minas, locale of Tiradentes' ill-fated plot in 1789 to make Brazil independent, should strike a blow for democracy. Virgílio's office at the German Transatlantic Bank in Rio became a busy place.

The nine-page *Manifesto dos Mineiros* was signed by ninety prominent men of Minas. Among them was ex-President Artur Bernardes, who thus subscribed to the Manifesto's condemnation of political practices before 1930. Dated October 24, 1943, the thirteenth anniversary of the fall of Washington Luís, the document was widely circulated. Citing Tiradentes and the Atlantic Charter, the Mineiros declared that "a people reduced to silence and deprived of the faculty of thinking or expressing itself is a corroded organism. . . . If we fight against fascism at the side of the United Nations so that liberty and democracy may be restored to all people, certainly we are not asking too much in demanding for ourselves such rights and guarantees."[3]

The Manifesto, with its reference to "illusory tranquillity and superficial peace," was resented by Vargas. In his speech inaugurating the new Finance Ministry building, he assailed those who would stir up internal dissension: "We do not have time now to fritter away on the interpretation of ideological formulae or on the examination of what might be politically suitable in the way of elections." Every effort should be directed to winning the war. After that, Vargas said, "in an atmosphere of peace and order, with maximum guarantees for liberty of expression, we shall adjust the political structure to reflect fully the wish of the people. And to the organized working classes we shall give priority in finding national rep-

---

[2] Carolina Nabuco, *A Vida de Virgílio de Melo Franco,* p. 155.
[3] *Ibid.,* pp. 139–149.

resentation: the employers, workers, businessmen, farmers—new classes, full of vigor and hope." He derided "those restless makeshift reformers, well-known on the political scene for their backward tendencies," who were "unpatriotically disturbing" the war effort.[4]

Virgílio de Melo Franco lost the job Vargas had found him at the German Transatlantic Bank. Resigning also a number of directorships, he wrote to the Finance Minister that he was ashamed to be losing only some business posts whereas for the same ideas hundreds of young men were losing their lives. Vargas and "Governor" Valadares let the ax fall. Manifesto signers who held positions in federal- or state-controlled enterprises lost their jobs. So did some professors. A bank whose directors signed the Manifesto was put in the hands of the Minas government on the ground that it had been controlled by capitalists residing in German-occupied France.[5]

Enemies of the Vargas regime in São Paulo, Rio Grande, and Bahia had been reported to be drafting manifestos similar to that of the Mineiros. These manifestos never appeared, but some trouble developed in São Paulo when students observed November 10, 1943, by declaring that the FEB should not be sent abroad but should be used in Brazil to overthrow the Government. Those responsible were jailed.

Aranha, a strong proponent of democracy, decided to accept the vice-presidency of the Society of the Friends of America. But in October 1943 the Rio police prevented the Friends from holding the meeting at which Aranha was to be installed. Dutra and the Society's president, General Rabelo, kept jabbing at each other, Dutra finally persuading Vargas to issue a statement warning Rabelo "to refrain from any extraneous activities which might affect the high interest of national defense or cause dissension in the Army."[6]

Aranha spent the next months working for better relations with the Soviet Union, never diplomatically recognized by Brazil although the two countries were now wartime allies. In February 1944 he declared that "personally I believe that if an opportunity should arise our diplomatic relations with the Soviet Union will be re-established."[7] Diplomats looked to the United States or Mexico to bring Brazil and Russia together. However, Communism's friends in Mexico were not optimistic about Vargas.

[4] Getúlio Vargas, *A Nova Política do Brasil*, X, 175–179.

[5] Despatch, Counselor of Embassy, Rio, to U.S. Secretary of State, November 24, 1943.

[6] Cable, Ambassador Caffery, Rio, to U.S. Secretary of State, October 28, 1943.

[7] *The New York Times*, February 24, 1944 (dateline Rio, February 23).

When Luís Carlos Prestes' mother was dying in Mexico, Mexico's influential ex-President Lázaro Cárdenas cabled Vargas, urging that her son be allowed to visit her.[8] The idea did not appeal to Vargas, and when Prestes' mother died, her last wish denied, Mexican Communists were furious at what they called Vargas' "coldness."

To give "paper legality" to the plans of the regime, Justice and Labor Minister Marcondes Filho delivered a speech containing his own "personal" interpretation of the 1937 Constitution. He explained that with the declaration of war in August 1942 the President had suspended the clause establishing the six-year term of office. This meant that when the war was over Vargas would still have one year and two months to serve, during which period he would have to call for a plebiscite.[9]

Vargas himself was anxious to hold on to power at least until peace negotiations had been concluded. He felt that Brazil's contribution to the United Nations and his own friendship with Roosevelt would give Brazil an important voice in postwar affairs. But in the meantime he wanted the world to know that he respected democracy and freedom as well as law and order. In April 1944, at the inauguration of Rio's elaborate Brazilian Press Association building, he made this clear. *The New York Times* put the news on its front page: "Vargas Promises Brazil Democracy."

The right time, Vargas said, would be "when we are again in full possession of the benefits derived from peace." Then "we shall complete the institutional organs which are not yet operating. Through the freest and most complete means the people will then, without any kind of fear, declare themselves and choose their representatives, democratically and within law and order. Her war agreements honored, her normal rhythm restored, Brazil in peace will be governed in accordance with national desires."[10]

Press Club president Herbert Moses and hundreds of Rio newspapermen applauded for five minutes. But Vargas' record was such that commentators in the cafés described his promise as "qualified." *Continuismo* was denounced.[11]

Amid controversies about Soviet recognition and the Communist-infiltrated Society of the Friends of America, observers saw a movement of political support for Aranha, his prestige enhanced by international

[8] Carlos de Lima Cavalcanti, interview, August 1, 1963.
[9] Despatch, Counselor of Embassy, Rio, to U.S. Secretary of State, November 13, 1943.
[10] Getúlio Vargas, *A Nova Política do Brasil*, X, 282.
[11] *The New York Times*, July 13, 1944.

events. But, unlike the short, quiet War Minister, with whom his personality was in striking contrast, Aranha was becoming the hero of those who opposed the Vargas dictatorship.

Aranha and the Society of the Friends of America, still hoping to hold a public ceremony, found themselves harried not only by the police and Dutra's generals. The DIP ordered the press never to mention the society. After stories of the Foreign Minister's humiliations had gone the rounds, rumors had him losing his post. He got no backing from the President and finally wrote Getúlio, saying: "Nothing is left for me but that I leave the Ministry of my own accord, of which I am advising you and will advise our embassies." Ten days passed with no word from Vargas. There were none of those urgent appeals which had followed earlier resignations. The picture was clear enough. When Aranha quit on August 24, 1944, a long and valuable association was broken.

Góis, sulking in Montevideo, received the news in a letter from Aranha. He, too, decided to resign. But Getúlio, hardly eager to have this influential military figure also join the opposition, called him to Rio.

Once Góis had reached the capital, he got together with the astute Dutra, fresh from the fighting fronts of Italy. The military was in a hurry to associate itself with democracy. Góis explained to Dutra that on his train ride from Montevideo he had sounded out generals in the southern states and found them all wanting a constitutional regime for Brazil. Dutra told Góis that the two of them were the most responsible for installing the Estado Nôvo. Pointing out that in seven years Vargas had never spoken about the plebiscite or elections, and that the war was approaching its end, Dutra suggested that Góis ask Vargas his intentions. Concluding that Dutra was a "timorous" sort of person, Góis accepted the mission.[12]

Góis saw Vargas on November 1, 1944, and described a discontented country. There being nothing timorous about him, he told the dictator that he had come from Montevideo "to do away with the Estado Nôvo."[13]

So Vargas had the word of the military. When Góis went on to suggest calling a constitutional assembly Vargas observed that it would be better to use some juridical process more "harmonious with Brazilian reality." He would ask Marcondes Filho to submit proposals after consulting Dutra and Góis.

[12] Lourival Coutinho, *O General Góes Depõe*, p. 404.
[13] *Ibid.*, p. 405.

On the seventh anniversary of the Estado Nôvo, Vargas addressed leaders of the Armed forces. Again ruling out a constitutional assembly, he proposed achieving postwar democracy by implementing the applicable provisions of the authoritarian Constitution of 1937. Vargas took pains to point out how well Brazil had done since being faced, seven years earlier, with the agitation of "utopian ideologies and alien interests." Thanks to November 10, 1937, Brazil had come to enjoy one of the finest periods of "its history as a free people." Industrialization and the discovery of petroleum had been important. The nation was well organized to go ahead.[14]

On the next day Getúlio moved to make his government more popular among workers. He widely increased the benefits of the Worker Accident Law, and legislated a "readaptation program" to train people. He set up a minimum salary for journalists, and prepared steps for unionizing the traditionally neglected rural workers.[15]

In his workroom in Guanabara Palace in November 1944 he listened to Francisco Campos explain that politics is the art of adapting, and that he would be lost unless he immediately espoused democracy and freedom of the press. "Chico Ciência" even told Vargas to assume the "leadership of the opposition against the Government." But Campos did not expect Getúlio to do anything. The un-Caesarlike Vargas, he felt, had a mind which went blank whenever a crisis occurred. ("The motor would stop working.")

The Constitution notwithstanding, Campos said that prevailing conditions no longer allowed Vargas to name ten members to the Federal Council. Closing his hand, Vargas said he could not open it, thus making it clear that he was not disposed to surrender the prerogative they were discussing.

Later, in a strongly worded memorandum, Campos suggested that modifications be made to the 1937 Constitution; further, an assembly should be called to approve the modified Constitution or to make a new one. Vargas passed Campos' recommendations on to Dutra, who agreed with them.[16]

[14] Getúlio Vargas, *A Nova Política do Brasil,* XI, 45–50.
[15] *The New York Times,* November 12, 1944.
[16] Francisco Campos, interview, September 3, 1963.

2. The Winds Blow Strong

Seeking a suitable standard-bearer, the opposition was handicapped because many of its leaders had not been treated by the dictatorship, the
DIP included, in a manner calculated to give them popular stature. Juarez
Távora, who had been military attaché in Chile, joined with ex-*interventor* Juraci Magalhães, then serving as a major in Recife, to work on a
good possibility—Brigaderio Eduardo Gomes, the Air Force hero in command in the Northeast.[1] Virgílio de Melo Franco sped to São Paulo in
December 1944 to round up support for Gomes. But the aggressive Virgílio, who had been predicting an uprising, had been under surveillance
by Benjamim Vargas' tough Personal Guard; when he returned to Rio, the
police reminded him that the dictatorship was not dead by putting him
in jail for ten days.

Brazilian writers raised their voices when they gathered in São Paulo
on January 22, 1945, for the one-week meeting of the First Brazilian
Writers' Congress. The commission of the Congress which drew up
"basic principles" was liberally sprinkled with Communists. The principles included "democratic legality as a guarantee of liberty of expression" and "a government elected by the direct secret vote of the people."[2]

In January 1945 Vargas was sorry to see his friend Caffery shifted to
Paris. To take his place as ambassador in Rio, Roosevelt sent Adolf A.
Berle. Berle's arrival was hailed by the Brazilian press, which had been
none too fond of Caffery. Sumner Welles, valiant defender of the dictatorship as nonfascist, was no longer in the State Department, and
Edward R. Stettinius, Jr. had become Secretary of State, succeeding the
aging Hull.

From Yalta, Stettinius flew to Rio, arriving in the heat of mid-Febru-
ary. His gift for Getúlio was a powerful radio receiving set, which prompted the dictator's ever more vocal detractors to quip that its purpose was to
permit the recipient to find out what was going on in the world.[3]

With Vargas and Acting Foreign Minister Pedro Leão Veloso, Stettinius was a lunch guest of Alzira and Ernâni do Amaral Peixoto at Petrópolis. The Brazilians were asked to renew diplomatic relations with Russia. The wartime unity of the United Nations was to become the basis

[1] Carolina Nabuco, *A Vida de Virgílio de Melo Franco,* pp. 159–160.
[2] José Eduardo do Prado Kelly, interview, August 29, 1963.
[3] Rosa Meireles da Costa Leite, interview, September 6, 1963.

of a world organization for providing eternal peace, and in the new organization Russia was to have a strong voting position.

Stettinius and Veloso flew to the Mexico City inter-American conference, where Brazil and other nations opened the door to permit Argentina to rejoin their councils. Of common concern was the establishment of a regional association for the settlement of hemispheric disputes.

In Brazil, control was slipping from Getúlio's hands. The press, deciding to wait no longer for Vargas to take hints, threw down the gauntlet. On February 22 Rio's *Correio da Manhã* published an interview which José Américo gave to Carlos Lacerda. In it the liberal politician from the Northeast, whose aspirations had been snuffed out when Vargas canceled the 1938 election, hailed principles formulated at the São Paulo Writers' Conference.

The DIP took no action, and from that moment on Brazilian newspapers rioted in freedom for the first time since 1937. Everything was discussed: the recognition of Russia (on behalf of which Góis joined Aranha); amnesty for political prisoners and exiles; and, above all, the need of elections and complete freedom of speech. No Cabinet statement about "future elections" sufficed. "Action, not words" was demanded. Socialist João Mangabeira, long disregarded by the controlled press, was quoted as saying: "We have no elections, we and the African tribes."

In February 1945, while so many were enjoying the experience of raising their voices in discontent, José Américo urged that Eduardo Gomes be the presidential candidate of the opposition. Aranha, too, backed Gomes. This he did before the end of February in an interview explaining his resignation as Foreign Minister. "All went splendidly until I detected that internal politics was trying to dominate my foreign-policy activities." Aranha added that he was not an enemy of Vargas, but opposed the regime which Vargas represented.

On February 28 Vargas bent before the winds blown by the military, the Brazilian press and public opinion, and outside forces. "Considering the manifest tendencies of Brazilian public opinion" he and his Cabinet signed a lengthy decree, Constitutional Amendment No. 9, calling for the election of a President of Brazil (for a six-year term), federal and state legislators, and state governors. The new federal Congress and the President would have powers to change the Constitution, but the President could submit the projected changes to a nationwide plebiscite. Within ninety days the President would announce the election dates.[4]

[4] Fernando H. Mendes de Almeida (ed.), *Constituições do Brasil,* pp. 533–546.

The Rio press screamed that the amendment implied a continuation of the unpopular 1937 Constitution. The decree, the *Diário Carioca* said, is a "reform in a fascist mold," and another paper called it "deceptive."

Vargas at Rio Negro Palace in Petrópolis tried to please both the military and the press. Marcondes Filho, who had drawn up the new constitutional amendment but never had got along well with the War Minister,[5] was replaced as Justice Minister by Agamenon Magalhães, Dutra's Pernambuco friend. Then Vargas sent word to Herbert Moses that he would hold his first press conference in several years. About one hundred newsmen made their way up the mountainside.

They heard the harassed dictator assail "Nazi-fascists." "As has been proved," he said, they helped put on the attack in May 1938. He described "Nazi-fascism" as characterized by an official party, and by the absolute power of the state over the spiritual and economic life of the individual, even to the extent of repudiating religion and upholding race prejudice. None of this, Vargas explained, had occurred under the Brazilian regime. "Just because we left out the classic formulation of a representative government, we have been called totalitarian."[6] In practice, Vargas pointed out, the plebiscite had been put off for reasons which the Army had appreciated "so patriotically": in 1938 because of internal conditions, and after that because of world conditions.[7]

Having dutifully heard Vargas on the past, the newsmen asked questions about the future. In reply to one question Vargas said that a constitutional assembly was unnecessary because Congress would have the power to modify the 1937 Constitution.

What about the DIP? This, Vargas answered, would limit itself to promoting Brazilian culture.

What about Russia? Vargas said that the undesirable Comintern had been dissolved, and that Brazil would be attending peace conferences with Russia, which had nobly defended her territory and now sought diplomatic relations with Brazil. "It is impossible to continue ignoring Russia."

Journalists asked about amnesty for Luís Carlos Prestes. Getúlio cautiously asserted that his government had always been sympathetic to amnesty, but added that he had to consider the repercussions in the Armed Forces and on Brazilian life. He had pardoned a number of political

[5] Lourival Coutinho, *O General Góes Depõe*, p. 411.
[6] *The New York Times*, March 3, 1945.
[7] Getúlio Vargas, *A Nova Política do Brasil*, XI, 100–101.

prisoners and was agreeable to studying individual cases, including that of Prestes.

Would Vargas be a presidential candidate? In dodging this one, the dictator did little to allay suspicions. He was busy, he explained, arranging for the nation to hold an election and have political parties. The parties would choose the candidates. "Let's wait. Who knows but some name will appear . . . the name, not yet considered, of one who can bring tranquillity."

The press conference did not result in fewer attacks. Newspapers referred to the constitutional amendment by such phrases as "a constitutional monkeyshine," and the Brazilian Bar Association proclaimed that there was "nothing democratic" about it. In a widely publicized manifesto Francisco Campos said that his 1937 Constitution was not fascist, but had been misused by the Vargas regime. He, too, derided the latest amendment. "The time has come," he said, "for Vargas to think of Brazil and not himself."

From a rostrum on the steps of Rio's Opera House a battery of speakers, including Flôres da Cunha, participated in Rio's first political rally since 1937. They called for amnesty for political prisoners and exiles; also diplomatic relations with the Soviet Union. Maurício de Lacerda, feeling as combative as when attacking Bernardes and Washington Luís in the 1920's, said that the Brazilian people had demanded the abdication of Pedro II and were now demanding the abdication of the dictator, Getúlio Vargas.

3. Prestes Walks Out into a Spirited Political Fray

In March 1945 Getúlio appointed João Alberto Rio police chief. The former economic co-ordinator announced that Luís Carlos Prestes, his revolutionary chief in the 1920's, would be allowed to receive visitors.

For some time Prestes had been seeing one visitor, Orlando Leite Ribeiro. Leite Ribeiro, after conspiring with Prestes in the late 1920's, had risen in the Foreign Office during the dictatorship and was well regarded by Getúlio. When Brazil declared war against the Nazis, Leite Ribeiro told Vargas that Prestes had found a reason for supporting him. At the time, the news hardly interested Vargas, but with "democracy" the "fashionable word,"[1] and with the opposition vociferous, there were possibili-

---

[1] Vargas' remark to Clemente Mariani. Information from interview with Mariani, August 22, 1963.

ties which Getúlio encouraged Leite Ribeiro to explore with the prisoner who still faced almost forty years in jail.

The Communist Party of Brazil had been battered by Filinto Müller. What remained was split into two factions. One supported Vargas and the other felt it "more important to fight fascism in Brazil than to go to war in faraway places."[2] A word from Prestes' cell would be of inestimable value to one group or the other, particularly at a time when Communism seemed certain of growing. Moreover, Prestes' word was respected by many non-Communists in the working class. The little "Cavalier of Hope," pale and restless, had become "a great martyr," and was known as "South America's most famous political prisoner."

While Getúlio was turning the Prestes matter over in his mind, Rio's press was whooping it up for the austere Eduardo Gomes. The conservative, bourgeois-backed *brigadeiro* was described as "the people's candidate." The candidacy presented a problem to Getúlio. Should an electoral campaign become overheated, the military, with its first presidential candidate since the election of Hermes da Fonseca in 1910, would be unlikely to step in to stop the Air Force hero. Agamenon Magalhães suggested Dutra as an opponent to Gomes. So did Valadares. Notable for his loyalty to Vargas, Dutra should be able to attract much of the military which might otherwise join the opposition, and he could only support the regime of November 1937, having been one of its pillars. He hardly seemed destined to outshine Getúlio; if Vargas lacked some glamour, Dutra's lack was in the extreme.

Vargas liked the idea. To the candidacy of the *brigadeiro* he would, as he put it, reply with a sword to fight a sword. Dutra accepted so quickly that he startled the cautious President. As in 1937, Vargas turned to Valadares to launch the candidacy, and on March 12 the Minas governor journeyed to São Paulo to collect signatures on his pro-Dutra manifesto. Gomes supporters said that Dutra had been chosen by Vargas for the "ignominious" purpose of splitting the military.

Dutra told newsmen of the fine sentiments which would guide him if elected: protection for the working class, unrestricted freedom of opinion, and closer ties with the United States. As for Getúlio, he became sixty-two on April 19, but this anniversary was not among his happiest birthdays. For years it had been pointed out, for all who could read, that Vargas alone could bring Brazil to greatness; but if the press, suddenly free, was

[2] Agildo Barata, *Vida de um Revolucionário*, p. 320.

any indication of how people felt, his work had made him a disliked man who could do nothing right.

Surrounded by his family, including Lutero (just back from Italy), Getúlio observed his birthday at Amaral Peixoto's summer place. A newspaperman, so close a friend as to be present at the lunch, asked Getúlio why he did not announce his own candidacy. Getúlio replied: "You are seeing a man who no longer knows what his duty is. I am faced with a dilemma. I feel it necessary to endure a little longer, await the end of the war, prepare the nation for peace, pass the government to my successor, and retire definitely from politics. At most this will take a year. But I have become tired and am annoyed at so much infamy and villainy and my wish is to resign, turning the government over to those who are so anxious to have it." Then he paused and concluded: "If I did that, I would leave a powder keg behind me."[3]

Eduardo Gomes was suggesting that Vargas pack his bags and let the Supreme Court judges run the country until an elected President could take over. But Getúlio had no wish to retire to green pastures under pressure. And the trouble with his setting the date was that it was too easy to see that powder keg which made another year necessary.

Góis has stated that when he was called to Petrópolis he found Vargas "visibly emotional."[4] Góis suggested that Vargas could be a candidate, but Getúlio said he would prefer to rest than work with a congress. The President then went on to discuss the two national political parties he proposed to establish. One of these, to be made up of the bureaucratic machinery established by the dictatorship throughout the states, would support Dutra. The other, a Labor Party, was to be founded by Marcondes Filho and José Segadas Viana of the Labor Ministry.

Before the parties were formally organized, Getúlio arranged for the renewal of diplomatic relations with Moscow and proclaimed amnesty for Brazil's 563 political prisoners.

When liberty came to them all, Police Chief João Alberto smilingly escorted the "Cavalier of Hope" to freedom. The first public act of the Communist leader was to appear with Ambassador Berle on a balcony of the American Embassy at a ceremony honoring the memory of Franklin D. Roosevelt, who had died a week before. Then, on April 26, Prestes made his political views known in a statement to the press.

[3] Alzira Vargas do Amaral Peixoto, Ch. 8 of "A Vida de Getúlio . . .," in *Fatos & Fotos*, August 3, 1963.
[4] Lourival Coutinho, *O General Góes Depõe*, p. 412.

He was in no hurry for elections, for if they were called too soon the Communist Party could not accomplish its "full purpose," which was to achieve political power peacefully. Both Gomes and Dutra, Prestes said, were "on similar political planes"; a third candidate was needed . . . someone nonpolitical, preferably an engineer.

The inclination of most Communists had been to support Gomes, and Prestes' rejection of both candidates came as a bombshell. But the new line became effective immediately, and International Communist backing went to the pro-Vargas wing of the Brazilian party.[5] One of the Communists who had helped draw up the declaration of principles at the São Paulo Writers' Congress had recently given an interview declaring that Communists should ally themselves with movements against the dictatorship. Now, in a piece of self-criticism, he analyzed everything with "cold logic" and found that Prestes was right.

[5] Agildo Barata, *Vida de um Revolucionário*, p. 323.

4. National Political Parties

Valadares and other politicians associated with the dictatorship organized the PSD (Partido Social Democrático), which was to support Dutra.

The opposition, seeking to bring into one fold all groups opposed to the Vargas regime, agreed on two essential matters: a candidate, Eduardo Gomes, and a party name, the UDN (União Democrática Nacional). Otherwise there were squabbles. On April 7, 1945, José Américo from the Northeast, and Flôres da Cunha and Raul Pilla from Rio Grande, came to the new Brazilian Press Association building to help establish the UDN. They found that Artur Bernardes, seventy, was angry because a majority did not favor him as presiding officer;[1] the delegates turned, instead, to another Mineiro, Pedro Aleixo. Miguel Costa's Socialists were upset at being snubbed by the São Paulo Republican and Democratic Parties.[2]

On April 11, when Brazil's political prisoners were about to get their freedom, the Supreme Court decided that the anti-Vargas exiles could return to Brazil. Among those who had already returned was Júlio de Mesquita Filho, seeking to get his newspaper back. Armando de Sales had reached São Paulo a few days before the Supreme Court decision and was

[1] Carolina Nabuco, *A Vida de Virgílio de Melo Franco*, p. 176.
[2] Carlos Castilho Cabral, *Tempos de Jânio e Outros Tempos*, p. 39.

in a sanatorium, where he died before the end of 1945. As soon as the justices handed down their ruling the UDN phoned Otávio Mangabeira in New York, and he prepared to make his first plane trip so as to play a role in the opposition party.

Luís Carlos Prestes thought that he, and not Vargas, had the support of the "popular masses."[3] But the press felt that the Vargas regime was making strides into Prestes' territory, and it accused Labor Minister Marcondes Filho of encouraging strikes. The wage increases of late 1943 had helped send living costs up a record 27 per cent in 1944, and Santos stevedores and São Paulo bus drivers were tying up traffic, asking for a 10 per cent raise. The press pointed out that strikes were constitutionally illegal and concluded that the dictatorship was creating "electoral confusion."

Vargas was in a stew about the public attacks and activities of his opponents. When Dutra looked over the speech that Vargas had prepared to deliver to the workers on May 1, 1945, he found it full of unkind words about the opposition, but without any reference to the government candidate. Góis mentioned the omission to Getúlio, who, Góis has written, smiled "malevolently" and asked if the complaint had not originated with Dutra.[4] Góis admitted as much and Vargas agreed to do something.

Thus the sixty thousand in Vasco da Gama Stadium heard Vargas declare that Dutra deserved the confidence of the nation. Once again Vargas reviewed his achievements since 1930. Then he spoke of the two political currents, one which was using a party program to incorporate these achievements, and the other, a bunch of vilifiers, "counseling disobedience, indiscipline and subversion." This opposition, using the most violent attacks and "unbridled demagoguery," was turning to arms, Vargas charged. But he made it clear that "plotters and reactionaries" would fail. Fearless of threats, Getúlio would maintain order and, after the election, turn over his office to his legally elected successor.[5]

Brigadeiro Gomes was quick to point out that the opposition, far from inciting disorder, was seeking the re-establishment of constitutional order. Vargas, he said, was accusing the opposition of plotting so that he might have a pretext for regaining his absolute power. After assuring

---

[3] Lourival Coutinho, *O General Góes Depõe*, p. 419.
[4] *Ibid.*, p. 414.
[5] Getúlio Vargas, *A Nova Política do Brasil*, XI, 142–151.

Brazilians that dictatorships, like epidemics, pass away, he quoted Edmund Burke to warn that "the price of liberty is eternal vigilance."[6]

On May 28, within the ninety days prescribed by the constitutional amendment of February 28, Vargas signed an electoral decree. The election of December 2, 1945, was to be for a President, who was to serve six years as provided by the 1937 Constitution, and for federal legislators. The decree was not, as described by Virgílio de Melo Franco, something which would serve 100 per cent the interests of the Vargas regime. In setting May 6, 1946, as the date for the election of governors and state assemblies, the regime was doing what the opposition wanted. Vargas-appointed *interventores* might well be out by May 1946, whereas it was felt that on December 2, 1945, they might assure themselves future control of their states.

The decree stipulated that political parties must be national and it prohibited them from using civic militias or uniforms. Already Plínio Salgado had instructed his followers to reorganize as a political party, causing Prestes, in his address to a great throng on May 22, to warn against a revival of fascism. Vargas' Labor Ministry officials had plans ready for launching the PTB, or Brazilian Labor Party (Partido Trabalhista Brasileiro).

On July 1 the PSD fulfilled its appointed duty, holding an open-air rally at which nineteen speakers praised Dutra. On the seventeenth it held its first national convention in Rio's Municipal Theater and nominated the War Minister for the Presidency. Goís, who had helped found the PSD, backed his Army companion, although he was also well impressed with Gomes. But not all the people around Vargas liked the choice of Dutra, and intrigue followed. Dutra was warned of what had happened to José Américo after Valadares and Vargas had picked him in 1937, and the sensitive Vargas heard that Dutra was organizing the Army to prevent any possibility of having the election called off.

Vargas made no more public references to Dutra's virtues, and in private expressed dissatisfaction with him. Not that Dutra was making statements irritating to Vargas and his friends, as José Américo had done in 1937. Dutra's sin, in the eyes of Vargas, was meeting with politicians and military people who opposed the regime. Advising Goís that he was withdrawing his support of Dutra, Getúlio stated that the candidate had the "implicit obligation not to be in contact with declared enemies of the gov-

6 Carolina Nabuco, *A Vida de Virgílio de Melo Franco*, pp. 174–176.

ernment."[7] Dutra resigned his Cabinet post on August 3 to start campaigning. Vargas accepted his suggestion that Góis take over the War Ministry, but on more than one occasion it seemed to Góis that Vargas was trying to get him to break with Dutra.[8] At one time Vargas dangled before Góis the possibility that he enter the presidential race as a substitute for Dutra.

When Valadares advised the President to stick by the Dutra candidacy ("You have no alternative"), Getúlio calmly asked the Minas *interventor*: "Shall we launch your candidacy?" Valadares answered in a questioning tone: "Only now, with two military men in the race, have you thought of that?"[9]

To Cordeiro de Farias, back from Italy, Getúlio expressed interest in an agreement between Dutra and Gomes whereby they would both withdraw in favor of a single candidate. Cordeiro, who was Getúlio's pipeline to Gomes, discussed the matter in weekly evening sessions at Guanabara Palace. Vargas said he would handle Dutra and he authorized Cordeiro to work things out with Gomes. When Cordeiro asked Vargas to suggest names of possible compromise candidates, Vargas listed Góis, Air Minister Salgado Filho, Police Chief João Alberto, and Cordeiro, carefully explaining that Cordeiro was his favorite. To Gomes, who had no intention of withdrawing, Cordeiro expressed the thought that Vargas was offering the suggestions as part of some maneuver.[10] Before the coup of 1937, Vargas had spoken of the need of setting aside the two chief candidates and choosing a third.

The UDN was reorganized and Otávio Mangabeira chosen as party president. His socialist brother, João Mangabeira, helped establish a "Democratic Left," but it stood by Gomes. So did Bernardes, although he parted from the UDN to found a national Partido Republicano.

[7] Lourival Coutinho, *O General Góes Depõe*, pp. 414–415.
[8] *Ibid.*, pp. 416–417.
[9] Benedicto Valladares, *Tempos Idos e Vividos: Memórias*, pp. 274–275.
[10] Osvaldo Cordeiro de Farias, interview, July 30, 1963.

5. Presidential Bouquets for the Queremistas

Getúlio ignored a complaint filed in the Supreme Court charging him with illegal seizure of power on November 10, 1937. He declared in June 1945 that Brazil, like other members of the United Nations, was at war with Japan. He wanted to give Brazil a badly needed antitrust law, but the decree he issued put vast powers in the hands of some of the Cabinet officers and was attacked by his detractors. Described as "the act of a dictator who disdains public opinion," it was, they said, to be used to harry government foes. Undictatorlike, Vargas kept postponing the effective date of the decree. He even sought to have the UDN join in a "coalition government," but the opposition refused.

Getúlio's troubles had been considerable, but around mid-year his spirits were lifted. Maybe he was not the devil after all. During a short trip to Minas he was acclaimed with that old chant, "We want Getúlio."[1]

In July and August, Cariocas showed wild enthusiasm for returning FEB contingents and for Getúlio. General Mark Clark, about whom Brazilians also went wild, reached Rio in July to greet the first ship bringing war heroes from Italy. With Vargas and Clark in the reviewing stand, crowds shouted themselves hoarse while 5,000 Brazilian soldiers, together with 42 members of Crittenberger's Mountain Division, paraded through Rio's streets, and while the greatest fleet of planes ever seen in Brazil flew overhead displaying captured enemy flags. Pipe-smoking snakes, their mouths and nostrils exhaling smoke, glared from many a poster. Explaining the emblem of the FEB, Cariocas recalled that pro-Nazis had once said: "The day you see a Brazilian soldier in Europe you'll see a snake smoking a pipe."

When more contingents arrived in August, Vargas, accompanied by military chieftains like Góis and Mascarenhas de Morais, went to the dock to welcome each ship. The Brazilian President received the greatest ovation of his life.[2]

Laborers kept up the cry "Queremos Getúlio" ("We want Getúlio"), and on August 13 made it the theme of a huge rally in Rio, promoting their slogan on posters, armbands, and scarves.[3] The Queremistas, as these vocal elements were called, were affiliated with the PTB (Labor Party) or the Communist Party, and they expressed their dissatisfaction with the military candidates by another slogan: "Constituinte com Getúlio." Brazil, they felt, should postpone the presidential election and have a constitutional assembly which would work with Vargas.

It was as though Vargas were a candidate. Vargas' refusal to declare himself was characteristic but the Queremistas tried to make the pressure

[1] José Caó, *Dutra*, p. 230.
[2] Alzira Vargas do Amaral Peixoto, Ch. 8 of "A Vida de Getúlio . . .," in *Fatos & Fotos*, August 3, 1963.
[3] José Caó, *Dutra*, p. 231.

irresistable. Foes pictured Vargas as stimulating the demonstrations. They remarked that Vargas cronies had been in touch with Prestes,[4] and they noted that laborite Hugo Borghi, a Vargas friend doing well speculating in cotton, was a prominent Queremista. Surely, the conjecture went, Getúlio had a trick up his sleeve.

The candidacy of Dutra, no orator, was at a low ebb. Finding PSD leaders talking about replacing Dutra, Góis investigated and was told by Valadares that Vargas had nothing to do with the idea. Just the same, Góis let Getúlio know that if he tried to drop Dutra he would have to find another War Minister,[5] a threat which implied more than Góis' resignation. But rumors persisted, owing in part to UDN people who belittled Dutra as 'the "interim candidate" and spoke of Valadares' willingness to sacrifice him.[6]

September 2 was the deadline for resignations of officeholders who wished to be presidential candidates. It passed with Getúlio still in office. But skeptics, impressed by the *constituinte* signs painted on sidewalks and walls by Queremistas, pointed out that Vargas was in a position to issue a decree changing the rules. So on Independence Day, September 7, Getúlio repeated that he would limit himself to presiding over an honest election.[7]

The Queremista movement reached a high point on October 3, fifteenth anniversary of the 1930 outbreak. Defying orders of João Alberto, an estimated 100,000 Queremistas held a mass meeting and then, early in the evening, marched five miles to Guanabara Palace. They bore a statement declaring that the Brazilian people, gathered in state capitals, cities, and towns, had resolved that the December 2 election should be for a constitutional assembly and that the presidential election should take place at a date set by the assembly.

Getúlio, restless, was rehearsing the words he felt like using in announcing his resignation to the mass of humanity in the Palace garden. He would tell the people that he had always sought to satisfy them, but that now "powerful reactionary forces, some hidden, some in the open, prevent me. In this dramatic period of my life I prefer to resign, descend these stairs, and add my voice to the majority of Brazilians."[8]

[4] Lourival Coutinho, *O General Góes Depõe*, p. 428.
[5] *Ibid.*, pp. 425–426.
[6] Carolina Nabuco, *A Vida de Virgílio de Melo Franco*, p. 179.
[7] Getúlio Vargas, *A Nova Política do Brasil*, XI, 183.
[8] Alzira Vargas do Amaral Peixoto, Ch. 8 of "A Vida de Getúlio . . .," in *Fatos & Fotos*, August 3, 1963.

But before making an appearance he conferred with Góis, João Alberto, and Agamenon Magalhães, and they dissuaded him from resigning. Instead, he declared to his huge audience that "events no longer depend on my will, which is the will of the people."[9] Some of the crowd heard Vargas reaffirm "before God" that he was not a candidate, but his words were often drowned by thousands of voices shouting in unison the demand for Getúlio and a constitutional assembly. Eleven months earlier Getúlio had rejected the idea of a constitutional assembly, but to the Queremistas he admitted that the solution they wanted opened the way for better things than the path which his government was following. His duty, Vargas said, was to fulfill the legal arrangements which had been set up. But if it would help the realization of the people's aspirations, he would not hesitate to free himself of that duty by resigning, retiring to obscurity, without bitterness and with his usual love of the noble, brave, and generous Brazilian people.

"The calling of a *constituinte* is a profoundly democratic act that the people have a right to demand. When the will of the people is not satisfied, there always remain ferments of disorder and revolt. And we must resolve our political problem within law and order. I must tell you that there are powerful reactionary forces, some hidden, some open, opposed to the calling of a *constituinte*. I can affirm that, as far as things depend on me, the people can count on me."[10]

Maybe there was something to that curious suggestion of Francisco Campos about how the President should join the opposition to the government.

[9] *Ibid.*
[10] Getúlio Vargas, *A Nova Política do Brasil,* XI, 191.

6. "The Power of the Masses"

In September, Ambassador Berle reflected that if the elections were called off an uprising by supporters of Gomes would create a delicate situation at the air bases because of the presence of numerous members of the United States military.[1] The Ambassador prepared a speech praising "the solemn promise of free elections" and showed it to Getúlio, who said he was tired and ready to quit. Vargas had no criticism to make of Berle's paper, which contained thoughts he himself had expressed from time to

[1] Adolf A. Berle, interviews, March 8, 1963, and June 5, 1963.

time. Addressing newsmen at Petrópolis on September 29, Berle used the words he had already gone over with Vargas.

The resulting headlines were sensational. Vargas, highly irritated, told Alzira that he had not expected Berle would deliver the talk to the "opposition." He called in Góis and complained of United States "intervention." When Góis pointed out that Berle had first cleared the speech, Vargas said that he had been tired at the time and had found it difficult to understand Berle's Portuguese, so that he could not be sure that the press reports corresponded with what he had heard.[2]

This incident was followed by the headlines which resulted from Getúlio's dramatic words of October 3 to the Queremistas. While the military ministers met to assert jointly that the scheduled election would take place, the press accused Vargas of having used "slippery words." Rumors had Vargas resigning, especially after the press reported that twenty-six trunks had left Guanabara Palace for São Borja.

But Getúlio reminded Brazil that he was still a political factor. On October 10 he changed the election law to give the *interventores* what they had been wanting, state elections on December 2. Opposition leaders, once hopeful of winning some governorships and state legislatures, let out a howl. Bernardes called the new decree "a coup against Brazilian democracy,"[3] and Juraci Magalhães suggested that the UDN, in protest, refuse to put up any candidates for state or municipal offices.[4] The Queremistas felt the atmosphere improved for getting the presidential election postponed.

In his speeches Vargas now urged the workers and common people to join the PTB so as to avoid backing politicians who, once elected, might forget their promises.[5] The PTB, generally regarded as the headquarters of Queremismo, named Vargas its honorary president.

As frequently as Queremistas put on rallies, Góis issued statements assuring Brazilians that the scheduled elections would occur. Finally the military and the Rio police forbade any more meetings called to oppose the presidential election. In canceling such a meeting planned for October 27, the police cited the "political tension," and Góis warned that the rally might lead to civil war.[6]

[2] Lourival Coutinho, *O General Góes Depõe*, p. 432.
[3] *The New York Times*, dateline Rio, October 10, 1945.
[4] Carolina Nabuco, *A Vida de Virgílio de Melo Franco*, p. 185.
[5] Getúlio Vargas, *A Nova Política do Brasil*, XI, 197–199; José Caó, *Dutra*, p. 233.
[6] *The New York Times*, dateline Rio, October 28, 1945.

Workers in Argentina marched on Buenos Aires, making their power felt to such an extent that anti-Peronistas in the military who had imprisoned Perón simply stood by while Perón entered Buenos Aires in triumph on October 17, 1945.[7] Batista Luzardo, Brazilian ambassador to Argentina, described the event in this manner to Vargas, who then spoke to Góis about the "power of the masses." Góis silenced the President by asserting that it had not been the masses which had brought Perón back; rather, the War Minister said, it had been the pro-Perón military.[8]

[7] See Robert J. Alexander, *Prophets of the Revolution*, p. 251.
[8] Lourival Coutinho, *O General Góes Depõe*, p. 439.

7. Vargas Resigns

With the police forbidding the Queremistas to hold their meetings, Vargas prepared to play another card. Rio mayor Henrique Dodsworth would become Foreign Minister, allowing João Alberto to succeed him as mayor. The switch was interesting to João Alberto, who had political ambitions,[1] and meant that Getúlio could name a new Police Chief, friendly to the Queremistas. For this key post the President selected his brother Benjamim.

By October 25 these plans were ready to be implemented, but not until the evening of October 28 did Vargas authorize João Alberto to reveal the impending changes to his friends in the military. Almost all of them felt that Benjamim's appointment showed that Getúlio intended to call off the presidential election.[2]

On the morning of the twenty-ninth João Alberto broke the news to Góis as the two drove downtown. In reply to a question by an infuriated Góis, João Alberto revealed that his delay in advising the War Minister had been at the request of Vargas. Góis considered that Vargas, in naming Benjamim, had broken "all understandings" and was dealing this "blow" only in order to stay in power. In the course of his tirade against Vargas, Góis resolved to resign. But, he added to João Alberto, Vargas was making a big mistake and it would backfire. "He can last no longer in a government which, with superhuman effort, I have been sustaining."[3]

[1] Henrique Dodsworth, *Depoimento sôbre Getúlio Vargas*, p. 7.
[2] Osvaldo Cordeiro de Farias, interview, July 30, 1963; Eusébio de Queiroz Filho, interview, June 26, 1963; Lourival Coutinho, *O General Góes Depõe*, p. 442.
[3] Lourival Coutinho, *O General Góes Depõe*, p. 442.

In his office Góis dictated a sharply worded letter of resignation and sent coded messages to regional commanders ordering implementation of a defense plan he had earlier drawn up for use in case of an anti-government uprising. The commander of the First Military Region (Rio district) was to carry it out with help from the Navy, the Air Force, and the Military Police. Generals around Góis, contending that Vargas had lost his authority and that they had the responsibility of avoiding civil war, asked Góis to assume command of all the forces of land, sea, and air. When Góis accepted, the War Ministry became a crowded and busy place.

Dutra reported that Justice Minister Agamenon Magalhães and João Alberto were on their way to Guanabara Palace to try to dissuade Vargas from naming Benjamim. Although Dutra got Góis to tone down his resignation letter, Góis went ahead with his military measures for "defense." Dutra decided to collaborate "as a soldier" who was "no longer a candidate," and he visited the São Cristóvão barracks to prepare the units there.[4] Góis lunched and napped in his office until 3:00 P.M., and then the excitement began.

Among those waiting to see the new commander of all the military forces was Benjamim Vargas, who, surrounded by Queremistas, had earlier descended on the police headquarters. Now the new police chief called on the "War Minister" to express a desire to co-operate wherever possible. But Góis rudely told Benjamim to find another War Minister, and when Benjamim pleaded for a harmonious understanding, Góis told his visitor that he could tell his brother that this was impossible.

While special editions of the afternoon papers were announcing Benjamim's appointment, leaders of the Navy and Air Force agreed to back the Army, whereupon Góis arranged to have the Marines patrol areas around the docks and take control of telegraph and postal services. Threats of a general strike on behalf of Vargas strengthened Góis' determination to have all communications and transportation under military control. Some of the tanks which began rumbling into Rio surrounded the War Ministry and others were sent by Góis to Guanabara Palace.

At the Palace, Orlando Leite Ribeiro brought Vargas a message from Prestes, offering to stir up public agitations. Although Getúlio sensibly rejected this,[5] Prestes stayed close to the Palace ready to act in case Vargas decided to resist the group which had taken control.[6]

[4] *Ibid.*, p. 447.
[5] Osvaldo Cordeiro de Farias, interview, July 30, 1963.
[6] Luís Carlos Prestes, interview, September 5, 1963.

Vargas sent his chief military aide to the War Ministry with invitations for Dutra to call on him at 7:00 P.M. and Góis at 9:00. Góis declined and Dutra accepted. There were generals who feared that the Vargas invitation was a trap, and so when Dutra left for Guanabara Palace the men at the War Ministry made a hostage of Justice Minister Agamenon Magalhães, who had dropped in to try to work out some solution.

Making his way through the tanks around Guanabara Palace, Dutra met with Vargas, who reviewed various possibilities. But when Dutra suggested withdrawing the appointment of Benjamim, Getúlio told him: "If I am not free to choose even a chief of police whom I can trust, this means I am no longer President."[7]

After Dutra reported back at the War Ministry, Agamenon Magalhães suggested that Góis call on the "President." Góis again declined, pointing out that he, Góis, was chief of Brazil at the moment.[8] Determined that the time had come for Vargas to go, Góis named Cordeiro de Farias his Chief of Staff and ordered him to deliver the ultimatum to Vargas: Vargas should resign in exchange for full guarantees for himself, his family, and his friends. Cordeiro, citing his warm relations with Getúlio, demurred, but Góis insisted, and for all to hear he repeated his message to Vargas and found it acceptable to the military men around him. These now included Eduardo Gomes, who had rushed to Rio, interrupting his campaigning in the south.

The two presidential candidates agreed that in the short interval until one of them took office the Presidency should be in the hands of Chief Justice José Linhares.

After Cordeiro and Agamenon Magalhães left for Guanabara Palace, Góis presided over a meeting of military officers and heard a lot of unfavorable things about Vargas. Sins of the Estado Nôvo were hashed over: people had been unjustly imprisoned, exiled, or deprived of political rights; Vargas was accused of having planned a rebellion for that very day, October 29, with the help of PTB and Communist strikers; the poor, who occupied the *favelas* (slums) on the Rio hillsides, were to be organized to participate in disturbances or even terrorism.[9]

While this discussion was going on Cordeiro carried out his unpleasant

[7] Alzira Vargas do Amaral Peixoto, Ch. 8 of "A Vida de Getúlio . . .," in *Fatos & Fotos,* August 3, 1963; José Caó, *Dutra,* p. 241.

[8] Lourival Coutinho, *O General Góes Depõe,* p. 455.

[9] *Ibid.,* p. 459.

mission at Guanabara Palace. Going in to speak alone with Vargas, he found him friendly but serious, and in the middle of the conversation they were joined by brother Benjamim.[10]

The generals, Cordeiro said, dominated the situation and had the Palace surrounded; appealing to Vargas' patriotism, they were telling him to resign. Vargas acknowledged his lack of military strength but liked the idea of resisting and said that he would die fighting against an unconstitutional *coup d'état*, leaving Góis responsible for the massacre of the President and his family.

But Cordeiro pointed out that Góis and the military had nothing like that in mind. It was simply a question of Vargas' leaving in a dignified manner or else being forced into a ridiculous situation, with water, power, and supplies cut off from the Palace. Vargas withdrew from the office to think things over for fifteen minutes and returned with his decision: "I would prefer that you all attack me and that my death remain as a protest against this violence. But as this is to be a bloodless coup, I shall not be a cause of disturbance."[11]

Thus Vargas submitted, expressing a wish to retire to Rio Grande and emphasizing how important it was that "public order" be maintained.

[10] Osvaldo Cordeiro de Farias, interview, July 30, 1963.

[11] *Ibid.*; Alzira Vargas do Amaral Peixoto, Ch. 8 of "A Vida de Getúlio . . .," in *Fatos & Fotos*, August 3, 1963.

BOOK X

OUT OF POWER,

1945–1950

"Brazil is being ruled by a capitalist democracy which . . . facilitates trusts, monopolies, and black markets, and exploits the miseries of the people. . . . I have chosen between the powerful and the humble and I prefer the latter."

1. The Election of December 2, 1945

CHIEF JUSTICE José Linhares was attending a party when representatives of the Armed Forces surprised him with the news that he was about to become President of Brazil. When he reached the War Ministry at 2:00 A.M. to be invested with his new powers his formal evening attire was a contrast to all the uniforms around him.

Inquiring about conditions throughout the country, Linhares learned that most of the *interventores* had resigned. In Belo Horizonte, Valadares had adhered to the anti-Vargas movement after consulting Dutra.[1] In Rio, Army men had raided the Communist Party headquarters and arrested a few PTB and Communist leaders, but Prestes had found asylum at the Mexican Embassy. House arrest had been applied to Agamenon Magalhães and Marcondes Filho.

UDN leaders were enchanted with the changes, particularly as the make-up of the new Cabinet became known. Linhares had already drawn up a list by the time he sat down at noon on October 30 with Góis, Dutra, and Gomes in what was supposed to be a meeting where both candidates would approve the selections. Dutra, alarmed at the list, succeeded in getting PSD-supporting Góis to accept the War Ministry.

[1] Lourival Coutinho, *O General Góes Depõe,* p. 467.

In Guanabara Palace, Getúlio was preparing to make a rapid departure. "Do what is necessary to take care of your mother," he told Alzira, "for I'm leaving alone." It was after midnight, Cordeiro de Farias had just left the Palace, and Getúlio was handing Alzira an envelope. He had not died heroically, defending the common people against reactionaries, but a final message might yet be useful if his plane should crash. "Open this only if something happens to me during the trip; otherwise burn it," he said to his daughter.[2]

Later in the day he handed João Alberto (again police chief) a short manifesto to the Brazilian people. Its staccato sentences lacked the polish of some of the ghost-written speeches which at the height of his power had gained Vargas membership in the exclusive Brazilian Academy of Letters. He explained that he was abstaining from analyzing the causes of his resignation, for to do so might irreparably shock the nation. "History and time will speak for me." He held no grudges. "The workers, the humble, those who never lacked my affection and help—in short, the people, must understand me. And all will do me justice."[3]

Receiving a journalist, he observed that he needed a rest, and added: "I am getting it two months sooner than I had thought." Asked whether he planned to return to politics, he smiled and said "That depends entirely on events."[4] While the new Cabinet held its first meeting on the morning of October 31, Alzira and João Alberto drove with Getúlio to the airport to see him off. Inaccurately the press quoted him as saying: "Though they send me away, I shall nevertheless return."

Many felt that Vargas and his principal collaborators should be deprived of their political rights and that Vargas himself should be exiled abroad or to the remote Brazilian interior. But while Vargas was boarding the plane for Rio Grande, Góis was torpedoing these ideas at the Cabinet meeting. He revealed to fellow ministers that the ultimatum which Cordeiro had taken to Guanabara Palace had provided "full guarantees" for Vargas, his family, and his friends.

In other respects the UDN did well. Linhares quickly closed the notorious National Security Tribunal and repealed the Vargas antitrust decree. When the Cabinet ruled that the elections to be held on December 2 would be for President and the two legislative houses, which would have

[2] Alzira Vargas do Amaral Peixoto, Ch. 9 of "A Vida de Getúlio . . .," in *Fatos & Fotos,* September 7, 1963.

[3] Getúlio Vargas, *A Nova Política do Brasil,* XI, 206.

[4] *The New York Times,* October 31, 1945.

powers to draw up a new constitution, it postponed the state elections. The constitution makers were to decide about them. New state *interventores* were named, further setting back the fading presidential chances of Dutra. As Alzira saw it, the new government was replacing the old slogan "Constituinte com Getúlio" with a new one: "Constituinte com Brigadeiro Eduardo Gomes."[5] Dutra in moments of discouragement considered withdrawing his candidacy and breaking with the Linhares Government,[6] but in the end he would always decide to plod ahead, denying rumors that he was stepping aside.

The Communists, in spite of their objections to such an early race, nominated a presidential candidate. Their choice, engineer Iedo Fiuza, was not a Communist. As mayor of Petrópolis he had been a close personal friend of Getúlio and his backers hoped he would get Vargas' support.[7]

The Labor Party (PTB), recovering from the shock of October 29, was split. Those who looked to Aranha to interest himself in the party found him wrapped up in the UDN campaign for Gomes. His suggestion that the PTB back Gomes was well received by Segadas Viana, a principal organizer of the PTB and leader of an important wing. But many in the PTB still hoped to see Vargas back Dutra. The *brigadeiro* was pictured as unfriendly to the low-income groups, and there were stories about how the confident UDN leaders preferred to "march to victory" without any "votes of the dictatorship."

In the minds of some, such as *The New York Times* correspondent William S. White, there was doubt that Vargas' backing would help any candidate.[8] Unflattering stories about the fallen strong man, that "latter-day Machiavelli," were legion. He was pictured stamping about his hacienda, "a South American Caesar who understood everything but the passage of time."[9] He was accused of being in sympathy with the Farrell-Perón regime in Argentina, and his manifesto of October 30 was criticized for its "bad Portuguese."[10] Paulista politicians reiterated the need to banish him from the country.

Góis, who had agreed to make sure that Vargas' presence in Brazil

---

[5] Alzira Vargas do Amaral Peixoto, Ch. 9 of "A Vida de Getúlio . . .," in *Fatos & Fotos*, September 7, 1963.

[6] Lourival Coutinho, *O General Góes Depõe*, pp. 478–479.

[7] Osvaldo Peralva, interview, September 14, 1963.

[8] *The New York Times*, dateline Rio, November 5, 1945.

[9] *Ibid.*, dateline Rio, November 6, 1945.

[10] *Jornal do Comercio*, Rio, November 15, 1945.

would not endanger national security, stated that it would be "inconvenient or at least premature" for Vargas to run for the Senate. Word came from São Borja that Vargas would not accept such a candidacy. Nonetheless the PSD of Rio Grande do Sul nominated him, and the PTB in many other states followed this example, choosing him as its candidate for the Senate or lower house. According to the system of proportional representation, a party's strength in the Assembly would depend on the number of votes cast for that party's candidates; if a candidate were elected to more than one seat he could accept only one, but those seats he declined would be filled by alternates from his party. Prestes' prestige being high, the Communist Party put the "Cavalier's" name on the ballot in numerous states.

Flying for a visit to São Borja, Alzira and Ernâni do Amaral Peixoto found Getúlio alone, walking in the garden at his brother Protásio's home. The building of Getúlio's ranch house, Itu, had not been completed. Son Manoel Antônio and neighbor João ("Jango") Goulart were momentarily away from São Borja, getting a taste of local politics and the yen to organize a strong Gaúcho PTB. Protásio had some local PSD business. Darci was remaining in Rio to attend to her charities.

But Getúlio at this time was not to be alone much. Disrupting the tranquillity of Protásio's home, planes arrived, most of them full of PSD and PTB politicians who felt that Getúlio might prevent a Gomes landslide if he would back Dutra. Getúlio seemed disposed not to get involved. But, contemplating the victory plans of the UDN, he said to his daughter: "I feel like a small boy watching from outside the preparations for a banquet. The plates, cutlery, food, are all laid on the table. When the guests begin to take their places, the boy yanks the tablecloth, and good-by banquet!"[11]

Those who most strongly urged Vargas to yank the tablecloth were João Neves da Fontoura, serving as intermediary between Dutra and Vargas, and Hugo Borghi. Borghi, the wealthy Paulista promoter of Queremismo, represented the wing of the PTB which was fighting Segadas Viana. Recalling the money Borghi had made in cotton speculation in the last days of the Vargas regime (reportedly with Bank of Brazil credit), Segadas Viana described Borghi as "a case for the police."[12]

Getúlio agreed that he preferred Dutra to Gomes, and was persuaded

[11] Alzira Vargas do Amaral Peixoto, Ch. 9 of "A Vida de Getúlio . . .," in *Fatos & Fotos,* September 7, 1963.

[12] *Jornal do Commercio,* Rio, November 24, 1945, quoting José Segadas Vianna in *O Globo.*

to sign a message recommending Dutra. Publicized none too soon, it was the signal for state directorships of the PTB to organize for Dutra.

As December rolled on and the election count gradually became known, the full stature of Vargas as an influence in Brazil became obvious. Among the workers, especially in industrial São Paulo, the popularity of the ex-dictator was enormous. Elected senator from São Paulo and Rio Grande, Vargas was also elected federal congressman from six states and the Federal District. Dutra has acknowledged that his victory over Gomes (3,-250,000 to 2,040,000 votes) was due to Vargas' statement.[13]

While UDN leaders bemoaned the effectiveness of "demagoguery," Communists felt encouraged. Fiuza was given 10 per cent of the votes for President. In the Federal District, where Fiuza received 135,000 votes to 184,000 for Gomes and 166,000 for Dutra, Prestes was handsomely elected both senator and congressman. His victories in a few other congressional races helped the Communists gain fourteen seats (out of a total of 286) in the lower chamber.

[13] Eurico Gaspar Dutra, interview, July 28, 1963.

2. Getúlio Reacts to an Onslaught

Getúlio became senator-elect from Rio Grande, but, instead of hastening to take his seat in the Constitutional Assembly on February 1, 1946, he supervised the completion of his ranch house.

The Rio newspapers were infected by the spirit of 1945. Brazil, they said, badly needed "a new deal," free of secret police and "Vargas grafters," who were blamed for the pinching inflation. Although Ambassador Berle pronounced the election a fair one, there were stories about how the "Vargas machine" had driven ruthlessly over public opinion. The *brigaderio,* these observers asserted, had been defeated because "Vargas gangs" had conveyed truckloads of bibulous, bought voters to polling places in the country districts. Vargas was making no public statements, but he privately remarked on his ranch that if there had been any machines their drivers had not been in his hands.

The press went on to say that the honest Dutra was amenable to freeing himself from "Vargas pressure" in order to give the Brazilian people the fair break they "richly deserved after suffering so long." There was talk of a coalition between Dutra and the UDN.

While the Assembly wrestled with the job of writing another constitution, Dutra liberalized foreign exchange regulations so as not to handicap foreign investors, and he doomed the fancy casinos by making gambling illegal. The relative peace for which the Dutra regime became known was not yet evident. In March 1946 Senator Prestes was widely quoted as having stated that he and his followers would fight for Russia in case of a war between Brazil and Russia. After the police forbade a mass meeting in Rio on May 1, Prestes used inflammatory words in Pernambuco. All known Communists were thrown out of positions in the executive branch of the federal government. The first Russian envoy in twenty-nine years reached Brazil in May 1946, when Brazilian police were trying to ban all Communist public meetings and were dealing with railroad and port strikes. A little later Zenóbio da Costa, head of the First Military Region, "detained" two hundred Communists and had the police occupy the Communist Party headquarters. Prestes, furious at the Dutra Administration, said he would welcome an arrangement with Vargas so that together they might stem fascism.

On June 1, 1946, Vargas arrived in Rio, and was met at the airport by so large a throng that he had to use a jeep to leave the field at its far end. Being sworn in as senator a few days later, he was described as hiding his feelings with his famous smile. He said he would give all his attention to his new duties, shunning "partisan controversies."

But old wounds were opened as soon as Getúlio took his seat. Otávio Mangabeira, whose UDN had 103 *constituintes*, introduced a motion to applaud the Army for the step taken on October 29. A few days later anti-Vargas *deputados* were blasting the whole Vargas financial record. In one Assembly session fistfights followed hot words. Vargas, hearing his regime heaped with blame for all the ills of the nation, challenged his accusers to meet him outside the building, and stalked out.

He was back at São Borja before the Assembly produced the Constitution of September 18, 1946, and he never signed it. It provided for five-year terms for Presidents (thus reducing the six-year term to which Dutra thought he had been elected), with no immediate re-election. Much of the social legislation of the Estado Nôvo was included. The right of private property was upheld, but for public need or social interests property could be expropriated "with prior and just indemnification in cash." Brazil, under the 1946 Constitution, was assured a plenitude of election years, presidential and congressional elections not being simultaneous.

In São Borja, Getúlio heard about the inauguration of Volta Redonda but was not invited to be present at the fulfillment of his great dream.

Alzira has written that "Edmundo de Macedo Soares e Silva, whom Vargas had chosen, prepared and defended against all attacks in order to realize this project, was President Dutra's Transportation Minister and was afraid, when he made the inaugural speech, to mention the name of Getúlio Vargas amid such select company; he referred to the previous government as if he had sterilizing tongs in his voice."[1] On October 29, 1946, legislators who disliked Vargas started their series of annual "solemn sessions," commemorating the day with a great splurge of anti-Estado Nôvo oratory.

In Pôrto Alegre on November 30, 1946, Getúlio addressed a rally of the PTB, using the occasion to attack the Dutra Administration, blame foreign financiers for his downfall, and give a lecture on democracy.

The Administration, he said, had been assailing him with "impotent hate," was "piling up" the public debt, and had written a constitution which was merely a compilation of former ones.

"I was the victim of agents of international finance who intended to keep our country simply as an exporting colony for raw materials and a purchaser of industrial goods. . . . The trusts and monopolies could not forgive my government for having taken the CVRD [iron-ore company] away from a foreign syndicate." Nor could they forgive Vargas for "having nationalized the mineral wealth of our subsoil, and our waterfalls." Nor for discovering oil. Nor for creating Volta Redonda, and installing aluminum and cellulose plants.

There were, he said, two kinds of democracy: the "old liberal capitalist democracy, which is in rapid decline because it is rooted in inequality"; and "Socialist Democracy of the workers, to which I belong and for which I will fight on behalf of the people." Brazil, Vargas said, "is being ruled by a capitalist democracy, which, comfortably installed in life, facilitates trusts, monopolies, and black markets, and exploits the miseries of the people. This kind of democracy is like an old tree with dry leaves, which the people one day will shake in a hurricane of anger. . . . I have chosen between the powerful and the humble and I prefer the latter."[2]

A few days later, after newsmen queried Vargas about his explanation of his downfall, the press quoted him as saying that it was merely necessary to cite Ambassador Berle's speech at Petrópolis. Newspapers even

[1] Alzira Vargas do Amaral Peixoto, Ch. 9 of "A Vida de Getúlio . . .," in *Fatos & Fotos*, September 7, 1963.
[2] *The New York Times,* December 1, 1966.

reported that Vargas said he had told Berle that he disagreed with his speech when the Ambassador had shown it to him before delivering it. "This is ridiculous," Berle snapped as he read the stories.

In December 1946 Vargas returned to Rio to deliver his "maiden speech" in the new legislature. Pulling out a long prepared text, he launched into a defense of his regime, maintaining that he had prevented "a civil war" between Communists in the north and fascists in the south. Brazil, he pointed out, had been the first nation to withstand Hitler's power. Even Roosevelt had had to "swallow" the *Panay* incident, whereas the Estado Nôvo in 1938 had demanded the departure of the German ambassador. Vargas quoted a cable from F.D.R. expressing gratitude for the Brazilian defense of free peoples.

There was much heckling in the Senate, but it was otherwise outside, where a mob of two thousand had gathered. Vargas interrupted his three-hour speech to greet his admirers from a balcony of Monroe Palace, and he received thunderous applause from the crowd, which began singing the National Anthem in his honor.

3. President Dutra

With the promulgation of the 1946 Constitution, General Eurico Gaspar Dutra became a constitutional President . . . so constitutional in spirit that he has been described as "Brazil's foremost civilian President." Asked for his opinion he customarily opened a copy of the Constitution in book form, his constant companion. "What does the Constitution say?" he would ask.

Dutra reconstituted the whole Cabinet, and in doing so achieved a coalition with the UDN, two of whose members got Cabinet posts. The coalition, a defeat for the Vargas wing of the PSD, was useful to Brazil, for it meant that Dutra had a Congress with which he could usually get along.

UDN secretary Virgílio de Melo Franco argued vigorously that the UDN was a party of pure ideals and should not contaminate itself by co-operating with the PSD. But UDN directors, although they would complain now and then at finding an *interventor* friendly to Vargas, backed Otávio Mangabeira in his decision to deal with Dutra. Rebuffed, Melo Franco resigned as party secretary but worked for the UDN in Minas, where the PSD was seriously split between those favoring and those opposing the coalition.

As established by the Constitutional Assembly, state elections took place on January 19, 1947. Otávio Mangabeira was elected governor of Bahia with the support of much of the local PSD as well as his own UDN. Minas, too, got a UDN governor with the help of a wing of the PSD. In São Paulo, which had outstripped Minas to become Brazil's most populous state, the race for governor was between Hugo Borghi of the PTB and Ademar de Barros, whom Vargas had fired as *interventor*. Victory went to Ademar, backed by Communists and his new, untried PSP (Partido Social Progressista).

Prestes, who wanted to see the Communists gather one million votes, or about 20 per cent of the total, had to be content with half his hope. This meant that, as compared with 1945, the Communist Party was holding its own in a field now crowded with fourteen "national" political parties.

In Rio the Dutra Administration turned to balancing the budget and carrying out, undramatically, badly needed works which had not been possible during the war. Roads and schools were built. Ports, in wretched condition, were enlarged and dredged. Locomotives and tankers were acquired. The attention given to Brazil's transport system was one of the steps taken to improve the supply of foodstuffs, so neglected during the war that Brazilians got used to long line-ups for such staples as sugar, meat, and beans. Work was started on the long-promised Paulo Afonso hydroelectric plant on the São Francisco River.

In the face of a barrage of criticism from the PTB, the Administration tried to cope with financial problems. When Dutra took over, Brazil's reserves of gold and foreign exchange had reached the record high of over $800 million. Of this amount $350 million were in gold reserves, $260 million in blocked British sterling, and $50 million in other blocked currencies. The remainder, in United States dollar reserves, was totally inadequate for rehabilitating the transport system and covering the large pent-up demand for imports. Agricultural machinery, trucks, buses, automobiles, and luxury items came flowing in when at last they became available, but all had climbed in price since the Brazilian balances had been created. Brazil's sterling balances, their value cut when the British had to devalue the pound, were used to reduce foreign indebtedness and to nationalize some British-owned port facilities and railways.

A favorable trade balance, traditional with Brazil and necessary for servicing foreign debts, was realized during the five-year Dutra period, chiefly because few imports were available in 1946 and because of the improvement in the coffee picture. The Vargas-created National Coffee Department was closed down and its coffee stockpile was sold to pay off the foreign Coffee Realization Loan of May, 1930. The world found itself short of coffee and the price shot up to over fifty cents per pound late in 1949 and then went higher. In 1949 Brazilian coffee exports set an all-time record of 19.4 million bags.

Those two well-known ills, inflation and insufficient foreign exchange, received attention. Inflation was well stalled in 1948 and 1949 as the federal government, in contrast to Ademar de Barros' São Paulo state government, lived close to its income in 1947 and 1948. But when the presidential election approached, Congress ignored the pleas of budget balancers, and new money issues became necessary, as in 1946. Credit expansion, which had started late in 1948, continued in 1949 as coffee prices rose; this also contributed to the 10-per-cent increase in the cost of living in 1950.

Early under Dutra, Brazil co-operated with free trade policies advocated by the United States. But in February 1948 Congress acted on Dutra's request for legislation which would allow the government to control imports. The system of requiring import licenses became effective in the second half of 1949.

Dutra was not noted for being a loquacious President. When he did speak he was likely to denounce Communism. In May 1947, on the basis of its internal statutes, the Brazilian Communist Party was declared illegal by a three-to-two vote of the Superior Electoral Tribunal. In October 1947 the Senate voted to eject Communists from all elected offices. When this bill was ratified by the lower house early in 1948, Prestes and other Communist legislators, federal and local, lost their seats. The party having become illegal, Communist leaders acquired the habit of offering the votes of their followers in exchange for cash or other considerations.[1] In one local election three men running for the same office bought Communist support.[2]

Steps were taken to reduce Communist influence in labor unions. There being no place in the government-controlled set-up of *sindicatos, federações*, and *confederações* for a general overall union, the Communist-infiltrated Confederação dos Trabalhadores do Brasil was suspended, as were labor unions affiliated with it. To curb Communism in labor, the Dutra Administration used an article in the labor law requiring that union officials profess to support no ideology opposing the democratic regime.

[1] Osvaldo Peralva, interview, September 14, 1963.
[2] Osvaldo Peralva, *O Retrato,* p. 213.

When Moscow reacted with virulent press attacks against Brazil's President and Army, the Brazilian Administration, with the backing of Congress, broke diplomatic relations with Moscow. The step was welcome to the anti-Communist military close to Dutra and defined Brazil's position early in the Cold War.

4. Charges and Counter-Charges

In 1947, while Vargas was in São Borja on a leave of absence from the unfriendly Senate, his enemies in Rio concocted all sorts of accusations. Some headlines spoke of an anti-government conspiracy by Prestes and Vargas; others, with equal inaccuracy, reported that Vargas was making a deal for the support of Perón in Argentina. Dutra's War Minister announced that the Brazilian Senate would be asked to permit the Administration to question Senator Vargas for plotting to overthrow the government.

Getúlio was persuaded to test his political strength in what seemed a particularly favorable area. São Paulo state in November 1947 was to choose a vice-governor, mayors, and aldermen. Vargas would do more than issue statements urging the Paulistas to elect Carlos Cirilo Júnior vice-governor. He would personally campaign for him, adding the magic of Vargas appearances and oratory.

Cirilo's leading opponent, Luís Novelli Júnior, was President Dutra's son-in-law and the candidate of Ademar de Barros. The Communists by then had broken with Ademar, who had refused to do all they expected of him after they had helped elect him governor. Interest in the campaign was nationwide because Ademar, if he were to resign in order to run for President in 1950, would need a friendly vice-governor. Furthermore, Getúlio was campaigning for the first time since 1930, and this time at the side of Cirilo's Communist supporters.

It was a rough campaign in which Ademar's police did little to restrain well-organized, unruly, anti-Vargas mobs which sometimes fired at the speakers' stand. For Getúlio, who had to be hustled away from one mob, the result was as dismaying as the campaign. Novelli won. Getúlio, beaten and disillusioned, made definite his leave from the Senate, and retired once more to São Borja. Now he was left alone at his Itu ranch house, except for occasional visits of personal friends, and frequent visits from his young neighbor, Jango Goulart.

In Rio some of Getúlio's supporters in the PTB spent their time attacking Dutra. One who had served the dictatorship as head of the Lloyd

Brasileiro and the Central do Brasil Railroad managed to turn out six hundred articles in Rio dailies. The foreign exchange reserves, said Dutra's critics, were being squandered largely on luxury items. They added that the blocked pounds could have been used to better advantage than for the acquisition of railroad companies in poor condition.

Late in 1949 Vargas joined the fray, issuing from São Borja his year-end message for the Brazilian workers, "especially the humble ones." Speaking "from the bosom of the people" he could observe "the cynicism of the courtiers, the shady dealers who carry on under the shadow of high office."

From October 1945 until now we can see what has increased in this large nation: the cost of living rose 100 per cent, taxes increased about 148 per cent, government income almost tripled, and so did public expenditures and budget deficits. Paper currency increased by 9 billion cruzeiros. In compensation, something must have declined. Yes, national production went down. And the gold reserves, which backed our money, almost vanished.

Only reform, said Vargas, could save Brazil. Brazilians would have to regain confidence in themselves. Brazil needed a complete plan of national reorganization to fight underproduction, underconsumption, and the disorganization generated by a subdemocracy dominated by exploiting parasites and intermediaries. The job required technicians, not representatives of special interests.

Someone should defend the Brazilian people, "this good, generous, patient, suffering people, ridiculed by false promises and massacred when they protest. . . . My new way of life brings me close to the rural class, the field workers, who comprise some 70 per cent of our population. There must be an agrarian reform." And, "to help the urban worker, social legislation must be perfected."

"It seems to me I have done what I could. Now we must turn to stubborn battle, to youthful spirit, full of vitality. Only with such forces can miracles be wrought. By fighting we can win."[1]

By the time it was published this message had already been answered in part by Dutra's unsensational year-end analysis of achievements and failures. Production increases were cited, but Dutra admitted that Congress, in spite of all his urging, had indulged in a spending spree which made it necessary to print more currency. The Finance Minister was quick

[1] *Jornal do Commercio,* Rio, January 1, 1950, dateline Pôrto Alegre, December 31, 1949.

to deny Vargas' untrue charge about the gold reserves. Rio's *Jornal do Commercio* attributed Vargas' statement to disrespect and hate.

Analyzing the situation in one of his articles, Assis Chateaubriand wrote that state legislators were interested only in increasing taxes and raising salaries "for the recruitment of electoral clientele to the political parties. . . . The federal, state, and municipal legislative bodies have been the most important corroborators of the old affirmation of the dictator that Brazil is not a nation ripe for democracy."

Chateaubriand went on to observe that when the war was over

. . . our house was empty. We had no ships, railroad cars, locomotives, automobiles, or modern machines for constructing ports and roads; no tractors. . . . After the fall of the Estado Nôvo about $2 billion were spent on useful imports from the United States. In 1947 and 1948 Brazil imported 120,000 motor vehicles costing $250 million. All the omnibus equipment of Rio, São Paulo, and other state capitals was renovated and paid for in dollars. The federal government engaged in an act of patriotism and brilliance, of which Getúlio Vargas would not be capable, when it endorsed the loan to Brazilian Traction, which will save the Federal District, São Paulo, and the state of Rio from the tremendous power crisis which threatened. . . .

To say that Brazil is experiencing a crisis is economic heresy when her two key products, coffee and cotton, receive the highest prices they have ever fetched in international markets. This year coffee brings about $600 million and cotton $100 million. Let Vargas come and feel the pulse of São Paulo. Cereals being produced in the interior have brought an end to the long lines which waited for foods during the Estado Nôvo. . . .

Production in 1949 in São Paulo and Rio beat all records in power consumption. The consumption of cement and paper has doubled in three years.

No doubt Brazil owes to Vargas the paper and cellulose industry of the Klabin brothers in Paraná, a great industrial accomplishment. Also Volta Redonda. That is all.

Vargas is bitter about a Brazil that expands with liberty under the spur of free enterprise.[2]

Chateaubriand himself might write in this vein, but the stories from São Borja which appeared in his newspapers had a different slant. Samuel Wainer, sent in February 1949 to provide coverage as the Chateaubriand chain's "special ambassador to the province of Itu," had once been a foe of the dictatorship. His reports from São Borja in 1949 and 1950 marked his as no foe of the ex-dictator.

[2] *Ibid.*, January 3, 1950, dateline Santos, December 31, 1949, reprinted from *Diário de São Paulo*.

5. Pre-Campaign Political Maneuvering, 1950

As was inevitable, great pressure was put on Getúlio to try to recapture the Presidency. Although he had serious reservations, a principal one being that it would be very difficult to govern "with a Congress like the one we have," Getúlio was so provoked by his enemies that he came to be persuaded to do what his supporters urged.[1] Wounded and disregarded, he had not been happy in retirement. To be carried to Catete Palace "on the arms of the people" would serve as a great vindication.

The ex-dictator kept his feelings to himself and was careful to rely, during the complex precampaign maneuverings, on his political acumen and well-developed sense of timing. After workers expressed disappointment that in his 1949 year-end message he had not announced his candidacy, Getúlio proclaimed that the PTB would "back no candidate who does not support the program of the party."

Local leaders of the PTB, shaken by the internal dissensions and defeats of 1947, began to make trips to São Borja to get the word of the Labor Party's "elder statesman." Getúlio politely listened to the names of possible presidential candidates and to the various formulae for making selections. Unhurried, he realized that the practical question of whether he could return depended to some extent on the outcome of talks between anti-Vargas politicians who were trying to get together.

When the press asked President Dutra about the presidential succession, he remarked with characteristic simplicity that the answer lay in the hands of the political parties and that he had lost contact with such matters. "I don't understand politics," he added.[2] But leaders of the parties which had collaborated in the Government—PSD, UDN, and Bernardes' PR (Partido Republicano)—made frequent trips to the presidential palace and at length heard Dutra insist that his support would go to a man of his own party, the PSD.

Neither Dutra nor the PSD could turn to São Paulo, for Ademar and his PSP were fighting the federal Administration. Therefore the formula of the "Government people" became a PSD man from Minas,[3] where the UDN and a wing of the PSD had been co-operating. The trick lay in finding a PSD name which, in addition to being acceptable to the two

---

[1] Lourival Coutinho, *O General Góes Depõe*, p. 499.
[2] *Jornal do Commercio*, Rio, February 9, 1950.
[3] Clemente Mariani, interview, August 22, 1963.

wings of the party in Minas, would induce the UDN and PR of Minas to put loyalty to state and antipathy to Vargas ahead of party. Early in 1950 Milton Campos, UDN governor of Minas, presided over a series of meetings where one name after another was suggested. Many of them were unknown outside the state and none of them satisfied both wings of the PSD and the UDN as well.

Getúlio's friends in the PSD had no desire to see the kind of PSD-UDN combination which was being discussed in Minas. A faction of the PSD, which included son-in-law Ernâni do Amaral Peixoto, began angling for a coalition with the PTB. At the suggestion of Vargas, representatives of the parties he had created attended meetings to draw up a joint program.

São Paulo's ambitious Governor Ademar de Barros had been on such poor terms with the Dutra Administration that it had taken all the President's reverence for the Constitution to hold back those in Rio who favored a federal intervention in São Paulo. Ademar's government, getting what it felt to be insufficient federal financial assistance, took to issuing short-term bonds, which damaged the state's credit. But the state advanced industrially, and the Governor busily inaugurated highways, hospitals, and schools.

To become a presidential candidate Ademar would have to turn over the state government before April 4 to Vice-Governor Novelli, who had become his political foe. Appreciating that Dutra's son-in-law, if he became acting governor, might even seek to jail him on the charge of mishandling public funds, Ademar declared he would stay in his post "for the good of São Paulo and Brazil." He would not, he declared, "make the mistake made by Armando de Sales Oliveira."[4]

In March 1950 Ademar was in São Borja discussing a political deal with Getúlio. Milton Campos was getting nowhere in his efforts to satisfy all the Minas currents. Outside Minas, leaders were becoming increasingly critical of these negotiations, which were being tied to arrangements involving candidates for the Minas governorship.

One of the critics, UDN President José Eduardo do Prado Kelly, began to gaze soulfully in the direction of Eduardo Gomes, who, ignoring all political maneuvering, was already running for President as candidate of the Movimento Nacional Popular. Unlike the men on the long list of names the PSD Mineiros were digging up, Gomes seemed to Prado

---

[4] *Jornal do Commercio*, Rio, January 28, 1950.

Kelly the best representative of the real party spirit. And, for whatever it was worth, his candidacy again had the support of the big conservative Rio newspapers.

Prado Kelly received a report which seemed to justify his fears: a PSD-PTB coalition had been reached, with Ovídio de Abreu, a Valadares candidate, running on a ticket whose vice-presidential candidate would be PTB Acting President Salgado Filho.[5]

Every day there were reports, with few names missing consideration in the simultaneous drives to cook up alliances. Prado Kelly, convinced that what he had learned was well-founded, rushed to Minas and Bahia to confer with Milton Campos and Otávio Mangabeira, and then announced that the UDN was again supporting Eduardo Gomes.[6]

The failure of the PSD and UDN to get together opened the door for Vargas to consider seriously the pleas that he himself run. Ademar was offering PSP support, in return, of course, for all he could get. The São Paulo governor never could persuade Getúlio to sign a formal agreement to support him for President five years later.[7] He had to content himself with pleasant words and the assurance that in the 1950 election the São Paulo PTB would back the PSP man he wanted in the governorship.

The president of the PSP of Rio Grande imprudently told the press that Getúlio and Ademar had reached important understandings and that Getúlio was a candidate. The report was promptly denied by Vargas, and Ademar's man amended his statement, explaining that Vargas was not really running, but that fate would make him the candidate of the democratic and popular fronts.

[5] José Eduardo do Prado Kelly, interview, August 29, 1963.
[6] *Ibid.*
[7] Samuel Wainer, interview, July 31, 1963.

6. Getúlio Announces His Candidacy

Getúlio was not in the habit of celebrating his birthday publicly. But on April 19, 1950, he made an exception, attending a political rally honoring his sixty-seventh birthday at the neighboring ranch of Jango Goulart. Here he acceded to the pleas of demonstrators urging that he run for President. He said he would sacrifice himself for the cause of the workers, and concluded with these words: "Take me with you."[1]

[1] Alzira Vargas do Amaral Peixoto, Ch. 10 of "A Vida de Getúlio . . .," in *Fatos & Fotos*, September 14, 1963.

The PSD would not support Gomes. Apart from backing Vargas, a position which held no appeal for the Dutra people, the best thing it could do for Getúlio's candidacy would be to select a man who was little known, who would alienate PSD Getulistas, and who would appeal to the same voters Gomes sought to attract. At the suggestion of PSD representatives from Rio Grande do Sul, the national directorship of the PSD did just this in May.[2] It seized on the name of Cristiano Machado, a *deputado* from Minas who had been mayor of Belo Horizonte in the late 1920's and, as Minas Interior Secretary, had worked for the 1930 revolution. Dutra gave his blessing.

Vargas said he had nothing against Machado. But the Vargas wing of the PSD of Rio Grande, led by João Neves, refused to support the Mineiro, arranging instead to break the party there into two factions. Writing about the nation as a whole, Rio's *Jornal do Commercio* editorialized that "the people who want to subordinate the PSD to Getúlio Vargas are now rebelling at the selection of Cristiano Machado."[3]

Juraci Magalhães, UDN candidate for governor of Bahia, shared a feeling of Góis and some others in the PSD that the UDN in the end might well turn to Machado. Explaining to Gomes that he had visited Bahia municipalities and noted considerable support for Vargas, Juraci added that "both you and Cristiano will be beaten if you remain split."[4]

But it was too late for Gomes to abandon such keen supporters as Prado Kelly, and the UDN met in convention to launch his candidacy officially. Then in June the PTB delegates unanimously nominated Vargas, and from São Paulo Ademar announced his support of Vargas, "candidate of the PTB and PSP." Next, 1,400 PSD delegates, with most of the Rio Grande contingent missing, met at Tiradentes Palace and nominated Machado.

Bernardes' Partido Republicano gathered in July to support Machado and give him a running mate, Altino Arantes, who had governed São Paulo thirty years earlier. A UDN vice-presidential candidate was found in Odilon Braga, the Mineiro who had left the Vargas Cabinet when the Estado Nôvo was established. Uncompromisingly UDN, the UDN ticket should have pleased Virgílio de Melo Franco had he lived to campaign for it.

Before throwing his Gaúcho hat into the ring Getúlio thought of every-

---

[2] *Jornal do Commercio,* Rio, May 15 and 16, 1950.
[3] *Ibid.,* May 28, 1950.
[4] Juraci Magalhães, interview, August 3, 1963.

thing. The military which ousted him in 1945 was not overlooked, and emissaries from Itu came to Rio to chat with Góis. The ailing General suggested that Vargas would do well to stop his attacks on Dutra because they might be interpreted as dislike of the military. After Vargas agreed, more emissaries came, some from Itu and one representing Ademar, to see how Góis felt about being Vargas' running mate.[5]

Ademar de Barros would not have minded seeing the PTB-PSP "populist front" cemented in the normal way, with a vice-presidential candidate from the party he dominated. The deal made at Itu did not call for that,[6] and so Vargas for a while sounded out Góis in messages. But the PTB, recalling October 1945, abhorred the thought of Góis.[7] Nor was Góis interested in deepening the split in his own party, the PSD. In a note to Itu, Góis cited his failing health and lack of interest in the Vice-Presidency; he also sent word that the Army would abide by the Constitution and would not oppose Vargas if he were elected.

The PTB-PSP vice-presidential candidacy went, then, to Deputado João Café Filho, who had founded the PSP in the Northeast in 1945 and later joined with Ademar so that the party's membership might exceed the minimum of fifty thousand required for being considered national.[8] A journalist who had shown some socialistic leanings and in 1937 had been exiled for his dislike of the Estado Nôvo, Café Filho confounded the opposition by his willingness to appear on the ballot with Vargas.

The *Diário Carioca* proclaimed it a "great disappointment" to have as Vargas' teammate this former champion of liberty who had so emphatically exclaimed "Remember 1937!" But the same newspaper became upset also with its own candidate, Eduardo Gomes. How could a man of such "fine tradition" accept "the support of the old Green Shirts?" Plínio Salgado, having returned from Portugal in 1945 and founded the PRP (Partido de Representação Popular), "to combat fascism, communism, and Nazism" and to push for "corporate state government," threw his support in 1950 to the UDN.

The elections were scheduled for October 3, 1950, and Getúlio left Itu in August for São Paulo and Rio before campaigning in the north. In the Rio residence of PTB President Danton Coelho, Góis and Vargas

---

[5] Lourival Coutinho, *O General Góes Depõe*, p. 496.

[6] João Café Filho, interview, September 6, 1963, and his memorandum of same date (answering questions).

[7] *Ibid.*

[8] *Ibid.*

faced each other for the first time since Góis had overturned the dictator. The two men met with an emotional embrace and expressions of pleasure at the reconciliation before Vargas got to talking politics with the General.

Getúlio felt confident of winning, and would fool those who thought he was "weak." Agents were at work in various states offering PTB backing to non-PTB local candidates in return for votes for Vargas. Thus, Vargas explained to Góis, arrangements had been made in Minas which would assure the defeat of Machado in the presidential contest and give victory to Juscelino Kubitschek, the PSD gubernatorial candidate.[9] When Góis asked Vargas if he could tell this to Cristiano Machado, Getúlio asked Góis only not to reveal his source. Thus Machado heard about those state deals which were to bring about what was called the *cristianização* ("Christianization") of the PSD.

[9] Lourival Coutinho, *O General Góes Depõe*, pp. 501–502.

7. "On the Arms of the People"

Getúlio put on a strenuous and effective campaign. From the moment he left Rio for the north in mid-August until he returned to São Borja on the last day of September, he had no rest from speaking engagements, jostlings, and travel. There were the small planes, in the likes of which two gubernatorial candidates lost their lives; there were the poorly lit airfields and the many bad roads. State capitals and remote towns heard Getúlio stand on his record, criticize the Dutra regime, and pledge himself, with the help of the people, to carry on the program he had begun in 1930.

São Paulo, which he visited briefly in the first part of August and for a week in September, was filled with Vargas propaganda before he appeared. But the façade of São Paulo University was draped with black crepe and the University flag flown at half mast. *O Estado de S. Paulo* refused to use Vargas' name, instead referring always to "the former dictator."

The Vargas campaign was backed by an abundance of volunteer workers: typists, propagandists, and people who offered automobiles and space in homes and offices. Scores of old associates, such as Luís Simões Lopes and Lourival Fontes, worked for Vargas' return to power. It being necessary for candidates to print their own ballots, one supporter had 200 million Vargas *cédulas* printed, and pilots were persuaded to carry stacks of them to far-away places. Anticipating several million votes, the Vargas people were also anticipating a prevalent trick of destroying opponents' ballots.[1]

The Peronista press in Argentina had been busy attacking the pro-United States Dutra regime. As was probably inevitable, the Brazilian press accused the Argentine press of reflecting Vargas' "political affinity with Perón" and mixing into Brazilian politics in favor of Vargas. Although Vargas never met Perón, Jango Goulart was on warm terms with the Argentine ruler and had sold him Brazilian lumber.

When Dutra's chief military aide affirmed that foreign financial assistance was being received by Brazilian candidates, the Argentines reacted. Dutra's aide then denied having said that such contributions came from Perón. But Buenos Aires' *Democracia,* principal organ of Peronism, accused Dutra's aide of "irresponsible insolence" and declared his rectification "no less offensive than his original assertion."[2] Although the Argentine ambassador in Rio officially denied that the government of Argentina was involved in the Brazilian political campaign,[3] Getúlio's enemies kept this issue alive.

The Communists learned from Prestes that the principal candidates were "reactionaries." Vargas was a "tyrant landowner," Machado a "banker-agent of Yankee imperialism," and Gomes the "instrument of the most reactionary high clergy and the puppet of rich landowners." Good Communists, Prestes said, should cast blank ballots. He kept in hiding, accused of sedition, after issuing his August 1950 manifesto calling for a violent agrarian revolution and the confiscation of key enterprises, especially foreign corporations.

Their party outlawed, Communists inscribed their names as candidates of legal parties. When the Superior Electoral Tribunal refused to remove the names of suspected Paulista Communists running for local offices on the ticket of the Social Labor Party, Communists hailed the decisions as a "setback for those bandits, Getúlio and Ademar."[4] The Liga Eleitoral Católica (LEC), much more fussy than the Electoral Tribunal, listed 623 objectionable candidates, including Vargas' running mate.

The amiable Machado promised that if elected he would carry on with Dutra's Five-Year Plan, which was to spend $500 million to improve

---

[1] Napoleão Alencastro Guimarães, interview, August 21, 1963.

[2] *The New York Times,* datelines Rio, August 10, 1950, and Buenos Aires, August 19, 1950.

[3] *Jornal do Commercio,* Rio, August 13, 1950.

[4] *The New York Times,* dateline Rio, September 22, 1950.

health, transportation, and the supply of energy. He urged the creation of more rural banks to help revive "stunted" agricultural production. The unsmiling *brigadeiro* offered a government in which all groups and parties would collaborate.

Getúlio sympathized with the good Brazilian people, afflicted by "sufferings," "privation," and a living-cost increase which he variously described as 300 per cent and 400 per cent. In the last four years, he said, the printing presses had turned out under Dutra as much new currency as they had turned out under him in fifteen years. But, he added, his own issues had been used for war costs and for creating such assets as the steel and iron-ore companies.[5]

Vargas in November 1945 had stated that he would go along with the people against Dutra if Dutra should ever fail to keep his promises. "And now I am with you to fulfill my word," campaigning "without benefit of the coffers of the Bank of Brazil."

Brazil, Getúlio said, must be rescued from the stagnation and apathy in which she was foundering. Offering to renew what he called an interrupted upsurge in progress and production, Vargas kept reiterating that he was not a man of empty promises. Pointing to his record, he told Santa Catarina's workers that under his regime coal had come to be produced "properly and methodically." For the Northeast there had been roads and dams; also the Alcohol and Sugar Institute. The Paulo Afonso hydroelectric project he described as "one of the few things initiated by my Government which the new Government did not discontinue." In the course of fulfilling the pledges made when he campaigned in 1930 he had created the Labor Ministry and given the working man up-to-date labor legislation.

"My adversaries," Getúlio declared in Recife, "call me Father of the Poor, and Father of the Rich. But I never have been factious or an extremist. Above all, I tried to act justly and to realize the common good. Rich and poor are equally Brazilian."

The issue of nationalism he confined to minerals and oil, which, he said, his Government had made a part of the national patrimony. Foreign capital was welcome but it should not be used "to turn our natural resources over to the control of foreign companies." In particular he discussed petroleum, "which my Government proved exists." "Those who turn their petroleum over to others alienate their own independence."

[5] For Vargas' 1950 campaign speeches, see Getúlio Vargas, *A Campanha Presidencial.*

He praised Roosevelt and talked about the FEB. Saying that "my Government got Brazil to participate in the United Nations," he promised to support the world organization. Speaking to audiences which were hearing about the Marshall Plan and the war in Korea, he said that

Brazil must not be asked to collaborate and make sacrifices, with the benefits distributed to others. We have important and urgent problems to solve. Petroleum is one of these. If they want our efficient co-operation, they must first help us find the solution, in accordance with Brazilian interests, which must have preference.

Election day would be the twentieth anniversary of the outbreak of the 1930 revolution. As he went from city to city, reminding his hearers of his previous visits, he evoked the names of local heroes who had helped make the revolution. At Belo Horizonte, whose main square had become a bedlam of loudspeakers and swirling election ballots, Getúlio recalled Antônio Carlos "with his prophetic 'Let us make the revolution before the people make it'," and Olegário Maciel, "the perfect reflection of the Mineiro's quality of fulfilling his word."

At Ponta Grossa, Paraná, he recalled his arrival twenty years earlier, at the head of the revolutionary forces which had made their headquarters there. The wild acclaim had then made Getúlio certain of victory. And so it did again, with the familiar refrain, "We want, we want, we want Ge-Ge-Getúlio," ringing in his ears. This time, he said, it would be a different type of victory, won by the secret vote, an achievement of the revolution.[6]

The anti-Vargas press suggested that the former dictator was uttering his political swan song and would soon be retired for good. But the voters decided otherwise:

For President
Getúlio Dorneles Vargas	3,849,040
Eduardo Gomes	2,342,384
Cristiano Machado	1,697,193

For Vice-President
João Café Filho	2,520,790
Odilon Braga	2,344,841
Altino Arantes	1,649,309

In São Paulo, Vargas picked up a million votes, almost double the combined vote of his opponents, while Minas split pretty evenly among Vargas, Gomes, and Machado.

[6] Getúlio Vargas, *A Campanha Presidencial*, pp. 501–502.

Ademar's triumph in São Paulo was complete, with his gubernatorial candidate winning by a large margin. In the state legislature and in the Paulista bloc in the national congress Ademar's PSP gained first place, followed by the PTB. In other states things went well for Getulismo and the PSD.

The last hurdle was the legal contest brought on when opponents of Vargas maintained that the "majority" mentioned in the 1946 Constitution meant an absolute majority. The Superior Electoral Tribunal in January, 1951, thirteen days before inauguration day, ruled that the Constitution meant a majority over one's closest opponent. Vargas and Café Filho were declared elected.

BOOK XI

CONSTITUTIONAL PRESIDENT,

1951–1954

"I do not come to sow illusions, nor should you expect of me the marvels and miracles of a newly arrived Messianism."

1. Inauguration

OPTIMISM WAS IN the air in January 1951 as Brazil awaited the new administration and as the President-elect worked for a coalition government. *The New York Times* pointed out that Vargas was "handicapped by great expectations," but it went on to say that it was an asset to be succeeding Dutra, "a colorless, inert President who did little to counter the sharp post-war inflation."[1]

Vargas, speaking in January at his first postelection press conference, insisted that he was not a "miracle man." He would try to lower living costs by combating black markets, eliminating handicaps to production, and improving transportation. As he saw it, only a union of "all national political forces" could hold back Communism, which showed signs of disrupting Brazil and bringing total war to the world. The United States, also concerned with international Communism, had already called a meeting of the American Foreign Ministers for March. To allow preparation for this meeting, Vargas early advised his recent campaign manager, João Neves, that he was again to assume the Foreign Ministry post, which he had left when Dutra had made the deal with the UDN.

[1] *The New York Times* editorial, January 31, 1951.

While dignitaries from forty nations were arriving to honor Brazil's new administration, Getúlio, animated by the prospect of giving Brazil a constructive five years, took up residence in a hotel near Rio's soaring Corcovado Peak and chatted with politicians about filling government posts. He had made an ally of Plínio Salgado's PRP, and of the major parties lacked the co-operation of only the UDN. The PSD, PTB, and PSP were all pleased to be represented in the Cabinet. But when a member of the UDN from the Northeast agreed to serve as Agriculture Minister he was roundly denounced by the leaders of his party.

A lunch with President Dutra was arranged at Góis' home, and there Vargas' exceptionally good mood was in contrast to that of the man he had so mercilessly criticized.[2] The reserved outgoing President was not happy about Vargas' selections to head the military ministries.

Newton Estilac Leal, chosen to be War Minister, had had vast experience, starting as a rebel *tenente* in the 1920's, but top officers of the Military Club opposed him for consorting with leftists. Colonel Nero Moura, who was to be Air Minister, had headed the excellent Brazilian Air Force in Italy; on October 29, 1945, he had resigned from active duty as a protest against the overthrow of Vargas. The *brigadeiros* were as unhappy about his selection as the generals were about Estilac, but Getúlio felt that both these appointees were popular among officers of lower rank.[3]

The Klabin paper company's able Horácio Lafer, a Paulista PSD leader, became Finance Minister. At one time Getúlio had in mind giving this key job to the biggest contributor to his electoral campaign,[4] industrialist Ricardo Jafet of São Paulo's sizable Syrian Lebanese community. Instead, Jafet became president of the Bank of Brazil. As many foresaw, the appointments of Lafer and Jafet would disrupt the traditional harmony between the Finance Ministry and the Bank.

Vargas was already organizing a mission to attract foreign investments. An agreement between United States Ambassador Herschel V. Johnson and Dutra's Foreign Minister, Raul Fernandes, would establish a joint Brazil-United States commission to push Brazilian economic development. Vargas, eager to see this implemented, had preinaugural talks with

[2] Lourival Coutinho, *O General Góes Depõe*, p. 512.

[3] *Ibid.*, p. 513; Glauco Carneiro, "A Face Final de Vargas" (V) in *O Cruziero*, February 20, 1965.

[4] Glauco Carneiro, "A Face Final de Vargas" (V) in *O Cruzeiro*, February 20, 1965.

Johnson and Nelson Rockefeller, who was in Rio for the ceremonies.

On January 31, after the oath of office had been administered in Tiradentes Palace, Vargas addressed a frenzied throng outside. He told of his silence in the face of the slander, hatred, and injustice that had been heaped upon him when he had left office in 1945. The people, he said with pleased assurance, had reacted, carrying him back to the Presidency.[5]

Then the new President rode triumphantly in an open car, while guns saluted, confetti was thrown, and admiring crowds, swarming wherever he went, gave Rio another great traffic jam. Carnaval was coming and new sambas were dedicated to Getúlio.

At Catete Palace, Vargas uttered a word of faint praise for Dutra, whom he described as deserving the country's thanks for having "led an administration which culminated in a model election." When reporters brought up the name of Adolf Berle, Getúlio told them that "the traditional and permanent relations of friendship and co-operation between the United States and Brazil were in no way affected by the attitudes of any individual officials who may have misinterpreted those ideals and served them badly."[6]

The press soon learned that Lourival Fontes, former chief of the DIP, was on the job as head of the President's office staff. Texts, such as those reporting Vargas' words "praising" Dutra, were not, Fontes said, to be distributed by the government-run news agency until the Presidency had approved their release.[7] The press shrugged its shoulders at this Vargas attempt to avoid being misquoted.

The ceremonies over, Vargas sped up the mountain road to Petrópolis and there held the new administration's first Cabinet meeting. Although Lafer outlined his financial program, the press coverage of the meeting was limited to the official news organ and the Chateaubriand chain's Samuel Wainer.[8]

Wainer, whose news stories in 1949 and during the 1950 campaign had helped Vargas, reminded the new President of all the difficulties he could expect from the unfriendly press. Thus, at Wainer's suggestion, the pro-Vargas Rio daily, Última Hora, was born, with Wainer as its director. Making full use of his Vargas connection, and explaining to industrialists and bankers that the President was vitally interested in Última Hora,

[5] Getúlio Vargas, O Govêrno Trabalhista do Brasil, pp. 25–29.
[6] The New York Times, dateline Rio, January 31, 1951.
[7] Ibid., dateline Rio, February 1, 1951.
[8] Samuel Wainer, interview, July 31, 1963.

Wainer obtained ample capital and, from the Bank of Brazil, generous loans.[9]

Getúlio, a careful reader of all of Rio's important dailies, told Wainer that criticism by the opposition press could be useful if it were written in good faith. "Rulers often are unaware of matters which are harmful to the public."[10] But he soon concluded that the majority of Rio's dailies generally disregarded anything constructive that the government was doing and spent their time picturing the regime as inactive and responsible for everything that went wrong.[11]

[9] Glauco Carneiro, "A Face Final de Vargas" (II) in *O Cruzeiro*, January 30, 1965.
[10] *Ibid.*
[11] Glauco Carneiro, "A Face Final de Vargas" (III) in *O Cruzeiro*, February 6, 1965.

2. The Headaches of 1951–1952

The high hopes of January 1951 were followed by disappointment. However, it was possible for a while to blame the Dutra Administration for Brazil's mounting financial difficulties. These, Vargas announced in March, "exceed anything we expected."[1] It was also possible to rely on phrases about good-sounding programs calling for efficiency, morality, austerity, and attention to rubber, "production of which was discontinued without foresight."[2]

Brazil heard plenty of words from the President, many of them over the radio. On February 18, 1951, to repay the people for their acclaim at his inauguration, he gave a "party" attended by 130,000 in the huge new Maracanã Stadium. Stage celebrities and soccer stars entertained the crowd, and Getúlio told of plans to halt inflation and replace chaos with order. On May Day, addressing the workers as of old at Vasco da Gama Stadium, he promised price controls and wage increases, and appealed for labor backing to assist him in combating the "exploiters" who caused high living costs.[3]

In the middle of 1951 Congress authorized Vargas to fight inflation by establishing ceiling prices and punishing speculators in foods. Finance Minister Lafer instructed banks to refuse loans to merchants who took

[1] Getúlio Vargas, *O Govêrno Trabalhista do Brasil*, p. 52.
[2] *Ibid.*, p. 57.
[3] *Ibid.*, pp. 321–333.

advantage of market conditions to raise prices. Minimum wages were increased as a Christmas present.

The 1951 cost-of-living increase, which could hardly be controlled by ceiling prices and certainly not by higher wages, was a reflection of the budget deficits of the last two Dutra years and the expansion of credit spurred by rising coffee quotations.

Lafer applied himself heroically to the task of balancing the federal budget. But his anti-inflationary efforts were sabotaged by Jafet's credit policy at the Bank of Brazil. In 1951 and 1952, while the federal budget showed a surplus, some 24 billion cruzeiros of new currency were issued; Bank of Brazil loans outstanding increased by 15 billion cruzeiros, one billion going to the Jafet steel mill. Unknown to Vargas, some who were close to the 'inner circle" took advantage of their positions to help arrange Bank of Brazil loans. The greatest scandal was that which enriched a group which bought up poor cotton and sold it to the Bank at the price of good cotton.[4]

In 1952, following the late 1951 wage increases and the abandonment of some ineffectual price ceilings, living costs rose 23 per cent. In protest there were meat boycotts by housewives and even some looting of food shops. Above all, there was bitterness. To make things worse, in 1951 Brazil's Northeast had its first severe drought since 1942. After a visit to the region, Lafer criticized the traditional emphasis on hydraulic works as the remedy for the Northeast's problems and persuaded Vargas to establish a regional credit institution, the Bank of the Northeast of Brazil.[5]

The lack of foreign exchange was no deterrent to making purchases abroad, even at the high prices caused by the Korean War. Vargas' financial team, which included Luís Simões Lopes of the Office of Exports and Imports, felt that the Korean War might well become global, in which case, as in World War II, it would be practically impossible to get anything. In 1951 and particularly in 1952 the excess of imports over exports was unprecedented, leaving Brazil owing more than $600 million to commercial creditors abroad.

In his 1951 year-end message to the nation Vargas announced that foreign investors had been "bleeding Brazil" by sending excessive profit remittances abroad "illegally and scandalously."[6] The Dutra regime had

[4] Lourival Fontes, interview, July 27, 1963.

[5] Stefan H. Robock, *Brazil's Developing Northeast: A Study of Regional Planning and Foreign Aid*, pp. 91–93; Albert O. Hirschman, *Journeys toward Progress*, p. 61.

[6] *The New York Times*, dateline Rio, December 31, 1951.

limited these remittances to 8 per cent annually, and on January 4, 1952, Vargas decreed that the 8 per cent was allowable only on the capital originally brought in and registered, not on reinvested profits.

Profit remittances had been large.[7] The crux of the matter lay in the difference between the official exchange rate of 18.5 cruzeiros per dollar and the "black market's" more realistic appraisal of 35 cruzeiros. It was attractive to buy dollars for remission abroad at the cheap official rate, but it was hardly interesting to use the official rate as a basis for investing dollars in Brazil. Foreign investors seemed agreeable to accepting a fair and free exchange rate provided that reinvestments be included in the formula limiting remittances. The Brazilian government hesitated to part from the official rate. Although such a move would give exports, highly overpriced in world markets, a badly needed boost, it might be inflationary at home. While the debate went on, foreign investors held off placing new capital in Brazil.

By handling the matter as he did in his year-end radio address, Vargas opened a Pandora's box, and the technical aspects of the debate were drowned out by the cries of economic ultranationalists. One of these was War Minister Estilac Leal. Another was ex-President Artur Bernardes, who spoke of "insidious infiltration by foreign investment."[8] Senator Bernardes was well practiced at this game and used it to attack Vargas, explaining that the Estado Nôvo had been installed in 1937 "to protect foreign trusts," and that Vargas' proposed new petroleum law was "inspired by the trusts." Vargas was working on a proposal for the creation of a petroleum extraction company which would be at least 51 per cent owned by the government and which would not have a monopoly; under government control private companies would also be able to extract petroleum, and foreign investments in petroleum would not be excluded.[9]

Lafer asserted that there were good and bad foreign investors, but also pointed out that Communists were quick to seize on any minor disagreement between Brazil and the United States. Juarez Távora warned that the Communist threat was worse than any danger of exploitation by foreign trusts.

---

[7] In *New Perspectives of Brazil* (p. 129) Eric Baklanoff reports that "In the seven years between 1947 and 1953, the inflow of venture capital averaged only 15 million dollars per year, while profit remittances averaged 47 million dollars."

[8] *The New York Times,* dateline Rio, February 2, 1951.

[9] Napoleão Alencastro Guimarães, interview, August 21, 1963; Juarez Távora, interview, May 22, 1965; Vargas' message to Congress, December 6, 1951 (Project 1516; in Câmara dos Deputados, *Petróleo, Projetos 1516/51, 1517/51, 1595/52*).

When Vargas took over in 1951, the Communists in their Rio daily, *Imprensa Popular,* said that "the old tyrant now succeeds the iniquitous dictator Dutra." In March 1951, as the American Foreign Ministers gathered in Washington, the Communists organized disturbances in Rio, São Paulo, and Belo Horizonte. Brazil having been invited to send a small force to Korea,[10] Communists shouted "Not one soldier for Korea" and promoted a "Continental Peace Congress."

The Korean matter was discussed by the National Security Council, with Vargas presiding. Góis, whom Vargas had appointed Chief of Staff of the Armed Forces, expressed his conviction that Brazilian troops, without lengthy preparation, would not be effective in Korea. Then he was sent to Washington to discuss co-operation in case the new conflict became general.

On March 15, 1952, Foreign Minister João Neves and Ambassador Johnson signed a United States-Brazil Military Aid Pact in which both countries promised armed support if needed for hemispheric defense, the United States offering aid in weapons and equipment in exchange for access to raw materials. This pact, displeasing to the Communists, Perón and some PTB lawmakers, was finally ratified by Congress over a year after it was signed, but the obstruction and discussion so concerned Góis that at one point he suggested to Vargas that it might be best that Congress reject the pact.[11]

An abortive raid on an Army ammunition depot in Natal in March 1952 as the Communist Party of Brazil prepared to mark its thirtieth anniversary, brought an alert against possible Red outbreaks. While the police searched unsuccessfully for Prestes, the Communists encouraged anti-inflation riots and looting. João Neves declared that the Communist drive for influence was more determined than it ever had been.

Communists infiltrated sectors of the PTB[12] and were delighted to note that in labor circles the new administration did not apply the stern anti-Communist policy of the Dutra regime. The decree of September 1, 1952, whereby Labor Minister Danton Coelho struck out the requirement that union officials support no ideology contrary to the democratic regime,[13] was considered a major Communist victory.

Communist sympathizers were finding such a good friend in War Minister Estilac Leal that Zenóbio da Costa, commander of troops in the

[10] Lourival Coutinho, *O General Góes Depõe,* p. 517.
[11] *Ibid.,* p. 520.
[12] *Ibid.*
[13] Arnaldo Sussekind, interview, September 11, 1963.

Rio area, resigned his post in protest. Seeking to heal the rift in the Army, Getúlio accepted the resignation of both Zenóbio and Estilac late in March 1952. The President's chief military aide became War Minister, and Góis, who was quite unwell, resigned as Chief of Staff. Anti-Estilac Leal generals then organized a "Democratic Crusade" to have the Army purged of pro-Communists. Combating it, Estilac rallied anti-United States forces and declared that his downfall was the result of a campaign organized and paid for by foreign interests.

3. Missing F. D. R.

On December 31, 1952, in his annual radio address to the nation, Getúlio promised better times, explaining that the measures taken in the second half of 1952 had virtually overcome the crisis. "We have freed ourselves from the chronic evil of continuous deficits, the cause of finanical anarchy." He referred optimistically to a potential new source of foreign currency: "The reserve of atomic minerals constitutes a wealth of which we cannot evaluate the full significance."[1]

Mentioning the Joint Brazil-United States Economic Development Commission, Vargas said that it had obtained for Brazil foreign loans totaling over $100 million, with roughly twice as much still to come. These figures agreed with understandings already reached, it being expected that around $300 million would be provided by the World Bank (IBRD) and the Export-Import Bank for projects approved by the Commission.

When João Neves was in Washington for the 1951 Foreign Ministers Meeting, Brazilian technicians had discussed at the World Bank the Joint Commission's forthcoming work. Although the $300 million figure had then been subject to reservations about changes in Brazil's foreign-currency position and "credit-worthiness," these reservations had been left out of assurances given Lafer in Washington in September 1951.[2] Lafer needed to know, because the local currency requirements, estimated as equivalent to $550 million, were to be obtained by increasing taxes, an unpopular step which Lafer took after his Washington talk.

In the meantime the Joint Economic Development Commission was formally installed in the magnificent, marble-walled Salão Nobre of the Brazilian Finance Ministry in July 1951, with speeches stressing its char-

---

[1] *The New York Times,* dateline Rio, December 31, 1952.

[2] Joint Brazil-United States Economic Development Commission, *The Development of Brazil,* p. 72.

acter of action or implementation. Merwin Bohan, chief of the United States team, had an office adjoining that of the keenly interested Lafer. Ari Torres headed a team which included the cream of Brazil's financial, economic, and engineering personnel.

The Commission, which had the advantage of development studies prepared by the Abbink Mission of 1948, gave emphasis to transportation and electric-power projects which could be realized reasonably quickly, would complement private investment, and would eliminate bottlenecks or promote economic growth. On the Commission's recommendation it was agreed that the federal railways would be incorporated into one organization, and the National Economic Development Bank was established to handle the financing of the development program. The Commission approved and forwarded to Washington forty-one detailed projects calling for 14 billion cruzeiros in local currency costs and $387,300,000 in foreign currencies.

The effort had been a well-planned and well-executed exercise in international co-operation. When Vargas mentioned it on the radio at the end of 1952 Merwin Bohan was in Washington trying to lay the groundwork for the Joint Commission to bow out in a blaze of glorious goodwill early in the forthcoming Eisenhower Administration. With a sense of shock at what he felt to be a lack of good faith, Bohan learned at the World Bank that conditions had changed: balance-of-payment questions, credit worthiness, and other obstacles had come in the way.[3]

Brazil's credit worthiness had slipped badly with the purchases abroad in 1952. Lafer and Vargas' new ambassador to Washington, rich young banker Walter Moreira Sales, were eager for a bail-out loan to help liquidate the backlog of commercial arrearages. Four hundred million dollars were owed to United States exporters, who exerted strong pressure. Early in the Eisenhower administration the Export-Import Bank came through with $300 million to help pay them off.

The decision to lend Brazil this $300 million, and the practical withdrawal of the Export-Import Bank from the field of economic development financing, made the outlook for the Joint Commission's projects discouraging.[4] Although in February 1953 the Vargas Administration established a "free" cruzeiro market which could be used for the unlimited remission of profits by foreign investors, this did not persuade the World Bank to alter its view that Brazil needed to clean up its house. Recommen-

[3] Letter from Merwin L. Bohan, December 17, 1963, pp. 8–9.
[4] *Ibid.*, p. 9.

dations for a number of the Joint Commission projects fell on sterile ground.

Milton Eisenhower, concluding a South American tour late in July 1953 with a five-day visit in Brazil, did not find Rio's climate friendly. The *Diário Carioca* quoted him as saying that if Brazil wanted to be aided, it must aid itself, and the *Correio da Manhã* accused the Eisenhower Administration of reneging on Truman promises. Milton Eisenhower states: "The Brazilians were furious and made no effort to hide their anger."[5] He tried to tell them that "the kind of technical advice you received is as good as money," but this hardly mollified disappointed members of the Joint Commission. Milton Eisenhower called on Vargas. "He was," he writes, "a short, oldish, roving-eyed man. His vivacious and attractive daughter was at his side constantly, and I soon concluded that Vargas . . . was not well."[6]

Vargas had slipped on a well-polished palace floor, fracturing a leg and arm, but his indisposition was not only physical. Alzira had rushed to Rio from a short vacation to find Getúlio irritable and deeply depressed. In splints which pained him, he was afflicted by insomnia and worries and was thinking of resigning. "His illness," Alzira concludes, "was loneliness. He refused to receive visitors and was getting no human warmth. We devised a plan to keep him occupied, and for someone to be with him, especially at night when insomnia led him to somber thoughts."[7]

The work of the Joint Commission was over. Valentim Bouças drove Bohan to Catete for a farewell talk with Getúlio, who hid well the disappointment he felt at the outcome. The President expressed a keen desire "to have all of the work of the Joint Commission published—so that I may deliver a set to President Eisenhower, in order that there be no lack of continuity in carrying out the reciprocal commitments assumed by our two countries."[8]

During 1952 and 1953 foreign currency of $181 million was made available to Brazil for fifteen of the Joint Commission projects, leaving, at the end of 1953, twenty-six projects, calling for $206 million, awaiting action. Although eventually most of the balance was provided by the

[5] Milton S. Eisenhower, *The Wine Is Bitter*, p. 152.

[6] *Ibid.*, p. 198.

[7] Alzira Vargas do Amaral Peixoto, Ch. 11 of "A Vida de Getúlio . . .," in *Fatos & Fotos*, September 21, 1963.

[8] Merwin L. Bohan, interview, August 20, 1964.

Export-Import Bank, the conditions under which the Joint Commission wound up its work contributed to a feeling in Brazil that an unsatisfactory change had been taking place in the United States attitude. World War II having ended, the days of a special role for Brazil in United States thinking seemed to be over. The United States was giving enormous attention to the Marshall Plan and was particularly concerned with the struggle against international Communism on other continents. Vargas missed Franklin D. Roosevelt.

While Washington rumbled with McCarthyism, nationalist sentiments made headway in Latin America, Brazil not excepted. The United States, which in Brazil was receiving sincere criticism from some of its friends, came also to be a target of irrational ultranationalism.

Following the death of Stalin in 1953, the Brazilian Communist Party —always taking its orders from Russia—changed its line drastically from the violent revolutionary one called for in 1948 and 1950. Adapting itself better to the realities of Brazilian politics, it would "attack American imperialism and not all imperialisms."[9] It would encourage anti-United States nationalists.[10]

The petroleum question was discussed everywhere. "Nationalism" was so popular that in 1953 UDN congressmen took the lead in sponsoring a bill which would be as "nationalistic" as possible, and in this they were encouraged by some of the men who were close to Vargas. Vargas' original project, allowing private companies, fell by the wayside. No politician, Vargas included, could appear less "patriotic" than anyone else. With Vargas urging congressmen to act and warning of "hidden forces," the Câmara and Senate passed a bill which put all petroleum production in the hands of state-owned and state-run Petrobrás. At Vargas' request the UDN's Juraci Magalhães left the presidency of the government-run iron ore company to become the first president of Petrobrás.

[9] Osvaldo Peralva, *O Retrato*, p. 27 n.
[10] Rollie E. Poppino, "Communism in Postwar Brazil," pp. 4-5.

4. Trying Another Team

There were many bills in which Vargas was deeply interested, but few were passed by Congress. Among those which lay dormant was his ambitious project for reforming public administration. This would do away with needless departments and create some new ministries to supervise numerous entities which were reporting directly to the President.[1]

While the press attacked the President for doing nothing, the cost of living increased at a much faster rate than it had in the last years of the Dutra administration.

Francisco Campos, summoned to Catete for a talk, found Getúlio in "lamentable" condition, deeply depressed, and regretting ever having left Itu.[2] When Góis spoke with Vargas, it was after junior Army officers had shown the General that it was practically impossible for them to live on their pay. As usual, Góis had plenty of suggestions for the President: big reforms, changes in the Constitution, and a totally new Cabinet.[3]

Vargas was ready for a sweeping Cabinet change. Finance Minister Lafer, after complaining of the Bank of Brazil's lavish credit operations and condemning its cotton transactions, had persuaded Vargas to drop Jafet, but he himself was running into criticism. The sound money man was accused of opposing relief in the Northeast, and was blamed for the painful economic situation. The "parallel" or "free" exchange market, which he had instituted, showed that the currency had so depreciated that it took forty-five cruzeiros to buy a dollar. Other Cabinet ministers were having such troubles that their effectiveness in dealing with Congress was reduced.

The Cabinet revision began in June 1953. José Américo, co-ordinator of the Northeast Drought Control Program, had been having a disagreement with the Transport Minister and was named to replace him. Then Osvaldo Aranha became Finance Minister and João Goulart Labor Minister. A few days later, changes were made in most of the other nonmilitary Cabinet posts. Vicente Ráo, an old Paulista foe of the Estado Nôvo, became Foreign Minister.

Getúlio was not surrounding himself with "yes men." Aranha, who had become Dutra's ambassador to the United Nations and then headed the General Assembly, had been at odds with Vargas ideas since 1944. But the sentiments which sprang from a long and deep personal friendship, as well as a desire to help, induced him to take the Finance post against the advice of Góis. Besides, Aranha could see the post as offering him an opportunity to achieve the Presidency as Vargas' successor.[4] Var-

---

[1] Glauco Carneiro, "A Face Final de Vargas" (XII) in *O Cruzeiro*, April 24, 1965.

[2] Francisco Campos, interview, September 3, 1963.

[3] Lourival Coutinho, *O General Góes Depõe*, p. 526.

[4] Afonso Arinos de Melo Franco, interview, August 20, 1963.

gas, too, liked this idea, and was prepared to push Aranha's candidacy in 1955.[5]

Aranha's measures to conserve foreign exchange were well received. His ruling of October 1953 ended the system of import licenses, whose distribution—after Luís Simões Lopes left the Office of Exports and Imports—had been afflicted by corruption. Under Aranha's new arrangement the possibility of acquiring foreign exchange for imports was made available to all by means of the government's auctioning of the rights to buy such exchange. In accordance with the nature of the goods to be imported, various categories of these auctions were established; at the same time exporters were given bonuses above the official rate of 18.5 cruzeiros per dollar, exports also falling into categories with different bonuses for each.

Less successful was the Aranha policy of "protecting" coffee. For a while the purchases made on the New York Coffee Exchange by firms of specialists on behalf of Brazil seemed to have a favorable effect, particularly with the news of a frost in Paraná. But it was not a serious frost. World production had more than caught up with consumption, as became all too evident. In spite of a lot of buying done on Aranha's instructions, a New York price of eighty-seven cents per pound could not be maintained, and early in July 1954 the "defense" was switched from New York to Brazil. The recently created Brazilian Coffee Institute (IBC) would buy in Brazil all coffee that producers and merchants could not dispose of at the equivalent of an eighty-seven cent price in New York, the corresponding cruzeiro price being paid in Brazil by the IBC. Although in this way Brazil started filling warehouses and keeping coffee off the world market, the world price continued to fall, with producers in Colombia, Africa, and elsewhere increasing their exports.

São Borja neighbor Jango Goulart, who resided at Catete Palace and seemed to be regarded by Getúlio as almost a member of the family, was head of the PTB. Ambitious at thirty-seven to take over the Labor Ministry, he sponsored the maritime strike which embarrassed Labor Minister José Segadas Viana. In doing this, Goulart co-operated with Communist elements in the maritime union.

In the Cabinet shuffle of June 1953, Goulart replaced Segadas Viana and then settled the strike to the advantage of the maritime workers. Next he proposed a great increase in the minimum wage, and gave encouragement to "leftist" unions which had been closed by the Dutra Adminis-

---

[5] Tancredo Neves, interview, October 7, 1965.

tration. Communists, thanks to the Danton Coelho decree of September 1952, were gaining union posts.[6]

Even before Vargas held the first meeting of his new Cabinet on August 7, 1953, there were strong objections to Goulart in the Rio press (notable exceptions being *Última Hora* and *O Mundo*). He was accused of ousting independent union leaders, encouraging workers to agitate and strike, and setting about to organize Brazilian labor into something resembling the General Labor Confederation of Argentina, described as Perón's principal prop. Some journalists visualized a coup by "elements close to Vargas."

Getúlio assured Brazilians that the Constitution would prevail, and Goulart announced that he had no subversive designs. However, doubts existed on the part of some of the members of the Grupo da Sorbonne, associated with the Superior War College which had been established during the Dutra Administration.[7] These men disliked Goulart's idea of creating a *república sindicalizada,* or trade union republic.[8] They resented what they felt to be his tendency to encourage undemocratic or anti-constitutional forces in order to bring about social-economic change,[9] and they also feared Perón's efforts to bring Brazil into an anti-United States bloc (ABC) with Argentina and Chile.

Under these circumstances the *memorial* which was signed in February 1954 by eighty-two Army men, all of them colonels or lieutenant-colonels, created a crisis. This *memorial,* after senior Colonel Amauri Kruel had revised the draft in an effort to make it nonpolitical,[10] was mostly a complaint against the War Minister; nevertheless, it included brief references to the proposed minimum-wage increase and to corruption in government.

Goulart had been completing work on the decree which would double the minimum wage for workers, bringing it in the Federal District to 2,400 cruzeiros per month, equal to the salary of an Army second lieutenant. He announced that he would submit his resignation so as not to embarrass the President, and Getúlio prepared to deal with this new crisis. Advised by Lourival Fontes that there were three possible solutions, the

[6] Arnaldo Sussekind, interview, September 11, 1963.
[7] Afonso Arinos de Melo Franco, interview, August 20, 1963.
[8] Hélio Silva, interview, July 27, 1963.
[9] Afonso Arinos de Melo Franco, interview, August 20, 1963.
[10] Amauri Kruel, interviews, November 15 and November 30, 1965.

right way, the wrong way, and the Army way,[11] Getúlio gave all appearances of placating the top Army officers. The War Minister, who called the Colonel's manifesto "an invaluable contribution" but had delayed ten days before showing it to Vargas, was reproached by the President for not having kept him informed; he was replaced by Zenóbio da Costa, who two years earlier had complained of Communism around Estilac Leal.

Posters were declaring that workers would get a fair deal "only with Getúlio and Jango," but Getúlio accepted the Goulart resignation. However, Goulart's influence in the Labor Ministry in no way diminished, and his 100-per-cent increase in minimum wages was made effective May 1, 1954. Vargas, discussing the wage increase with the colonels who had signed the *memorial,* spoke of the plight of workers in the face of eight years of inflation.[12]

Brazil was preparing for the political campaign which was to end on October 3, 1954, with the election of most of the governors, two thirds of the senators, and all the federal *deputados.* UDN congressmen were working on plans to impeach the President, who was to be charged with intriguing with Perón.

Already, in March 1954, Carlos Lacerda's oppositionist *Tribuna da Imprensa* had printed what it claimed was a secret speech by Perón to the Argentine War College. In this story President Vargas was described as having sent Geraldo Rocha of *O Mundo* to explain to Perón that he could not fulfill agreements leading to a Brazilian alliance with Argentina and Chile because of his difficult political situation.[13] In April, after the Argentine Embassy called this article an insidious slander, ex-Foreign Minister João Neves spoke to the press. He said that Batista Luzardo, Brazil's ambassador to Argentina, had bypassed him to negotiate with Perón about the ABC alliance, and he pictured Goulart as frequently visiting Perón and praising the Argentine ruler and the "popular masses" of his country.[14]

There was, however, no basis at all for charging Vargas with secretly negotiating with Perón about the ABC matter or any other matter, and in June 1954 the President's political opponents tried another approach. They accused him of mishandling public funds.

[11] Lourival Fontes, interview, July 27, 1963.
[12] Afonso César, *Política, Cifrão e Sangue: Documentário do 24 de Agôsto,* pp. 157–160.
[13] Carlos Lacerda, *O Caminho da Liberdade,* p. 191.
[14] *Ibid.,* p. 36.

Politics had become infested with—almost synonymous with—corruption.[15] The regime included some who took advantage of their positions. Getúlio, who was strictly honest, encouraged investigations designed to reveal wrongdoings. When he heard that Samuel Wainer, director of *Última Hora,* had used his Vargas connection to borrow 265 million cruzeiros from the Bank of Brazil, the President, feeling betrayed, broke with him. Part of the final tragedy lay in the conduct of some of the men whom Getúlio had put in good posts. Lourival Fontes writes that Vargas "did not have a thousand eyes" and had to use the human material that was available.[16] But he could have been more careful.

The congressional opposition lined up sixteen *deputados* to make anti-Vargas speeches, but, after the PSP decided not to support impeachment, on June 16 the *deputados* resolved by a vote of 136 to 37 not to forward the matter to the Senate. Some agreed with a thought attributed to Dutra: "Let's tolerate Getúlio to the bitter end."

The election campaign promised to be a rough one in which Getúlio's image would be further impaired. The growing lack of respect for his Government was reflected on Sunday, August 1, when Vargas appeared for the races at Rio's conservative Jockey Club and was booed. People were charging that the funds of the Pension Institutes were being handled improperly and that the Federal Supply and Price Commission was costly and ineffective. In three years bread and rice prices had climbed 100 per cent. Reflecting the inflation, the cruzeiro had fallen on the free market to sixty to the dollar.

Most violent in attacking Vargas, Goulart, Jafet, and Wainer was the *Tribuna da Imprensa.* Its owner, Carlos Lacerda, seemed well in the lead in his congressional race against Getúlio's son, Lutero.

[15] See Afonso Arinos de Melo Franco, *Estudos de Direito Constitucional,* pp. 165–196; also Glauco Carneiro, "A Face Final de Vargas" (XIV) in *O Cruzeiro,* May 8, 1965.

[16] Glauco Carneiro, "A Face Final de Vargas" (XIV) in *O Cruzeiro,* May 8, 1965.

5. "Major Vaz Is Dead"[1]

Fear that Lacerda's life was in danger was well founded, and members of the Air Force decided to take turns accompanying him as he campaigned. When he returned to his Tonelero Street apartment in Rio's Copacabana district about 1:00 o'clock on the morning of August 5 Air Force Major Rubens Vaz was with him.

After the car pulled up in front of the apartment shots were fired, hitting Lacerda in the foot and killing Major Vaz. The criminal escaped in a waiting taxi, but not before he wounded an approaching policeman who fired on the car.

This crime filled the newspapers. On the fifth Lacerda wrote in the *Tribuna da Imprensa*: "I accuse only one man as responsible. . . . He is the protector of thieves whose impunity gives them the audacity for such acts. This man is named Getúlio Vargas."

Getúlio, dismayed at the crime, told associates that on the eve of elections his most dedicated enemy could not have made it worse for the government. Outside Catete Palace, then the President's residence, several hundred marchers bore banners calling for the punishment of the assassins.

The Vaz funeral was attended by Dutra, Eduardo Gomes, and hundreds of military officers, and after it was over six hundred officers from all branches of the Armed Forces gathered at the Air Force Club to voice their indignation. To the police investigation was added an Air Force investigation, which had the government's support.

The taxi driver, whose cab had been hit by bullets, quickly confessed to the police that he had transported two men to and from the scene of the crime. At first he denied knowing them. But as he stationed his car at the Catete Palace cab stand and customarily served the presidential "Personal Guard," suspicions grew. On August 7 he admitted that one of the men was Climério, a member of the guard, who had offered 20,000 cruzeiros for the transportation. Climério was a crony of Gregório Fortunato, the Negro who headed the "Personal Guard."

[1] See F. Zenha Machado, *Os Últimos Dias do Govêrno de Vargas*; Afonso César, *Política, Cifrão e Sangue*; Hugo Baldessarini, *Crônica de uma Época: Getúlio Vargas e o Crime de Toneleros*; *O Globo*'s *O Livro Negro da Corrupção*; and J. V. D. Saunders' "A Revolution of Agreement among Friends: The End of the Vargas Era" in *The Hispanic American Historical Review*, XLIV, No. 2 (May, 1964).

Gregório Fortunato, an uneducated peon from São Borja, had great influence, and considered himself the loyal defender of the regime. Known now as the "Black Angel of Catete," he had fought at the side of Benjamim Vargas against the Paulistas in 1932, had joined the Personal Guard when Benjamim formed it in 1938, and had become its commander when Benjamim left the position in 1950. Exploiting the confidence shown in him by the President, he was flattered by opportunists of all social classes; he fattened on "commissions" from "bankers" of the unlawful "animal game" lottery, and accepted large fees for arranging import permits and Bank of Brazil loans. A few months before the shooting he had been decorated by the War Minister.

Gregório was asked by Vargas' chief military aide to order Climério to Catete. Instead the Black Angel found 50,000 cruzeiros—part of a gratification received for arranging a Bank of Brazil loan—and gave them to a subordinate to take to Climério with a message to flee.

Advised that Climério was implicated, Getúlio agreed to disband the eighty-three–man Personal Guard. The guard, he told his chief military aide, only served to keep poor supplicants from visiting him. "I have never feared the people: they constitute the best friend I have."[2] Then he added: "Apprehend anyone in the Palace, even without consulting me." Gregório was confined to his suite of rooms at Catete.

News of the involvement of the presidential bodyguard sent Vargas' prestige plummeting. The *Tribuna da Imprensa* editorial of August 9 said that "if there remained any shadow of patriotism in him, the man today would hand over his authority to his legal substitute." Similar thoughts were expressed by Afonso Arinos de Melo Franco and other UDN congressmen.

But Getúlio resolved not to resign. When Communications Minister José Américo went to Catete to suggest that the President yield to the opposition, Getúlio insisted on "dignifying the mandate received from the people." Speaking with Lourival Fontes he said: "Today I am Constitutional President. I shall not remain in the government a day more or less than my mandate. I shall fight in the streets, and shall leave only when dead. I shall resist in the government, for that is my duty."[3] When Cardinal Jaime de Barros Câmara called, evoking memories of Cardinal Leme's visits to President Washington Luís in 1930, Vargas stated that he would neither resign nor prevent the truth from being discovered.

[2] F. Zenha Machado, *Os Últimos Dias do Govêrno de Vargas*, p. 23.
[3] *Ibid.*, p. 34.

Vargas went to Belo Horizonte to inaugurate the Mannesmann steel tube plant, leaving a restless Rio. On August 11, at Rio's renowned Candelária Church, Cardinal Câmara, with three bishops in attendance, celebrated Mass for the soul of Major Vaz. On President Vargas Avenue, outside Candelária, thousands assembled. After the service many moved down Rio Branco Avenue to the square in front of the Municipal Theater, traditional rallying point for demonstrations. On their way they tore down posters urging the re-election of Deputado Lutero Vargas. With the help of tear gas the police dispersed repeated anti-government manifestations.

In Belo Horizonte on August 12 Getúlio spoke of the benefits his Government had brought Minas. His preoccupation with the public good, he said, required him to serve out his term. Condemning those who used lies to bring discord, chaos, and anarchy to Brazil, he predicted a healthy reaction on the part of patriotic public opinion. "The insults they hurl at me, the stones they throw at me, the lies and calumnies, will not succeed in dispiriting me, in disturbing my serenity, or in wresting me away from the principles of love and Christian humility according to which I have molded my life and which make me forget offenses and pardon injustices. On the other hand, I will not tolerate those who are agents of crime or instruments of corruption."[4]

[4] *The New York Times,* dateline Rio, August 12, 1954.

6. A Sea of Mud

Getúlio's return to Rio on Friday, August 13, coincided with sensational developments in the murder investigation. The well-organized manhunt, in which the Armed Forces were using cars, helicopters, and planes, yielded a thirty-three–year–old mulatto, Alcino João do Nascimento, who turned out to be the killer.

At Galeão Air Base, headquarters of the Air Force Investigation, he confessed that in June a counterfeiter had put him in touch with presidential guard Climério, who had contracted with him to assassinate Lacerda in return for 500,000 cruzeiros and a good job as a police investigator. After the crime, he said, Climério had given him 10,000 cruzeiros, saying that the money came from Lutero Vargas.

Lutero, who was not involved, went to Galeão and, setting aside his congressional immunity, offered to give any information that might be helpful. On that same evening, August 13, he addressed the nation by radio. He spoke of the "insanity of bad Brazilians, working for personal hatreds, trying to involve my name in their fraudulent plot."[1] In conclusion he said: "I swear before God and the nation that I had no part, either through act or omission, in this deplorable event."

In the search for Climério, areas in Rio de Janeiro, São Paulo, Paraná, and Rio Grande do Sul (including São Borja) were combed. A lead from a Catete taxi driver sent investigators to a banana grove in the state of Rio. Roads were blocked and a helicopter hovered overhead while military vehicles and two hundred well-armed men closed in. On the chilly morning of August 18, at the end of what has been described as "the greatest manhunt in Brazilian annals,"[2] a hungry and exhausted Climério was captured. "Those in whom I most trusted betrayed me," he said.[3]

Climério was found in possession of 53,000 cruzeiros bearing the same serial number as 225,000 found on Gregório. After both men had been transferred to Galeão, Climério accused Gregório of having asked him to arrange the murder of Lacerda. The investigating commission of the Air Force reported that the specific orders for the crime had come from Gregório. Climério and the murderer, they found, had been given to understand that Lutero Vargas was interested and would use his parliamentary immunity somehow to protect the assassin.[4]

In the Chamber of Deputies minority leader Afonso Arinos de Melo Franco referred to the "guild of criminals" in the government. Majority leader Gustavo Capanema maintained that the UDN, not the people, agitated for Vargas' resignation. Army generals were inclined to respect the Constitution, and observers saw Getúlio weathering the storm. When Air Minister Nero Moura resigned, the President appointed as his successor Brigadeiro Epaminondas Gomes dos Santos, who had earlier urged Air Force officers not to become "an electoral tool of the UDN."

But the storm became worse after the investigators, searching for papers in Catete Palace, went off with Gregório's private files. As was later reported by the chief of the Military Police Investigation (ap-

---

[1] F. Zenha Machado, *Os Últimos Dias do Govêrno de Vargas*, p. 49.

[2] J. V. D. Saunders in *The Hispanic American Historical Review*, XLIV, No. 2 (May, 1964), 199.

[3] F. Zenha Machado, *Os Últimos Dias do Govêrno de Vargas*, p. 54; J. V. D. Saunders in *The Hispanic American Historical Review*, XLIV, No. 2 (May, 1964), 200.

[4] Report of Air Force investigators read to Air Force Club, August 21, 1954, in F. Zenha Machado, *Os Últimos Dias do Govêrno de Vargas*, p. 150.

pointed by Air Minister Nero Moura), the investigators, asked to look into crimes against persons, "uncovered crimes against the patrimony, crimes against public faith, and crimes against public administration."[5]

The papers in Gregório's files disclosed influence peddling, as well as bribery of officials to get import licenses covering $13 million.[6] One of the papers was a receipt dated August 27, 1953, signed by Getúlio's son Manoel Antônio Vargas, acknowledging payment of 3,920,000 cruzeiros by Gregório, who thereby became the owner of the São Manoel property at São Borja. In making this purchase Gregório had been assisted by a 3,000,000 cruzeiro loan from the Bank of Brazil.

The Air Force colonel in charge of the Military Police Investigation was called to Catete by Getúlio. While the findings were being described, the President remarked: "What an incredible thing! What a miserable thing!" After the colonel had finished, Getúlio said: "I have the impression I am upon a sea of mud."

[5] The report of Air Force Colonel João Adil de Oliveira, chief of the Military Police Investigation, was submitted to Air Minister Eduardo Gomes on September 19, 1954. The text may be found in F. Zenha Machado, *Os Últimos Dias do Govêrno de Vargas*, pp. 177–194 and in Hugo Baldessarini, *Crônica de uma Época: Getúlio Vargas e o Crime de Toneleros*, pp. 207–221. Gregório Fortunato maintained that General Ângelo Mendes de Morais and Deputado Euvaldo Lodi had influenced him in deciding to act against Lacerda's life. In 1956 Gregório Fortunato was sentenced to twenty-five years' imprisonment; Climério Euribes de Almeida and Alcino João de Nascimento each got thirty-three-year sentences. In 1962 Gregório Fortunato was murdered by a fellow prisoner.

[6] F. Zenha Machado, *Os Últimos Dias do Govêrno de Vargas*, p. 69; Hugo Baldessarini, *Crônica de uma Época: Getúlio Vargas e o Crime de Toneleros*, pp. 179–180.

7. Getúlio Refuses To Resign

On the night of August 21 officers of the Air Force gathered to hear their investigators tell of evidence found in Gregório's files. The final words of the report reminded the officers that "our mission recalls the memory of a fallen comrade, and proves the degraded state of the nation." The Air Force Club president closed the meeting abruptly, before a motion could be made, and the *brigadeiros* resolved to meet on Sunday morning, the twenty-second.

Carlos Lacerda, in nightly broadcasts attacking Vargas, was using the radio more effectively than it had ever been used before in Brazilian politics. The Brazilian Lawyers' Association and the board of the University of the Federal District declared that Vargas should resign. Former Presidents Bernardes and Dutra made the same suggestion.[1] "Resignation," Dutra told reporters, "is the only solution that can calm the nation. . . . It cannot be denied that the President has public opinion against him at this moment; and a government without public opinion in its favor has no choice but to resign, even if it has the material elements for resisting."

Vice-President Café Filho reached the conclusion that his having been elected on the same ticket with Vargas might present a complication and therefore proposed to the military authorities the joint resignation of Vargas and himself. But Zenóbio insisted that as War Minister it was his duty to maintain the President in office. When Café Filho discussed the joint resignation idea with Vargas the President said he had made up his mind not to resign.[2] Privately Vargas was not at all happy that the Vice-President was going around making such a suggestion to senators and others.[3]

That was the situation when the Air Force *brigadeiros* met on the twenty-second, shaken by the report they had heard the night before. After Eduardo Gomes proposed that Vargas resign, all present agreed, and the Army and Navy were advised. A short document was signed by the thirty *brigadeiros* and given to Armed Forces Chief of Staff Mascarenhas de Morais for delivery to Vargas.

Neither the latest cries of the opposition nor those bitter years following 1945 indicated that retirement to the "green fields" would be anything Getúlio would care to put up with. Alzira was aware that her father had death in mind. At Catete on the night of August 13 she had received a shock when a Palace assistant had shown her a note written in pencil by Getúlio: "I leave to the fury of my enemies the legacy of my death. I take with me the regret of not having been able to do for this good and generous Brazilian people, and principally the poorest, all that I wanted. Lies, slander, the vilest fabrications were concocted by the spite of rancorous and gratuitous enemies . . ."[4]

[1] *The New York Times,* dateline Rio, August 22, 1954.

[2] Page 7 of memo received from João Café Filho, September 6, 1963; F. Zenha Machado, *Os Últimos Dias do Govêrno de Vargas,* p. 66.

[3] Tancredo Neves in *O Cruzeiro,* September 18, 1954, quoted in F. Zenha Machado, *Os Últimos Dias do Govêrno de Vargas,* p. 66.

[4] Alzira Vargas do Amaral Peixoto, Chs. 12 and 13 of "A Vida de Getúlio . . .," in *Fatos & Fotos,* September 28 and October 5, 1963.

Mentioning this note to her father on the fourteenth, Alzira heard him say: "It is not what you are thinking, my dear. If I could be sure that my resignation would mean peace and calm for the Brazilian people and that I should be allowed to end my days in tranquillity and dignity, I should not have a moment's hesitation. I've had enough and I am tired; I am too old to take the iniquities and injustices with which they try to hurt me. But as I am sure that what they want is to humiliate me, I shall not resign. I shall only leave here dead." Alzira told him that he was quite right and that "we are all ready to fight at your side." But Getúlio went on to say: "I don't want the sacrifice of anybody. I intend to resist alone in order to make my attitude a protest. Don't worry, daughter, I am not contemplating suicide."[5]

On the evening of the twenty-second, Mascarenhas brought Getúlio the message of the *brigadeiros*: "The undersigned FAB officers, reaffirming their determination to remain within order, discipline, and constitutional precepts, feel that the present national crisis can be satisfactorily resolved only by the resignation of the President of the Republic."

Getúlio said: "I cannot agree with this, Marshal. They want me to slip away from here as though I were a criminal. I have committed no crime. I'll stay in power. If necessary I'll leave bathed in blood, but I cannot be made to flee like that. . . . I shall fulfill my mandate until the end with the collaboration of the Armed Forces. But even if I should be abandoned by the Navy, Army, and Air Force and by my own friends, I'll resist alone. . . . I have lived much. Now I can die. Never, however, will I give a demonstration of pusillanimity. And so, if they want to depose me, I shall issue a manifesto to the nation and die resisting, weapon in hand. . . . I am too old to be demoralized, and now I have no reason to fear death."[6]

After the ex-commander of the FEB left, Benjamim found his brother bent over his desk studying a paper. Getúlio, who had been working on it for days[7] with the help of journalist José Soares Maciel Filho, told Benjamim that it was a "political document" but did not show it to him.[8]

While Getúlio stayed up all night, which was not unusual, it became known that the admirals had met and decided to back the *brigadeiros*. As for the Army, whose strength made it the determining factor, War Minister Zenóbio da Costa issued a statement to the press at dawn on the

[5] *Ibid.*, Ch. 12, September 28, 1963; *Última Hora*, August 30, 1954.

[6] F. Zenha Machado, *Os Últimos Dias do Govêrno de Vargas*, pp. 81–82.

[7] José Soares Maciel Filho, interview, March 14, 1965.

[8] Queiroz Júnior, *Memórias sôbre Getúlio*, p. 169; F. Zenha Machado, *Os Últimos Dias do Govêrno de Vargas*, pp. 84–85.

twenty-third. He said he had just been checking things at Vila Militar and could assure everyone that "there is perfect agreement in the Army; at all costs the President will remain in office."[9]

At that moment a Manifesto to the Nation was being circulated for signatures of generals who did not agree with Zenóbio. Dated August 22, it spoke of the murder of Vaz, planned by Gregório Fortunato in the presidential Palace, and the escape of the murderers, made possible also in the Palace by people who had the President's full confidence. It cited criminal corruption among those closest to the President, and added that the "political-military crisis" was "irreparably worsening" the economic situation. The signers backed their Air Force and Navy comrades in concluding that tranquillity and unity could best be served by the President's resignation.[10]

Although signatures were not being added rapidly to the Manifesto, Zenóbio, when he learned of it, declared it a modification of "the agreement of honor" made earlier at a meeting of generals. On the twenty-third one general after another brought the War Minister advice. Some spoke of a growing split in the Army, and a few urged that a "dignified solution" would be to have Getúlio take a "leave of absence" from Brazil for the rest of his term. One general who held this view told Zenóbio that even if he won a bloody armed struggle peace would not be achieved. Finally, the War Minister received a visit from Mascarenhas de Morais. The Chiefs of Staff of the Army, Navy, and Air Force, Mascarenhas explained, felt that Vargas should be warned that the situation was more serious than the President's closest advisers seemed to consider it.

On the twenty-third Vargas held his usual 8:00 P.M. conference with Lourival Fontes, and the two men discussed the anti-Administration speech made by the Vice-President earlier in the day in the Senate. In justifying his proposed dual resignation, Café Filho had said: "Economic and financial problems get worse each day, acquiring an unprecedented aspect and threatening, in their inevitable social repercussions, to reach unforeseeable proportions."[11] Fontes and Vargas also spoke of a trip Getúlio was planning to make on the twenty-seventh to the north of Brazil. Getúlio said: "This trip will be good; it will restore my spirit and get me away from this bonfire."

[9] Queiroz Júnior, Memórias sôbre Getúlio, p. 165.

[10] Photo of Army manifesto and signatures (27) in Bento Munhoz da Rocha Netto, Radiografia de Novembro, 2nd ed., pp. 118–119.

[11] João Café Filho speech in F. Zenha Machado, Os Últimos Dias do Govêrno de Vargas, pp. 157–161.

After midnight Zenóbio and Mascarenhas were ushered into the President's third-floor study. With Benjamim at his side, Getúlio heard the report of the two Army leaders. Although he refused to resign or take a leave of absence, he resolved to discuss the situation at once with his Cabinet.

Aranha and Justice Minister Tancredo Neves, waiting for the Cabinet meeting to begin, joined Vargas, Zenóbio, and Mascarenhas. Vargas, they noted, pulled some papers from a drawer. Signing one of them, he folded it and put it in his pocket and then called for Goulart, who was scheduled to leave on a trip to Rio Grande later on the twenty-fourth.

Vargas gave Jango one of the documents, and then gave Tancredo Neves the pen he had used for the signing.[12] "Keep this as a remembrance of these days," he said to Tancredo. Then: "Don't worry, all will end well."

[12] Tancredo Neves, interview with Daphne F. Rodger, June 28, 1965.

8. The Last Cabinet Meeting

Governor Amaral Peixoto and Alzira drove through hostile crowds to Catete.[1] There Getúlio chatted with his son-in-law, and in his presence read over and signed another copy of the papers he had with him.[2] Then he said: "We can go down to the meeting." It was about 3:00 A.M.

Making his way downstairs in the elevator, Getúlio appeared thoroughly at peace and exceptionally friendly.[3] Smoking a cigar, he took his place at the head of the long banquet table around which his ministers were gathered, Aranha sitting on his right.[4] Alzira, disregarding her father's long-standing rule that such meetings should not be interrupted, pushed open the door and was followed by other members of the family, and by a number of close friends.

Getúlio asked each Cabinet officer what should be done. War Minister Zenóbio said that things were getting worse and that the large majority of officers commanding troops would be unlikely to follow him against the

[1] Alzira Vargas do Amaral Peixoto, Ch. 12 of "A Vida de Getúlio . . .," in *Fatos & Fotos*, September 28, 1963.

[2] *Ibid.*; F. Zenha Machado, *Os Últimos Dias do Govêrno de Vargas*, p. 101.

[3] Osvaldo G. Aranha, interview, July 2, 1963.

[4] *Ibid.*; Alzira Vargas do Amaral Peixoto, Ch. 12 of "A Vida de Getúlio . . .," in *Fatos & Fotos*, September 28, 1963.

Air Force and Navy. He would act if called on to do so, he said, but "much blood" would flow and the outcome was uncertain. The Navy Minister pointed out that the Navy "has already placed itself on the side of the Air Force." The Air Force Minister said he could do nothing about the position taken against the government by his branch of the service.[5]

Justice Minister Tancredo Neves made a long talk in favor of Vargas' staying in power, and called for a more spirited demonstration on the part of the military ministers. But the reports already given by them had created the impression that the government had lost control of the situation. José Américo favored a "conclusive" decision, a resignation by Vargas accompanied by a grand manifesto. Other ministers said that the decision was the President's and that they would back him to the end.

Aranha saw three possibilities: (1) "personal resistance, at the cost of life itself, and of which I obviously declare myself at once a supporter"; (2) the solution which he believed the President wished to avoid, a fight in which the faithful forces would combat those acting against the Constitution; and (3) the President's resignation, "a decision of an intimate nature, which it is not up to us to go into."[6]

In an aside to Aranha's son, one of the generals remarked that whoever first took a position at Vila Militar would prevail.[7] Alzira, who had followed the military's political maneuvers, was more optimistic than the War Minister about the situation at Vila Militar.[8] After hearing Cabinet ministers talk about consulting Congress and about a presidential leave of absence, she was unable to restrain herself and spoke out. As was her father's custom, she used no theatrics.

"General Zenóbio: this is not a simple political game. Lives are at stake, including mine, and so I consider myself entitled to speak. This is nothing but a Cabinet consipracy and it is not a movement affecting the Armed Forces. You know as well as I do that at Vila Militar nothing has altered since your visit there this afternoon, and without the Vila can anyone attempt a *golpe* in this country?"

To the Navy Minister she pointed out that the Marines, as she had

[5] José Américo de Almeida, *Ocasos de Sangue*, p. 21.

[6] F. Zenha Machado, *Os Últimos Dias do Govêrno de Vargas*, p. 108.

[7] Osvaldo G. Aranha, interview, July 2, 1963.

[8] Alzira Vargas do Amaral Peixoto, Ch. 12 of "A Vida de Getúlio . . .," in *Fatos & Fotos*, September 28, 1963. Jeremias de Mattos, interview, October 22, 1966.

learned from their commander, preferred not to march for or against anybody and would shoot only if attacked. To the Air Force Minister she said that the commander of the only effective fliers in Rio was loyal.

Turning again to Zenóbio, she concluded:

"Of the thirteen generals—because, General, there are only thirteen signers of the Manifesto—only one commands troops and those are not here in the capital; the others hold desk jobs. If you believe that the resignation of my father will bring peace, progress, and order to the country, that is the end of the matter. But are you sure?"[9]

After Zenóbio explained to Alzira that he was perfectly willing to act but only wanted to point out the consequences, Alzira apologized to her father and withdrew. Getúlio had watched her "as though he were absent and indifferent to everything,"[10] but this expression was not for her alone. Throughout the discussion he seemed to be paying no attention, giving only the impression that everything was occurring as might be expected.[11] He was in the same daze while some of the other visitors, inspired by Alzira's spirited words, broke in to make their comments.

When the Air Force Minister suggested that the whole matter could be settled simply by arresting Eduardo Gomes and Juarez Távora, the irritated Zenóbio asked: "And why don't you arrest them?" "Because I have no troops," was the answer. The Navy Minister said: "Mr. President, it appears that your fate is to be betrayed by the leaders of your Armed Forces," whereupon the President's chief military aide remarked that the failure of the Armed Forces to back the President would be unconstitutional and disastrous. Turning to the aide, Zenóbio asked why he did not command troops to defend the regime. In the conversation which followed the aide asked for troops, was offered a command in the resistance, and accepted.[12]

After Getúlio broke in to ask what the Cabinet members thought would be best for Brazil, a phone message brought news that one of the groups of generals thought Vargas should take a leave of absence. While some ministers discussed the technical aspects of this solution, favored by José Américo, others spoke of defending Vargas, and still others said they would support any decision Vargas might make.

[9] Alzira Vargas do Amaral Peixoto, Ch. 12 of "A Vida de Getúlio . . .," in *Fatos & Fotos*, September 28, 1963.

[10] *Ibid.*

[11] F. Zenha Machado, *Os Últimos Dias do Govêrno de Vargas*, p. 104.

[12] Alzira Vargas do Amaral Peixoto, Ch. 12 of "A Vida de Getúlio . . .," in *Fatos & Fotos*, September 28, 1963.

Because the Cabinet officers seemed to be supporting Vargas, Zenóbio decided that the military had no time to lose. Other generals were undoubtedly adding their signatures to the ultimatum calling for the President's resignation, and if the Cabinet decided to resist, he would have to arrest all who signed. Getting up from his chair, the War Minister asked the Navy and Air Force Ministers to assume their posts and announced that he would send troops into the streets to defend the President.[13] Then he left the room.

After a little more talk by Cabinet ministers Getúlio ended the debate about his future. Speaking calmly and slowly, he said: "As my ministry has reached no conclusion, I shall decide. I instruct my military ministers to maintain order within the country. If order is maintained, I shall withdraw. I shall ask for a leave of absence. If not, the rebels will find my body here."[14] Bidding his Cabinet good night, he left the room and, after a few embraces, made his way somberly upstairs to his private rooms.

Cabinet ministers called Zenóbio back and settled down to discuss what had happened. Tancredo Neves drew up the bulletin which the distraught Aranha, seeking Vargas' approval, took upstairs.[15] At 4:45 A.M. it was being broadcast to the nation: "President Vargas, with the full support of his ministers, has decided to take a leave of absence and turn the government over to his legal substitute, provided that order is maintained, the constitutional powers are respected, and honor is shown for the agreements solemnly assumed before the nation by the superior officers of our Armed Forces. Otherwise, he will remain immovable in his resolution to defend his constitutional prerogatives with the sacrifice, if necessary, of his life itself."

Café Filho, who was beginning to receive the congratulations of his friends at his modest Copacabana apartment, pointed out that his own offer to resign had been nullified by Vargas' refusal to accept his formula, and he expressed his interest in pacifying the nation and organizing a coalition government.

At Catete Palace sandbags were being placed in strategic positions, and revolvers were being issued to those who had not brought their own. For a while Vargas' friends conversed in groups. Vargas was sleeping and,

---

[13] Zenóbio da Costa declaration distributed to press August 26, 1954, in F. Zenha Machado, *Os Últimos Dias do Govêrno de Vargas*, pp. 161–168; F. Zenha Machado, *Os Últimos Dias do Govêrno de Vargas*, p. 108.

[14] *Ibid.*, p. 109; Alzira Vargas do Amaral Peixoto, Ch. 12 of "A Vida de Getúlio . . .," in *Fatos & Fotos*, September 28, 1963.

[15] Tancredo Neves, interview with Daphne F. Rodger, June 28, 1965.

as nothing sensational seemed to be occurring at Catete, his Cabinet ministers left to follow his example. Getting away from Catete they passed through crowds which were now even more furiously hostile to the government.[16]

[16] Osvaldo G. Aranha, interview, July 2, 1963.

9. The Shot

After leaving the Cabinet meeting Getúlio chatted in his upstairs office with Benjamim. They were soon joined by Alzira, ready to play her part with the other "occasional residents of Catete," those closest and most devoted to Getúlio, in defending her father "to the last drop of blood."

Taking a key from his jacket, Getúlio spoke to his brother and daughter. "This key," he said, "opens this safe. If anything happens to me, in there are some securities and important papers. One of you should remove them. The securities are for Darci and the papers are Alzira's. Now I am going to sleep."[1]

"Father, please stop all this," said Alzira. "Who is going to use the key if we all go together to our end?"[2]

"I am only letting you know," Getúlio remarked pleasantly. With a goodnight wish he retired to his large, cheerlessly furnished bedroom.

When Aranha came up with Justice Minister Tancredo Neves' text about the decision reached at the Cabinet meeting, Alzira took it to her father's bedroom and made a suggestion. But Getúlio was uninterested and refused to listen. "Let them do what they like; I don't want to read it. I am already asleep."

It was a short sleep. At 6:00 A.M. two Army men arrived at Catete to advise that Air Force investigators wanted Benjamim to testify immediately at the Galeão air base. Benjamim told them that he could not leave his brother at the moment. "I don't refuse to testify, but if they want to hear me, they can come here." After further discussion, Benjamim said he would consult Getúlio.

"At this hour? Why?" Getúlio asked.[3] Benjamim could only assume

[1] Alzira Vargas do Amaral Peixoto, Ch. 12 of "A Vida de Getúlio . . .," in *Fatos & Fotos*, September 28, 1963.
[2] F. Zenha Machado, *Os Últimos Dias do Govêrno de Vargas*, p. 111.
[3] *Ibid.*, p. 119.

that the military wanted to arrest him "because I am ready to resist with you." Getúlio backed Benjamim in his decision not to go.

Alzira, learning that her father was awake, went into the bedroom and spoke of some Army officers willing to act on his behalf. She asked him to support her in authorizing the arrest of Juarez Távora and Eduardo Gomes.

"You may, but it won't do any good," Getúlio replied good-humoredly. "Zenóbio has already been invited to be Café's War Minister."[4]

"Why didn't you tell me that yesterday? Everything would have been different."

"Let me sleep. It wouldn't have done any good."

Alzira left and her father rested, waiting for news from Zenóbio's meeting at the War Ministry.

Zenóbio told the generals that he had never been disloyal and explained that at the Cabinet meeting he had spoken of the seriousness of the situation only to spare bloodshed. When some generals objected to the conditional aspect of the Cabinet note and suggested that Vargas might well choose to remain in power, perhaps indefinitely, Zenóbio tried to reassure them. "The leave of absence of the President is definite. I learned that from the conversations of the ministers after the meeting, when I returned there at the request of Aranha."[5]

Benjamim was on the ground floor of Catete with Tancredo Neves and the President's chief military aide, awaiting news from the generals' meeting. It reached them at 7:00 A.M. Zenóbio, they were told, had assured the Army that Vargas' withdrawal was definite.

Benjamim reported to Getúlio, who asked: "Then this means I am deposed?"

"I don't know if you are deposed. I do know that it's the end. It was the easiest way to remove you from office."

Although Benjamim insisted that the source of their information was reliable and had been clear, Getúlio sent Benjamim off to check the information and report back. At 7:45 A.M., waiting for Benjamim to return, Getúlio rang for his valet and told him to advise Benjamim that he wanted to see him again.

Twenty minutes later Benjamim had not returned, and Getúlio, still in his white-and-gray-striped pajamas, crossed the corridor from his bed-

[4] Alzira Vargas do Amaral Peixoto, Ch. 12 of "A Vida de Getúlio . . .," in *Fatos & Fotos*, September 28, 1963.

[5] Zenóbio da Costa declaration distributed to press August 26, 1954, in F. Zenha Machado, *Os Últimos Dias do Govêrno da Vargas*, pp. 161–168.

room to his office. Alzira was surprised to see him, as her father was never in the habit of appearing thus attired in commonly used corridors, but he had already sent her to bed twice and this time she decided not to interfere.

From his study Getúlio returned to the bedroom. Finding his valet there, he sent him off. "Let me rest a little more," he said, sitting on the bed.

The next thing was a fatal shot.

10. Entering History

Those who rushed into Vargas' bedroom found his body reclining on the bed with one leg over the side. There was a bullet hole in the pajama top, made by the Colt 32 revolver lying nearby.

Embracing her father, the tearful Alzira cried "It can't be. It can't be. You promised me."[1] Lutero, disconsolate, pronounced him dead. Benjamim, who quickly phoned Zenóbio and Aranha, told the latter that Vargas had "died." On the drive to Catete, Aranha learned from his car radio that it had been suicide.[2]

The crowd around the Palace had become enormous and was now emotionally pro-Vargas, in complete contrast to its attitude when the ministers had passed through it earlier to reach and leave the Cabinet meeting. Almost as quickly as the suicide was announced, Rádio Nacional broadcast two sentences based on excerpts from the penciled note which a Vargas assistant had shown Alzira about ten days earlier. Brazilians, many weeping, heard: "To the fury of my enemies I leave the legacy of my death. I have the sorrow of not having done all that I wanted for the humble."

Reaching the bedroom, Aranha bent down before the corpse, and then embraced Benjamim, saying: "He died in order not to sacrifice us. He was an extraordinary man. He knew that we two would die for him."[3]

On a bedside table for all to see was a white envelope, and Governor Amaral Peixoto opened it, finding there the two-page typewritten document which Vargas had signed in his presence before the last Cabinet meeting. It turned out to be a farewell message to the Brazilian people, and Amaral Peixoto, after reading it, asked someone to take it to Rádio

[1] F. Zenha Machado, *Os Últimos Dias do Govêrno de Vargas*, p. 127.

[2] Osvaldo G. Aranha, interview, July 2, 1963.

[3] F. Zenha Machado, *Os Últimos Dias do Govêrno de Vargas*, p. 128.

Nacional's director, who was in the corridor. But before the message was broadcast to the people at 9:00 A.M., Aranha read it aloud to a group in the Palace.

Alzira, leaving the room, suddenly exclaimed: "The key! I want the key!" It had fallen from Vargas' pajama pocket and, after it was found under his body, Alzira opened the study safe and put the papers in a briefcase. Some days later, when she felt able to examine them, she found two copies of the so-called "testament-letter." These were in addition to the signed copy which her husband had opened right after the suicide and the one which her father had given Goulart. One of the copies from the safe was an unsigned carbon, and the other a draft signed by Getúlio, full of typing mistakes and corrections.[4]

The typewritten message, broadcast less than an hour after the suicide, helped ensure that Getulismo would continue in Brazil:

> *Once more the forces and interests which work against the people have organized themselves afresh and break out against me.*
>
> *They do not accuse me, they insult me; they do not fight me, they vilify and do not allow me the right to defend myself. They must silence my voice and impede my actions so that I shall not continue to defend, as I have always defended, the people and especially the humble. I follow my destiny. After decades of domination and plunder on the part of international economic and financial groups, I placed myself at the head of a revolution and won. I began the work of liberation and I installed a regime of social freedom. I had to resign. I returned to the government on the arms of the people. The underground campaign of international groups joined that of the national groups which were working against the regime of assuring employment. The excess-profits law was held up by Congress. Hatreds were unleashed against the just revision of minimum wages. I wished to bring about national freedom in the utilization of our resources by means of Petrobrás; this had hardly begun to operate when the wave of agitation swelled. Electrobrás was obstructed to the point of despair. They do not want the worker to be free. They do not want the people to be independent.*
>
> *I assumed the government in the midst of an inflationary spiral which was destroying the rewards of work. Profits of foreign companies were reaching as much as 500 per cent per annum. In declarations of import*

---

[4] Alzira Vargas do Amaral Peixoto, Ch. 13 of "A Vida de Getúlio . . .," in in *Fatos & Fotos*, October 5, 1963.

values, frauds of more than $100 million per year were proved. Came the coffee crisis and the value of our main product rose. We tried to defend its price and the reply was such violent pressure on our economy that we were forced to give in.

I have fought month after month, day after day, hour after hour, resisting constant, incessant pressure, suffering everything in silence, forgetting everything, giving myself in order to defend the people who now are left deserted. There is nothing more I can give you except my blood. If the birds of prey want someone's blood, if they want to go on draining the Brazilian people, I offer my life as a holocaust. I choose this means of being always with you. When they humiliate you, you will feel my soul suffering at your side. When hunger knocks at your door, you will feel in your breast the energy to struggle for yourselves and your children. When you are scorned, my memory will give you the strength to react. My sacrifice will keep you united and my name will be your battle standard.

Each drop of my blood will be an immortal flame in your conscience and will uphold the sacred will to resist. To hatred, I answer with pardon. And to those who think that they have defeated me, I reply with my victory. I was a slave of the people, and today I am freeing myself for eternal life. But this people whose slave I was will no longer be slave to anyone. My sacrifice will remain forever in their souls and my blood will be the price of their ransom.

I fought against the spoliation of Brazil. I fought against the spoliation of the people. I have fought with my whole heart. Hatred, infamy, and slander have not conquered my spirit. I have given you my life. Now I offer you my death. I fear nothing. Serenely I take my first step toward eternity and leave life to enter history.

EPILOGUE

FOLLOWING THE NEWS of Getúlio's suicide, mobs shouted against Eduardo Gomes and assaulted the Air Ministry building. Delivery trucks of *O Globo,* the prominent afternoon paper which had been attacking Vargas, were set afire. Authorities had their hands full defending the plant of *Tribuna da Imprensa,* which distributed no issue that afternoon; and they were particularly busy preventing rioters, led by Communist troublemakers, from moving on the American Embassy. In Pôrto Alegre the American Consulate was stormed, and in Belo Horizonte damage was inflicted on the quarters of the United States Information Agency.

But those not inclined to be violent made up the vast majority. Sorrowing, 100,000 of them waited to file past the body of the ex-President as it lay in state until 8:15 A.M. on August 25. Many waited all night but could not get into Catete Palace. They jammed the streets as the coffin was taken to Santos Dumont Airport in downtown Rio, and there they broke through lines of police to help carry it to the plane which was to take it to São Borja for burial.

Vice-President João Café Filho took over the Presidency. His earlier socialistic tendencies replaced by a profound respect for free enterprise,[1] he named a Cabinet which represented a breakaway from the men who had been influential during the last Vargas years. Café Filho's Finance Minister had called the large May 1 wage increase a disaster. The new Labor Minister, a man who had long supported Vargas, was an adversary of Goulart.

But the October 1954 elections for governors and congressmen showed

[1] Page 5 of memorandum given by João Café Filho during interview, September 6, 1963.

the strength of the forces with which Vargas had identified himself at the end. Writing of the workers' fury against the UDN, considered "guilty of the denouement," one author states that "August 24, 1954, decided the election of October 3, 1954."[2]

For the 1955 presidential election the PTB, at the suggestion of Aranha,[3] joined forces with the PSD, bringing the two Vargas-created parties together behind Kubitschek (PSD) for President and Goulart (PTB) for Vice-President. At the polls this Getulista combination defeated slates led by presidential candidates Juarez Távora of the UDN and of some smaller parties, Ademar de Barros of the PSP, and Plínio Salgado of the PRP. The victory was viewed fearfully by the men who in 1954 had forced Goulart out of the Labor Ministry.

In 1960 those who had long opposed Vargas experienced the thrill of victory in a presidential election. They did this by having the UDN back Jânio Quadros, who had done well in São Paulo politics but who lacked any close association with their party. He did have, however, an ability to get through to the poor classes which was by no means typical of the UDN. Disheveled, thin, and indignant, he would rant against the "corruption of the politicians," and promise to govern sternly.

Unable to have his way as much as he wanted and attacked by Carlos Lacerda for such acts as honoring Cuba's "Che" Guevara, the charismatic Quadros resigned on August 25, 1961, after seven months in the Presidency. He pictured his resignation as a courageous sacrifice. But, unlike Vargas in 1954, he planned to be alive to enjoy the popular manifestations aroused by it.

Quadros' farewell words bore the imprint of Vargas' last message and also brought to mind the references to "powerful reactionary forces, some hidden, some open," made in October 1945 when Vargas told the Queremistas that he might resign. On leaving office, Quadros explained that he had been "defeated by the reaction" after having "worked day and night, indefatigably, without prejudice or malice." "My efforts to achieve for this nation true political and economic liberty have been frustrated." Wanting "a Brazil for the Brazilians," he had been thwarted, he said, "by corruption, lies and cowardice which subordinated the general interests to the appetites and ambitions of groups of individuals, including foreign ones. . . . Therefore I find myself crushed. Terrible forces arose against me."

[2] José Viriato de Castro, *O Fenômeno Jânio Quadros*, p. 106.
[3] Osvaldo M. Penido, interview, September 6, 1963; Osvaldo G. Aranha, interview, July 2, 1963.

There was no reaction such as had followed Vargas' suicide. Tearfully departing by steamer, Quadros quoted a statement attributed to Vargas in 1945: "Though they send me away, I shall nevertheless return." Quadros did return to run again for the São Paulo governorship in 1962. Trying to explain his resignation, he criticized Adolf Berle, Ambassador John Moors Cabot, and Treasury Secretary Douglas Dillon. But even this appeal for votes was not enough to overcome a feeling that he had acted irresponsibly. In a close contest the Paulistas picked Ademar de Barros, who was waving the anti-Communist flag.

Jango Goulart had been elected Vice-President a second time in 1960 when he had narrowly defeated Quadros' undemagogic UDN running mate and a third candidate. He achieved the Presidency by Quadros' resignation. Often called the "political heir" of Vargas, Goulart chose not to administer but rather to agitate on behalf of the far Left. In the course of damaging the economy and endearing himself to Luís Carlos Prestes and a growing Brazilian Marxism, Goulart stirred up the maximum amount of unrest. His main objection to the Constitution, it came to be felt by many, was that it would not allow him to continue in office beyond January 1966, and he did little to discourage the idea that he wished to provoke a coup in order to head a countercoup. He warned of conspiracies, as Vargas had warned before ending elections in 1937; but most of the congressmen were not impressed with Goulart's suggestion that a "state of siege" be enacted to give him special powers.

Goulart was fond of presiding over street meetings to which truckloads of laborers were conveyed. At one such meeting, held in Rio on the night of August 23, 1963, the memory of Vargas was honored. At the noisy meeting of March 13, 1964, also in Rio, Goulart was urged by the speakers and the audience to bypass Congress in order to enact "basic reforms." On this occasion the President's brother-in-law, Deputado Leonel Brizola, suggested replacing Congress by a new assembly made up of "workers, peasants, sergeants, nationalist officers, and authentic men of the people."[4] Goulart called the Constitution obsolete, announced the expropriation of privately owned oil refineries, and attacked those who had forced Getúlio Vargas "to the supreme sacrifice."[5] Placards calling for legalization of the Brazilian Communist Party surrounded a large picture of Vargas and a sign bearing the words: "This people whose slave I was will no longer be slave to anyone."

[4] *Correio da Manhã*, March 14, 1964.
[5] Mário Victor, *5 Anos que Abalaram o Brasil*, pp. 475–476.

Thanks to Goulart, tools of Communism and advocates of the "Cubanization" of Brazil were in high positions in labor unions, in Petrobrás, and in the federal government.

In late March 1964, after Goulart appalled much of the nation by supporting sailors who had mutinied, Army Generals Olímpio Mourão Filho and Carlos Luís Guedes rebelled against him in Minas. It was a bold action, for most of the top Army commands, particularly in the militarily strong Rio area, had been placed in the hands of Goulart supporters. Anti-Goulart Army Chief of Staff Humberto Castelo Branco felt that the rebel generals in Minas were acting precipitously.[6]

The rebellion against Goulart was supported by important governors, such as Carlos Lacerda (Guanabara), Ademar de Barros (São Paulo), and José de Magalhães Pinto (Minas); also by many worried citizens who had been marching in anti-Goulart parades. It was assisted by the conspiracy which Army men without troops, like Odílio Denis, Nelson de Melo, and Osvaldo Cordeiro de Farias, had long been organizing.

After hours of uncertainty on March 31, the rebellion was joined by most of the troop commanders. Second Army Commander Amauri Kruel, a Vargas admirer and a personal friend of Goulart, joined it in São Paulo "to break the circle of Communism, which now compromises the authority of the government."[7] Troops under Fourth Army Commander Justino Alves Bastos arrested Pernambuco Governor Miguel Arrais and other Northeasterners who had seemed to them to be behaving like Communists. Pro-Goulart top Army chiefs in the Rio area were deserted by the officers they commanded. Goulart, remarking that "not one little shot" had been fired in his support, fled the country on April 2.

General Humberto Castelo Branco assumed the Presidency on April 15. Before he took office he listed his modest material assets, making it clear that there would be a healthy change from practices of the recent past. Nonpolitical technicians were assigned the difficult tasks necessary to straighten out the country. Not the least of these was to curb the great inflation which had become pronounced under Kubitschek and Goulart.

With the help of Francisco Campos, the 1946 Constitution was modified to give the new President more authority to get Congress to act. Military leaders, who took control after the victorious movement, declared that the Goulart Administration had "deliberately sought to bolshevize the nation." They cancelled the mandates of about fifty federal congress-

---

[6] José Stacchini, *Março 64: Mobilização da Audácia*, pp. 75–77.
[7] From manifesto of Amauri Kruel, April 1, 1964.

men and suspended for ten years the political rights of three hundred citizens (including ex-Presidents Kubitschek, Quadros, and Goulart). These steps were taken, the anti-Goulart military declared, "in the interest of peace and national honor."

Thus the curtain fell for the Gaúcho cattle raiser who considered himself to be Getúlio's political heir.

RÉSUMÉ

THE VARGAS STORY is, among other things, a story of success in politics.

In part, Vargas owed this success to the long and careful preparation which preceded each important step. He detested unnecessary risks.

He was aided by the patience which he trained himself to exercise. Never acting impulsively, be became known as a calm and cheerful cigar smoker, who knew the wisdom of caution. "Sometimes," he once said, "our friends want me to move a little fast; and then I must defend myself." Not infrequently he was accused of "leaving things as they are to see how they will turn out."

The Brazilian Catholic philosopher Tristão de Athayde emphasizes that Vargas, when he was careful not to seem to be forcing issues, and when he sought the cooperation of former adversaries, was adhering to rules which are important in Brazilian politics. He goes on to say that Vargas was a keen observer of facts and of human nature; that intelligence, observation, and instinct gave him an exceptional understanding of Brazil and of its future, and allowed him to take Brazil "across a kind of frontier."[1]

Vargas was wholly absorbed in his work. Thorough and practical, he well assessed prevailing moods, the strength of forces which sought to exert pressures, and the loyalties and weaknesses of men with whom he had to deal. He used standard political tools effectively. These were tools which some people, calling him Machiavellian, have liked to say that he used with cynicism.

Getúlio, who remarked that "the revolt of creatures against their crea-

[1] Tristão de Athayde, interview, November 4, 1966.

tors is traditional in Brazilian political life," knew how to handle those who seemed likely to make effective bids to outshine or replace him. He also acted on the awareness that appointments and favors can often win the goodwill of foes and of others who help he felt he needed. Additional tools were political deals, charges which were sometimes unfair to opponents, and appeals to nationalism.

Success in politics required more than the use of pragmatic tools. It required, and at the same time made possible, attention to the problems which confronted the nation. Vargas became identified with the transformation of Brazil.

As Brazilian Marxist economist Caio Prado Júnior sees it, the transformation which followed 1930 had to come. He feels that Vargas' contribution lay in knowing how to bring about the vast changes with the fewest possible shocks, thus preventing the period from being more agitated than it was.[2]

For steps which he took or did not take, Vargas was often criticized by observers who did not have his self-assigned task of retaining a dominant position. With that task in mind he found himself (as he remarked at the time of the Provisional Government) much less free to act than was generally supposed.

The 1930 revolution, popular with the masses, must be attributed to the positions taken by a few members of the small group of cultured elite who had governed the country until then. An important political faction felt so offended that, when a suitable occasion arose, it temporarily joined forces with rebellious *tenentismo*. The resulting violation of the 1891 Constitution encouraged further constitutional breaks.

The *tenentes* overruled the idea that the 1930 revolution simply corrected a fraudulent election. Brazil, the *tenentes* said, had to be remade rather than returned, via old political ways, to the lords of a few powerful states.

Vargas, the victor of the 1930 Revolution, moved too slowly for some and too swiftly for others. He sought to prevent any one force, the military included, from dominating him or Brazil. Keeping independent of currents which were powerful and ambitious. Vargas during the first phase of Getulismo (1930–1945) presided over tugs-of-war between rival groups, such as the contest between the *tenentes* and the politicians, and the contest between the Dutra wing and the Aranha wing.

[2] Caio Prado Júnior, interview, November 9, 1966.

His very political success during this first phase, allowing a fifteen-year rule which was mostly dictatorship, had drawbacks for Brazil. Some of the drawbacks are inherent in paternalism. Self-reliance and self-discipline were stunted. Labor and business leaders grew accustomed to turn for favors to a group which perpetuated itself in power. Constitutional provisions came to be regarded as arrangements of the moment, subject to the pleasure of this group.

Neither a citation of the fabricated "Cohen Plan" nor the mislabeling of presidential candidate Armando de Sales Oliveira as demagogic and subversive[3] was a good reason for ending elections in 1937. But Army leaders had other reasons for lending their support to this move. Brazil, they felt, had yet to be remade, and this work was left to the Estado Nôvo.

The 1937 coup cannot be considered entirely apart from the times and the Brazilian heritage. Much of that part of the world which had no long democratic experience and was suffering economically shared Francisco Campos' doubts about the ability of parliaments to deal with the situation. World prices for Brazilian commodities were lower than when "General Coffee" turned against Washington Luís.

Under the 1934 Constitution representatives of Flôres da Cunha converted various state legislative assembly halls into battlegrounds for power. As for the federal Congress, it was felt that the few politically important states were interested in using it, as in the past, to promote their own interests. Meanwhile, elsewhere in the world, totalitarian nations seemed to be surging ahead with a great sense of national purpose.

Considering world and Brazilian conditions, Afonso Arinos de Melo Franco believes that the Estado Nôvo was logical and inevitable, just as was its collapse in 1945. The Estado Nôvo, he says, was "based on reality."[4] In the opinion of Tristão de Athayde, the Estado Nôvo violated the Brazilian political principle of getting things done slowly and in a fraternal atmosphere.

There were resentments, some inspired by genuine dedication to freedom, and others by thwarted ambition. For the large mass of Brazilians, only a small fraction of whom had become imbued with a dedication to liberal political democracy, Vargas retained his appeal.

The artist at achieving and maintaining power was not one of those thunderous madmen of the age. Instead of banging tabletops, Brazil's leader sought to be the intelligent, pleasant listener. Vargas, who has been

[3] Getúlio Vargas, *A Nova Política do Brasil*, V, 29.
[4] Afonso Arinos de Melo Franco, interview, November 4, 1966.

described by Juarez Távora as broad-minded, understanding, and reasonable,[5] seemed a disappointment to Francisco Campos, advocate of the "Caesar" role.

Vargas did exercise control over the spoken and written word, and he did shove aside some hard-fighting democrats who valiantly refused to give up the idea that elections, legislatures, and free speech should prevail in Brazil. But the purpose of dictatorship was not the practice of vindictiveness. Nor was Vargas interested in power as a road to personal wealth or immoral living. The Estado Nôvo was established to carry out a program which the admirer of Júlio de Castilhos felt could not otherwise be executed.

The dictatorship allowed the government to annoy segments of opinion for what it felt to be the long-run good of Brazil. The state flags were burned. In the economically and politically troubled 1930's the green wave of Integralismo (popular in military circles) and the red wave of Communism were defied. Local armies were made loyal to the central government. Also, just when Axis prestige was at its height, Vargas decided to institute a campaign against long-ingrained foreign cultural influences and aggressive local Nazis.

The dictatorship, emphatically pro-Brazil, was neither rightist nor leftist. Although laborers were deprived of the right to strike, never did Getulismo hesitate in its course of giving—paternalistically—some dignity to millions of Brazilians who before 1930 had counted for nothing in the eyes of the government.

Besides seeking to end the fragmentation of Brazil, the program contributed to the development of a modern, diversified, industrialized economy. Wartime conditions set back some projects, such as the Paulo Afonso hydroelectric works. But the Vargas Government provided more than a steel mill and a paper plant and the discovery of petroleum. Celso Furtado has written that "the period which began in 1930 must be considered on the whole as the period when the industrial system was implanted." He explains this by saying that "the political opportunism of the new rulers, far less rigid in their ideological outlook than the men of Minas and São Paulo who had formerly governed the Republic, indirectly paved the way for industrialization."[6]

Vargas, freed for a while from the need of devoting practically all of

[5] Juarez Távora, interview, May 22, 1965.
[6] Celso Furtado, *Diagnosis of the Brazilian Crisis*, p. 100.

his attention to political pressure groups, concerned himself with measures which were aimed at bettering Brazil. His attention spanned from Rio's streets, which he took steps to widen, to Brazil's vast interior, which he sought to advertise. Large areas, which had been more or less ignored by state governments, were sliced away from states and made into five federally-supported "territories."[7]

The Brazil which emerged in 1945, with new ministries dedicated to Aviation, to Labor and Industry, and to Health and Education, and with its minimum wages, its Labor Law Consolidation, and its broad social security schemes, was an entirely different country from that which Washington Luís had left in 1930. Under Vargas the economic problems of the Northeast had come to receive the national attention which they merited; no longer did this attention depend on the slim hope of placing a Northeasterner in the Presidency. When democracy was achieved, it relied heavily on the secret vote, the requirement that political parties be national, and the Electoral Tribunals, carefully worked out legacies of dictatorship.

The fact that Getúlio Vargas never went on one of those ovation-studded visits to the United States or Europe was no handicap to him when he negotiated internationally. Vargas knew something about "squeezing the maximum" (as the American ambassador put it) out of the United States on the one hand and the fascist powers on the other.

With the world afire, again he moved too slowly to suit many. Yet again he moved too swiftly to suit others. Overruling Brazil's military leaders in January 1942, he declined to follow the examples of Argentina and Chile. Instead, he played Brazil's hand in support of the United States. His, too, was the decision which resulted in sending 25,000 Brazilian soldiers overseas.

Brazil's prestige in 1944 was such that the United States vigorously supported the idea that Brazil have a permanent seat on the United Nations Security Council, together with the United States, France, Great Britain, China, and the Soviet Union. However, Soviet opposition doomed this aspiration of Vargas and others.

When World War II was coming to an end, Getúlio was being described as "behind the times" because he had demonstrated reservations about the traditional form of liberal political democracy. Forced out of

---

[7] Juarez Távora, interview, May 22, 1965; Janari Gentil Nunes, interview, October 18, 1965.

power by a military which was determined by then to show its fondness for democracy, the erstwhile "Father of the Brazilians" became the object of attacks in the press, in Congress, and elsewhere. He reaped the bitter harvest of having vexed some important groups, including writers who had keenly resented the Estado Nôvo and its curbs on free expression. Groundlessly he was accused of conspiracy. After a political reverse in São Paulo in 1947, his striking showing in the 1945 congressional elections was forgotten. He was considered finished, was sometimes described as a pest, and was left in uncomfortable isolation.

Choosing in 1950 to enter the noisy arena in which the awards were likely to go to the users of demagoguery, Vargas achieved his popular vindication by a wide margin. He campaigned effectively and was helped by his past attention to urban labor. Those who had spent the Estado Nôvo years insisting that Brazil's need was electoral democracy now found that "the former dictator" and post-Vargas Getulista leaders were usually able to pull the rug out from under opponents—regardless of the fact that leading opponents (deeply devoted to the UDN) were the most honorable of men.

The proper conduct of government affairs was a matter to which Vargas gave careful attention. A civil service merit system was introduced in 1936, and this was expanded with the creation of DASP (Departamento Administrativo do Serviço Público) shortly after the Estado Nôvo was established. The bulk of the appointments in the ministries—theretofore subject to considerations related to politics and friendship—came to be based on competitive examinations. "This is a silent revolution," Vargas said as he witnessed the system under which, between 1936 and 1945, 200,000 people took competitive examinations which determined who filled 20,000 posts.[8] DASP reviewed ministerial budgets, coordinated purchasing by government entities, and did much to provide the administrative efficiency which was called for by the 1937 Constitution.

Vargas did not sign decree laws in order to favor friends or influential persons. Strictly honest about money matters, he had a strong dislike for the misuse of public office by anyone.[9] When he became President in 1951, rumors were circulating about what was said to have been the improper issuance of import permits by CEXIM. To head CEXIM, Vargas ap-

[8] Luís Simões Lopes, interview, December 17, 1966.

[9] Vicente Ráo, interview, November 17, 1966; Luís Simões Lopes, interview, December 17, 1966.

pointed Luis Simões Lopes, who in the past had ably run DASP and had
helped Vargas satisfy himself that decrees about to be issued were in the
public interest.

Some men disappointed Vargas, misusing the trust he put in them. This
happened toward the end of his life, when he sometimes gave the impression of being less effective than he had been earlier. After Simões Lopes
left CEXIM in 1953, financial dishonesty came to determine the distribution of many import licenses. This abuse was soon ended: the possibility
of acquiring foreign exchange for imports was made available to all by
means of the government's auctioning the rights to buy such exchange.

During "the short period of fifteen years" Vargas damaged the Communist movement not so much by police measures as by enacting labor
legislation and by founding the PTB. The last Vargas administration displeased the Communists in many ways, as when it signed the United
States-Brazil Military Aid Pact. The National Security Law of 1953 was
used to arrest Communists and even to dismiss some suspected members
of the Foreign Office. It was only after the suicide that Communist leaders,
pleased with parts of the farewell letter, decided to tear up resolutions,
adopted in August 1954, calling for the overthrow of Vargas. They found
it convenient to identify themselves with the posthumous popularity of
"The Father of the Poor," and to use Goulart for purposes of infiltration.

Nationalism was a concept of extreme importance in military, political,
and other circles. As the question of large-scale iron-ore exports was
studied, before and during the Estado Nôvo, it became evident that much
of the military felt that the exploitation of iron ore could and should be
dominated by Brazilians.[10]

Vargas appears to have felt that one could be patriotic without necessarily accepting the programs presented by many who sought to appear to
be "the most nationalistic" of Brazilians. During the dictatorship he could,
when he thought it helpful to Brazil, disregard constitutional provisions
about nationalizing all banks and sources of hydraulic energy. In the 1950
election campaign he stressed the need of foreign capital for Brazilian
industrial development, as long as foreigners did not dominate natural
resources.[11]

[10] Assis Chateaubriand statement to Charles A. Gauld, June 1965.
[11] Getúlio Vargas, *A Campanha Presidencial,* p. 258.

During his last administration Vargas approved the Amapá manganese ore-export project, which had been worked out under President Dutra and which has gone ahead under private ownership, 51 per cent of it Brazilian and 49 per cent United States, to be a model enterprise.[12] In taking this stand about Amapá ore Vargas had to overrule those nationalists who were demanding that the government expropriate the deposits.[13]

Vargas' original project for Petrobrás would have placed control of the petroleum industry in the hands of the Brazilian government but would neither have ruled out foreign investments in that field nor made Petrobrás a monopoly. This project collapsed as politicians appreciated the importance of showing themselves to be "extreme nationalists." (The UDN found itself with an opportunity to appear to be more "patriotic" than Vargas.) Unlike Goulart in later years, Getúlio gave Petrobrás a well-regarded administrator—an old foe of the Estado Nôvo, Juraci Magalhães.

The last Vargas administration cancelled the limitation on the remission of profits abroad and took other steps which helped to attract (notably under President Kubitschek) foreign capital for the further development of Brazil.[14]

There was, of course, always the need to reply to the charges of men like Artur Bernardes, who in 1952 described Vargas as the "protector of foreign trusts." The Communist Party of Brazil, agreeing with Bernardes and others who were known as nationalists, unleashed propaganda which stated that Vargas was the chief enemy of the Brazilian workers. But Vargas came out of it all leaving an image which he felt was more appropriate.

[12] About the enterprise, see Paul Vanorden Shaw, *Know-How Conquers Jungle*.
[13] Janari Gentil Nunes, interview, October 18, 1965.
[14] Eric N. Baklanoff, "Foreign Private Investment and Industrialization in Brazil" in *New Perspectives of Brazil* (Eric N. Baklanoff, ed.), p. 129.

SOURCES OF MATERIAL

Aside from information provided by newspapers and by the National Archives in Washington and Rio de Janeiro, information was obtained from conversations and written works such as those listed below. Among the books omitted from this list are many about the Constitucionalista uprising of 1932; a bibliography by Aureliano Leite on this event is given on page 17 of *O Estado de S. Paulo* of July 9, 1958.

For books listed here the spelling—including the use of accents—is that appearing in the title pages. Capitalization in titles follows the conventions of English usage.

Albuquerque, Epitacio Pessôa Cavalcanti de. *Getulio Vargas.* Preface by Gilberto Amado. Imprensa Nacional, Rio de Janeiro, 1938.

Aleixo, Pedro. Interview, October 14, 1965.

Alexander, Robert J. "Brazilian Tenentismo," *The Hispanic American Historical Review*, XXXVI, No. 1 (May, 1956), 229–242.

———. *Communism in Latin America.* Rutgers University Press, New Brunswick, New Jersey, 1957.

———. *Prophets of the Revolution.* Macmillan, New York, 1962.

———. *Labor Relations in Argentina, Brazil, and Chile.* McGraw-Hill, New York, 1962.

Alliança Liberal. *Alliança Liberal: Documentos da Campanha Presidencial.* Officinas Graphicas Alba, Rio de Janeiro, 1930.

Almeida, Fernando H. Mendes de (ed.). *Constituições do Brasil.* 4th ed. Edição Saraiva, São Paulo, 1963.

Almeida, Gil de. *Homens e Factos de uma Revolução.* Calvino Filho, Rio de Janeiro, 1934.

Almeida, J. Canuto Mendes de. *Saudacão a Getulio Vargas*, n.p. São Paulo, 1950.

Almeida, José Américo de. *Ocasos de Sangue.* Livraria José Olympio, Rio de Janeiro, 1954.

———. *A Palavra e o Tempo.* Livraria José Olympio, Rio de Janeiro, 1965.

Amado, Gilberto. *Perfil do Presidente Getulio Vargas.* Imprensa Nacional, Rio de Janeiro, 1937.

Amado, Jorge. *Homens e Coisas do Partido Comunista.* Edições Horizonte, Ltda., Rio de Janeiro, 1946.

————. *O Cavaleiro da Esperança: Vida de Luiz Carlos Prestes.* 10th ed. Coleção Novos Horizontes, 1956.

Amaral, Ignacio M. Azevedo do. *Ensaio sôbre a Revolução Brasileira, 1931–1934.* Imprensa Naval, Rio de Janeiro, 1963.

Amaral, Rubens do. *A Campanha Liberal.* Sociedade Impressora Paulista, 1930.

Amora, Paulo. *Bernardes: O Estadista de Minas na República.* Companhia Editôra Nacional, São Paulo, 1964.

Anhembi magazine (Paulo Duarte, director). São Paulo, 1950–1962.

Apulchro, Xisto. *A Verdade Historica: Da Convenção de Junho de 1921 á Revolução de Julho de 1922.* Rio de Janeiro, 1922.

Aranha, Osvaldo G. Interviews, July 2 and September 4, 1963.

Aranha, Oswaldo. *A Revolução e a América: O Presidente Getulio Vargas e a Diplomacia (1930–1940).* Departamento de Imprensa e Propaganda, Rio de Janeiro, 1941.

————. *"Os Pilatos Poderão Lavar as Mãos, Jamais, Porém, as Consciências":* *Importante Depoimento do Ministro Oswaldo Aranha sôbre o Sentido do Sacrifício de Getúlio Vargas,* transcribed from *Ultima Hora,* September 17, 1954.

Arantes, Altino. Interview, August 7, 1963.

Araripe, Tristão de Alencar. *Tasso Fragoso: Um Pouco de História do Nosso Exército.* Biblioteca do Exército, Rio de Janeiro, 1960.

Athayde, Austregésilo de. Interview, August 30, 1963.

Athayde, Tristão de. Interview, November 4, 1966.

Baklanoff, Eric (ed). *New Perspectives of Brazil.* Vanderbilt University Press, Nashville, Tennessee, 1966.

Baldessarini, Hugo. *Cronica de uma Época (de 1950 ao Atentado contra Carlos Lacerda): Getúlio Vargas e o Crime de Toneleros.* Companhia Editôra Nacional, São Paulo, 1957.

Banas, Geraldo. Interview, August 6, 1963.

Banco do Brasil. Annual Reports. Rio de Janeiro.

Barata, Agildo. *Vida de um Revolucionário: Memórias.* Editôra Melso, Rio de Janeiro [c. 1963].

————. Interviews, October 29 and November 4, 1965.

Barata, Hamilton. *O Assalto de 1930.* Civilização Brasileira, Rio de Janeiro, 1932.

Barbosa, Ary. *Uma Ingloria Pagina da Revolução.* Typographia Ypiranga, Petropolis, 1931.

Barbosa, João Alberto Leite. Interview, June 20, 1963.

Barreto Filho, Mello. *Anchieta e Getúlio Vargas.* Departamento de Imprensa e Propaganda, Rio de Janeiro, 1941.

Barros, Ademar de. Interview, August 5, 1963.

————. Typewritten memorandum with answers to questions, São Paulo, August, 1963. Original in Latin American Collection, The University of Texas.

Barros, João Alberto Lins de. *Memórias de um Revolucionário* (Part I, *A Marcha da Coluna*). Editôra Civilização Brasileira, Rio de Janeiro, 1953.

Barroso, Gustavo. *O Integralismo de Norte a Sul.* Civilização Brasileira, S.A. Rio de Janeiro, 1934.

————. *O Que o Integralista Deve Saber.* 2nd ed. Civilização Brasileira S.A. Rio de Janeiro, 1935.

Basbaum, Leoncio. *História Sincera da República.* 2nd ed. of Vol. II and 1st ed. of Vol. III. Editôra Edaglit, São Paulo, 1962.

Bastos, Abguar. *Prestes e a Revolução Social.* Editorial Calvino, Rio de Janeiro, 1946.

Bastos, Alves. *Palmo a Palmo: A Lucta no Sector Sul.* Soc. Impressora Paulista, São Paulo, 1932.

Bastos, Joaquim Justino Alves. *Encontro com o Tempo.* Editôra Globo, Pôrto Alegre, 1965.

Bastos, Reynaldo. *Getulio Vargas: O Reformador.* n.p., Rio de Janeiro, 1939.

Baum, Vicki. *The Weeping Wood.* Doubleday, Doran & Co., Garden City, New York, 1943.

Beals, Carleton. *The Coming Struggle for Latin America.* Halcyon House, New York, 1940.

Berle, Adolf A. Interviews, March 8, 1963 and June 5, 1963.

Bohan, Merwin L. Letter of December 17, 1963, to J. W. F. D. Latin American Collection of The University of Texas.

————. Interview, August 20, 1964.

Bouças, Valentim F. *Finanças do Brasil: Dívida Externa, 1824–1945.* Vol. XIX. Ministério da Fazenda, Rio de Janeiro, 1955.

————. Interviews, June 10 and August 19, 1963.

Branco, Manoel Thomaz Castello. *O Brasil no II Grande Guerra.* Biblioteca do Exército, Rio de Janeiro, 1960.

Branco, Carlos Castello. "Memórias do Senador Benedito Valadares." Article in *Jornal do Brasil*, Rio de Janeiro, July 19, 1966.

Brussolo, Armando. *Tudo Pelo Brasil!* Editorial Paulista, 1932.

————. *Basta de Mentiras! Considerações em Torno do Livro do Cel. Herculano.* São Paulo, 1933.

Burden, William A. M. *The Struggle for Airways in Latin America.* Council on Foreign Relations, New York [c. 1943].

Cabanas, João. *A Columna da Morte.* Livraria Editôra, Almeída & Torres, Rio de Janeiro, 1928.

————. *Os Phariseus da Revolução.* Freitas Bastos, Rio de Janeiro, 1932.

Cabral, Carlos Castilho. *Batalhões Patrioticos na Revolução de 1924.* Livraria Liberdade, São Paulo, 1927.

————. *Tempos de Jânio e Outros Tempos*. Editôra Civilização Brasileira, S.A., Rio de Janeiro, 1962.

Café Filho, João. *Do Sindicato ao Catete: Memórias Políticas e Confissões Humanas*. 2 vols. Livraria José Olympio, Rio de Janeiro, 1966.

————. Interview, September 6, 1963.

————. Typewritten memorandum with answers to questions, Rio de Janeiro, September, 1963. Original in Latin American Collection, The University of Texas.

Caffery, Jefferson. Interviews, June 3, 1963 and August 4, 1964.

Callage, Roque. *Episodios da Revolução*. Edição da Livraria do Globo. Barcellos, Bertaso & Cia., Pôrto Alegre, 1930.

Calmon, Pedro. *História do Brasil*. Vols. VI and VII. Livraria José Olympio, Río de Janeiro, 1961.

————. Interview, July 18, 1965.

Câmara dos Deputados. *Petróleo, Projetos 1516/51, 1517/51, 1595/52*. Departamento de Imprensa Nacional, Rio de Janeiro, 1952.

Camargo, Ayres de. *Patriotas Paulistas na Columna Sul*. Livraria Liberdade, São Paulo, 1925.

Camargo, Joracy. *Getúlio Vargas e a Inteligência Nacional*. Departamento de Imprensa e Propaganda, 1940.

Campos, Francisco. *O Estado Nacional, Sua Estructura, Seu Conteudo Ideologico*. Livraria José Olympio, Rio de Janeiro, 1940.

————. Interviews, September 3, 1963, and December 14, 1965.

Campos, Milton. Interview, October 21, 1965.

Campos, Newton de Siqueira. Interviews, July-September, 1963.

Caó, José. *Dutra*. Instituto Progresso Editorial S.A., São Paulo, 1949.

Capanema, Gustavo. Interview, October 23, 1965.

Carneiro, Glauco. *História das Revoluções Brasileiras*. 2 vols. Edições O Cruzeiro, Rio de Janeiro, 1965.

————. *O Revolucionário Siqueira Campos*. 2 vols. Edições O Cruzeiro, Rio de Janeiro, 1966.

————. Interview with Manoel Ananias dos Santos, "Eu Também Sou Sobrevivente dos '18 do Forte'." *O Cruzeiro* magazine, Rio de Janeiro, September 5, 1964.

————. Consultor, Osvaldo Galvão. "Revoluções Brasileiras," Chaps. XII–XIX (July 18, 1964–September 5, 1964) of series of articles in *O Cruzeiro* magazine, Rio de Janeiro.

————. In collaboration with Lourival Fontes. "A Face Final de Vargas: Os Bilhetes de Vargas." A series of 15 articles appearing in *O Cruzeiro* magazine, Rio de Janeiro, January 23, 1965–May 15, 1965.

Carneiro, Levi. *Pela Nova Constituição*. A. Coelho Branco Fº., Rio de Janeiro, 1943.

————. *O Livro de um Advogado.* A. Coelho Branco Filho, Rio de Janeiro, 1943.

————. Interview, June 26, 1963.

Carneiro, Nelson de Souza. *XXII de Agusto! O Movimento Constitucionalista na Bahia.* Companhia Editôra Nacional, São Paulo, 1933.

Carone, Edgard. *Revoluções do Brasil Contemporâneo, 1922–1938.* São Paulo Editôra (Coleçâo Buriti), São Paulo, 1965.

Carrazzoni, André. *Getúlio Vargas.* 2nd ed. Livraria José Olympio, Rio de Janeiro, 1939.

————. *Perfil do Estudante Getúlio Vargas.* 4th ed. Editôra A Noite, Rio de Janeiro, 1943.

Carvalho, Affonso de. *1ª Bateria Fogo! O Movimento Pacificador: Golpe de Vista da Revolução de 1930.* 3rd ed. Civilização Brasileira, Rio de Janeiro, 1931.

————. *Capacete de Aço.* Preface by Góes Monteiro. Civilização Brasileira, Rio de Janeiro, 1933.

Carvalho, Alvaro de. *Nas Vesperas da Revolução: 70 Dias na Presidencia do Estado da Parahyba, de 26 Julho a 4 de Outubro de 1930.* Empreza Graphica da "Revista dos Tribunaes," São Paulo, 1932.

Carvalho, Antônio Gontijo de. Interview, August 8, 1963.

Carvalho, J. Nunes de. *A Revolução no Brasil, 1924–1925.* 2nd ed. Typ. São Benedicto, Rio de Janeiro, 1930.

Carvalho, Luiz Antônio da Costa. *As Realizações do Governo Getulio Vargas no Campo do Direito.* Departamento de Imprensa e Propaganda, 1942.

Carvalho, M. Balbino de. *A Lucta no Graças.* Jacintho Ribeiro dos Santos, Rio de Janeiro, 1926.

Carvalho, Napoleão de. Interview, August 6, 1963.

Castro, Américo Mendes de Oliveira. *Tenentismo e Fascismo.* Typ. do Jornal do Commercio, Rio de Janeiro, 1932.

Castro, José Viriato de. *O Fênomeno Jânio Quadros.* 3rd ed. Palácio do Livro, São Paulo, 1959.

————. *O Ex-Leão de São Manoel: Ademar.* Palácio do Livro, São Paulo, 1960.

Castro, Sertorio de. *A República que a Revolução Destruio.* Freitas Bastos, Rio de Janeiro, 1932.

Cavalcanti, Carlos de Lima. Interviews, August 1 and August 29, 1963.

César, Afonso. *Política, Cifrão e Sangue: Documentário do 24 de Agôsto.* Editorial Andres, Ltda., Rio de Janeiro, n.d.

Cesarino Júnior, A. F. Interview, August 8, 1963.

Chagas, Paulo Pinheiro. *Os Dois Lados do Homem e da Lição Vargas.* Rio de de Janeiro, 1955.

Chevalier, Carlos. *Os 18 do Forte. Collectanea organisada pelo Capitão Carlos Chevalier sobre Siqueira Campos, Commandante dos 18 do Forte de Copacabana, 1922–1930.* Impressores F. Barretto & Cia., Rio de Janeiro, n.d.

Ciano, Galeazzo. *Ciano's Diary, 1937–1938.* Translated by Andreas Mayor. Methuen & Co., Ltd., London, 1952.

Coaracy, Vivaldo. *O Caso de São Paulo.* Liga de Defesa Paulista. Estabelecimento Graphico Irmãos Ferraz, São Paulo, 1931.

———. *A Sala da Capela.* Livraria José Olympio, São Paulo, 1933.

Comissão Mista Brasil—Estados Unidos para Desenvolvimento Econômico. *Projetos* (14 vols.), *Relatório Geral* (2 vols.), and *Estudos Diversos.* Rio de Janeiro, 1953 and 1954.

Conn, Stetson, and Byron Fairchild. *The Framework of Hemisphere Defense.* Department of the Army, Washington, 1960.

Conselho Nacional de Economia. *Exposição Geral da Situação Econômica do Brasil.* Departamento de Imprensa Nacional, Rio de Janeiro, 1952.

Cooke, Morris Llewellyn. *Brazil on the March: A Study in International Cooperation.* 2nd printing. McGraw-Hill, New York, 1944.

Costa, Bernardino Victoy. *Vargas: A Mocidade e a Pátria.* Rio de Janeiro, 1951.

Costa, José Augusto. *Criminosos de duas Revoluções, 1930–32.* São Paulo, *Paulo, de 5 de Julho de 1924.* Cia Graphico-Editôra Monteiro Lobato, São Paulo, 1924.

Costa, Edgard. *A Legislação Eleitoral Brasileira: Histórico, Comentários e Sugestões.* Departamento de Imprensa Nacional, 1964.

———. *Os Grandes Julgamentos do Supremo Tribunal Federal.* Vols. I, II, and III. Editôra Civilização Brasileira, S.A. Rio de Janeiro, 1964.

Costa, Fernando. *Realizações do Presidente Getúlio Vargas no Ministério da Agricultura.* Departamento de Imprensa e Propaganda, 1941.

Costa, João. Interview, August 29, 1963.

Costa, Joffre Gomes da. *Marechal Henrique Lott.* Rio de Janeiro, 1960.

Costa, José Augusto. *Criminosos de duas Revoluções, 1930–32.* São Paulo, 1933.

Costa, Licurgo. *Cidadão do Mundo.* Preface by Valentim P. Bouças. 3rd ed. Livraria José Olympio, Rio de Janeiro, 1943.

Coutinho, Lourival. *O General Góes Depõe . . .* 2nd ed. Livraria Editôra Coelho Branco, Rio de Janeiro, 1956.

Cunha, Vasco Leitão da. Interview, June 24, 1966.

Dantas, Mercedes. *A Força Nacionalizadora do Estado Novo.* Departmento de Imprensa e Propaganda, Rio de Janeiro, 1942.

Departamento de Imprensa e Propaganda. *Estado Nacional, 10-11-1937–10-11-1942: Cinco Anos de Unidade e de Ação.* Rio de Janeiro, 1942.

———. *Comemorações do Estado Nacional 1937–1942 na Voz das Classes e na Palavra do Chefe.* Rio de Janeiro, 1943.

Department of State. *Documents on German Foreign Policy, 1918–1945.* Series D (1937–1945), Vol. V. Government Printing Office, Washington, 1953.

————. *Foreign Relations of the United States.* Volumes on "The American Republics" (V [1939], V [1940], VI [1941], V [1942] V [1943]).

de Vicq de Cumptich, Vincent. Interview, July 9, 1963.

Dias, Everardo. *Histórica das Lutas Sociais no Brasil.* Editôra Edaglit, São Paulo, 1962.

Diniz, Almachio. *São Paulo e a Sua Guerra de Seccessão.* Irmãos Pongetti, Rio de Janeiro, 1933.

Diniz, Zolachio. *Getúlio Vargas* (Short Preface by João Neves da Fontoura). Editôra Secula XX, Rio de Janeiro, 1942.

Dodsworth, Henrique. *A Avenida Presidente Vargas.* Copyright *Jornal do Commercio,* Rio de Janeiro, 1955.

————. *Depoimento sôbre Getúlio Vargas.* Rio de Janeiro, 1964.

Doria, A. de Sampaio. *"Democracia"* and *"A Revolução de 1930"* (two works in single volume) Companhia Editôra Nacional, São Paulo, 1930.

Duarte, Paulo. *Agora Nós!* São Paulo, 1927.

————. *Que É Que Há?* 2nd ed. 1931.

————. *Palmares pelo Avesso.* Instituto Progresso Editorial, S.A., São Paulo, 1947.

————. *Prisão, Exílio, Luta . . .* Livraria Editôra Zelio Valverda S.A., Rio de Janeiro, 1946.

————. Interviews, August 9, 1963; November 23 and November 29, 1965.

Duarte, Silva. *A Revolução Victoriosa.* Livraria Zenith, São Paulo, 1930.

Dutra, Eurico Gaspar. See Oliveira, José Teixeira de.

————. Interview, "Dutra O Cidadão" (text by Lêdo Ivo) in *Manchete* magazine, Rio de Janeiro, May 22, 1965.

————. Interview, July 28, 1963.

————. Typewritten memorandum with answers to questions, Rio de Janeiro, August, 1963. Original in Latin American Collection, The University of Texas.

Dutra, Firmo. Interview, July 25, 1963.

Dyott, G. M. "Miranda, o Salteador, Sanguinario, Implacavel, Culto e Cavalheiresco," in *O Cruzeiro,* June 22, 1935.

Eisenhower, Milton S. *The Wine Is Bitter.* Doubleday, Garden City, New York, 1963.

(Election Campaign of 1930). *A Plataforma Getúlio Vargas Repellida pela Opinião Nacional.* 156-page collection of newspaper articles of January, 1930, attacking the Vargas platform. n.d.

Ellis Junior, Alfredo. *A Nossa Guerra.* Editôra Piratininga S.A. São Paulo, 1933.

————. "Confederação ou Separação". 3rd ed. Editorial Paulista, São Paulo, 1934.

Facó, Rui. Brasil Século XX. Editorial Victória Limitada, Rio de Janeiro, 1960.

Fairbairn, Arnoldo Hasselmann. Interview, December 6, 1965.

Fairchild, Byron. See Conn, Stetson.

Farias, Osvaldo Cordeiro de. Interview, July 30, 1963.

Fernandes, Annibal. Pernambuco No Tempo do "Vice-Rei" . . . Schmidt, Rio de Janeiro, n.d.

Ferraz, Otávio Marcondes. Interview, August 8, 1963.

Ferreira Filho, Artur. História Geral do Rio Grande do Sul, 1503–1960. 2nd ed. Editôra, Globo, S.A., Pôrto Alegre, 1960.

Ferreira, Waldemar Martins. História do Direito Constitucional Brasileiro. Max Limonad, São Paulo, 1954.

————. Interview, August 6, 1963.

Figueiredo, Euclydes. Contribuição para a História da Revolução Constitucionalista de 1932. Livraria Martins, São Paulo, 1954.

Fonseca, Hermes Ernesto da. Interview, September 7, 1963.

Fontes, Lourival. See Carneiro, Glauco. "A Face Final de Vargas."

————. Interview, July 27, 1963.

Fontoura, João Neves da. Por S. Paulo e pelo Brasil! n.p., 1932.

————. Acuso! n.p., Rio de Janeiro, 1933.

————. A Voz das Opposições Brasileiras. Edições Cultura Brasileira, São Paulo [c. 1935].

————. Borges de Medeiros e Seu Tempo (Memórias, Vol. I). Editôra Globo, Pôrto Alegre, 1958.

————. A Aliança Liberal e a Revolução de 1930 (Memórias, Vol. II). Editôra Globo, Pôrto Alegre, 1963.

Franco, Afonso Arinos de Melo. Um Estadista da República. 3 vols. Livraria José Olympio, Rio de Janeiro, 1955.

————. Estudos de Direito Constitucional. Rio de Janeiro, 1957.

————. A Alma do Tempo: Memórias. Livraria José Olympio, Rio de Janeiro, 1961.

————. A Escalada: Memórias. Livraria José Olympio, Rio de Janeiro, 1965.

————. Interviews, August 13 and August 20, 1963; November 4, 1966.

Franco, Virgilio A. de Mello. Outubro, 1930. 2nd ed. Schmidt, Rio de Janeiro, 1931.

————. A Campanha da U.D.N. (1944–1945). Livraria Editôra Zelio Valverde, S.A., Rio de Janeiro, 1946.

————. Sob o Signo da Resistência. Livraria Editôra Zelio Valverde S.A., Rio de Janeiro, 1947.

Freire, Gilberto. Interview, September 29, 1964.

Freire, Josué Justiniano. *A Odysséa do 12° Regimento.* Oficina de Encad. e Pautação do E.C.F.E., Rio de Janeiro, 1933.

Frischauer, Paul. *Presidente Vargas: Biografia.* Translation into Portuguese by Mário da Silva and Brutus Pedreira. Companhia Editôra Nacional, São Paulo, Rio de Janeiro, Recife, Pôrto Alegre, 1943.

Gabaglia, Laurita Pessôa Raja. *Epitacio Pessôa.* 2 vols. Livraria José Olympio, Rio de Janeiro and São Paulo, 1951.

———. *O Cardeal Leme.* Livraria José Olympio, Rio de Janeiro, 1962.

Galvão, Francisco. *Diretrizes do Estado Novo.* Departamento de Imprensa e Propaganda, 1942.

Ganzert, Frederic W. "Wartime Economic Conditions," *Brazil* (ed. by Laurence F. Hill). University of California Press, Berkeley and Los Angeles, 1947.

Gauld, Charles A. *Brazilian Federal Publications, 1930–1940.* The Latin American Economic Institute, Boston, 1941.

———. *The Last Titan: Percival Farquhar.* Institute of Hispanic American and Luso-Brazilian Studies, Stanford University, 1964.

Gentil, Alvides. *As Ideias do Presidente Getulio Vargas.* Livraria José Olympio, Rio de Janeiro, 1939.

Gleason, S. Everett. See Langer, William L.

Globo, O. *O Livro Negro da Corrupção.* Special edition of *O Globo* newspaper about assassination of Major Vaz in August, 1954, and subsequent disclosures. n.d.

Goes, Eurico de. See Costa, Cyro.

Gomes, Eduardo. *Campanha de Libertação.* Livraria Martins, São Paulo, 1946.

———. Interview, July 20, 1963.

Gonçalves, Landri Sales. Interview, September 2, 1963.

Goulart, Gastão. *Verdades da Revolução Paulista.* 1933.

Greenen, Henrique. *Aventuras de uma Familia Durante a Revolução de 1924.* Romero & Comp., São Paulo, 1925.

Guimarães, Napoleão Alencastro. Interview, August 21, 1963.

Gunther, John. *Inside Latin America.* Harper, New York, 1941.

Hambloch, Ernest. *His Majesty the President of Brazil.* Dutton, New York, 1936.

Henriques, Affonso (Affonso Henriques Correia). *Vargas, o Maquiavélico.* Palácio do Livro, São Paulo, 1961.

———. *Ascensão e Queda de Getúlio Vargas.* 3 vols. Distribuidora Record de Serviços de Imprensa, Ltda., Rio de Janeiro, 1966.

Hill, Frank Ernest. See Wilkins, Mira.

Hill, Laurence F. (ed.) *Brazil.* University of California Press, Berkeley and Los Angeles, 1947.

Hilton, Stanley E. "Germany's Trade Drive in South America, 1934–1939: The Case of Brazil," *Hispanic American Historical Review* (forthcoming).

Hirschman, Albert O. *Journeys toward Progress.* The Twentieth-Century Fund, New York, 1963.

Hull, Cordell. *The Memoirs of Cordell Hull.* 2 vols. Macmillan, New York, 1948.

Hyde, H. Montgomery. *Room 3603.* Third Printing. Farrar and Straus, New York, 1963.

Instituto Brasileiro de Geografia e Estatística. *Anuário Estatístico do Brasil.* Ano V, 1939/1940; Ano VI, 1941/1945; also subsequent years. Rio de Janeiro.

James, Bascombe W. Interview, June 17, 1963.

Jardim, Renato. *A Aventura de Outubro e a Invasão de São Paulo.* 3rd ed. Civilização Brasileira, Rio de Janeiro, 1932.

————. *Um Libello a Sustentar.* Civilização Brasileira, S.A., Rio de Janeiro, 1933.

Joint Brazil–United States Economic Development Commission. Report: *The Development of Brazil.* Institute of Inter-American Affairs, Foreign Operations Administration, Washington, D.C., 1954.

Josefsohn, Leon. *Getúlio, Êste Desconhecido.* Rio de Janeiro, 1957.

Karam, Elias. *Um Paranaense nas Trincheiras da Lei.* Oficinas Graficas da "A Cruzada," Curitiba, 1933.

Kelly, José Eduardo do Prado. Interview, August 29, 1963.

King, Winfield C. *Brazil's Coffee Industry.* U.S. Department of Agriculture, March, 1962.

Klinger, Bertoldo, Euclydes Figueiredo, and others (including Argemiro de Assis Brasil). *Nós e a Dictadura,* n.p., 1933.

Klinger, Bertoldo. *Parada e Desfile duma Vida de Voluntário do Brasil.* Emprêsa Gráfica "O Cruzeiro" S.A., Rio de Janeiro, 1958.

————. Interview, August 28, 1963.

Kruel, Amauri. Interviews, November 15 and November 30, 1965.

Lacerda, Carlos. *O Caminho da Liberdade.* 2nd ed. Rio de Janeiro, 1957.

Lacerda, Maurício de. *Entre Duas Revoluções.* Livraria Editôra Leite Ribeiro, Rio de Janeiro, 1927.

————. *Historia de uma Covardia.* Rio de Janeiro, 1927.

————. *Segunda Republica.* Freitas Bastos, Rio de Janeiro, 1931.

Lafayette, Pedro. *Os Crimes do Partido Comunista.* Editôra Moderna, Rio de Janeiro, 1946.

Lafer, Horácio. Interview, August 7, 1963.

Langer, William L. and S. Everett Gleason. *The Undeclared War, 1940–1941.* Published for the Council on Foreign Relations by Harper, New York, 1953.

Lee, Fernando. Interview, August 6, 1963.

Leite, Aureliano. *Dias de Pavor*. Cia Graphico-Editôra Monteiro Lobato, São Paulo, 1924.

———. *Memórias de um Revolucionário: A Revolução de 1930*, Pródromos e Conseqüências, n.p., São Paulo., 1931.

———. *Martirio e Glória de São Paulo*. São Paulo, 1934.

Leite, Carlos da Costa. Interview, September 6, 1963.

Leite, Rosa Meireles da Costa. Interview, September 6, 1963.

Lelis, João. *A Campanha de Princêsa (1930)*. Publicações A União, João Pessôa, Paraíba, 1944.

Leonardos, Thomas. "Palestra Proferida na Escola Superior de Guerra, em 9 de Junho de 1964." A mimeographed speech. Rio de Janeiro.

———. *Às Vésperas da Quinta República: Sugestões para o Presidencialismo Brasileiro*. Emprêsa Gráfica O Cruzeiro, S.A., Rio de Janeiro. [1962.]

Lessa, Origenes. *Ilha Grande*. Companhia Editôra Nacional, São Paulo, 1933.

Levy, Herbert. Interview, August 9, 1963.

Lima, Afonso de Albuquerque. Interview, September 12, 1963.

Lima, Azevedo. *Seis Mezes de Dictadura: Julho a Dezembro de 1924*. Empresa Editôra Getulio Costa & Cia., São Paulo, 1925.

———. *Da Caserna ao Carcere*. 2nd ed. Livraria H. Antunes, Rio de Janeiro, 1931.

Lima, Cláudio Araujo. *Mito e Realidade de Vargas*. 2nd ed. Editôra Civilização Brasileira S.A., São Paulo, 1955.

Lima, Herman. *História da Caricatura no Brasil*. Livraria José Olympio, Rio de Janeiro, 1963. (See Vol. I, pp. 326–354.)

Lima, José Queiroz. Interviews, July 22, 1963, and August 19, 1963.

Lima, Lourenço Moreira. *A Coluna Prestes: Marchas e Combates*. 2nd ed. Editôra Brasiliense, Ltda., São Paulo, 1945.

Lima Sobrinho, Alexandre José Barbosa. *A Verdade sôbre a Revolução de Outubro*. Gráfica-Editôra Unitas, Ltda., São Paulo, 1933.

Loewenstein, Karl. *Brazil under Vargas*. Macmillan, New York, 1942.

Lopes, Lucas. Interview, July 9, 1963.

Lopes, Luís Simões. Interview, December 17, 1966.

Lopes Filho, Ildefonso Simões. *Defendendo Meu Pai*. 2nd ed. Oficinas Graphicas da Livraria do Globo, Barcellos, Bertaso & Cia., Pôrto Alegre, 1935.

Loureiro, Waldemar. *Assalto aos Cartorios*. Rio, 1936.

Louzado, Alfredo João. *Legislação Social-Trabalhista: Coletânea de Decretos Feita por Determinação do Ministro do Trabalho, Indústria e Comércio*. 1933.

Luis, Pedro. *Getúlio Vargas. Separata do Livro "Acusados Políticos e Réus Militares" (Ontem e hoje): Documentos para a História*. Propriedade de "Nova Jurisprudência Ltda.," São Paulo e Rio de Janeiro, Editôra Comercial Americana Ltda., São Paulo, 1946.

Luna, Luiz. *Lampião e Seus Cabras*. Editôra Leitura, S.A., Rio de Janeiro, 1963.
Machado, F. Zenha. *Os Últimos Dias do Govêrno de Vargas*. Editôra Lux Ltda., Rio de Janeiro, 1955.
Maciel Filho, José Soares. Interview, March 14, 1965.
Magalhães, Elyeser. Interview, August 15, 1963.
Magalhães, Jacy Montenegro. Interviews, July 28 and August 15, 1963.
Magalhães, Juraci. Interviews, August 3, 1963, October 1, 1964, and October 13, 1964.
Marcondes Filho, Alexandre. *O Momento Constitucional Brasileiro*. Imprensa Nacional, Rio de Janeiro, 1943.
————. Typewritten memorandum with answers to questions, São Paulo, September 3, 1963. Original in Latin American Collection, The University of Texas.
————. Interview, August 8, 1963.
Mariani, Clemente. Interview, August 22, 1963.
Marques, Cicero. *O Ultimo Dia de Governo do Presidente Washington Luis no Palacio Guanabara*. Soc. Impressora Paulista, São Paulo, n.d.
Martins, Enéas. Interview, August 26, 1963.
Matos, Almir. *Em Agôsto Getúlio Ficou Só*. Centro Popular de Cultura da UNE. Editôra Problemas Contemporâneos, Rio de Janeiro, 1963.
Mattós, Jeremias de. Interview, October 22, 1966.
McAshan, S. Maurice, Jr., Interview, May 27, 1963.
Medeiros, Maurico de. *Outras Revoluções Virão*. Freitas Bastos & Cia., Rio de Janeiro, 1932.
Medeyros, J. Paulo de. *Getulio Vargas: O Reformador Social*. 1941.
Melo, Olbiano de. *A Marcha da Revolução Social no Brasil*. Edições O Cruzeiro, Rio de Janeiro, 1957.
Menezes-Wanderley, Rubey de. *A Expiação*. Rio de Janeiro, 1931.
Mesquita Filho, Júlio de. *"Memórias de um Revolucionário": Notas para um Ensaio de Sociologia Política*. Editôra Anhambi Limitada, São Paulo, 1954.
————. Interview, August 7, 1963.
———— and others. *Centenário de Júlio Mesquita*. Editôra Anhambi, S.A., São Paulo, 1964.
Minas, João de. *Jantando um Defunto*. Edições Alpha, Rio de Janeiro, 1928.
Ministério da Fazenda. *Finanças do Brasil*. Secretaria do Conselho Técnico de Economia e Finanças. Jornal do Commercio, Rio de Janeiro, 1940.
————. *Programas Econômicos e Financeiros na Vigência da Constituição Federal de 1946*. Serviço de Estatística Econômica e Financeira (do Conselho Nacional de Estatística I.B.G.E.), n.d.
————. *Comentários sôbre o Ultimo Discurso Proferido pelo Senador Getúlio Vargas*. Rio de Janeiro, 1950.
Ministério das Relações Exteriores. *Relatório de 1941*; also *Relatório de 1942*. Imprensa Nacional, Rio de Janeiro, 1944. (Also other years.)

————. *O Brasil e a Segunda Guerra Mundial.* 2 vols. Imprensa Nacional, Rio de Janeiro, 1944.

————. *Brasil, 1946.* (Issued in English. Also other years.)

Miranda, Alcibiades. *A Rebellião de São Paulo.* Curityba, n.p., 1934.

Miranda, Emídio da Costa. Interview, July 19, 1963.

Moniz, Heitor. *Communismo.* I. Amorim & Cia. Ltda. Rio de Janeiro, [c. 1937].

Montalvo, Ricardo J. *Getulio Vargas.* M. Gleizer, Buenos Aires, 1939.

Monteiro, Joaquim Ribeiro. "A Revolução de 30 na Bahia." Manuscript. Copy in Latin American Collection, The University of Texas.

————. Interview, August 29, 1963.

Monteiro, Pedro Aurélio de Góes. *A Revolução de 30.* Adersen, Rio de Janeiro.

————. See Coutinho, Lourival.

Monteiro, Pedro Aurélio de Góes, João Neves da Fontoura, and Henrique Dodsworth. *Uma Grande Data.* Speeches. Departamento de Imprensa e Propaganda, Rio de Janeiro, 1941.

Moraes, J. B. Mascarenhas de. *A F.E.B. pelo Seu Comandante.* Instituto Progresso Editorial, S.A., São Paulo, 1947.

Moraes Neto, Pruente de. Interviews, August 31 and September 10, 1963.

Moura, Jaïr Pinto de. Preface by Romão Gomes. *A Fogueira Constitucionalista.* Editorial Paulista, São Paulo, 1933.

Mourão Filho, Olímpio. Interviews, October 9, 1965 and November 29, 1966.

Müller, Filinto. Interview, October 15, 1965.

Nabuco, Carolina. *A Vida de Virgílio de Melo Franco.* Livraria José Olympio, Rio de Janeiro, 1962.

Nabuco, Mauricio. Interview, August 13, 1963.

Nasser, David, *Falta Alguem em Nuremberg.* Edições do Povo, Rio de Janeiro, 1947.

————, *A Revolução dos Covardes.* Emprêsa Gráfica "O Cruzeiro" S.A., Rio de Janeiro, 1947.

[Nasser, David]. *Eu Fui Guarda-Costas de Getúlio.* (Author's name not shown.) Emprêsa Gráfica "O Cruzeiro," S.A., Rio de Janeiro, 1949.

Nasser, David. *O Anjo Negro de Getúlio.* Edições O Cruzeiro, Rio de Janeiro, 1966.

Neves, Tancredo. Interviews, June 28 and October 7, 1965.

Nogueira Filho, Paulo. *Ideais e Lutas de um Burguês Progressista: O Partido Democrático e a Revolução de 1930.* 2 vols. Editôra Anhambi, S.A., São Paulo, 1958.

————. *Ideais e Lutas de um Burguês Progressista: A Guerra Cívica, 1932,* Vol. I, *Ocupação Militar.* Vol. II, *Insurreiçao Civil.* José Olympio, Rio de Janeiro, 1965, 1966.

————. "Ideais e Lutas de um Burguês Progressista: Pródomos da Guerra Cívica dos Paulistas." Manuscript.

[Nogueira Filho, Paulo]. *Paulo Nogueira Filho, Cidadão Emérito de São Paulo.* São Paulo, 1961.

Nogueira Filho, Paulo. Interviews, August 14, 1963 and November 18, 1965.

Normano, John F. *The Economic Ideas of Dr. Getúlio Vargas.* The Latin American Economic Institute, Boston, 1941.

Noronha, Abilio de. *Narrando a Verdade.* Companhia Graphico-Editôra Monteiro Lobato, São Paulo, 1924.

————. *O Resto da Verdade.* Empresa Editôra Rochéa, São Paulo, 1925.

Nunes, Janari Gentil. Interview, October 18, 1965.

Oliveira, Armando de Salles. *Discursos.* São Paulo, 1935.

Oliveira, José Teixeira de. *O Govêrno Dutra.* Editôra Civilização Brasileira S.A., Rio de Janeiro, São Paulo, Bahia, 1956.

Oliveira, Nelson Tabajara de. *1924: A Revolução de Isidoro.* Companhia Editôra Nacional, São Paulo, 1956.

Oliveira, Odilon Aquino de. See Tenorio, Heliodoro.

Oliveira Filho, Benjamim de. *M.M.D.C.* Schmidt, Rio de Janeiro, 1932.

Ónody, Oliver. *A Inflação Brasileira (1820–1958).* Rio de Janeiro, 1960.

Osorio, Manoel. *A Guerra de São Paulo.* Empreza Editôra "Americana," São Paulo, 1932.

Pacheco, Armando. *Getulio Me Disse . . .* Editôra Aurora, Rio de Janeiro, 1949.

Paim Filho, Firmino. Manifesto published in *O País,* October 9–10, 1930.

Patric, Anthony. *Toward the Winning Goal.* Rio de Janeiro, 1940.

Peixoto, Alzira Vargas do Amaral. *Getúlio Vargas, Meu Pai.* Pocket-book edition. Editôra Globo, Pôrto Alegre, 1960.

————. "A Vida de Getúlio Contada por Sua Filha, Alzira Vargas, ao Jornalista Raul Guidicelli" (the *Fatos & Fotos* magazine series starting June 15, 1963, and ending with Chap. 13 on October 5, 1963). Rio de Janeiro.

————. Interview, July 11, 1963.

Peixoto, Augusto Amaral. Interview, August 17, 1963.

Peixoto, Silvio. *Aspectos Históricos do Estado Novo.* Departmento de Imprensa e Propaganda, Rio de Janeiro, n.d.

Penido, Osvaldo M. Interview, September 6, 1963.

Peralva, Osvaldo. *O Retrato.* Editôra Globo, Pôrto Alegre, 1962.

————. Interview, September 14, 1963.

Pereira, Astrojildo. *Formação do PCB (1922–1928).* Editorial Vitória Limitada, Rio de Janeiro, n.d.

Pessôa, Alfredo. *Um Homem que Governa.* Zelio Valverde, Rio de Janeiro, 1942.

Pessoa, Epitácio. *Obras Completas de Epitácio Pessoa.* (Vols. XXI and XXII, *Pela Verdade,* were published in 1957.) Instituto Nacional do Livro, Ministério da Educação e Cultura, Rio de Janeiro.

Pessôa, Laurita. See Gabaglia, Laurita Pessôa Raja.

Picchia, Menotti Del. *A Revolução Paulista,* n.p., São Paulo, 1932.

Pilla, Raul. Interview, October 13, 1965.

Pimenta, Mattos. *Um Grito de Alerta no Tumulto da Revolução*. Ariel, Editôra Ltda., Rio de Janeiro, 1931.

———. *A Epopéa Paulista*. Ariel, Editôra Ltda., Rio de Janeiro, 1933.

Pimpão, Hirosê. *Getulio Vargas e o Direito Social Trabalhista*. Rio de Janeiro, 1942.

Pinto, Heraclito Fontoura Sobral (Procurador Criminal da República). *Por Libello-Crime Accusatório*. (Accusation against 1922 revolutionaries.) Imprensa Nacional, Rio de Janeiro, 1927.

Pinto, H. Sobral, and R Lopes Machado. *O Caso da "Narrativa do Motim a Bordo do Encouraçado São Paulo, Exarada no Livro da Torre 3"; Allegações de Defesa, pelos Advogados H. Sobral Pinto, R. Lopes Machado*. Justiça Militar, Rio de Janeiro, 1932.

Pinto, Herondino Pereira. *Nos Subterraneos do Estado Novo*. Rio de Janeiro, 1950.

Polícia de São Paulo. *Movimento Subversivo de Julho* [1924]. Casa Garraux, 1925.

Poppino, Rollie E. "Communism in Postwar Brazil." Paper presented at American Historical Association session, Chicago, December 29, 1962.

———. *International Communism in Latin America: A History of the Movement, 1917–1963*. The Free Press of Glencoe, 1964.

Portella, Fernando. Interview, June 10, 1963.

Porto, Eurico Bellens. *A Insurreição de 27 de Novembro* [1935]. Polícia Civil do Districo Federal, Rio de Janeiro, 1936.

Prado Júnior, Caio. Interviews, November 17, 1965 and November 9, 1966.

Prestes, Luís Carlos. Interview, September 5, 1963.

Procurador Criminal da Republica, em Commissão no Estado de São Paulo. *Successos Subversivos de São Paulo, Denuncia*. Imprensa Nacional, Rio de Janeiro, 1925.

Pupo Neto, Trajano. Interview, August 8, 1963.

Queiroz Filho, Eusébio de. Interview, June 26, 1963.

Queiroz Júnior, José. *O Suicidio de Getúlio através da Psicanalise*. Editorial "Copac" S.A., Rio de Janeiro, 1947.

———. *222 Anedotas de Getúlio Vargas*. Companhia Brasileira de Artes Gráficas, Rio de Janeiro, 1955.

———. *Memórias sôbre Getúlio*. Editorial Copac, Rio de Janeiro, 1957.

Ramos, Graciliano, *Memórias do Cárcere*. 4th ed. 2 vols. Livraria Martins, São Paulo, 1960.

Ramos, Rodrigo Otávio Jordão. Interview, September 13, 1963.

Ráo, Vicente. Interviews, August 10, 1963 and November 17, 1966.

Reis, Malvino. Interview, September 2, 1963.

Reis, Raul. Interview, August 15, 1963.

Renard, Antoine. *São Paulo É Isto!* São Paulo, 1933.

Revista do Globo (Edição Especial). *Revolução de Outubro de 1930: Imagens e documentos*. Barcellos, Bertaso & Cia., Pôrto Alegre, 1931.

(Revolt of 1924). Various authors. *1922—5 de Julho—1924*. Volume commemorating the events of 1924. Introduction by J. Nunes de Carvalho. Editôra Henrique Velho, Rio de Janeiro, 1944.

Reyes, Plinio. *A Sedição Militar de Matto Grosso em 1922*. Typographia Piratininga, S. Paulo, 1922.

Ribeiro, Alvaro. *Falsa Democracia: A revolta de São Paulo em 1924*. F. de Piro & Cia., Rio de Janeiro, 1927.

Roberto, Paulo. *O Sorriso do Presidente*. Grafica Olimpica, [Rio de Janeiro], 1940.

Robock, Stefan H. *Brazil's Developing Northeast: A Study of Regional Planning and Foreign Aid*. The Brookings Institution, Washington, D.C., 1963.

Rocha, Geraldo. *Na Hora da Borrasca Não se Muda o Timoneiro!* . . . Rio de Janeiro, 1937.

Rocha Netto, Bento Munhoz da. *Radiografia de Novembro*. 2nd edition. Editôra Civilização Brasileira S.A., Rio de Janeiro, 1961.

Rodriques, Lysias. *Gaviões de Penacho: A Lucta Aérea na Guerra Paulista de 1932*. 1934.

Rodrigues, Mario. *Meu Libello*. Editôra Brasileira Lux, Rio de Janeiro, 1925.

Rosa, Pedro Santa. *Revolução Unica em Dois Millenios*. Typ. São Benedicto, Rio de Janeiro, 1931.

Sá, Hernane Tavares de. *The Brazilians*. The John Day Co., New York, 1947.

Sales, Apolonio. Typewritten memorandum with answers to questions. Rio de Janeiro, June, 1963.

Salgado, Plínio. *A Psicologia da Revolução*. Civilação Brasileira S.A., Rio de Janeiro (1933).

———. *O Integralismo perante a Nação*. 3rd ed. Livraria Clássica Brasileira S.A., Rio de Janeiro, 1955.

———. Interview, October 14, 1965.

Santos, Francisco Martins dos. *O Fato Moral e o Fato Social de Década Getuliana*. Zelio Valverde, Editor, Rio de Janeiro, 1941.

Santos, João Oliveria. *Análise das Tendências do Mercado Internacional do Café*. 2nd ed. Instituto Brasileiro de Café, Washington, D.C., July, 1962.

Saraiva, João. *Em Continencia á Lei*. 1933.

Saunders, J. V. D. "The Death of Vargas," in *The Mississippi Quarterly*, IX (Spring, 1956), 117–131.

———. "A Revolution of Agreement among Friends: The End of the Vargas Era," in *The Hispanic American Historical Review*, XLIV, No. 2 (May 1964), 197–213.

Seabra, J. J. *Esfola de um Mentiroso*. Rio de Janeiro, 1936.

Shaw, Paul Vanorden. *Know-How Conquers Jungle.* ICOMI, Rio de Janeiro, 1963.

Silva, Gastão Pereira da. *Getulio Vargas e o Aspecto Intelectual de Sua Obra.* Gráfica Guarany, Ltda. Rio de Janeiro, 1942.

Silva, Hélio. *1922: Sangue na Areia de Copacabana,* Vol. I in *O Ciclo de Vargas.* Editôra Civilização Brasileira S.A. Rio de Janeiro, 1964.

————. *1926: A Grande Marcha,* Vol. II in *O Ciclo de Vargas.* Editôra Civilização Brasileira S.A., Rio de Janeiro, 1965.

————. *1930: A Revolução Traída,* Vol. III in *O Ciclo de Vargas.* Editôra Civilização Brasileira, S.A., Rio de Janeiro, 1966.

————. *1931: Os Tenentes no Poder,* Vol. IV in *O Ciclo de Vargas.* Editôra Civilização, S.A., Rio de Janeiro, 1966.

————. "Lembrai-vos de 1937." Articles in newspaper *Tribuna da Imprensa,* Rio de Janeiro, October 1, 1959–October 27, 1959.

————. "Assim Foi Deposto Getúlio." Article in *Tribuna da Imprensa,* Rio de Janeiro, October 29, 1959.

————. "Rapsódia Verde." Manuscript in Hélio Silva's possession.

————. Interviews, July 27, August 3, August 24, and September 3, 1963.

Silva, Herculano de Carvalho e. *A Revolução Constitucionalista.* Civilização Brasileira, Rio de Janeiro, 1932.

Silva, José Pereira da. *Getulio Vargas.* Selma Editôra, Rio de Janeiro, 1934.

Silva Filho, Sinval de Castro e. "Evolução Histórica das Formas de Govêrno: Intentona Comunista de 1935; Exaltação dos Heróis." Speech given on November 27, 1937. Manuscript. Copy in Latin American Collection, The University of Texas.

————. Interview, September 5, 1963.

Soares, Dorval. Interview, July 24, 1963.

Soares, Gerson de Macedo. *A Acção da Marinha na Revolução Paulista de 1924.* Editôra Guanabara, Rio de Janeiro, 1932.

————. *O Contra-Torpedeiro Baleado.* Livraria Editôra Marisa, Rio de Janeiro, 1933.

Sodré, Nelson Werneck. *História Militar do Brasil.* Editôra Civilização Brasileira, Rio de Janeiro, 1965.

————. *História da Imprensa no Brasil.* Editôra Civilização Brasileira, Rio de Janeiro, 1966.

Souza, Carlos Martins Pereira e. Interview, June 12, 1963.

Souza, J. P. Coelho de. *O Pensamento Político de Assis Brasil.* Livraria José Olympio, Rio de Janeiro, 1958.

Souza, Leal de. *Getúlio Vargas.* Gráfica Olimpica, Rio de Janeiro, 1940.

Souza, Manoel Rodrigues de. *Por Que Getulio Vargas Suspendeu o Funcionamento do Congresso em 1937?* Rio de Janeiro, 1957.

Stacchini, José. *Março 64: Mobilização da Audácia.* Companhia Editôra Nacional, São Paulo, 1965.

Szulc, Tad. *Twilight of the Tyrants.* Henry Holt, New York, 1959.

Sussekind, Arnaldo. Interview, September 11, 1963.

Távora, Araken. *O Dia em Que Vargas Morreu.* Editôra de Repórter, Ltda., Rio de Janeiro, 1966.

Távora, Juarez. *À Guisa de Depoimento sobre a Revolução Brasileira de 1924,* Vol. I, O Combate, São Paulo, 1927; Vol. III, Mendonça, Machado & C., Rio de Janeiro, 1928.

————. *Petróleo para o Brasil.* Livraria José Olympio, Rio de Janeiro, 1955.

————. Interviews, May 20 and May 22, 1965.

Teixeira, Oswaldo. *Getulio Vargas e a Arte no Brasil.* D.I.P., 1940.

Tejo, Limeira. *Jango.* Editorial Andes Ltda., Rio de Janeiro, 1957.

Tenorio, Heliodoro, and Odilon Aquino de Oliveira. *São Paulo contra a Dictadura.* 2nd ed. Distribuição "ELO"; Simão & Del Picchia, São Paulo, 1934.

Tiller, Ann Quiggins. "The Igniting Spark—Brasil, 1930," in *The Hispanic American Historical Review,* XLV, No. 3 (August, 1965), 384–392.

Tinoco, Brígido. *A Vida de Nilo Peçanha.* Livraria José Olympio. Rio de Janeiro, 1962.

Tinoco, Godofredo. *Tempo Bom.* Tip. Jornal do Commercio, Jacinto R. Santos, Rio de Janeiro, 1931.

Tolentino, José. *Nilo Peçanha, Sua Vida Publica.* Armando Martins, Petropolis, n.d.

Townsend, Charles H. T., Jr. "Progress in Developing Superior Hevea Clones in Brazil" in *Economic Botany,* XIV, No. 3 (July–September, 1960), 189–196.

[Tribunal Superior Eleitoral]. *O Partido Comunista: Sua Condenação pela Justiça Brasileira.* Imprensa Nacional, Rio de Janeiro, 1947.

United States Army, Headquarters IV Corps. *The Final Campaign across Northwest Italy.* Milan, Italy, 1945.

Valladares, Benedicto. *Tempos Idos e Vividos: Memórias.* Civilização Brasileira, Rio de Janeiro, 1966.

————. Interview, October 21, 1965.

Vampré, Leven. *São Paulo: Terra Conquistada.* Sociedade Impressora Paulista, São Paulo, 1932.

Vargas, Alzira. See Peixoto, Alzira Vargas do Amaral.

Vargas, Getúlio. *De 1929 a 1934.* Calvino Filho, Editor, Rio de Janeiro, 1934.

————. *A Nova Política do Brasil.* 11 volumes. Livraria José Olympio, Rio de Janeiro, 1938–1947.

————. *O Estado Novo e o Momento Brasileiro; Entrevista Concedida à Imprensa pelo Presidente Getulio Vargas na Data do Primeiro Aniversario da Instituição do Regime de 10 de Novembro.* Rio de Janeiro, n.d.

[Vargas, Getúlio.] *Promessas e Realizações; A Solução das Grandes Theses Juridicas, Politicas e Sociaes no Governo Getulio Vargas*. Imprensa Nacional, Rio de Janeiro, 1938.

Vargas, Getúlio. *As Diretrizes da Nova Política do Brasil*. Livraria José Olympio, Rio de Janeiro, 1942.

[Vargas, Getúlio.] *O Pensamento Político do Presidente . . . Comemorativa do 60° Aniversário do Presidente Getúlio Vargas*. Various authors. Imprensa Nacional, Rio de Janeiro, 1943.

Vargas, Getúlio. *A Política Trabalhista no Brasil*. Livraria José Olympio, Rio de Janeiro and São Paulo, 1950.

———. *A Campanha Presidencial*. Livraria José Olympio, Rio de Janeiro, 1951.

———. *O Govêrno Trabalhista do Brasil*. Livraria José Olympio, Rio de Janeiro, 1952.

———. *Mensagem ao Congresso Nacional, Apresentado pelo Presidente da República por Ocasião da Abertura da Sessão Legislativa de 1953*. Departamento de Imprensa Nacional, Rio de Janeiro, 1953.

———. *A Política Nacionalista do Petróleo no Brasil*. (Apresentação de Alfredo Marques Vianna; depoimento de J. Soares Pereira). Edições Tempo Brasileiro Ltda., Rio de Janeiro, 1964.

Vargas Netto, Manuel. *General Vargas*. Rio de Janeiro, 1943.

Vergara, Luiz. *Fui Secretário de Getúlio Vargas*. Editôra Globo, Pôrto Alegre, 1960.

Verissimo, Erico. *O Arquipélago* (part of *O Tempo e o Vento*). 2nd printing. Editôra Globo, Pôrto Alegre, 1961.

Vianna, Hélio. *História da República: História Diplomática do Brasil*. 2nd ed. Edições Melhoramentos, São Paulo, [1961].

Vicente, João. *Revlução de 5 de Julho [1922]*. 1925.

Victor, Mário. *5 Anos que Abalaram o Brasil*. Editôra Civilização Brasileira, S.A., Rio de Janeiro, 1965.

Vidal, Adhemar. *1930: Historia de João Pessôa e da Revolução na Parahyba*. Companhia Editôra Nacional, São Paulo, 1931.

Vidal, Olmio Barros. *Um Destino a Serviço do Brasil*. Gráfica Olímpica, Rio de Janeiro, 1945.

Vieira, Luiz. *Getúlio Vargas: Estadista e Sociólogo*. Departamento de Imprensa e Propaganda, Rio de Janeiro, 1951.

Wainer, Samuel. Interview, July 31, 1963.

Walters, Vernon. "Why Brazil is Different." Manuscript. Copy in Latin American Collection, The University of Texas.

———. Interview, May 14, 1965.

Wanderley, Rubey. *Getúlio Vargas: Político e Escritor*. 2nd ed. Képler, Rio de Janeiro, 1951.

Welles, Sumner. *Seven Decisions That Shaped History.* Harper, New York, 1951.

Whitaker, José Maria. *Relatório da Administração Financeira do Govêrno Provisório de 4 de Novembro de 1930 a 16 de Novembro de 1931: Exposição Apresentada pelo Dr. José Maria Whitaker em 4 de Fevereiro de 1933.* Ministério da Fazenda. Imprensa Nacional, Rio de Janeiro, 1937.

————. Interview, August 7, 1963.

Wilkins, Mira and Frank Ernest Hill. *American Business Abroad: Ford on Six Continents.* Wayne State University Press, Detroit, 1964.

Wirth, John D. "Tenentismo in the Brazilian Revolution of 1930," in *The Hispanic American Historical Review,* XLIV, No. 2 (May, 1964), 161–179.

Wythe, George. *Brazil: An Expanding Economy.* The Twentieth Century Fund, New York, 1949.

Young, Jordan. "Military Aspects of the 1930 Brazilian Revolution," in *The Hispanic American Historical Review,* XLIV, No. 2 (May, 1964), 180–196.

374